ACCOUNTING, COSTING
AND MANAGEMENT

Accounting, Costing, and Management

Riad Izhar, B.Sc., Cert. Ed.

Oxford University Press

To my father and mother

Acknowledgements

The publisher would like to thank the following for granting permissions to reproduce examination questions.

The Association of Accounting Technicians
The London Chamber of Commerce
The Institute of Chartered Accountants
The Chartered Association of Certified Accountants
The Chartered Institute of Management Accountants
The University of London Examinations Board
The Associated Examining Board

The publishers would like to make it clear that the answers provided for examination questions in this book are the author's model answers and have not been supplied by the examination boards or professional associations.

Every effort has been made to gain permissions on examination questions before publication. Further source credits will be made in future impressions if contact is made with the publisher.

Oxford University Press, Great Clarendon Street, OX2 6DP
Oxford New York
Athens Auckland Bangkok Bogotá Buenos Aires
Calcutta Cape Town Chennai Dar es Salaam
Delhi Florence Hong Kong Istanbul Karachi
Kuala Lumpur Madrid Melbourne Mexico City
Mumbai Nairobi Paris São Paulo Singapore
Taipei Tokyo Toronto Warsaw

and associated companies in
Berlin Ibadan

Oxford is a trade mark of Oxford University Press

Reprinted 1991, 1993, 1994, 1996, 1999, 2000

ISBN 0 19 8327463

Typeset by Burns & Smith, Derby

Printed in Hong Kong

Foreword

The content of this book has been influenced by two considerations:

1. There is a large number of books on bookkeeping and financial accounting, and an almost equally great number on cost and management accounting. In most examinations, however, the student is required to possess a knowledge of both financial *and* cost/management accounting. My aim has been to produce one book that covers both these areas of accounting.

2. Accounting is a subject which has to be learnt by attempting questions. Reading and initial learning are necessary, but not enough in themselves to enable the reader to answer numerical questions, which constitute most of the examination questions and the bulk of the accountant's work. Most books describe and illustrate the principles and techniques followed by questions. Answers are given to only some of the questions, often in a condensed form at the back of the book. As a result the student cannot easily check his work. I have tried to attach more importance to the process of attempting and checking answers to questions, especially past examination questions. At the end of each chapter is a large selection of questions, mostly from recent examination papers, followed by detailed answers with working and explanations to some. Answers to the rest (those marked with a *) are published in a separate book which I have called the *Tutor's Solutions Manual*. This ensures that the student working on his own has access to a set of answers which he can use to check his work and evaluate his progress. At the same time it can be used by tutors as a class text since the questions without answers at the end of each chapter can be set as homework. There is no need for the tutor to work through the homework questions himself as detailed answers are contained in the Tutor's Solutions Manual. Anwers to the questions are my own and not the bodies from which they are taken. I have tried to set the questions at the end of the each chapter in order of increasing difficulty. A number of essay questions have also been included. I have not answered these formally as the relevant material is covered in the text.

The book assumes an elementary knowledge of bookkeeping but for those who do not have this, I have in Chapter 1 attempted to explain and illustrate the basic principles of double-entry bookkeeping. This book is intended for students of the following:

GCE Advanced level Accounting (especially Associated Examining Board and London Board)
Chartered Association of Certified Accountants, Foundation stage
Institute of Chartered Accountants, Foundation stage
Chartered Institute of Management Accountants, Foundation stage
Association of Accounting Technicians, Intermediate and Final
London Chamber of Commerce and Industry, Higher Stage Accounting

I have been careful to choose a reasonable selection of questions from each of these bodies. In addition it is hoped that the book will be of use to students on the first and second years of a degree course and the Higher National Diploma, although no questions have been included from these examinations.

Accounting is a technical subject but where possible I have tried to explain the rationale/reasoning behind the techniques to aid understanding. Where examples have been used to illustrate principles the figures have been kept simple to make them easier to understand.

Where I have used the word 'he' this is to be taken as 'he/she'. This abbreviation does not reflect a bias on my part, but is used purely as a matter of convenience.

I would like to thank my colleague Noel Trimming, BSc (Econ), ACIS, for willingly and freely responding to queries that arose during the course of the writing of this book, and to Oliver Thompson for reading the original manuscript and making several suggestions as to its improvement. My appreciation also goes to the Associated Examining Board and University of London Schools Examining Board for the General Certificate of Education, Chartered Association of Certified Accountants, Chartered Institute of Management Accountants, Association of Accounting Technicians, London Chamber of Commerce and Industry, and the Polytechnics of the City of London, Central London, and South Bank for the Foundation examination of the Institute of Chartered Accountants for granting their permission to use past examination questions.

Bloomsbury, London RIAD IZHAR

Contents

Introduction

Like many other disciplines, accountancy covers a wide spectrum of knowledge. It is usual to sub-divide the subject into three principal areas: *financial accounting*, *costing*, and *management accounting*. This book follows this pattern — Part I looks at financial accounting, Part II cost accounting, and Part III management accounting. Financial accounting is concerned with the *recording* and *reporting* of business activities while cost and management accounting emphasize the role of accounting as a *tool of management*.

The raw material for financial acounting is *bookkeeping*, which is the day-to-day recording of business transactions, usually in *double-entry* form. Accounting is the preparation of periodic financial statements from the books. Of these, the two most important are the annual *income statement* showing the profit or loss on a year's trading and the *balance sheet* which shows the financial position of the business at the year-end. Bookkeeping is considered in Chapter 1, annual financial statements of the simplest form of business organization, the sole proprietor, in Chapter 2. More complicated business structures such as the *partnership* and *limited company* are looked at in Chapters 8 and 10 respectively. Consideration is also given to the accounts of non-profit making organizations such as clubs and societies in Chapter 7. Chapters 3-6 look at some specific aspects of bookkeeping and accounts preparation, namely depreciation, control accounts, incomplete records, and the correction of errors. Part I concludes with a look at the accounting tools commonly used to *analyse* business performance, namely funds flow statements (Chapter 11) and ratios (Chapter 12).

Financial accounting is concerned with reporting on the *past* chiefly for the benefit of the business owners, creditors, and potential investors. In contrast, management accounting is concerned with the *future* and seeks to provide internal management with the financial information it needs to run the business on a day-to-day basis. The work of the management accountant does not involve the recording of historic transactions and preparation of year-end financial statements, but is concerned with providing relevant information to aid managerial *decision-making*, *planning*, and *control* — using techniques such as relevant costing (Chaper 20), budgeting (Chapter 21), standard costing and variance analysis (Chapter 22), break-even analysis (Chapter 23), and capital investment appraisal (Chapter 24). These are dealt with in Part III of the book.

Cost accounting provides the link between financial and management accounting. As its name suggests, it is concerned with the *recording*, *classification*, and *determination of costs*. This is necessary if we are to be able to prepare the year-end financial statements. Costing can therefore be thought of as a bookkeeping exercise. However, in addition to this, costing is also the basis of management accounting. It reveals to management not only total costs (which the financial accountant is mainly interested in) but also costs of individual departments, of different products and the effect on costs of pursuing a certain course of action - all information needed for the successful day-to-day management of a business.

The recording and determination of costs is more complicated for manufacturing than for trading and service organizations, because it is necessary to account for factory costs in addition to warehouse and office costs. The financial accountant's presentation of factory costs is looked at in Chapter 13, manufacturing accounts. The next few chapters look at the problem of the determination of unit production cost, consisting of labour (Chapter 14), material (Chapter 15), and overheads (Chapter 16). Accounting for overhead presents the cost accountant with special difficulties. The two rival approaches, absorption and marginal costing, are described, compared and evaluated in Chapter 19. Chapters 17 and 18 look at the nature of the costing system required in specific industrial situations such as shipbuilding and construction work (job and contract costing), and continuous flow mass-production industries (process costing).

PART I
Financial Accounting

CHAPTER 1

Bookkeeping — A Quick Consideration

The recording of business transactions is known as bookkeeping. Bookkeeping dates back many centuries. The ancient Egyptians used to record important transactions in hieroglyphics, the Romans in Latin. Thus if Caligula bought a stallion from Claudius he might have written 'from Claudius the purchase of one stallion, price __'. This system is characterized by *single-entry* and recording in the form of a statement. Today bookkeeping is recorded more scientifically as *double-entry* and in the form of *accounts*. Each transaction is seen as having a two-fold effect on the business. Necessity is often the mother of invention and the double-entry system was developed in 15th century Italy when the expansion of commerce and trade made necessary a system of recording that was more fool-proof and which would reveal more information than the simple single-entry system. Its first formal exposition was in Venice in 1494 by one *Luca Paciolo*. Although the system has been further developed since then, its basic principles remain the same.

The Accounting Equation

The assets of a business are financed by *people*. They may be either owners or lenders. These persons have a claim on the assets. This claim represents a *liability* to the business. Since all money spent on assets, must have been provided by someone it follows that ASSETS = LIABILITIES. The liability to the owner is known as the *capital* of the business. The formula then becomes ASSETS = CAPITAL + LIABILITIES. Since the relationship between assets, capital, and liabilities is an Equation, it follows that a change in one item must have an *equal and oppposite effect* on another. For example, an increase in an asset must result in a similar increase in a liability, increase in capital or decrease in another type of asset. A business transaction will affect *two* items, not one. It is therefore recorded as a double-entry. In a double-entry system each account has two sides — a left-hand *debit (Dr)* side representing *receipt* of money or value, and a right-hand *credit (Cr)* side representing *giving* of money or value. Increases in assets, being receipt of money or value to a business, are shown on the *debit* side of an account. Decreases are shown on the credit side. The opposite rules apply for capital and liabilities.

Assets

Dr	+	£	*Cr*	–	£

Capital

Dr	–	£	*Cr*	+	£

Liabilities

Dr	–	£	*Cr*	+	£

Thus, if a person starts a business on 5 May 19_5 with £10 000 capital the double-entry is:

Cash (asset)

5 May 19_5	Capital	10 000			

Capital

			5 May 19_5	Cash	10 000

The name of the account in which the double-entry is performed is included in each account. This is to build in a system of cross-referencing in the accounts.

If on 6 May part of the money is used to buy premises for £5 000:

Cash (asset)

			6 May 19_5	Premises	5 000

Premises (asset)

6 May 19_5	Cash	5 000			

Both are asset accounts but while one is increased (debited) the other is decreased (credited).

The beauty of the double-entry system is the balance and symmetry which exists in the books at any one time. For every debit there is a corresponding credit. Because of this balance it is possible to *check* the accuracy of the entries by seeing whether the total of the debits equal the total credits. This is done in a *trial balance.*

The balance between the two sides also makes it possible to prepare periodic statements of affairs showing the total of assets on one side, balanced by capital and liabilities on the other. This is done in a so-called *balance sheet.*

As soon as a business starts trading, two additional types of account are needed — for *expenses* and for *revenue.* Revenue receivable *adds* to the capital value of a business. Revenue is therefore *credited.* Expenses have the opposite effect and are therefore debited.

Expenses

Dr	+	£	*Cr*	−	£

Revenue

Dr	−	£	*Cr*	+	£

Thus, if on 7 May wages are paid for £200 cash:

Wages (expense)

7 May 19_5	Cash	200			

Cash (asset)

			7 May 19_5	Wages	200

And if on 8 May sales of £300 are made on credit to K. Farmer:

Sales (revenue)

			8 May 19_5	K. Farmer	300

K. Farmer, debtor (asset)

8 May 19_5	Sales	300			

To perform the double-entry for a transaction proceed as follows:

(1) Identify which two accounts are involved.

(2) Classify them as being either asset, capital, liability, expense or revenue and follow the rules of debits and credits laid out above. If your initial answer comes out as two debits or two credits, check it — it is wrong. All transactions have a debit and a corresponding credit effect on the accounts.

Balancing Off Accounts

Consider the following account:

Cash

19_5		£	19_5		£
May 5	Capital	10 000	May 6	Premises	5 000
8	Sales	1 500	7	Purchases	1 000
9	Loan	2 500			

It would be useful to know the net cash of the business at a point in time. This can be done by *balancing off* the account. This involves adding up both sides and inserting the *difference* on the smaller side to make it equal to the larger side.

Cash

19_5		£	19_5		£
May 5	Capital	10 000	May 6	Premises	5 000
8	Sales	1 500	7	Purchases	1 000
9	Loan	2 500	9	Balance c/d	8 000
		14 000			14 000
May 10	Balance b/d	8 000			

The difference, in this case £8 000, is known as the *balance* on the account. It is carried down (c/d) to the start of the next day by entering on the opposite side of the account. The above account is said to have a debit balance because the total of debits exceed credits.

Where the total of debits is exactly equal to credits the account has a nil balance and there is no need to carry or bring down balances. Where an account has only one entry it is not necessary to balance it since the entry represents the balance on the account.

Trial Balance

If the balances on all accounts in the books are listed, the total of debit balances should equal the total of credit balances. This check is performed in the trial balance. Since the trial balance is a summary of the books and contains all accounts it can be used as the basis from which to prepare the final accounts, being the income statement and balance sheet. This is looked at in Chapter 2.

Example

On 1 January William set up in a business as a retailer. His transactions for the first two weeks are as follows:

Jan

1 Started business by putting £10 000 in a bank account
2 Withdrew £2 000 cash from the bank
3 Bought goods for cash, £1 000
4 Bought a second-hand van on credit from Sun Motors for £400
5 Sold goods for cash, £200
7 Paid wages £60, in cash
9 Bought goods on credit from A. Supplier for £400
11 Sold goods on credit to B. Customer for £500
12 Sent Sun Motors a cheque for £100
13 Sent A. Supplier a cheque for £390 in full settlement for the goods bought on 9th. Discount received on prompt payment, £10.
14 Paid wages £60, in cash
14 Received a cheque for £200 from B. Customer

Record the above transactions in double-entry form, balance the accounts at 14 January and extract a trial balance at the close of business on that date.

Answer

The classification of each account as being either asset, capital, liability, expense or income is shown in brackets after the account name. This is not done in practice.

WILLIAM

Ledger

Capital

			£				£
				Jan	1	Bank	10 000

Bank (asset)

			£				£
Jan	1	Capital	10 000	Jan	2	Cash	2 000
	14	B. Customer	200		12	Sun Motors	100
					13	A. Supplier	390
					14	Balance c/d	7 710
			10 200				10 200
Jan	15	Balance b/d	7 710				

Cash (asset)

			£				£
Jan	2	Bank	2 000	Jan	3	Purchases	1 000
	5	Sales	200		7	Wages	60
					14	Wages	60
					14	Balance c/d	1 080
			2 200				2 200
June	15	Balance b/d	1 080				

Purchases (expense)

			£				£
Jan	3	Cash	1 000				
	9	A. Supplier	400	Jan	14	Balance c/d	1 400
			1 400				1 400
Jan	15	Balance b/d	1 400				

Motor van (asset)

			£				£
Jan	4	Sun Motors	400				

Sun Motors (liability)

			£				£
Jan	12	Bank	100	Jan	4	Motor van	400
	14	Balance c/d	300				
			400				400
				Jan	15	Balance b/d	300

Sales (revenue)

			£				£
				Jan	5	Cash	200
Jan	14	Balance c/d	700		11	B. Customer	500
			700				700
				Jan	15	Balance b/d	700

Wages (expense)

			£				£
Jan	7	Cash	60				
	14	Cash	60	Jan	14	Balance c/d	120
			120				120
Jan	15	Balance b/d	120				

A. Supplier (liability)

			£				£
Jan	13	Bank	390	Jan	9	Purchases	400
	13	Discount received	10				
			400				400

B. Customer (asset)

			£				£
Jan	11	Sales	500	Jan	14	Bank	200
					14	Balance c/d	300
			500				500
Jan	15	Balance b/d	300				

Discount received (revenue)

			£				£
				Jan	13	A. Supplier	10

WILLIAM
Trial balance as at 14 Jan

	Dr £	*Cr* £
Capital		10 000
Bank	7 710	
Cash	1 080	
Purchases	1 400	
Motor van	400	
Sun Motors		300
Sales		700
Wages	120	
B. Customer	300	
Discount received		10
	11 010	11 010

If you are not familiar with double-entry bookkeeping attempt question 1.1 now before reading on.

The Full Double-entry Bookkeeping System

A full system contains several books, each with a different function. They are:

Purchase Day Book (Journal)
Sales Day Book (Journal)
Return Outwards Journal
Return Inwards Journal
The Journal
Cash Book
Petty Cash Book
} Books of Original entry

Cash Book
Purchase Ledger
Sales Ledger
General Ledger
} Divisions of the Ledger

In large businesses, because of the number of accounts it is not possible to keep them all in one ledger. The ledger has to be split or sub-divided on some logical basis. The usual sub-division is in terms of function. The individual accounts for debtors and creditors are kept in separate books called the *Sales Ledger* and *Purchase Ledger*. Cash and bank, being the two busiest accounts are allowed a book on their own called the *Cash Book*. Petty cash expenses are recorded in a separate book, the Petty Cash Book. This leaves the remaining sub-division, called the *General Ledger,* to contain the remaining asset, capital, and liability accounts and all the income and expense accounts.

An important feature of the above system is that transactions are initially recorded in a *day book, journal, or cash book* before being *posted* to an account in the ledger. As an example, a purchase day book looks as follows:

Purchase Day Book

Date	*Supplier*	*Invoice number*	*Folio*	£
Jan. 1	K. King	213	PL 11	80
2	L. Lord	214	PL 13	75
3	M. Ltd	215	PL 14	200
.	.	.	.	.
.	.	.	.	.
.	.	.	.	.
Total credit purchases for the month			GL 40	5 000

The invoice number represents the source document from which the entry has been made. The *folio* indicates the place in the ledger where the posting has been made e.g. K. King's purchase to page 11 of the purchase ledger. The double-entry for transactions recorded in the book of original (first) entry is performed *periodically*, for example at the end of each month. From the purchase day book the individual suppliers' accounts are credited in the purchase ledger. The *total* of purchases, £5 000, is debited to purchases account in the general ledger. The advantages of this system are that the purchase clerk need disturb the general ledger clerk only once a month instead of every day and the size of the purchases account is much reduced since only one entry need be made instead of *all* purchases individually. The same benefits accrue from maintaining a sales day book.

The cash and petty cash books are both books of original entry *and* part of the double-entry system, since they contain accounts. The books remain in single entry until the end of a period, commonly the month, when the double-entry is completed by posting to the purchase ledger, sales ledger, and general ledger. To facilitate such postings the books are often *analysed into columns* recording similar income and expenses.

Illustration

Petty Cash Book

Dr			*Cr*	*Stationery*	*Coffee*	*Sundry*
£	*Date*	*Item*	£	£	£	£
	Jan					
70	1	CB				
	2	Paper	3	3		
	3	Sugar	2		2	
	4	Flowers	5			5
			.	.	.	.
			.	.	.	.
			.	.	.	.
			.	.	.	.
			.	.	.	.
			.	.	.	.
			60	20	10	30
60	31	CB		GL 55	GL 12	GL 56
	31	Bal c/d	70			
130			130			
	Feb					
70	1	Bal c/d				

At the end of the month the stationery account, in page 55 of the general ledger is debited with £20, coffee in page 12 with £10, and sundry expenses in page 56 with £30. Analysis into columns reveals the monthly total easily without having to work out the amount of each expense from the total column. Of course, the total of the analysed columns £20 + £10 + £30, equals the £60 in the total column.

Presentation of the petty cash book is a little different from other accounts in that the date and account name of the debit entries are recorded in the middle of the account instead of the left. The entry on the 1st January represents receipt by the petty cashier of £70 from the main cashier to finance the month's expenditures. At the end of the month the amount spent, £60 is received to restore the petty cashier's balance to £70. This periodic topping-up is known as the *imprest system.*

Transactions which are not initially recorded in any of the purchase, sales and returns day books, cash book, or petty cash book, are entered in the *Journal.* This may be used to record the purchase and sale of fixed assets on credit, the correction of errors and miscellaneous transactions of a complicated nature such as the admission of a new partner in a partnership and issue of shares by a company. A journal is useful in that entries in ledger accounts in respect of the above have some point of reference, with an explanation of the reason for the ledger entry — called the *narrative*. This is particularly useful when a bookkeeper leaves and the incoming bookkeeper has to familiarize himself with the existing contents of the accounts.

Control Accounts

Businesses often build into their recording system a *check* on entries in the individual debtor and creditor accounts in the sales and purchase ledgers. As an example, when individual debtors are debited at the end of the month, from the sales day book, the *total* of these postings are debited in an independent account in another book. This is the *sales ledger control account* kept in the general ledger. The debit to control is not part of the double-entry system. If this procedure is followed for all transactions connected with credit customers the *total* of the balances in the sales ledger at any one time should equal the *single balance* on the sales ledger control account. If it does not, the sales clerk is alerted to errors. Control accounts are an important part of a recording system, and are considered in more detail in Chapter 4.

Computers and Bookkeeping

While bookkeeping was originally done in actual books, with the application of computers to business in recent decades a lot of it is now recorded on *cards* and *magnetic tape*. The principles of double-entry have not been affected though, and operators who understand it are still needed to organize the input and understand the output. The main impact of computerization has been that much of the manual task of physical recording has been eliminated. A computerized system is able to handle larger amounts of data and process them more quickly.

Case Study

Following the questions on this chapter is a case study. In it you are required to keep a full set of books for a restaurant for a month's trading. Following chapter 2 is Part II of the case study — preparation of the final accounts.

Questions

1.1* Record Muriel's transactions for the month of May, balance off all accounts, and extract a trial balance as at 31 May 19_8.

May

1 Started business with £5 000 in the bank and £2 000 cash
2 Bought goods for cash £400, on credit from L. Jones £200, from A. Smith £300
4 Bought fixtures on credit from Desk Ltd. £600
7 Sold goods for cash £250, on credit to B. Black £350, K. White £450
9 Paid L. Jones
10 Received a loan from A. Friend by cheque £1 000
12 Returned some fixtures, invoiced at £100, to Desk Ltd
14 Paid Desk Ltd. a cheque for £500
14 Paid rent by cheque £175
17 Bought goods for cash £500, on credit from L. Jones £400
23 Sold goods for cash £275, on credit to B. Black £375, K. White £475
29 Received a cheque from B. Black £725
31 Paid monthly salary by cheque for £450, rent by cheque £175

(20 marks)

Author's Question

1.2 Transactions
(1) the purchase of goods on credit from suppliers
(2) the sale of goods on credit
(3) cheques received from credit customers
(4) payments to suppliers by cheque for goods previously supplied
(5) allowances to credit customers upon return of faulty goods
(6) daily cash takings paid into the bank
(7) monthly salaries paid to employees
(8) the year end stock valuation

For each of the above types of transactions identify
(a) the originating document for the data
(b) the book of original entry for the transaction, and
(c) the way in which the data will be incorporated into the double entry system.

(20 marks)

Association of Accounting Technicians, Preliminary

1.3 (a) The owner of a newly formed small trading business has asked for advice regarding the establishment of a full double-entry accounting system.

List the books required to provide full accounting records and state briefly the purpose of each book. (10 marks)

(b) The owner of a company with over 5 000 credit customers seeks advice on a suitable system for checking the accuracy of the ledger entries relating to these customers.
Describe how control can be exercised in such a situation. (10 marks)

(20 marks)

Advanced level Accounting, London

Case Study — Kilburn Tandoori

Part I, Bookkeeping

On 1 February 19_8 Mr and Mrs Shah bought an existing eating house to convert it to an Indian restaurant. The initial capital of £50 000 banked on 1 February was used the next day to make the following payments: £40 000 for purchase of premises, £4 000 for furniture and fittings and £6 000 for conversion costs.

Customers were required to settle bills by cash or cheque after the meal, and weekly credit accounts were opened for two nearby offices who entertained their guests at the restaurant on a regular basis. A 3 per cent cash discount was offered for payment within one week. All cash and cheques were banked daily. All payments, except petty cash expenditures, were made by cheque. Mr Shah paid his suppliers a week following delivery, thereby obtaining a 2 per cent cash discount from each.

The following is a week-by-week summary of the first month's trading:

	Week			
	1	*2*	*3*	*4*
	£	£	£	£
Credit purchases from suppliers				
Williams Farms		500	450	550
T. Green & Sons	80	100	110	100
Hakim Meat	300	350	350	350
Robinson Wines	50	110	175	150

Other Payments				
Cook's wages	100	100	110	100
Waiters' wages	180	180	200	200
Cash register machine		200		
Rates				270
Drawings		55	10	70
For petty cash expenditure	30	30	30	30
Cash Receipts	625	830	1055	1210
Cheques Received	810	1050	1100	1175
Invoiced to credit customers				
Sun Finance Co.		110	155	150
Chrome Metals PLC		60	80	100
Cheques received from credit customers				
Sun Finance Co.			107	150
Chrome Metals PLC				138
Summary of petty cash expenditure				
Cleaning materials	5	7	7	8
Fresh flowers	10	4	5	6
Napkins	12	14	15	15

The owners employ you to maintain a full double-entry bookkeeping system. *Write up the books for the first month's trading.*

Notes

(1) Since the information given is on a week-by-week basis it is best to write up the books also on a weekly basis.

(2) Classify the £6 000 conversion costs as premises, the £200 cash register as fixtures and fittings.

(3) The petty cash expenditures for cleaning materials, fresh flowers, and napkins should be grouped into one account called general expenses.

(4) In your discount calculations round off to the nearest whole £.

Solutions

1.2

Transaction no.	*(a) Document*	*(b) Book of original entry*	*(c) Double-entry*
1.	Purchase invoice	Purchase day book	*Dr* monthly total to purchase a/c, GL *Cr* individual amounts to suppliers' a/cs, PL Additional entry — *Cr* purchase ledger control account, GL, with monthly total
2.	Sales invoice	Sales day book	*Dr* individual amounts to debtors' a/cs, SL *Cr* monthly total to sales a/c, GL Additional entry — *Dr* sales ledger control account, GL, with monthly total
3.	Cheque received	Cash book	*Dr* Bank *Cr* Debtors, SL Additional entry — *Cr* sales ledger control with total
4.	Cheque sent	Cash book	*Dr* Creditors, PL *Cr* Bank Additional entry — *Dr* purchase ledger control with total

Transaction no.	*(a) Document*	*(b) Book of original entry*	*(c) Double-entry*
5.	Credit note	Return inwards Journal	*Dr* monthly total to return inwards a/c, GL *Cr* individual customers, SL Additional entry — *Cr* sales ledger control with total
6.	Paying-in slip	Cash book	*Dr* Bank *Cr* Cash
7.	Wages slip	Cash book	*Dr* Wages and salaries, GL *Cr* Bank
8.	Stock sheets	The Journal	*Dr* Stock, GL *Cr* Trading a/c, in the year-end income statement

CHAPTER 2

Final Accounts — The Income Statement and Balance Sheet

Every so often the businessman will ask questions like 'How much profit have I made over the past year?' and 'What is my business worth today compared to last year?' The answer to these important questions cannot be obtained from the books. For them he has to prepare annual accounting statements, of which there are two — the *income statement* which seeks to answer the first question and the *balance sheet* which answers the second. These statements cannot be prepared unless the bookkeeping has been performed throughout the year. The books are therefore the *raw material* for the final accounts.

At the end of a financial year the accountant will:

(1) Check the cash book with the bank statement by performing a *bank reconciliation statement.*

(2) Check the individual debtor and creditor accounts in the sales and purchase ledgers with their respective *control accounts.*

(3) Prepare a *Trial Balance* from the general ledger to check its arithmetic accuracy.

(4) Adjust certain expense accounts in the general ledger for accruals and prepayments, and create provisions for depreciation and doubtful debts.

(5) Prepare the final accounts.

Businesses are organized either as sole traders, partnerships, or limited companies. The final accounts in this chapter are addressed in terms of sole traders. However, the principles and procedure of preparing them are equally applicable to all forms of business organizations. The differences lie in the appropriation of profit, sources of finance (capital structure), and presentation of the accounts. Partnerships are looked at in Chapter 8, company accounts in Chapter 10.

Before looking at the final accounts let us now see what happens in the ledger accounts at the end of a financial year.

Purchases, Sales Ledgers

The personal account of each creditor and debtor is *balanced off* and a schedule or list of balances produced and totalled. These figures are checked with the control account. If there is a discrepancy, the bookkeeper has to undertake the tedious but necessary task of checking each individual account to identify and correct the errors.

General Ledger

All the accounts in the general ledger (being income, expense, asset, liability, and capital accounts) are totalled and *balanced*. The year-end trial balance is now extracted. If it does not balance, each account will have to be examined carefully to locate the errors. Some errors will be found quickly, others will prove more difficult to find; for these it is possible to cheat and force the trial balance to balance by inserting the difference in a *suspense account*, as long as the size of the difference is not material. (Suspense accounts and the correction of errors are looked at in Chapter 6.) All is now set for the year-end adjustments and preparation of the final accounts.

Purchases, Sales Accounts

The balances on these accounts are initially represented in the trial balance. On balancing of the trial balance they are *written off* to the trading account. At the start of the next financial year a business is not interested in last year's purchases and sales figures, so these accounts are closed. The process is a double-entry. The entries are represented below using hypothetical figures.

In the Journal, for purchases:

Dr Trading account	£13 000	
Cr Purchases		£13 000

And in the ledger:

Purchases

19_6		£	19_6		£
Jan. 14	Bank	600			
:	:	:			
:	:	:			
:	:	:			
:	:	:			
:	:	:			
:	:	:	Dec. 31	Trading	13 000
Total for the year		13 000			13 000

The debit side of the trading account therefore represents expenses.

In the *journal*, for sales:

Dr Sales	£20 000	
Cr Trading		£20 000

And in the ledger:

Sales

19_6		£	19_6		£
			Jan. 10	Bank	450
			:	:	:
			:	:	:
			:	:	:
			:	:	:
			:	:	:
Dec. 31	Trading	20 000	:	:	:
		20 000	Total for the year		20 000

The credit side of the trading account then represents revenue.

Expense Accounts

Again the totals are initially included in the year-end trial balance. They are then written off to the profit and loss acount (P&L), for the same reason that purchases and sales are written off to the trading account. The double-entry is:

Dr P&L account
Cr Expense account

The final accounts are based upon the *accruals concept*. This states that costs and revenues should be recognized when they are incurred or earned and not when they are paid or received. The *amount charged* to P&L in respect of an item of expenditure is then not necessarily the amount of *cash paid.*

Example

Donald rents business premises at a cost of £1 000 per month, payable quarterly. His financial year corresponds to the calendar year. Cheques for £3 000 are paid on 3 April, 3 July, and 3 October 19_1. At 31 December the amount due for the final quarter is accrued (outstanding), payable on 3 January 19_2. The ledger account would look as follows:

Rent

19_1		£
3 April	Bank	3 000
3 July	Bank	3 000
3 Oct	Bank	3 000

The balance on the account is £9 000, and this would be the amount shown for rent in the year-end trial balance. However, it would be wrong to charge only £9 000 to the P&L account. The £3 000 rent of the last quarter has been *incurred in this year* and the *benefit has been received in this year.* It should therefore be charged against this year's income. The completed account looks as follows:

Rent

19_1		£	19_1		£
3 April	Bank	3 000			
3 July	Bank	3 000			
3 Oct	Bank	3 000			
31 Dec	Balance c/d	3 000	31 Dec	P&L	12 000
		12 000			12 000
			19_2		
			1 Jan	Balance b/d	3 000

By adjusting the expense account for the accrual we have achieved two things:

1. the charge for rent in the P&L account is now the correct charge.
2. the account has a credit balance of £3 000 reflecting the liability existing at the year-end. This will be shown in the balance sheet under current liabilities.

If, at the end of an year, an expense is prepaid, as is often the case, for example with rates and insurance, the prepaid element should be carried down as a *debit* balance at the start of the next year. This has the effect of *reducing* the charge to P&L. The amount prepaid is shown in the balance sheet as a current asset.

In constructing a ledger account with an accrual or prepayment it is best to follow the steps below:

1. Bring forward any accrual or prepayment from last year.
2. Debit the account with cash and cheques paid.
3. Credit the account with the amount incurred i.e. which should have been paid. This is the transfer to P&L.
4. Balance the account. The balancing figure is the accrual or prepayment.

The procedure for revenue is the same except that cash received is credited to the account, the transfer to P&L debited. See questions 2.3 and 2.4.

The accruals concept is also known as the *matching concept* since an attempt is made to match all revenues attributable to a financial period to all expenses attributable to that period.

Provision for Doubtful Debts

Accounting profit is taken at the time of sale and before payment. If a debt is proving difficult to collect with the possibility that it will turn out to be a bad debt, the profit figure should be adjusted for this. The double-entry is:

Dr P&L
    Cr Provision for doubtful debts

No entry need be made in any individual debtor account. This is necessary only when a debt actually goes bad. The balance on the provision for doubtful debts account is deducted from the debtors figure to give a more realistic value of debtors in the balance sheet. Such an exercise is in line with the concept of *prudence* (or *conservatism*) which states that a loss should be provided for as soon as it is anticipated and that it is preferable to understate rather than overstate profits and assets.

Example

On 1 January 19_6 the balance on a provision for doubtful debts account stands at £70. At 31 December 19_6 it is decided to set the year's provision at 3 per cent of debtors, which total £3 000. Show the provision for doubtful debts account.

Provision for doubtful debts

19_6		£	19_6		£
			1 Jan	Balance b/d	70
31 Dec	Balance c/d	90	31 Dec	P&L	20
		90			90
			19_7		
			1 Jan	Balance b/d	90

Note that the charge to P&L is not the whole of the provision, but just the *increase* in provision required from the balance existing at the start of the year. If the provision is to be decreased this is credited to P&L, as a miscellaneous income.

There are two approaches to estimating the provision:

1. *specific provision* — each debtor account is examined individually, those which appear to be doubtful being listed.
2. *general provision* — a percentage of the total debtor figure is taken, based on past experience.

A combination of the two methods is sometimes used.

Provision for Depreciation

A further adjustment is needed to reflect the fall in value of fixed assets during the year. This is known as *depreciation* and the amount charged is an expense to P&L. The double entry is:

Dr P&L
    Cr Provision for depreciation

Depreciation is a popular topic with examiners and one that deserves detailed consideration. We shall return to it in the next chapter.

In the trial balance extracted from the books at the end of the year the balance on the provision accounts (depreciation and doubtful debts) are one year old since the year-end adjustments are made *after* trial balance extraction. The stock and capital accounts are also one year old. The value of capital at the year-end is revealed only after preparation of the income statement and balance sheet.

Final Accounts — the Income Statement

The purpose of the income statement is to determine the profit or loss for the year. It is divided into two parts — the *trading account*, which measures the profit on trading alone before taking overhead expenses into account (known as *gross profit*) and the *profit and loss account* which reveals the true profit of the business after charging the overheads (known as *net profit*). Such a division is useful for analysis of the results at the end of the year and for comparison to previous years.

The specific nature of the income statement prepared depends on the nature of the business. Since the trading account is concerned with the buying and selling of *goods*, it is prepared only by trading firms such as wholesalers, retailers, and manufacturers. Firms in the service industry such as hairdressers, lawyers, and mini-cab drivers do not prepare a trading account, since they are not dealing in goods. Only a profit and loss account, showing fee income less business expenses, is needed. The income statement of manufacturing concerns starts with a *manufacturing account* which calculates the cost of production of goods in the factory. The gross profit on trading is shown in the trading account. Overheads are then deducted in the profit and loss account. Manufacturing accounts are looked at in Chapter 13.

Capital and Revenue

The income statement seeks to deduct *revenue expenditure* from *revenue income* to arrive at profit. *Capital items* are excluded. Revenue items are those transactions whose influence on the business is short-term i.e. less than one financial year. Examples include the payment of wages (revenue expenditure) and the receipt of cash for goods sold (revenue income). Capital items, on the other hand, have a long-lasting effect on the business i.e. *more* than one financial year. A good example is the purchase of an item of fixed asset. Since this benefits a firm for more than one financial year it would be unfair to charge its cost *wholly* to the year of purchase. Instead it should be charged *over the expected lifetime of the asset* — through depreciation. This produces a fairer result than if the whole of the asset is charged to just one year.

The distinction between capital and revenue is in fact an application of the accruals concept, which you will remember states that expenditure should be charged to the year(s) in which the benefit is received. An alternative financial statement, which does not exclude capital items, is the *funds flow statement*. This is considered in Chapter 11.

Final Accounts — the Balance Sheet

The balance sheet is a statement of financial position of the business at the year-end. It shows details of the accounting equation that holds for all businesses, namely that Assets = Capital + Liabilities, and Capital = Assets — Liabilities. The upper half shows the various assets employed (uses of funds) less current liabilities, giving *net assets*. The lower half shows the various sources of funds from owners (capital) and long-term liabilities, representing total *capital employed*. The figure for net assets is equal to capital employed.

In bookkeeping terms the balance sheet is simply a list of balances remaining in the books after effecting the year-end adjustments and closing the income and expense accounts to the income statement. It is *not* part of the double-entry — hence the absence of the word 'account' from its name. In contrast the manufacturing, trading, and profit and loss accounts *are* part of the double-entry.

Horizontal Format

Traditionally the final accounts used to be prepared in double-entry, T-account, or horizontal format. This practice has in recent been replaced by the *vertical* style of presentation. Accounts are prepared mostly for the benefit of non-accountants such as businessmen, shareholders, and managers. Non-accountants, not being versed in the principles of double-entry, prefer to look at figures in columnar or tabular form rather than in debit-credit form. The vertical style of presentation has been adopted throughout this book.

Let us now look at an example of year-end adjustments and preparation of the final accounts from a trial balance.

Question

Claire Voyant is the owner of a shop selling beauty products and cosmetics for women. At 31 December 19_6, the end of her financial year, the following balances have been extracted from the books:

Trial balance as at 31 December 19_6

	Dr	*Cr*
	£	£
Bank balance	4 900	
Capital		14 500
Cash	2 000	
Discounts allowed	560	
Discounts received		500
Drawings	2 500	
Fixtures and fittings — cost	14 000	
Provision for depreciation on fixtures		3 500
Light and heat	900	
Provision for doubtful debts		60
Purchases	13 000	
Rent and rates	1 700	
Sales		20 000
Stock	2 000	
Trade creditors		6 850
Trade debtors	2 000	
Wages	1 850	
	£47 150	£47 150

The following matters are to be taken into account before preparation of the final accounts:

(1) The stock-take on 31 December 19_6 valued the shop's stock at £3 000, at cost.
(2) At 31 December 19_6 rent and rates were prepaid by £200 and there was an outstanding bill of £150 for wages.
(3) The fixtures and fittings are to be depreciated by £500.
(4) The provision for doubtful debts is to be 5% of the debtors at the year-end.

Required:
Miss Voyant's final accounts for the year ended 31 December 19_6.

Answer

The reference numbers on the left hand side will be used to explain the items after the account.

CLAIRE VOYANT

Trading and Profit and loss Account for the year ended 31 December 19_6

		£	£
	Sales		20 000
1.	Less cost of goods sold		
	Opening stock	2 000	
	Purchases	13 000	
		15 000	
	Less closing stock	3 000	
			12 000
2.	*Gross profit*		8 000
3.	Discounts received		500
			8 500
4.	*Less Expenses*		
	Discounts allowed	560	
	Light and heat	900	
	Rent and rates (1 700 – 200)	1 500	
	Wages (1 850 + 150)	2 000	
	Depreciation	500	
	Provision for doubtful debts*	40	
5.	*Net profit*		5 500
			£3 000

* Provision required	100
Existing provision	60
Increase required	40

CLAIRE VOYANT

Balance Sheet as at 31 December 19_6

		£	£	£
	Assets employed:			
6.	*Fixed assets*			
	Fixtures and fittings, at cost		14 000	
	Less accumulated depreciation (3 500 + 500)		4 000	
				10 000
7.	*Current assets*			
	Stock		3 000	
	Trade debtors	2 000		
	Less provision for doubtful debts	100	1 900	
	Prepayment		200	
	Bank balance		4 900	
	Cash		2 000	
			12 000	
8.	*Less Current liabilities*			
	Trade creditors	6 850		
	Accrued expense	150	7 000	
9.	*Working capital*			5 000
10.	*Net assets*			£15 000

	Financed by:	
	Capital, 1 January 19_6	14 500
	Add profit	3 000
		17 500
11.	Less drawings	2 500
12.	*Capital employed*	£15 000

Note carefully the difference in heading in the two statements. The income statement is headed 'for the year ended'. This is because it is a summary of the results of trading over a period, in this case from 1 January to 31 December. The balance sheet, on the other hand, is headed 'as at' because it represents the financial affairs of the business *at a given point in time*; the year-end.

A few words now on the items in the final accounts.

The Income Statement

1. *Cost of goods sold.* The figure for purchases is adjusted for the accruals concept to arrive at the cost of goods chargeable to this year. The £2 000 stock left over from last year was sold this year — therefore we charge it to this year's account. The £3 000 closing stock at the end of this year will be sold next year — therefore we take it out of purchases, to be charged as opening stock to next year. The resulting figure represents the cost of the goods sold in this year.

   Any carriage paid on goods delivered (*carriage inwards*) is normally added to purchases and counted as part of cost of goods sold. Carriage paid on goods sent to customers (*carriage outwards*) is a selling expense and entered in the profit and loss account.

2. *Gross profit.* This is the profit on trading alone before taking into account any overhead expenses. The trading account ends with the figure for gross profit.

3. *Discounts received.* The first item in the profit and loss account is *miscellaneous revenues* such as discounts received, rent receivable and profit on sale of fixed assets.

4. *Expenses.* The main body of the P&L account lists the various overhead expenses of the business, adjusted for accruals and prepayments.

5. *Net profit.* This represents the true profit of the business after all expenses have been met. For a sole trader it constitutes the income of the owner. A proportion is therefore subject to income tax.

The Balance Sheet

The top half shows the various ways in which the capital invested in the business has been employed — as between fixed assets, current assets and current liabilities.

6. *Fixed assets.* These are long-term assets held not with a view to resale but for permanent use in the business. Examples include land and buildings, plant and machinery, motor vehicles, and fixtures and fittings.

7. *Current assets.* These are short-term assets held with a view to conversion into cash. They are arranged in order of increasing liquidity. Thus cash, which is the perfect liquid asset is shown last, stock which is the least liquid shown first.
8. *Current liabilities.* These are short-term obligations due within the next 12 months. The main one is trade creditors for goods supplied but not yet paid for.

9. *Working capital.* This constitutes the excess of current assets over current liabilities. The *working capital cycle* consists of the conversion of stock and creditors to debtors when the stock is sold, and finally to cash when payment is received. Payment to creditors reduces the cash balance, but with new stock coming in they are soon sold bringing in further cash. And so the cycle continues. It can be represented as:

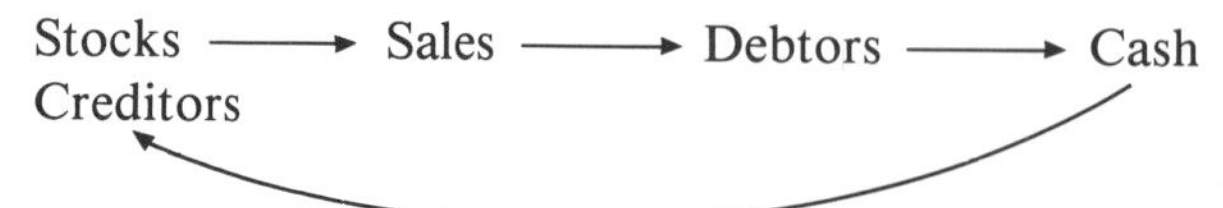

When sales are made for cash, debtors are eliminated and the cycle is shortened by the period of credit normally extended to customers.

Working capital can be distinguished from *fixed capital*, which is the amount of money invested in fixed assets — in this case £10 000.

10. *Net assets.* This represents total assets − Current liabilities. It is equal to capital employed.

The lower half of the balance sheet shows the various sources of finance.

11. *Drawings.* The figure for drawings over time should move with changes in profit over time, since drawings represent the owner's financial reward of running the business at a profit. If the owner does not withdraw the full amount of profit for a year he/she has effectively *re-invested* or '*ploughed back*' part of the profit into the business to help it grow. In our example Miss Voyant has ploughed £500 of the year's profit back into her shop, and this has increased capital from £14 500 to £15 000.

12. *Capital employed.* This represents the total amount of money invested into the business to date. It will increase if the owner:
    (i) injects additional capital
    (ii) borrows long-term, from a friend or bank
    (iii) does not withdraw all of a year's profit but retains some for use in the business.

    Capital employed is always equal to net assets. An increase in capital employed will lead to a similar increase in net assets since the additional money will be used in some way — to buy fixed assets, stock, to reduce liabilities, or simply to increase the bank balance.

Examination Questions

Examination questions on final accounts usually give a year-end trial balance or list of balances with additional information on year-end adjustments. From this you have to prepare an income statement and balance sheet. In practice, accountants go from the trial balance to the final accounts by effecting the year-end adjustments in an *Extended Trial Balance*. This method, however, takes a lot of time and space and is not really suitable for examination purposes, unless specifically asked for. A quicker method is to place a letter in front of each item in the trial balance to indicate its position in the final accounts — T for trading, P for P&L, and B for balance sheet. As you use each item, cross out the letter from the trial balance. At the same time, as you make each year-end adjustment, tick it off. This is also a good way of ensuring that you have taken all items into account in preparing your final accounts. Later you will reach a stage where you are confident enough to prepare the accounts without the need for any markings. Through having done many questions you will know instinctively what items to look out for and in which order.

Following the chapter is Part II of the case study for Kilburn Tandoori. It requires you to effect the adjustment required before preparing the final accounts. The solution to both parts I and II then follow.

Accounting Concepts and Conventions

Accounting statements are based upon a number of basic concepts. Two of these we have already met in this chapter — the *accruals concept* (as applied to expenses, fixed assets, and stock) and *conservatism* (as applied to debtors). Conservatism applied to expected losses is known as the concept of *prudence,* applied to expected gains, the *realization* concept. This states that profit is to be regarded as earned *when goods are delivered to the customer* — not when the goods are manufactured or bought by the seller, not even when the goods are ordered. The principle here is not to anticipate a profit until it actually materializes. A number of other concepts underlie a set of accounts. These are now considered.

The Money Measurement Concept

The language of accountants is Money. All business transactions are expressed in the common denominator of money. Thus the sale of ten units of a good for £5 each is recorded in the accounts not as the sale of ten physical units but as £50 earned from sales. While this has the advantage of being able to add many diverse business activities together, it suffers from the limitation that not all events can be quantified in money terms. Thus financial statements cannot record the amount of goodwill from customers, 'know-how', and patents a business possesses, human assets such as quality of the workforce and atmosphere at the place of work. *The accounts therefore do not tell the full story of a business.* Another problem with the practice is that money is not a stable unit of measurement — its value changes with inflation or deflation.

The Business Entity Concept

The accounts show the financial affairs of the *business only*, and does not extend to the private financial affairs of the owner or owners. Thus if a sole trader wins a million pounds on the football pools this is not entered as income in the accounts of the business. Only if he puts some of his winnings as additional capital into the business are the accounts affected. To take another example, if he takes some business stock home for personal use the figure for purchases should be reduced by this amount (since the stock is not being used for business, but private purposes) and the figure for drawings increased.

The Going Concern Concept

Accounts are prepared on the assumption that the business is a going concern i.e. *that it will continue to operate in the foreseeable future.* It does not record asset values at the price they would fetch if the business was sold off. Assets are stated at *cost less accumulated depreciation* and this figure is often different from their market value if the business was wound up. Departure from this concept is justifiable only if a business is in difficulty and liquidation is a distinct possibility. In this case the assets should be valued at the prices they are expected to fetch on liquidation. The departure from the concept should be stated in the accounts, giving reasons for it.

The Cost Concept

The practice of showing assets at cost is known as the cost concept. Accountants do not like subjectivity in their figures. The advantage of following the simple rule of recording everything at historic cost is that it is *objective* — immediately verifiable by reference to *facts.* A limitation however is that assets which did not cost anything are not shown in the accounts e.g. goodwill.

The other limitation of historic cost is that it fails to represent the affairs of a business realistically in a period of rising prices. Here true asset values exceed historic cost and the gap between the two becomes increasingly large with the simple passage of time. This limitation was highlighted in the mid-seventies when the UK and most of the Western economies suffered from a period of high inflation. The response of the accounting profession was to develop alternative systems of accounting which could accommodate the problem of rapidly rising prices. Of these the two which gained most exposure were *current cost accounting* (CCA) and *current purchasing power* (CPP). However these alternative systems were not without their own difficulties, not the least of which was their sheer complexity, and the profession was not united on which system to adopt. With the hesitation, and the bringing under control of inflation in the UK in the early eighties, neither system was chosen. As a result financial statements today are still prepared under historic cost. Some of the larger companies prepare current cost or alternative inflation accounting statements in addition to historic cost.

Consistency

There are some matters in the accounts for which there is more than one acceptable treatment. Examples include the different possible methods for depreciation and stock valuation, and the treatment of research and development expenditure. This would not be so important were it not for the fact that the different methods often lead to significantly different profit and balance sheet figures. This problem highlights the fact that accounting is not an exact science (although accountants sometimes like to think that it is). To try and overcome the problem, the principle of *consistency* states that *like items should be treated in a like manner within one accounting period and from one period to the next.* If this was not done it would be possible for management to effectively *choose* the profit figure of a year by selecting those methods of treatment and interpretation of events which suited them best. Also, the profit and other figures in the accounts between years would not be directly *comparable.* A change from consistency is allowed only if the change leads to a truer and fairer representation of the affairs of a business. If a change is made a note of it should be included in the accounts along with an explanation of the reason for the change.

Another advantage of consistency is that if similar events are treated in a like manner by *all* firms the accounts of *different businesses* would be directly comparable. Because this is not done in practice, inter-firm comparisons are fraught with difficulties. In an attempt to encourage greater consistency between firms the *Accounting Standards Committee* (ASC) was formed in the UK in 1970, of which all the six major accounting bodies are now members. The procedure of the ASC has been to issue an *Exposure Draft* on a subject first, inviting comments from businesses, accountants, academics and other interested parties. In the light of the comments modifications are made where they are felt necessary, and a formal *Statement of Standard Accounting Practice* (SSAP) issued, which accountants and businesses are then expected to observe. Areas in which statements have been issued so far include stocks and work-in-progress valuation (SSAP9), sources and application of funds statements (SSAP10), depreciation (SSAP12), and inflation accounting (SSAP16).

With the inter-dependence that exists between Western economies and the close economic and political co-operation, consistency of accounting treatment of matters *across national boundaries* is also desirable. This is particularly so for multinational companies — those operating in more than one country. In recognition of this the *International Accounting Standards Board* (IASB) was formed in 1973 through co-operation by most of the major Western economies including the USA, UK, West Germany, France, Japan, Australia and Canada. Progress on the international front is invariably slow but a number of *International Accounting Standards (IAS)* have been issued so far including ones on difficult areas such as stock valuation (IAS 2) and depreciation (IAS 4).

Standardization v. Flexibility

The drive for standardization has not been without its problems or critics. The main objection has come from those who believe that standardization is *not necessarily desirable*, because accounts are meant to represent the financial affairs of businesses in all different kinds of industries. A particular method of treatment while appropriate in one industry is not necessarily appropriate in another. Adherence to an unsuitable standard results in a worse position than if no standard existed.

Materiality

The accountant should concern himself only with items *material* in relation to the size of the business. For example, the purchase of a stapler which lasts for 3 years should, according to the accruals concept, be charged against income also over 3 years. Since the cost of a stapler is minimal however, it would not be worth the time and effort in maintaining separate accounts for stapler at cost and provision for depreciation of stapler. The benefit involved in doing this is far outweighed by the cost. The principle of materiality can then be applied to write off the whole of the cost in the year of purchase. This will not affect the accounts in any material way. There is no single dividing line between what is material and immaterial — this is dependent on the cost of recording and size of the business. Thus while a figure of £1 000 may be material for a small sole trader it is quite immaterial for a multi-national public company where the final accounts are probably expressed in millions of pounds rather than pounds.

Although the concepts presented in this chapter are generally accepted by the accounting profession today, they are not to be regarded as *Laws*. There are no natural laws in accounting — it is a man-made subject. Nor should the concepts be regarded as being immune to criticism and change. Concepts have evolved over time as the 'best way of doing things' in the light of past experience. Changes in conditions, attitudes and experiences may well cause a concept to be modified or even abandoned — as the historic cost concept nearly was in the late-seventies.

Also, while the above concepts are applicable in the majority of accounting situations, they are not *all* applicable in *all* situations. The over-riding requirement of a set of accounts is that they present a *true and fair view* of the financial affairs of a business. If adherence to a concept leads to a less than true and fair view, departure from it is justified so long as this is stated in the accounts. Thus the going concern concept should not be applied for a business facing the prospect of closure, the realization concept can be overlooked in the case of long-term contracts (explained in Contract Costing, Chapter 17), as can the cost concept for freehold property for which market value has risen significantly above historic cost.

Questions

2.1* The following trial balance has been extracted from the ledger of Mr Yousef, a sole trader.

Trial balance as at 31 May 19_6

	Dr	*Cr*
	£	£
Sales		138 078
Purchases	82 350	
Carriage	5 144	
Drawings	7 800	

	Dr	Cr
	£	£
Rent, rates and insurance	6 622	
Postage and Stationery	3 001	
Advertising	1 330	
Salaries and wages	26 420	
Bad debts	877	
Provision for bad debts		130
Debtors	12 120	
Creditors		6 471
Cash on hand	177	
Cash at bank	1 002	
Stocks as at 1 June 19_5	11 927	
Equipment		
at cost	58 000	
accumulated depreciation		19 000
Capital		53 091
	216 770	216 770

The following additional information as at 31 May 19_6 is available:

(a) Rent is accrued by £210.
(b) Rates have been prepaid by £880.
(c) £2 211 of carriage represents carriage inwards on purchases.
(d) Equipment is to be depreciated at 15% per annum using the straight line method.
(e) The provision for bad debts to be increased by £40.
(f) Stock at the close of business has been valued at £13 551.

Required:
Prepare a Trading and Profit and Loss Account for the year ended 31 May 19_6 and a Balance Sheet as at that date.

Association of Accounting Technicians, Preliminary **(20 marks)**

2.2 Charles is a wholesaler of accounting stationery. He conducts his business from a small warehouse which he owns. Part of the building is sub-let to another trader at an annual rent of £2 600. The following year-end trial balance has been extracted from his books at the close of business on 30 June 19_3:

Trial balance as at 30 June 19_3

	Dr	Cr
	£	£
Bad debts	500	
Bank	4 400	
Capital		55 000
Debtors	10 000	
Drawings	13 000	
Creditors		9 500
Heating and lighting	1 500	
Motor vehicles, at cost	22 000	
Provision for depreciation		7 000
Motor vehicle expenses	4 000	
Postage and stationery	1 600	
Purchases	66 000	
Rent and rates	8 000	
Rent received		2 000
Returns inwards	5 000	
Salaries and wages	11 500	
Sales		115 000
Stock	16 000	
Warehouse (land and buildings)	25 000	
	188 500	188 500

Additional information:

(1) Stock at 30 June 19_3, £20 000
(2) Heating and lighting accrued at 30 June 19_3, £500.
(3) The fall in value of the delivery vans during the year is estimated at £5000.
(4) Charles frequently takes home stationery for personal use. The total value of goods taken over the year is estimated at £2 000.

Required:
Charles' trading and profit and loss account for the year ended 30 June 19_3 and a balance sheet as at that date.

(20 marks)

Author's Question

2.3 The following balances stood in the books of Penelope at 1 January 19_2.

	Dr	*Cr*
	£	£
Electricity		50
Insurance	95	
Rent receivable	50	
Provision for doubtful debts		70

During 19_2 the following transactions took place:

3 Mar.	Paid insurance. This covers the period 1 Feb. to 31 July.	570	
2 Apr.	Paid electricity	200	
4 Apr.	Received rent		150
4 July	Paid electricity	180	
6 July	Received rent		150
3 Sept.	Paid insurance. This covers the period 1 Aug. to 31 Jan. 19_3.	600	
8 Oct.	Received rent		150
9 Oct.	Paid electricity	150	

Additional information:

(1) Penelope sub-lets parts of her premises for £50 a month.
(2) The electricity bill for the final quarter is estimated to be £170.
(3) At the end of the year Penelope wishes to make a provision for doubtful debts of 4% of debtors. Debtors at 31 December 19_2 stand at £2000.

Prepare:

(a) the following ledger accounts in Penelope's books:
    electricity (3 marks)
    insurance (3 marks)
    rent receivable (3 marks)
    provision for doubtful debts (3 marks)
(b) relevant extracts from the final accounts for the year ended 31 December 19_2. (6 marks)

(18 marks)

Author's Question

2.4*Colin rents premises at a rental of £1 000 per annum. He sublets part of the premises to Hill at £300 per annum and another part to Pine at £200 per annum. On 1 January 19_3 Colin had paid his own rent up to date; Hill's rent was 3 months in arrears and Pine had paid his rent to 31 March 19_3.

During the year 19_3;

(1) Colin paid his rent at the end of each quarter except the amount due at 31 December 19_3 which was outstanding;

(2) Colin received the following amounts from Hill: 31 January £150; 1 April £75; 5 July £75; 4 December £150; and
(3) Colin received the following amount from Pine, 10 October £100.

Required:
The accounts for rent payable and rent receivable in Colin's ledger for the year ended 31 December 19_3 on the basis that personal accounts are kept for Hill and Pine.

Institute of Chartered Accountants, Foundation, part-question **(7 marks)**

2.5*Given below is the Trial Balance of Derwent at 31 March Year 5:

	£000 *Dr*	*£000* *Cr*
Purchases and Sales	284	354
Drawings and Capital	12	152
Freehold Shop at Cost and accumulated depreciation thereon	78	30
Fixtures, Fittings at Cost and accumulated depreciation thereon	30	11
Debtors and Creditors	54	34
Stock at Cost (1 April Year 4)	64	
Wages	37	
Insurance	3	
Other expenses	28	
Bank		9
	590	590

The following additional information is available:

(1) Depreciation is to be provided at the rate of 10% on both the cost of fixtures and fittings and the cost of the freehold shop, at 31 March Year 5.

(2) Insurance includes £2 000 paid in respect of the year to 30 September Year 5.

(3) Stock at 31 March Year 5 comprised three categories (I, II and III) valued as follows:

	I *£000*	II *£000*	III *£000*
Cost	32	35	30
Net realizable value	44	30	40

(4) Wages owing at 31 March, Year 5 amounted to £2 000.

(5) Debtors include £4 000 regarded by the year-end as irrecoverable and it has been decided to provide for further bad debts at the rate of 2% on the balance.

(6) Derwent has employed an advertising agency to carry out a campaign during the three months to 31 March, Year 5. He has not yet either paid (or recorded) the £10 000 estimated cost of this campaign and expects to benefit from it during the middle part of his next financial year.

(7) Other expenses include £12 000 spent on adapting his shop to satisfy new government fire regulations.

Required:
(a) Prepare Derwent's Trading and Profit and Loss Account for the year ended 31 March, Year 5 and his Balance Sheet at that date. (12 marks)
(b) Briefly explain your treatment in (a) above of additional information (3), (6) and (7), justifying the treatment, in each case, by reference to relevant accounting concepts and conventions. (6 marks)

London Chamber of Commerce and Industry, Higher **(18 marks)**

2.6 After completing a training course at a technical college, Michael Faraday set up in business as a self-employed electrician on 1 January 19_5. He was very competent at his job but had no idea how to maintain proper accounting records. Sometime during 19_5 one of his friends asked Michael how well his business was doing. He replied 'All right...I think...but I'm not quite sure'.

In the ensuing conversation his friend asked whether he had prepared accounts yet, covering his first quarter's trading, to which Michael replied that he had not. His friend then stressed that, for various reasons, it was vital for accounts of businesses to be prepared properly.

Shortly afterwards Michael came to see you to ask for your help in preparing accounts for his first quarter's trading. He brought with him, in a cardboard box, the only records he had, mainly scribbled on scraps of paper.

He explained that he started his business with a car worth £700, and £2 250 in cash of which £250 was his savings and £2 000 had been borrowed from a relative at an interest rate of 10% per annum. It was his practice to pay his suppliers and expenses in cash, to require his customers to settle their accounts in cash and to bank any surplus in a business bank account. He maintained lists of cash receipts and cash payments, of supplies obtained on credit and of work carried out for customers and of appliances sold, on credit.

The list of credit suppliers comprised:

Date supplied	*Supplier*	*Amount owed*	*Date paid*	*Amount paid*	*Remarks*
19_5		£	19_5	£	
January	Dee & Co	337.74	March	330.00	Received discount £7.74
	AB Supplies	528.20	March	528.20	
February	Simpson	141.34	March	138.00	Received discount £3.34
	Cotton Ltd	427.40	March	130.00	Payment on account
			April	297.40	Remainder
	Dee & Co.	146.82	March	140.00	Received discount £6.82
March	AB Supplies	643.43	April	643.43	
	Simpson	95.60			Not yet paid

The purchase in January from Dee & Co. was of tools and equipment to enable him to carry out electrical repair work. All the remaining purchases were of repair materials, except for the purchase in February from Cotton Ltd. which consisted entirely of electrical appliances for resale.

In addition to the above credit transactions, he had brought repair materials for cash, as follows:

19_5	£
January	195.29
February	161.03
March	22.06

Other cash payments comprised:

19_5		£
January	Rent of premises for January to June 19_5	400.00
	Rates of premises for January to March 19_5	150.00
	Stationery	32.70

	Car running expenses	92.26
February	Sundries	51.54
	Car running expenses	81.42
March	Sundries	24.61
	Car running expenses	104.52
	Transfer to bank	500.00

He had also withdrawn £160.00 in cash at the end of each month for living expenses.

The list of credit customers comprised:

Date of sale	*Customer*	*Amount owed*	*Date received*	*Amount received*	*Remarks*
1985		£	19_5	£	
January	D. Hopkins	362.80	February	357.00	Allowed discount £5.80
	P. Bolton	417.10	March	417.10	
February	G. Leivers	55.00	March	55.00	
	M. Whitehead	151.72	April	151.72	
	N. John Ltd.	49.14	April	49.14	
	A. Linneker	12.53	March	12.53	
March	E. Horton	462.21	April	462.21	
	S. Ward	431.08	March	426.00	Allowed discount £5.08
	W. Scothern & Co.	319.12			Not yet received
	N. Annable	85.41			Not yet received

The above amounts relate to charges for repair work which he had carried out, except that the amounts shown in February for G. Leivers, N. John Ltd. and A. Linneker are for sales of electrical appliances.

In addition to the above credit transactions, he had cash takings, as follows:

19_5		£
January	Repair work	69.44
February	Repair work	256.86
March	Repair work	182.90
	Appliances	112.81

He estimated that, at the end of March 19_5, his stock of electrical repair materials was £691.02 and of electrical appliances for resale was £320.58, his tools and equipment were worth £300.00 and his car, £600.00. Apart from loan interest, the only accrual was for heating and lighting £265.00.

Required:

(a) Prepare
  (i) purchase daybook with analysis columns for type of purchase, and
  (ii) sales daybook with analysis columns for class of business undertaken. (6 marks)

(b) Open, post to 31 March 19_5 only, and balance a columnar cash book suitably analysed to facilitate ledger postings. (8 marks)

(c) Open, post to 31 March 19_5 only, and balance a creditors ledger control account and a debtors ledger control account. Use the closing balances in your answer to (g) below. [NB. Individual accounts for creditors and debtors are NOT required]. (3 marks)

(d) Open, post and balance sales and cost of sales accounts, each with separate columns for 'Repairs' and 'Appliances'. (3 marks)

(e) Prepare M. Faraday's trading account for the quarter ended 31 March 19_5, distinguishing between gross profit on repairs and on appliance sales. (3 marks)

(f) Prepare M. Faraday's general profit and loss account for the quarter ended 31 March 19_5. (4 marks)

(g) Prepare M. Faraday's balance sheet as at 31 March 19_5. (7 marks)
(34 marks)

Chartered Association of Certified Accountants

2.7 Discuss, using examples, the use and significance of the following generally accepted rules in drawing up accounts:
(a) Consistence (6 marks)
(b) Prudence (conservatism) (7 marks)
(c) Going concern (6 marks)
(d) Materiality (6 marks)
(25 marks)

Advanced level Accounting, AEB

2.8 (a) The auditors' report to the shareholders of a public limited company included the following two paragraphs:

'The accounts have been prepared on a going concern basis and the validity of this depends on the company's bankers continuing their support by providing adequate overdraft facilities.'

'Because of the materiality of the matters referred to in a previous paragraph we are unable to form an opinion as to whether the accounts give a true and fair view of the state of affairs of the company.'

You are required to explain the following terms:
(i) Going concern basis.
(ii) Materiality. (10 marks)

(b) Some companies provide current cost accounting information in addition to the historical cost financial statements. Explain the purposes of this additional information. (10 marks)
(20 marks)

Advanced level Accounting, London

2.9 The annual final accounts of businesses are normally prepared on the assumption that the business is a going concern.

Explain and give a simple illustration of:
(a) the effect of this convention on the figures which appear in those final accounts (8 marks)
(b) the implications for the final accounts figures if this convention were deemed to be inoperative. (9 marks)
(17 marks)

Chartered Association of Certified Accountants

2.10 Historical cost has been described as one of the fundamental assumptions underlying financial accounting.

Required:
An explanation of:
(a) What is meant by historical cost; (5 marks)
(b) The advantages of using historical cost; (6 marks)
(c) The disadvantages of using historical cost; (6 marks)
(d) To what extent historic cost is modified in practice (8 marks)
(25 marks)

Advanced level Accounting, AEB

Case Study — Kilburn Tandoori

Part II, Final Accounts

On completion of writing up the books, the following matters are brought to your attention:

(a) Stocks of food and drink at 28 February 19_8 are valued at £250.
(b) Mr Shah owes a waiter £20 in respect of overtime worked in week 4.
(c) The rates payment covers the period 1 February to 31 April.
(d) Electricity consumed in the month is estimated to be £100.
(e) Being a prudent man Mr Shah instructs you to create a provision for doubtful debts of 4 per cent of debtors.
(f) It is decided to write off fixtures and fittings by equal instalments over 10 years.

You are required to:

1. adjust the books for the above
2. prepare the restaurant's Trading and Profit and Loss Account for the first month and a Balance Sheet as at 28 February 19_8

Solutions

2.2

CHARLES

Trading and Profit and Loss Account for the year ended 30 June 19_3

	£	£
Sales (115 000 – 5 000)		110 000
Less cost of goods sold		
Opening stock	16 000	
Purchases (66 000 – 2 000 drawings)*	64 000	
	80 000	
Less closing stock	20 000	
		60 000
Gross profit		50 000
Rent receivable		2 600
		52 600
Less Expenses		
Bad debts	500	
Heating and lighting (1 500 + 500)	2 000	
Motor vehicle expenses	4 000	
Postage and stationery	1 600	
Rent and rates	8 000	
Salaries and wages	11 500	
Depreciation on vehicles	5 000	
		32 600
Net profit		£20 000

Balance Sheet as at 30 June 19_2

	£ *Cost*	£ *Dep'n*	£ *Net*
Fixed assets			
Land and buildings	25 000	—	25 000
Motor vehicles	22 000	12 000	10 000
	47 000	12 000	35 000

Current assets			
Stock		20 000	
Debtors		10 000	
Rent receivable		600	
Bank		4 400	
		35 000	
Less Current liabilities			
Creditors	9 500		
Accrued expense	500		
Working capital		10 000	
			25 000
Net assets			60 000
Financed by:			
Capital, 1 July 19_1			55 000
Add profit for the year			20 000
			75 000
Less drawings (13 000 + 2 000 stock)			15 000
			£60 000

* Business entity concept — The cost of stationery withdrawn by Charles has to be deducted from purchases at it was not used for business purposes.

2.3 (a)

PENELOPE

Ledger

Electricity

19_2		£	19_2		£
2 Apr.	Bank	200	1 Jan.	Bal b/f	50
4 July	Bank	180			
9 Oct.	Bank	150			
31 Dec.	Balance c/f	170	31 Dec.	*P&L*	∴ 650
		700			700
			19_3		
			1 Jan.	Bal b/f	170

Insurance

19_2		£	19_2		£
1 Jan.	Bal b/f	95			
3 Mar.	Bank (1 Feb–31 July)	570	31 Dec	*P&L*	∴ 1 165
3 Sept.	Bank (1 Aug–1 Jan.)	600	31 Dec.	Bal c/f ($600 \times \frac{1}{6}$)	100
		1 265			1 265
19_3					
1 Jan.	Bal b/f	100			

Rent receivable

19_2		£	19_2		£
1 Jan.	Bal b/f	50	4 Apr.	Bank	150
			6 July	Bank	150
			8 Oct.	Bank	150
31 Dec.	P&L (50 × 12 months)	600	31 Dec.	*Bal* c/f	∴ 200
		650			650
19_3					
1 Jan.	Bal b/f	200			

Provision for doubtful debts

19_2		£	19_2		£
			1 Jan.	Bal b/f	70
31 Dec.	Bal c/f (2 000 × 4%)	80	31 Dec.	*P&L*	∴ 10
		80			80
			19_3		
			1 Jan.	Bal b/f	80

(b)

PENELOPE

Profit and Loss Account Extract for the year ended 31 December 19_2

	£	£
Miscellaneous income		
Rent receivable		600
Expenses		
Electricity	650	
Insurance	1 165	
Provision for doubtful debts	10	

Balance Sheet Extract as at 31 December 19_2

	£	£
Current assets		
Debtors	2 000	
Less provision for doubtful debts	80	1 920
Rent receivable		200
Insurance prepaid		100
Current liabilities		
Electricity accrued		170

2.6 This is an excellent question highlighting the fact that the raw material for final accounts is the keeping of proper bookkeeping records. It is also fairly realistic. Clients of small High Street firms of accountants tend to be small businesses, most of whom do not operate a full double-entry bookkeeping system (see Chapter 5).

MICHAEL FARADAY

(a)

Purchase day book

(i)

Date	*Supplier*	*Repair materials* £	*Appliances for resale* £
January	AB Supplies	528.20	
February	Simpson	141.34	
	Cotton Ltd.		427.40
	Dee & Co,	146.82	
March	AB Supplies	643.43	
	Simpson	95.60	
		1555.39	427.40

Note — The purchase of tools and equipment, being *capital expenditure*, should not be entered in the Purchase Day Book. It goes straight to the Ledger.

— Day Books are for *credit* transactions only. The book of first entry for *cash* purchases is the Cash Book.

(ii)

Sales day book

Day	*Customer*	*Repair work* £	*Sales of appliances* £
January	D. Hopkins	362.80	
	P. Bolton	417.10	

		£	£
February	G. Leivers		55.00
	M. Whitehead	151.72	
	N. John Ltd.		49.14
	A. Linneker		12.53
March	E. Horton	462.21	
	S. Ward	431.08	
	W. Scothern & Co.	319.12	
	N. Annable	85.41	
		2 229.44	116.67

(b)

Cash Book

Dr. Date	*Item*	*Discount allowed*	*Total*	*Debtors*	*Repair work*	*Sales of appliance*	*Sundry*
19_5		£	£	£	£	£	£
Jan.	Capital		250.00				250.00
	Loan		2 000.00				2 000.00
	Repairs		69.44		69.44		
Feb.	D. Hopkins	5.80	357.00	357.00			
	Repairs		256.86		256.86		
March	P. Bolton		417.10	417.10			
	G. Leivers		55.00	55.00			
	A. Linneker		12.53	12.53			
	S. Ward	5.08	426.00	426.00			
	Repairs		182.90		182.90		
	Appliances		112.81			112.81	
		10.88	4 139.64	1 267.63	509.20	112.81	2 250.00
April	Balance b/d		578.01				

Cr. Date	*Item*	*Discount received*	*Total*	*Creditors*	*Repair materials*	*Expenses*	*Drawings and bank*
19_5		£	£	£	£	£	£
Jan.	Repair materials		195.29		195.29		
	Rent		400.00			400.00	
	Rates		150.00			150.00	
	Stationery		32.70			32.70	
	Car expenses		92.26			92.26	
	Drawings		160.00				160.00
Feb.	Repair materials		161.03		161.03		
	Sundries		51.54			51.54	
	Car expenses		81.42			81.42	
	Drawings		160.00				160.00
March	Dee & Co.	7.74	330.00	330.00			
	AB Supplies		528.20	528.20			
	Simpson	3.34	138.00	138.00			
	Cotton Ltd.		130.00	130.00			
	Dee & Co.	6.82	140.00	140.00			
	Repair materials		22.06		22.06		
	Sundries		24.61			24.61	
	Car expenses		104.52			104.52	
	Drawings		160.00				160.00
	Bank		500.00				500.00
		17.90	3 561.63	1 266.20	378.38	937.05	980.00
	Balance c/d		578.01				
			4 139.64				

(c)

Creditors ledger control account

19_5		£	19_5		£
March	Cash	936.20	March	Credit purchases	
	Discounts received	10.16		(1 555.39 + 427.40)	1 982.79
	Balance c/d	1 036.43			
		1 982.79			1 982.79
			April	Balance b/d	1 036.43

Debtors ledger control account

19_5		£	19_5		£
March	Sales	2 346.11	March	Cash	1 267.63
				Discounts allowed	10.88
				Balance c/d	1 067.60
		2 346.11			2 346.11
April	Balance b/d	1 067.60			

(d)

Sales

		Repairs	*Appliances*			*Repairs*	*Appliances*
19_5		£	£	19_5		£	£
March	Trading	2 738.64	229.48	March	Debtors	2 229.44	116.67
					Cash	509.20	112.81
		2 738.64	229.48			2 738.64	229.48

Cost of sales

		Repairs	*Appliances*			*Repairs*	*Appliances*
19_5		£	£	19_5		£	£
March	Creditors	1 555.39	427.40	March	Trading	1 242.75	106.82
	Cash	378.38		Closing stock c/f		691.02	320.58
		1 933.77	427.40			1 933.77	427.40

Although not asked for, the ledger accounts recording the purchase of tools and equipment look like this:

Dee & Co. — Tools creditor

19_5		£	19_5		£
March	Cash	330.00	Jan	Tools and equipment	337.74
	Discount received	7.74			
		337.74			337.74

Tools and equipment

19_5		£	19_5		£
Jan	Dec & Co.	337.74	March	P&L — depreciation	37.74
			March	Balance c/f	300.00
		337.74			337.74

(e)

M. FARADAY

Trading and Profit and Loss Account for the first quarter ended 31 March 19_5

	Repairs	*Appliances*	*Total*
	£	£	£
Sales	2 738.64	229.48	2 968.12
Less cost of sales	1 242.75	106.82	1 349.57
Gross profit	1 495.89	122.66	1 618.55

(f)

Discounts received (10.16 + 7.74)			17.90
			1 636.45

Less Expenses		
Rent ($400 \times \frac{3}{6}$)	200.00	
Rates	150.00	
Stationery	32.70	
Car expenses ($92.26 + 81.42 + 104.52$)	278.20	
Sundry expenses ($51.54 + 24.61$)	76.15	
Discounts allowed	10.88	
Depreciation on car ($700 - 600$)	100.00	
Depreciation on tools and equipment	37.74	
Heating and lighting	265.00	
Loan interest ($2000 \times 10\% \times \frac{3}{12}$)	50.00	
		1 200.67
Net profit		£ 435.78

(g)

M. FARADAY

Balance Sheet as at 31 March 19_5

	£	£	£
Fixed assets	*Cost*	*Dep'n*	*Net*
Car	700.00	100.00	600.00
Tools and equipment	337.74	37.74	300.00
	1 037.74	137.74	900.00
Current assets			
Stocks — repair materials		691.02	
appliances		320.58	
Trade debtors		1 067.60	
Rent prepaid		200.00	
Bank		500.00	
Cash		578.01	
		3 357.21	
Less Current liabilities			
Trade creditors	1 036.43		
Accruals ($265 + 50$)	315.00		
		1 351.43	
Working capital			2 005.78
Net assets			£2 905.78
Financed by:			
Opening capital ($700 + 250$)			950.00
Add profit			435.78
			1 385.78
Less drawings			480.00
Capital owned			905.78
Long-term liability			
10% loan			2 000.00
Capital employed			£2 905.78

Case Study — Kilburn Tandoori

Answer

The books of original entry should be written up first. These are the Purchase Day Book, Sales Day Book, Cash Book, and Petty Cash Book.

Purchase Day Book (Journal)

Week	*Supplier*	*£*
1	T. Green	80
	Hakim Meat	300
	Robinson Wines	50
2	Williams Farms	500
	T. Green	100
	Hakim Meat	350
	Robinson Wines	110
3	Williams Farms	450
	T. Green	110
	Hakim Meat	350
	Robinson Wines	175
4	Williams Farms	550
	T. Green	100
	Hakim Meat	350
	Robinson Wines	150
Credit purchases for the month		3 725

Sales Day Book (Journal)

Week	*Customer*	*£*
2	Sun Finance	110
	Chrome Metals	60
3	Sun Finance	155
	Chrome Metals	80
4	Sun Finance	150
	Chrome Metals	100
Credit sales for the month		655

Cash Book

Dr *Week*	*Item*	*Discount allowed* £	*Total* £	*Capital* £	*Sales* £	*Debtors* £
1	Capital		50 000	50 000		
	Cash		625		625	
	Cheques		810		810	
2	Cash		830		830	
	Cheques		1 050		1 050	
3	Cash		1 055		1 055	
	Cheques		1 100		1 100	
	Sun Finance	3	107			107
4	Cash		1 210		1 210	
	Cheques		1 175		1 175	
	Sun Finance	5	150			150
	Chrome Metals	2	138			138
		10	58 250	50 000	7 855	395
	Balance b/d		3 832			

Cr Week	*Item*	*Discount received* £	*Total* £	*Wages* £	*Creditors* £	*Fixed assets* £	*Petty cash book* £	*Drawings* £	*Rates* £
1	Premises		40 000			40 000			
	Furniture		4 000			4 000			
	Conversion costs		6 000			6 000			
	Wages		100	100					
	Wages		180	180					
	Petty cash		30				30		
2	T. Green	2	78		78				
	Hakim Meat	6	294		294				
	Robinson's	1	49		49				
	Wages		100	100					
	Wages		180	180					
	Petty cash		30				30		
	Drawings		55					55	
	Cash register		200			200			
3	Williams	10	490		490				
	T. Green	2	98		98				
	Hakim Meat	7	343		343				
	Robinson's	2	108		108				
	Wages		110	110					
	Wages		200	200					
	Petty cash		30				30		
	Drawings		10					10	
4	Williams	9	441		441				
	T. Green	2	108		108				
	Hakim Meat	7	343		343				
	Robinson's	4	171		171				
	Wages		100	100					
	Wages		200	200					
	Petty cash		30				30		
	Drawings		70					70	
	Rates		270						270
		52	54 418	1 170	2 523	50 200	120	135	270
Balance c/d			3 832						
			58 250						

Note
The entries for discounts allowed and discounts received in the Cash Book are *not* part of the double-entry. They are included merely to provide additional information to the cashier.

Petty Cash Book

Dr	Week		Cr Total	Cleaning materials	Flowers	Napkins
£			£	£	£	£
30	1	Cash book				
		Expenditures	27	5	10	12
30	2	Cash book				
		Expenditures	25	7	4	14
30	3	Cash book				
		Expenditures	27	7	5	15
30	4	Cash book				
		Expenditures	29	8	6	15
			108	27	25	56
12		Balance c/d	12			
120			120			
12		Balance b/d				

Postings to the ledgers are made at the *end of the month*, from the books of original entry. First, the individual creditor and debtor accounts in the Purchase and Sales Ledgers.

Purchase Ledger

Williams Farms

Week		£	Week		£
3	Bank	490	2	Purchases	500
	Discount	10	3	Purchases	450
4	Bank	441	4	Purchases	550
	Discount	9			
	Balance c/d	550			
		1 500			1 500
				Balance b/d	550

T. Green & Sons

Week		£	Week		£
2	Bank	78	1	Purchases	80
	Discount	2	2	Purchases	100
3	Bank	98	3	Purchases	110
	Discount	2	4	Purchases	100
4	Bank	108			
	Discount	2			
	Balance c/d	100			
		390			390
				Balance b/d	100

Hakim Meat

Week		£	Week		£
2	Bank	294	1	Purchases	300
	Discount	6	2	Purchases	350
3	Bank	343	3	Purchases	350
	Discount	7	4	Purchases	350
4	Bank	343			
	Discount	7			
	Balance c/d	350			
		1 350			1 350
				Balance b/d	350

Robinson Wines

Week		£	*Week*		£
2	Bank	49	1	Purchases	50
	Discount	1	2	Purchases	110
3	Bank	108	3	Purchases	175
	Discount	2	4	Purchases	150
4	Bank	171			
	Discount	4			
	Balance c/d	150			
		485			485
				Balance b/d	150

Note
The entries for 'Discount' represent discounts *received*. The books of original entry are; for purchases, the Purchase Day Book; for bank and discount, the Cash Book.

Sales Ledger

Sun Finance Co.

Week		£	*Week*		£
1	Sales	110	3	Bank	107
3	Sales	155		Discount	3
4	Sales	150	4	Bank	150
				Discount	5
				Balance c/d	150
		415			415
	Balance b/d	150			

Chrome Metals PLC

Week		£	*Week*		£
2	Sales	60	4	Bank	138
3	Sales	80		Discount	2
4	Sales	100		Balance c/d	100
		240			240
	Balance b/d	100			

Note
The entries for 'Discount' represent discounts *allowed*. The books of original entry are; for sales, the Sales Day Book; for bank and discount, the Cash Book.

General Ledger

Capital

	£		£
		Bank	50 000

Premises

	£		£
Bank	40 000		
Bank (conversion costs)	6 000		

Fixtures and Fittings

	£		£
Bank	4 000		
Bank (cash register)	200		

Total Creditors (PLCA)

	£		£
Bank	2 523	Purchases (as per PDB)	
Discounts received	52		
28 Feb. Balance c/d	1 150		
	3 725		3 725
		1 Mar. Balance b/d	1 150

	£		£
	Total Debtors (SLCA)		
Sales (as per SDB)	655	Bank	395
		Discounts allowed	10
		28 Feb. Balance c/d	250
	655		655
1 Mar. Balance b/d	250		
	Sales		
		Cash and bank	7 855
28 Feb. Trading	8 510	Sundry debtors, SL	655
	8 510		8 510
	Purchases		
Sundry creditors, PL	3 725	28 Feb. Trading	3 725
	Wages		
Bank	1 170		
28 Feb. Balance c/d	20	28 Feb. P&L	1 190
	1 190		1 190
		1 Mar. Balance b/d	20
	Rates		
Bank	270	28 Feb. P&L	90
		28 Feb. Balance c/d	180
	270		270
1 Mar. Balance b/d	180		
	Drawings		
Bank	135		
	General expenses		
PCB — cleaning	27	28 Feb. P&L	108
PCB — flowers	25		
PCB — napkins	56		
	108		108
	Discounts allowed		
Sundry debtors, SL	10	28 Feb. P&L	10
	Discounts received		
28 Feb. P&L	52	Sundry creditors, PL	52
	Electricity		
28 Feb. Balance c/d	100	28 Feb. P&L	100
		1 Mar. Balance b/d	100
	Provision for doubtful debts		
28 Feb. Balance c/d	10	28 Feb. P&L	10
		1 Mar. Balance b/d	10
	Provision for depreciation — fixtures and fittings		
28 Feb. Balance c/d	35	28 Feb. P&L	35
		1 Mar. Balance b/d	35
	Stock		
28 Feb. Trading	250	28 Feb. Balance c/d	250
1 Mar. Balance b/d	250		

The above represent the general ledger accounts as they would appear after:

(i) performing the double-entry of the transactions during the month
(ii) effecting the month-end adjustments

(iii) closing the income and expense accounts to the trading and profit and loss accounts, and
(iv) bringing down the balances remaining in the books of the asset, liability, and capital accounts.

On completion of (i) above and *before* (ii)

(1) the individual debtor and creditor accounts in the Sales and Purchase Ledgers should be checked with their respective control accounts
(2) a trial balance should be extracted from the general ledger to check that the total of the debit balances equals the total of the credit balances. This looks as follows:

Trial balance as at 28 February 19_8

	Dr	*Cr*
	£	*£*
Capital		50 000
Premises	46 000	
Fixtures and fittings	4 200	
Creditors		1 150
Debtors	250	
Sales		8 510
Purchases	3 725	
Wages	1 170	
Rates	270	
Drawings	135	
General expenses	108	
Discounts allowed	10	
Discounts received		52
Bank	3 832	
Cash	12	
	£59 712	£59 712

On balancing of the trial balance, steps (ii) and (iii) above can be performed. The resulting income statement looks like this:

KILBURN TANDOORI

Trading and Profit and Loss Account for the first month ended 28 February 19_8

	£	*£*
Sales		8 510
Less cost of goods sold		
Purchases	3 725	
Less closing stock	250	3 475
Gross profit		5 035
Discounts received		52
		5 087
Less Expenses		
Wages	1 190	
Rates	90	
General expenses	108	
Discounts allowed	10	
Electricity	100	
Provision for doubtful debts	10	
Depreciation on fixtures*	35	
		1 543
Net profit		£3 544

* £4 200 × 10% × $\frac{1}{12}$ = £35

The final task is (iv), followed by preparation of the balance sheet. This looks as follows:

KILBURN TANDOORI

Balance sheet as at 28 February 19_8

	£	£	£
Assets employed:			
Fixed assets			
Freehold premises			46 000
Fixtures and fittings, at cost		4 200	
Less depreciation		35	4 165
			50 165
Current assets			
Stock		250	
Trade debtors	250		
Less provision for doubtful debts	10	240	
Rates prepaid		180	
Bank		3 832	
Cash		12	
		4 514	
Less Current liabilities			
Trade creditors	1 150		
Accrued wages	20		
Electricity accrued	100	1 270	
Working capital			3 244
Net assets			£53 409
Financed by:			
Capital, 1 February 19_8			50 000
Add profit			3 544
			53 544
Less drawings			135
Capital employed			£53 409

CHAPTER 3

Depreciation

Fixed assets have been defined as long-term assets held, not with a view to resale, but for permanent use in the business. They represent investment in the business, known as *capital expenditure,* rather than revenue expenditure which are the necessary day-to-day expenses to keep the business working.

Such investments in assets have a finite life. The fall in value of fixed assets over time is known as *depreciation*. This has been defined in SSAP 12 (*Accounting for Depreciation*) 'as a measure of the wearing out, consumption, or other loss of value of a fixed asset whether arising from use, effluxion of time or obsolescence through technology and market changes'. Let us examine these causes:

(1) *Use.* There are two aspects to depreciation through use. Firstly, the mere fact that an asset becomes second-hand reduces its value. Secondly, use leads to loss in value from *wear-and-tear* (e.g. with machinery and vehicles) and exposure to the elements (e.g. rust with vehicles, weathering with buildings).

(2) *Time.* The simple passage of time also reduces the value of an asset, even if it is not used. This is especially so for assets with a definite finite life such as leasehold property.
(3) *Obsolescence.* Another cause of depreciation is an asset becoming out-of-date or obsolete, either through technological advances or a change in tastes and fashions. Thus the typewriter is being replaced by the technically superior word processor, the market value of a fleet of company cars drops on the day a new version comes onto the market.

Although capital expenditure produces an asset, it is still expenditure and will therefore need charging to the profit and loss account. In this sense capital expenditure is similar to revenue expenditure. The difference is that revenue expenditure is short-term and the benefit received in one accounting period — it is therefore written off (charged) against income in that period. Capital expenditure is long-term — the benefit is felt over several accounting periods. It is therefore also written off over several periods.

Benefits of Depreciation

1. On Reported Profit and Asset Values

This is best illustrated with an example: a business purchases a lorry to add to its fleet of vehicles for £20 000, expected useful life 5 years. The benefits are expected to accrue thus:

Year	1	2	3	4	5
Benefit (£)	4 000	4 000	4 000	4 000	4 000

If we charge the full cost of the lorry to P & L in year 1 with no charge in subsequent years we would be contravening the accruals (or matching) concept. This states that expenditure should be charged to P & L in the year or years in which the benefit of the expenditure is received.

Charge (£)	20 000	—	—	—	—

A charge such as above, in effect treating the lorry as a revenue item, clearly violates the accruals concept. It reduces profit by too much in year 1, leading to an understatement of profit, and fails to make any charge in years 2 to 5 leading to an overstatement in those years. To avoid this error a *proportion* of the cost should be charged to P & L each year. Doing this *gradually* reduces the book value of the asset shown in the balance sheet. This is more realistic than writing the whole of it out from the books in year 1 and showing the lorry to be worthless from years 2 to 5.

2. On Maintenance of Capital

Again an example will illustrate: John Smith sets up in business selling ice-cream by buying a van for £10 000. His annual takings over the first five years average £8 000, costs £3 000. John is happy with the apparent £5 000 annual profit and withdraws this amount from the business every year. At the end of 5 years his van breaks down and is declared a write-off. He now finds that his profitable business has suddenly ceased to exist. The mistake that John has made is that he failed to account for his capital consumption every year of

$$\frac{\text{£10 000}}{\text{5 years}} = \text{£2 000.}$$

What he was withdrawing was not only profit but also capital. John should have charged an additional £2 000 every year for *depreciation* of the van and taken only £3 000 as drawings from profit. If he had done this he would have accumulated £10 000 over 5 years — money which could have gone towards a replacement van thus ensuring continuity of the business. This example illustrates that failure to provide for depreciation will lead to a gradual erosion of a business' capital base.

Depreciation and Inflation

The purpose of depreciation is to *withhold from distribution funds sufficient to replace the asset when it is disposed of.* Depreciation calculations are based on historic cost. Sufficient funds should then be accumulated to replace the asset at that historic cost. But prices do not stand still in practice — they move upwards. The existence of inflation causes provisions based on historic cost to be inadequate. Profit is then overstated, and if the whole of profit is taken out as drawings (or distributed to shareholders in the case of companies) this leads to capital consumption.

To overcome this problem, the annual depreciation charge could be revised upwards, by basing it not on historic cost but *current replacement cost* at the time of making the provision. A guide to current cost can be gauged by looking at relevant indices of price movements. If this is done in every year the asset is held, when replacement is due, sufficient funds will be withheld in the business to replace the asset even at the inflated price.

What Depreciation is *not* — Common Misconceptions

1. A Fund for Replacement

A provision for depreciation does not *in itself* provide a fund for replacement. The effect of a provision is to reduce reported profit so reducing the outflow of cash from the business in the form of drawings or dividends. This amount is not specifically set aside in, for example, a sinking fund which is designed to mature at the end of the expected life of the asset. The money is used to finance the business in general e.g. the working capital cycle, or held as a general reserve. When cash is needed to replace the asset some assets are liquidated or the reserve drawn upon. There is no maintenance of a fund specifically for the replacement of the asset.

2. An Attempt at Asset Valuation

Depreciation is *not* an attempt to value an asset at the end of each financial year — it is a process of allocating the cost of the asset to the years which have benefited from its use. Valuing an asset is fraught with difficulties because there are several different possible bases of valuation, each providing different figures. The reason for the misconception is that balance sheets often use the term 'net book value' for fixed assets. Readers of accounts, being mostly non-accountants, interpret this as an attempt to value the asset at that moment in time. This it is not. What the accountant means by book value is historic cost less accumulated depreciation i.e. *that portion of the original cost which has still to be written off to P & L.*

3. An Outflow of Cash

Unlike other charges in the P & L account such as wages, rent and rates, provisions do not involve a cash outflow from the business. As we shall see later in this chapter, in making a provision for depreciation there is no double-entry with cash or bank. Let me illustrate with our earlier example of the lorry which was bought for £20 000, expected life 5 years. The annual provisions for depreciation are £4 000.

Year	1	2	3	4	5
Depreciation (£)	4 000	4 000	4 000	4 000	4 000
Cash flow (£)	(20 000)	—	—	—	—

We can see from above that the provisions in years 2 to 5 do not involve any cash outflow. The whole of the cash outflow is in year 1. By year 2 the lorry has been paid for, so the firm does not have to pay for it again in years 2-5. The annual provisions for depreciation are a mere *internal* book adjustment not involving any financial transactions with the outside world. (This point has particular significance for funds flow statements which we look at in Chapter 11.)

What is Capital Cost?

Owning and using an asset incurs several costs, both of capital and revenue nature. Since depreciation is the writing off of the capital cost it is important that the capital element can be accurately separated from the revenue element. Examination questions often pick up on this point. The purchase price of an asset is clearly capital, the day-to-day running expenses clearly revenue. Thus for a lorry the initial purchase price is capital expenditure; petrol, insurance and drivers' wages, revenue expenditure. There are a number of other costs where the distinction is not so obvious however.

Delivery charge. While transport costs are usually revenue, where they are incurred in connection with the acquisition of a capital item, they are capitalized. The general rule is that capital includes all costs incurred in acquiring an asset *and preparing it in a state ready for use.* Thus the capital cost of a piece of machinery includes delivery and installation charges in addition to the purchase price.

Repairs. For example, servicing a car or giving a machine an overhaul. This form of expenditure seeks to maintain the value of an asset, *not to add to its original value.* It is therefore treated as revenue and written off wholly to P & L in the years in which it is incurred.

Improvement. For example adding an extension to a building. Here the effect of the expenditure is to *add to original value,* so the cost should be capitalized and written off over the remaining life of the asset.

Methods of Depreciation

The question here is what should be the basis of the annual transfers to profit and loss account? Should it be simply *time*? If time, should an *equal* amount be written off each year? Should an attempt be made to reflect *usage*? Can the risk of obsolescence be built into the charge?

There are four main methods — *straight line, reducing (declining) balance, revaluation,* and *usage.* Of these, the first two are the most important.

Straight Line

In this method the asset is deemed to lose value *by an equal amount each year* — as in the lorry example above. The annual transfers to P & L is given by

$$\frac{\text{Cost} - \text{Residual value}}{\text{Useful life}}$$

While cost is known with certainty, the other two variables have to be estimated and are subjective. All methods of depreciation (except revaluation) suffer from this weakness of having to forecast. The assumption implicit in this method is that depreciation is a function of time. No account is taken of possible variations in use from year to year. The risk of obsolescence can be incorporated into the calculation by varying the estimate of useful life. Have a go at this exercise.

Exercise

Horace sets up in business offering a removal service with the purchase of a van for £10 000 on 1 January 19_1. He expects to use it for 3 years, then sell it for £4 000, using the proceeds to contribute to a new van. Show the annual depreciation charges and relevant balance sheet figures over the life of the van if Horace uses the straight-line method.

Answer

$$\text{Annual depreciation charge} = \frac{£10\,000 - £4\,000}{3 \text{ years}} = £2\,000$$

Year	Charge to P & L	Balance Sheet		
		Cost	Accumulated depreciation	Net book value
	£	£	£	£
19_1	2 000	10 000	2 000	8 000
19_2	2 000	10 000	4 000	6 000
19_3	2 000	10 000	6 000	4 000

Reducing Balance

Under this method the asset is deemed to lose *a greater part of its value in the early years of its use compared to later years.* The charge is calculated as a given percentage of the *previous year's net book value.* (Under straight line the change was based on cost.) This percentage is given by:

$$1 - \sqrt[n]{\frac{\text{Residual value}}{\text{cost}}}$$

where n = number of years.

In examinations at this level you will not be asked to calculate the annual percentage rate. You will be given it and merely have to *apply it* in depreciating the asset.

Exercise

For Horace's van show the annual depreciation charges and relevant balance sheet figures if he uses the reducing balance method, at 26%.

Answer

Year	Charge to P & L*	Balance Sheet		
		Cost	Accumulated depreciation	Net book value
	£	£	£	£
19_1	2 600	10 000	2 600	7 400
19_2	1 924	10 000	4 524	5 476
19_3	1 424	10 000	5 948	4 052

* Year 1 10 000 × 26% = 2 600
2 7 400 × 26% = 1 924
3 5 476 × 26% = 1 424

Note that: (i) the annual percentage rate that reduces the value of the van to exactly £4 000 in 3 years time is over 26% but under 27%.

(ii) in year 1 the reducing balance charge is greater than the straight line charge whereas in later years (2 and 3) the reverse is true.

Comparison

The straight line method is simpler to calculate. It is therefore cheaper to operate and there is less chance of making errors. Most firms in the UK use straight line. The reducing balance method however is felt to be more realistic in that in practice, assets tend to lose market value faster in the early years compared to later years. It is also more appropriate where the risk of obsolescence is high. Because most of the cost is written off in the early years, should the asset become obsolete the loss suffered is small. The third claimed advantage of reducing balance is that as assets get older the burden of repairs and maintenance gets progressively lighter. This results in a more even total charge for use of the asset. Under straight line the total charge increases, as illustrated below.

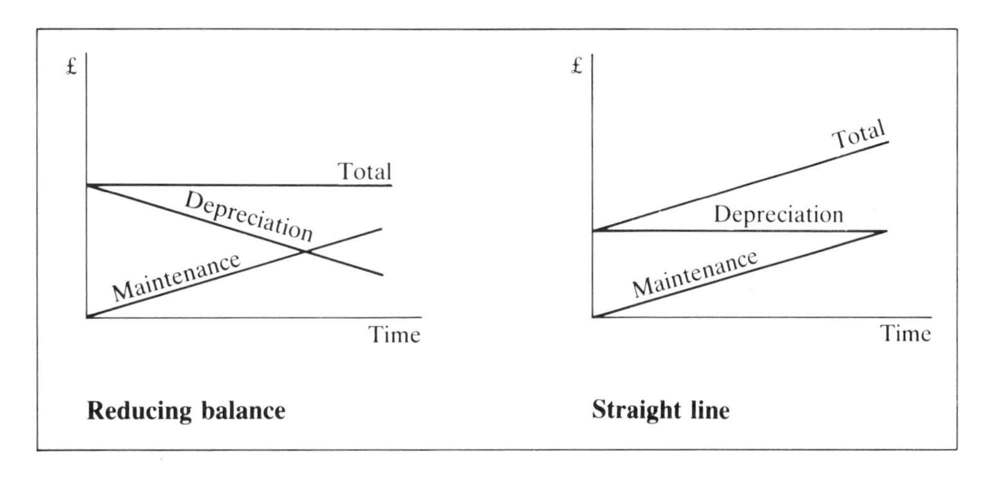

Despite its apparent advantages, reducing balance is not much used in the UK, but is popular in the USA. For examination purposes both are equally important.

Revaluation Method

This is the only method that attempts to relate the charge to the actual fall in value of the asset during the year. For this the asset has to be valued at the end of each year.

Illustration

Let us take a factory and its stock of loose tools.

		£
Valuation	1 January	10 000
Purchases	during year	2 000
Valuation	31 December	8 500

The depreciation is worked out as a balancing figure in the ledger account.

Loose tools — Net

	£		£
1 January Bal b/f	10 000	31 December P & L	∴ 3 500
Bank — purchases	2 000	31 December Bal c/f	8 500
	12 000		12 000

This method is conveniently applied to assets which are individually so small that it is not worth identifying for each the cost, estimated useful life, and residual value.

Usage Method

Where the main cause of depreciation is felt to be *use* rather than time the charge should also be based on use.

Illustration

Let us take a piece of specialized machinery which is bought for the production of 40 000 units of a good over 4 years — a specific long-term order.

Cost	£25 000
Expected usage	10 000 hours
Estimated residual value	£5 000

In Year 1, production level was 10 000 units, machine hours worked 2 600.

The depreciation charge could be based on either units produced or hours worked.

Charge per unit $= \dfrac{\text{Total chargeable}}{\text{Units}}$

$= \dfrac{£25\,000 - £5\,000}{40\,000} = £0.50$ per unit

Charge in year 1 = 10 000 units × £0.50
= £5 000

Charge per machine hour $= \dfrac{\text{Total chargeable}}{\text{Machine hours}}$

$= \dfrac{£25\,000 - £5\,000}{10\,000} = £2$ per hour

Charge in year 1 = 2 600 hours @ £2
= £5 200

See question 3.4

Which Method?

There is no one right method of depreciation. The method chosen will depend on the type of asset, factors which cause it to depreciate, risk of obsolescence and policy of firm. It will thus vary from asset to asset. For example a business may use straight line for leasehold property, reducing balance for motor vehicles, and the usage method for machinery. In recognition of this SSAP 12 deliberately holds back from recommending any one particular method.

The Accounting Entries Necessary for Depreciation

The double-entry for depreciation is made at the end of the year, just before preparation of the final accounts. The entry is the same regardless of the method of depreciation used. It is:

Dr Profit and loss
    Cr Provision for depreciation

There is a provision for depreciation account for each category of fixed asset. The *balance* on this account represents the total amount of the cost of the asset written off to date. Be careful about the distinction between the charge for the year and balance on the account. The annual charge is *written off to P & L* while the balance is shown in the *balance sheet.*

Illustration

Taking our van bought on 1 January 19_1 at a cost £10 000 and expected to last for 3 years, when it can be sold for £4 000. Using the straight line method:

Provision for depreciation

		£			£
31 Dec 19_1	Bal c/d (B)	2 000	31 Dec 19_1	P & L (A)	2 000
			1 Jan 19_2	Bal b/d (C)	2 000
31 Dec 19_2	Bal c/d (E)	4 000	31 Dec 19_2	P & L (D)	2 000
		4 000			4 000
			1 Jan 19_3	Bal b/d (F)	4 000

The six entries above are lettered in sequence. Only A and D represent double-entries (with P & L). The rest are for computation of the balance on the account.

Some firms, mostly small businesses, prefer to write down the value of an asset within the asset account itself, the double-entry being:

Dr Depreciation
Cr Asset

This is done for each category of asset. At the end of the year the total in the depreciation account is written off to P & L by:

Dr P & L
Cr Depreciation

Under this method the ledger accounts for the first two years of the van's life would look as follows:

Van

		£			£
1 Jan 19_1	Cash	10 000	31 Dec 19_1	Depreciation	2 000
			31 Dec 19_1	Bal c/d	8 000
		10 000			10 000
1 Jan 19_2	Bal b/d	8 000	31 Dec 19_2	Depreciation	2 000
			31 Dec 19_2	Bal c/d	6 000
		8 000			8 000
1 Jan 19_3	Bal b/d	6 000			

Depreciation

		£			£
31 Dec 19_1	Van	2 000	31 Dec 19_1	P & L	2 000
31 Dec 19_2	Van	2 000	31 Dec 19_2	P & L	2 000

This method used to be the only method until not so long ago. See question 3.4. Since then the practice of keeping a provision for depreciation account separate from the asset account has become more popular.

Grouping

Fixed assets of a similar type are normally grouped into one account. For example, a company with fifty pieces of machinery would not keep a separate account for each one — it would show them all in one account, probably calling it 'plant and machinery'. This would have its related provision for depreciation account. It would however maintain a *Fixed Assets Register* which shows details for each machine such as the make and the model, serial number, date of purchase, cost, and accumulated depreciation.

The Disposal of Assets

With the exception of freehold land, assets have a finite life and the entries made have to be written out of the books when an asset is either scrapped, sold, or part-exchanged for another asset. This involves a four-step procedure, laid out below.

Step 1
Write out the cost of the asset from the books. To do this we need to open a new account, called *Asset disposal.* The double-entry is:

Dr Asset disposal
    Cr Asset — at cost

Step 2
Write out the depreciation provided on the asset to date by:

Dr Provision for depreciation
    Cr Asset disposal

Step 2 is more tricky than step 1 because in questions the figure for accumulated depreciation to date is usually not given. However, it is possible to work it out from the cost and method and rate of depreciation used. In practice firms do not have to make this calculation because a record of the depreciation to date on each asset is kept in the fixed assets register.

Step 3
Enter the double-entry for the consideration received. If the asset is sold for cash:

Dr Cash
    Cr Asset disposal

If it is part-exchanged for another asset:

Dr Asset — at cost
    Cr Asset disposal

Step 4
Balance off the disposal account. If the accumulated depreciation and consideration received exceeds the cost a *profit* has been made on sale. This would be shown in the profit and loss account as a miscellaneous gain. The double entry is

Dr Asset disposal
    Cr P & L

Of course, if accumulated depreciation plus consideration is less than cost a book *loss* has been suffered, and therefore charged to profit and loss.

Losses and gains on disposal are not really attributable to the year of sale. They represent *adjustments* to the charge for depreciation on the asset. Where a profit has been made for example, the asset has been over-depreciated, so P & L is credited by the amount of the profit to reduce the total depreciation charged on the asset. The perfect solution to the error is to re-calculate the depreciation charges for the years the asset was held and adjust the profit figures accordingly. Such an exercise however, is laborious and impractical and SSAP 12 allows gains and losses to be wholly written off in the year of sale.

Assets Bought or Sold Part-Way Through the Year

A business whose financial year runs from 1 January to 31 December buys a machine on 1 July. In the year-end accounts should it charge a full year's depreciation on the asset or only for the time it was used i.e. 6 months? Strictly speaking, the charge should be pro-rota to the number of months of ownership.

The first approach is simpler to operate however and large firms where a slightly incorrect depreciation charge does not affect the accounts materially tend to charge a full year's depreciation on assets bought during the year. To compensate for this overcharge they make no charge for assets *sold* during the year, even though they were used for part of it. In this way the over and undercharges roughly cancel each other out, and the charge for depreciation is not materially different from the one that which would be obtained from a month-by-month calculation. The firm is, in effect, charging a full year's depreciation on all assets held at the end of each year.

Questions should indicate which system the business is applying. If they do not, follow this guideline:
- if no dates are given it is not possible to apply depreciation on a month-by-month basis
- if dates are given and no mention made of policy followed apply depreciation on a month-by-month basis. Do not forget to state the assumption made in your answer.

Subjectivity and Manipulation

As we know, depreciation is quite a subjective affair. The amount charged is affected by the estimates of useful life and residual value and also by the method used. Given that there is no one correct charge, it can be tempting for a business to *manipulate* reported profit by varying the amount of the charge from year to year. If higher profits are desired the charge could be lowered, for lower profits the charge increased. SSAP12, recognizing this, forbids a change in the depreciation rate or method unless the change is necessary to represent the affairs of the business more fairly. In any case, changing the rate or method for no good reason contravenes the principle of *consistency.*

Revising Estimated Life

Where an original estimate of useful life is proved too optimistic, perhaps due to unforeseen technical obsolescence, a business may make a change in the calculations. The remaining net book value (amount of cost still to be written off to P & L) should be written down to the residual value over the remainder of the new estimate of useful life. SSAP 12 recommends that,

'. . . businesses do not backdate charges for depreciation when useful lives are revised or any other charge connected with the asset made.'

Land and Buildings

Freehold land is unique in that it is probably the only asset that does not depreciate with time — in fact, it usually *appreciates.* For this reason SSAP 12 allows firms not to depreciate freehold land. Leasehold property however *does* have to be depreciated. The straight line basis should be used since the fall in value of the lease is a function of time. Whereas most land has unlimited life, buildings do not, and SSAP 12 requires buildings to be depreciated. The rate of depreciation is usually low, 2 per cent per year straight line being a common provision.

Questions

3.1 Parkinson Ltd. depreciates its plant and machinery at 20 per cent a year on the straight line basis, for each month of ownership. From the information that follows on the next page you are required to prepare:

(a) the plant account — at cost
(b) provision for depreciation account
(c) balance sheet extracts for the years 19_4, 19_5 and 19_6, and
(d) the plant disposal account for 19_6

Information

19_4	1 January	Bought plant costing	£2 000
	1 July	Bought plant costing	£3 000
19_5	1 October	Bought plant costing	£1 800
19_6	31 March	Sold plant which had been bought on 1 July 19_4 for £3 000, for the sum of £1 750	
	1 August	Bought plant costing	£1 000

All acquisitions were paid for on the date of purchase by cheque, except for the 1 August 19_6 plant which was bought on credit from Steel plc.

(20 marks)

Author's Question

3.2* Fastfreeze Ltd. completed its third year in business as a manufacturer of frozen foods on 31 May 19_5.

A machine was purchased on 1 June 19_2 at a cost of £16 000 and now needs replacing. Installation costs of £4 000 were incurred in June 19_2 and in addition a service contract was entered into for the life of the machine at a cost of £1 000 per annum. A replacement machine will cost £30 000 plus £5 000 installation costs and will require no service agreement. The existing machine has a trade-in value of £3 000. It is company policy to use the reducing balance method of depreciation at a rate of 20% per annum.

Required:

(a) The provision for depreciation account for *each* of the three years ended 31 May 19_3, 19_4 and 19_5. (5 marks)
(b) A statement showing the total charge against profits in the financial year ending 31 May 19_6 if the replacement machine were to be purchased on 31 December 19_5. (4 marks)

Advanced Level Accounting, AEB, part-question **(9 marks)**

3.3 At the beginning of the financial year on 1 April 19_5, a company had a balance on plant account of £372 000 and on provision for depreciation of plant account of £205 400.

The company's policy is to provide depreciation using the reducing balance method applied to the fixed assets held at the end of the financial year at the rate of 20% per annum.

On 1 September 19_5 the company sold for £13 700 some plant which it had acquired on 31 October 19_1 at a cost of £36 000. Additionally, installation costs totalled £4 000. During 19_3 major repairs costing £6 300 had been carried out on this plant and, in order to increase the capacity of the plant, a new motor had been fitted in December 19_3 at a cost of £4 400. A further overhaul costing £2 700 had been carried out during 19_4.

The company acquired new replacement plant on 30 November 19_5 at a cost of £96 000, inclusive of installation charges of £7 000.

Required:

Calculate:

(a) the balance of plant at cost at 31 March 19_6 (3 marks)
(b) the provision for depreciation of plant at 31 March 19_6 (10 marks)
(c) the profit or loss on disposal of the plant (4 marks)

(17 marks)

Chartered Association of Certified Accountants

3.4 Heath and Rowe are partners sharing profits/losses in the ratio of 3:2 respectively. Their financial year ends on 31 December.

At 1 January 19_2 the firm owned two light aircraft: A, which had been bought on 1 January 19_0 for £32 000, and B, bought on 1 July 19_1 for £58 000. Up to 31 December 19_1 the depreciation charge on them had been calculated at an annual rate of 20% on a straight line basis, assuming residual values of £4 000 for A and £6 000 for B. No separate provision account was maintained.

On 1 January 19_2 the partners decided that:

(1) A separate depreciation provision account would be kept.

(2) Depreciation should be provided on the basis of an hourly rate related to estimated flying hours, but with estimated residual values unchanged. Appropriate figures were:

	A	B
Total estimated flying hours during economic life	14 000	13 000
Actual flying hours from date of purchase to 31 December 19_1	5 200	1 250

(3) Adjustments should be made in the firm's books to put (1) and (2) into effect, retrospective to 1 January 19_0.

On 27 May 19_2 the firm bought aircraft C for £60 000. Its estimated flying hours were 15 000, and its residual value £7 500.

In September 19_2 aircraft A was converted into a training plane at a cost of £6 900 and, in addition, £3 200 was spent on a major engine overhaul. It is not anticipated that either of these factors will affect the estimated flying hours of the aircraft or its residual value.

Total flying hours during 19_2 were:
A. 2 350 (including 1 900 before September)
B. 1 980
C. 2 200

Required:

(a) A journal entry to give effect to items (1), (2) and (3). (Narrations are *not* required.) (8 marks)

(b) The following ledger accounts for the year 19_2:
(i) Aircraft
(ii) Provision for depreciation of aircraft. (10 marks)

(c) Comment briefly on the partners' decision in item (3), in the light of SSAP 12. (2 marks)

(20 marks)

London Chamber of Commerce and Industry, Higher

3.5* Kirkpatrick Limited, sellers and repairers of motor vehicles, commenced business on 1 January 19_2. The company's balance sheet as at 31 December 1983 included the following items in the fixed assets section:

	At cost	*Aggregate depreciation*	*Net*
	£	£	£
Motor vehicles	21 000	7 560	13 440

All the motor vehicles included were acquired when the company commenced business, the vehicles were XYZ123 costing £10 000, ABC 456 costing £7 000 and PQR789 costing £4 000. The company's policy up to 31 December 19_3 has been to provide depreciation at the rate of 20% per annum using the reducing balance method. However, it has now been decided to adopt the straight line method of providing for depreciation and to adjust the motor vehicles provision for depreciation at 1 January 19_4 in accordance with the new policy. In future, depreciation will be provided annually at the rate of 20% of the original cost of motor vehicles at each accounting year end.

During 19_4, the following transactions took place involving motor vehicles (fixed assets):

31 March	Vehicle XYZ123 was badly damaged in a road accident. The insurance company decided that the vehicle was beyond repair and therefore paid Kirkpatrick Limited £7 100 in full settlement.
30 June	Vehicle RST765 bought for cash from Express Traders Limited. Kirkpatrick Limited paid a cheque for £8 300 in full settlement of the amount due which included the insurance of the vehicle for the year commencing 30 June 19_4 of £500.
30 Sepember	Kirkpatrick Limited exchanged vehicle PQR789 for a new vehicle DEF432 and paid a cheque for £3 000 in full settlement. The list price of the new vehicle was £5 000.
10 October	Paid Quickspray Limited £200 for repainting DEF432 in the company's colours before it was used by Kirkpatrick Limited.

Required:

(a) Prepare the journal entries (or entry) required for the transaction of 30 September 19_4;
Note: Narratives are required. (5 marks)

(b) Prepare the following accounts in the books of the company for the year ended 31 December 19_4:
Motor vehicles—at cost
Motor vehicles—provision for depreciation
Motor vehicle disposals
Note: a separate account is opened for each vehicle disposal. (15 marks)
(20 marks)

Association of Accounting Technicians, Intermediate

3.6 What is the relationship between depreciation and:
(a) asset valuation
(b) capital consumption
(c) cash flow
(d) inflation (4 × 5 marks
(20 marks)

Author's Question

3.7 (a) Explain whether the policy for providing for depreciation on fixed assets in the annual income statement has any connection, direct or otherwise, with either the recovery of the original cost of the assets or the annual cash flow of a company. (7 marks)

(b) Outline
(i) the arguments for using historical cost for depreciation purposes;
(ii) the deficiencies of this method which might be overcome by using the current replacement cost in a time of rising prices. (11 marks)

(c) State the implications, and comment on the consequences, of a decision by a company to reduce the percentage figure used in depreciation calculations at the end of the financial year for which profits are lower than in previous years. (7 marks)
(25 marks)

Advanced Level Accounting, AEB

3.8 Evaluate the different methods of providing for depreciation. **(20 marks)**

Author's Question

Solutions

3.1

PARKINSON LTD.

Ledger

(a)

Plant — at cost

		£			£
19_4			19_4		
1 January	Bank	2 000			
1 July	Bank	3 000	31 December	Bal c/d	5 000
		5 000			5 000
19_5			19_5		
1 January	Bal b/d	5 000			
1 October	Bank	1 800	31 December	Bal c/d	6 800
		6 800			6 800
19_6			19_6		
1 January	Bal b/d	6 800	31 March	Disposal	3 000
1 August	Steel plc	1 000	31 December	Bal c/d	4 800
		7 800			7 800
19_7					
1 January	Bal b/d	4 800			

(b)

Provision for depreciation

		£			£
19_4			19_4		
31 December	Bal c/d	700	31 December	P & L (W_1)	700
19_5			19_5		
			1 January	Bal b/d	700
31 December	Bal c/d	1 790	31 December	P & L (W_2)	1 090
		1 790			1 790
19_6			19_6		
31 March	Disposal (W_4)	1 050	1 January	Bal b/d	1 790
31 December	Bal c/d	1 733	31 December	P & L (W_3)	993
		2 783			2 783
			19_7		
			1 January	Bal b/d	1 733

Depreciation workings

	Purchase date	Cost	Dep'n
		£	£
W_1 *For 19_4*	1 Jan 19_4	2 000 × 20%	400
	1 July 19_4	3 000 × 20% × $\frac{6}{12}$	300
			700
W_2 *For 19_5*	1 Jan 19_4	2 000 × 20%	400
	1 July 19_4	3 000 × 20%	600
	1 Oct 19_5	1 800 × 20% × $\frac{3}{12}$	90
			1 090
W_3 *For 19_6*	1 Jan 19_4	2 000 × 20%	400
	1 July 19_4	3 000 × 20% × $\frac{3}{12}$	150
	1 Oct 19_5	1 800 × 20%	360
	1 Aug 19_6	1 000 × 20% × $\frac{5}{12}$	83
			993
W_4 *On plant sold*		3 000 × 20% × $1\frac{9}{12}$ =	1 050

(d)

Plant disposal

19_6		£	19_6		£
31 March	Cost	3 000	31 March	Depreciation (W_4)	1 050
			31 March	Bank	1 750
			31 March	P & L - loss on sale	200
		3 000			3 000

(c)

PARKINSON LTD

Balance Sheet Extracts as at	*31.12.19_4*	*31.12.19_5*	*31.12.19_6*
	£	£	£
Plant - at cost	5 000	6 800	4 800
Less accumulated depreciation	700	1 790	1 733
Net book value	4 300	5 010	3 067

3.3 (a)

Plant — at cost

		£			£
1 April 19_5	Bal b/f	372 000	1 Sept 19_5	Disposal	44 400
30 Nov 19_5	Bank	96 000	31 March 19_6	Bal c/f	423 600
		468 000			468 000
1 April 19_6	Bal b/f	423 600			

(b)

Provision for depreciation — plant

		£			£
1 Sept 19_5	Disposal (W_1)	25 200	1 April 19_5	Bal b/f	205 400
31 Mar 19_6	Bal c/f	228 880	31 Mar 19_6	P & L (W_2)	48 680
		254 080			254 080
			1 April 19_6	Bal b/f	228 880

(c)

Plant disposal

		£			£
1 Sept 19_5	Cost	44 400	1 Sept 19_5	Depreciation	25 200
			1 Sept 19_5	Bank	13 700
			1 Sept 19_5	P & L (loss)	5 500
		44 400			44 400

Workings

W_1 *To find accumulated depreciation on plant sold*

	£	*Acc. dep'n* £
Bought 31 Oct 19_1	40 000	
Depreciation 31 March 19_2	8 000	8 000
	32 000	
Depreciation 31 March 19_3*	6 400	14 400
	25 600	
New motor Dec 19_3	4 400	
	30 000	
Depreciation 31 March 19_4*	6 000	20 400
	24 000	
Depreciation 31 March 19_5	4 800	25 200

* Repairs and the overhaul are *revenue expenditure* and therefore do not affect the capital cost of the plant.

W_2 *Depreciation charge for the year ended 31 March 19_6*

£[423 600 − (205 400 − 25 200)] × 20%

= £48 680

3.4 (a) The answer has to be done in three stages:

1. calculate depreciation provided so far under straight-line
2. calculate the charges under the new method,
3. effect the change through the journal.

Stage 1: Reconstruction of aircraft account to date.

Aircraft — Net

		£			£
1 Jan 19_0	Bank - A	32 000	31 Dec 19_0	P & L (W_1)	5 600
			31 Dec 19_0	Bal c/d	26 400
		32 000			32 000
1 Jan 19_1	Bal b/d	26 400	31 Dec 19_1	P & L (W_2)	10 800
1 July 19_1	Bank - B	58 000	31 Dec 19_1	Bal c/d	73 600
		84 400			84 400

Workings

			£
W_1	For A	$\frac{32\,000 - 4\,000}{5}$	5 600
W_2	For A		5 600
	For B	$\frac{58\,000 - 6\,000}{5} = 10\,400$	
		For 6 months, * $10\,400 \times \frac{6}{12}$	5 200
			10 800

* It is assumed that Heath and Rowe have been charging depreciation pro-rata to the number of months used.

Stage 2: Calculation of charges under the new method.

For A: $\frac{28\,000}{14\,000}$ = £2 per hour

Total to date, 5 200 hours × £2	10 400
Provided by old method	11 200
Decrease in provision required	(800)

For B: $\frac{52\,000}{13\,000}$ = £4 per hour

Total to date, 1 250 hours × £4	5 000
Provided by old method	5 200
Decrease in provision required	(200)

Stage 3: Effecting the change

Since the partners want to maintain a separate provision for depreciation account, the depreciation charged to the aircraft account has to be taken out (*dr*) and credited to a newly created provision for depreciation account. The decrease in the charge under the new method will increase the retained profits of the firm. These changes are initially recorded in the journal before being posted to ledger accounts.

The Journal

	£	£
Dr Aircraft, A £11 200 + B £5 200	16 400	
Cr Provision for depreciation, A 10 400 + B £5 000		15 400
Cr Profit and loss		1 000

(b)

Ledger

Aircraft — at cost

		£			£
1 Jan 19_2	Bal b/d	90 000			
27 May 19_2	Bank - C	60 000			
1 Sept 19_2	Bank - A	6 900	31 Dec 19_2	Bal c/d	156 900
		156 900			156 900
1 Jan 19_3	Bal b/d	156 900			

Provision for depreciation — aircraft

		£			£
			1 Jan 19_2	Bal b/d	15 400
31 Dec 19_2	Bal c/d	36 170	31 Dec 19_2	P & L (W_3)	20 770
		36 170			36 170
			1 Jan 19_3	Bal b/d	36 170

Note: The £3 200 overhaul on aircraft A should not be capitalized. It is *revenue expenditure,* and as such should be wholly written off to P & L.

Working

W_3

		£
For A:	2 350 hours @ £2	4 700
	Annual depreciation rate on conversion = $\frac{\text{Cost}}{\text{Remaining estimated flying hours}}$	
	$\frac{6\,900}{14\,000 - 5\,200 - 1\,900} = \frac{6\,900}{6\,900} = £1$ per hour	
	Depreciation = 450 hours × £1	450
For B:	1 980 hours × £4	7 920
For C:	$\frac{60\,000 - 7\,500}{15\,000} = £3.50$ per hour	
	2 200 hours × £3.50	7 700
Total charge for 19_2		20 770

(c) The partner's decision has contravened SSAP 12. According to the standard, a firm should not backdate charges for depreciation when a change connected with an asset is made, such as the method of depreciation or a revision of estimated useful life. The partners should have charged the *unallocated cost* of aircrafts A and B over their *remaining flying hours.* However, partnerships are under no legal obligation to follow SSAPs, so the change is not objectionable if the partners believe it to lead to a fairer allocation of the cost of the aircraft over time.

CHAPTER 4

Control Accounts

Businesses maintain separate accounts for each credit customer and supplier, usually in a sales ledger and purchase ledger, to ascertain the amounts owing from and to each at any one time. Where there is a large number it is quite possible for the sales/purchase clerk to make the occasional error. At the end of the month, before sending statements of accounts to debtors and cheques to creditors it is advisable to perform a check on the figures. This is done by the maintenance of Control Accounts.

How they Work

Every time entries are made in, for example, the sales ledger (usually monthly, from the sales day book and cash book) the *total* of these entries are recorded in an independent account called the sales ledger control account (SLCA), kept in the general ledger. If this is done for *all* entries the *total* of the individual balances in the sales ledgers at any one time should equal the *single balance* on the control account. If it does not, the bookkeeper is alerted to errors. It is useful to have such an alarm system before sending out the monthly cheques and statements of accounts.

Control accounts are used in a wide variety of accounting situations. Their main use in financial accounting is in respect to debtors and creditors, but they are also used in cost accounting e.g. cost ledger control, wages control, production overhead control. In this chapter we will look at their application to financial accounting, — the principles when using them in cost accounting, are the same. At the end of the year, once the individual debtor and creditor accounts have been checked against their respective controls, the single balance on the control is the one that appears in the trial balance. This is a better option than including all the many individual balances in it. Consider the length of the trial balance of a large company with thousands of individual debtors and creditors prepared without control accounts! The balances on the control account is also the figure that appears in the balance sheet — as trade debtors and trade creditors.

The practice of treating control accounts as part of the double-entry varies from firm to firm. In some the individual accounts are regarded as the double-entry, with the control being a checking account, not part of the double-entry. In others the control account assumes the responsibility of being part of the double-entry system, the individual accounts in this case being regarded as back-up. In such cases the control account is more properly thought of as being a Total Debtors or Total Creditors Account.

Usefulness

While control accounts are not strictly necessary to operate a double-entry accounting system, businesses with a large number of credit customers and suppliers take the trouble of maintaining them because in addition to the above function they offer a number of other advantages. These are as follows:

(1) If the trial balance fails to balance the only books that need to be checked are the general ledger and cash book. The possibility of errors in the sales ledger and purchasers ledger can be ruled out since they have already been reconciled before inclusion in the trial balance. In the absence of control accounts in the event of the trial balance not balancing the bookkeeper would have no clue as to which book or books the errors are in. *All* would need checking. In this way, control accounts can, and in practice do, lead to a considerable saving in time and effort.

(2) In the absence of control accounts, if it is desired to check entries in the debtors and creditors accounts a trial balance for the whole business involving *all* books has to be extracted; a lengthy and time-consuming exercise, which is done only once or twice a year. By building an independent check on debtors and creditors into the recording system, their entries can now be checked without the need to involve all books. Since the process is quicker and cheaper, checks can be performed more regularly.

(3) It is possible to find the figure for total debtors or total creditors simply by balancing one account. This is quicker and easier than having to balance all the individual accounts.

(4) Control accounts are usually kept by a person other than the sales/purchase ledger clerk. In this way the chance of deliberate fraud is reduced.

Contents

The items in the control accounts are exactly those which appear in the individual accounts. The only difference is in the amounts, the control containing the *total* of the individual accounts.

A typical sales ledger control account looks as follows:

Sales ledger control

	£		£
Balance b/f	x	Return inwards (from RIJ)	x
Credit sales (from SDB)	x	Cheques received } from CB	x
Dishonoured cheques	x	Discounts allowed } from CB	x
		Bad debts	x
		PL contra (explained later)	x
		Balance c/f	x
	x		x

SDB = Sales day book
RIJ = Return inwards journal
CB = Cash book

Note:

(1) items that increase the amount receivable from debtors are debited, whilst those that decrease the amount are credited
(2) cash sales do not feature
(3) provisions for doubtful debts are not entered in individual debtor accounts and therefore do not appear in the control.

A sales ledger control account may have a small credit balance in addition to the main debit balance. This will arise when:

(a) goods have been returned by a customer for which we have not sent the refund or credit note
(b) an account has been overpaid in error. See question 4.2.

A typical purchase ledger control account looks as follows:

Purchase ledger control

	£		£
Returns outwards (from ROJ)	x	Balance b/f	x
Cheques paid } from CB	x	Credit purchases (from PDB)	x
Discount received } from CB	x	Dishonoured cheques	x
SL contra	x		
Balance c/f	x		
	x		x

PDB = Purchase day book
ROJ = Return outwards journal

Again, note that:

(1) items that increase the amount payable to creditors are credited, whilst those that decrease the amount are debited
(2) cash purchases do not feature

A purchase ledger control account may have a small debit balance in addition to the main credit balance. This will arise when:

(a) we have not yet received a refund or credit note for goods returned to suppliers
(b) we have overpaid an account in error.

Contra Entries

Sometimes a business both sells goods to, *and* purchases from, another business.

Example

One of our customers, Mr. K, also supplies some materials to us. There will therefore be an account for K in both our sales ledger *and* purchase ledger. If Mr. K is owed £400 for materials supplied but also owes *us* £1 000 it would be silly of us to pay him £400 and then receive £1000 from him. It makes more sense to *'set off'* his indebtedness against ours, with the following book entry:

Dr K. Ltd. Creditor (PL)	£400	
Cr K. Ltd. Debtor (SL)		£400

The net result is that K. now owes us £600. Such a set off is known as a *contra entry* (₵ being its symbol). Of course, the entries made in the individual accounts should be repeated in the control accounts.

Large firms

In large firms, the sheer number of individual debtors or creditors may make it impossible to keep them all in a single book. The individual ledgers then have to be split up. How this is done will vary according to the nature of the business. Common divisions are by geographical area, type of product and alphabetically. There will be a separate control account for each sub-division of the ledger. See question 4.1.

Examination questions

Questions on control accounts tend to be of two types.

(1) A list of balances regarding debtors and creditors is given. From this you have to construct control accounts.
(2) A control account balance is given which differs from the total of individual balances. A number of errors are listed. You have to reconcile the control account to the individual accounts by adjusting them for the errors.

Type (1) questions are straight-forward. Look out for information supplied but not needed such as cash sales and provision for doubtful debts.

Type (2) questions can be tricky. To answer them, a proper understanding of the bookkeeping for purchases and sales is required. A common difficulty is in recognizing whether an error affects the individual account, control account, neither, or both.

Illustration

Sales day book

19_5			£
June	4	Green & Co.	50
	11	Mr Brown	100
	13	Hart & sons	75
	25	XYZ Co.	25
			250

From this book of original entry the double-entry takes place at the end of the month.

Dr individual debtors (SL) £50, £100, £75, 25
Cr Sales (GL) with the total, £250

At this time
Dr Sales ledger control (GL) with the total, £250

From this you should be able to see that:

(1) If there is a casting error in the sales or purchases total, only the control account needs to be adjusted. The individual accounts in the sales ledger are not affected.

(2) If there is an error of entry in an individual debtor's account (eg. transposition posting to wrong side, or casting) *only that individual account* should be adjusted. The control account is unaffected.

(3) If a transaction has been completely omitted from the books, it will need entering belatedly in *both* the individual and total account.

(4) If the entry in the individual account has been made but the additional entry to control forgotten (in respect of, for example, a contra) then only the control account will need updating.

(5) If the balance of a debtor's account has been omitted from the list of sales ledger balances this will affect *neither* the individual *nor* the total account. The omitted balance should simply be included in the revised list of individual balances.

Questions

4.1 The sales ledger records of a company reveal the following information for the month of May 19_5:

	A–J	*K–N*	*O–S*	*T–Z*
	£	£	£	£
Opening Debit balances	12 903	14 520	8 300	14 600
Opening Credit balances	—	194	150	—
Sales invoice	18 470	19 300	6 400	7 100
Cheques received	9 652	21 500	7 200	18 400
Sales returns	—	1 306	—	175
Bad debts written off	500	—	—	—
Cheques dishonoured	—	—	200	—
Closing Credit balances	150	—	200	—

(a) Prepare control accounts for the four ledger sections for the month ended 31 May 19_5. (20 marks)

(b) The total of the individual ledger balances in the K–N section of the ledger at 31 May 19_5 was £11 820. Give two possible reasons why this figure differs from that disclosed by the control account for this section of the ledger. (4 marks)

(c) A customer, P. Parker, supplies goods to the company, and has a balance in the purchases ledger totalling £400. His sales ledger balance at 31 May 19_5 is £600. What would be the effect on the two balances if the company 'set off' one balance against the other? (2 marks)

(d) What advantages, if any, are to be gained from splitting the sales ledger control accounts into alphabetical sections? (4 marks)

(30 marks)

Advanced Level Accounting, London

4.2* Mainway Dealers Limited maintains a debtors (sales) ledger and a creditors (purchases) ledger. The monthly accounts of the company for May 19_6 are now being prepared and the following information is available.

		£
Debtors' ledger as at 1 May 19_6:	Debit balances	16 720
	Credit balances	1 146
Creditors' ledger as at 1 May 19_6.	Debit balances	280
	Credit balances	7 470
Credit sales May 19_6		19 380
Credit purchases May 19_6		6 700
Cash and cheques received May 19_6:	Debtors' ledger	15 497
	Creditors' ledger	130
Cheques paid May 19_6:	Debtors' ledger	470
	Creditors' ledger	6 320
Credit notes issued May 19_6 for goods returned by customers		1 198
Credit notes received from suppliers May 19_6 for goods returned by Mainway Dealers Limited		240
* Cheques received and subsequently dishonoured May 19_6: Debtors' ledger		320
Discounts allowed May 19_6		430
Discounts received May 19_6		338
Bad debts written off May 19_6		131
* Bad debt written off in December 19_5 but recovered in May 19_6 (R. Bell)		142
Debtors' ledger as at 31 May 19_6:	Debit balances	To be determined
	Credit balances	670
Creditors' ledger as at 31 May 19_6:	Debit balances	365
	Credit balances	To be determined

It has been decided to set off a debt due from a customer, L. Green, of £300 against a debt due to L. Green of £1,200 in the creditors' ledger.

* Included in cash and cheques received May 19_6 £15 497.

The company has decided to create a provision for doubtful debts of $2\frac{1}{2}$% of the amount due to Mainway Dealers Limited on 31 May 1986 according to the debtors' ledger control account.

Required:

(a) Prepare the debtors' ledger control account and the creditors' ledger control account for May 19_6 in the books of Mainway Dealers Limited. (20 marks)

(b) An extract of the balance sheet as at 31 May 19_6 of Mainway Dealers Limited relating to the company's trade debtors and trade creditors.

(5 marks)

(25 marks)

Association of Accounting Technicians, Intermediate

4.3 J. Johnstone, a trader, has asked K. Miles, a recently employed office junior, to provide information from which the sales ledger control account for the month of October can be prepared. K. Miles has presented the following information for the month of October:

Balances on sales ledger		£
1 October:	(debit)	8 600
	(credit)	290
31 October:	(debit)	10 000
	(credit)	120
Credit sales		11 710
Cash sales		5 690
Cash received from debtors		7 150

Provision for doubtful debts	310
Discount allowed	1 210
Discount received	730
Sales returns	160
Bad debts written off	470

The balances on the sales ledger control account agreed with the balances in the sales ledger on 1 October. The credit balance on 31 October of £120 referred to an overpayment by a credit customer. After J. Johnstone prepared the sales ledger control account for the month of October the following errors were discovered:

(1) An invoice for a credit sale of £130 to T. Wright had been lost.
(2) The total for the sales day book has been overcast by £360.
(3) The receipt of a cheque for £580 from D. Noble had been correctly entered in the cash book but had been credited to Noble's account in the sales ledger as £850.
(4) A credit balance of £520 on M. Leigh's account in the purchases ledger had been transferred to M. Leigh's account in the sales ledger and the transfer had not been entered in the sales ledger control account.

Required:

(a) The sales ledger control account prepared by J. Johnstone based on the original information given to him by K. Miles. (6 marks)
(b) The adjustments required, if any, in the sales ledger control account prepared in (a) to correct the errors listed above. (9 marks)

(15 marks)

Advanced Level Accounting, AEB

4.4* The following balances have been included in a sales ledger control account for the year ended 31 January 19_5.

	£
Balance at 1 February 19_5	12 087
Sales (note 1)	117 635
Receipts from customers (note 2)	90 019
Discounts allowed (note 3)	3 000
Goods returned by customers	4 200
Bad debts written off (note 4)	1 550

Balances extracted from the sales ledger at 31 January 19_6 were

	£
Debit	35 588
Credit (note 5)	185

Notes:

(1) It was discovered that a batch of sales invoices totalling £3,400 had been omitted from the accounting records.
(2) Cash sales of £600 had been included in this total.
(3) Discounts allowed of £350, included in this total, had been omitted from the personal ledger.
(4) The personal ledger accounts of the 'bad debtors' had been debited with £1 550, whilst the correct entry had been made into the control account.
(5) Credit balances in the sales ledger of £400 had been transferred during the year into the purchases ledger. No record of this transfer had been made in the control account, although the personal accounts had been correctly adjusted.

(a) Prepare the sales ledger control account for the year ended 31 January 19_6. (9 marks)
(b) Prepare a statement reconciling the sales ledger balances with the control account balance. (4 marks)

(c) Under which balance sheet heading should *credit* balances contained within a limited company's sales ledger be shown? **(2 marks)**

(15 marks)

Advanced Level Accounting, London

4.5* The Sales ledger control account of a trading business for the month of November 19_3 was prepared by the accountant, as shown below:

Sales Ledger Control

	£		£
Opening debit balance b/d	27 684.07	Opening credit balance b/d	210.74
Credit Sales	31 220.86	Allowances to customers	1 984.18
Purchase ledger contras	763.70	Cash received	1 030.62
		Cheques received	28 456.07
Discounts allowed	1 414.28	Cash received (on an account previously written off as a bad debt)	161.20
Closing credit balance c/d	171.08		
		Closing debit balance c/d (balancing figure)	30 416.18
	£61 253.99		£61 258.99
Opening debit balance b/d	30 416.18	Opening credit balance b/f	171.08

The book-keeper balanced the individual customers' accounts and prepared a Debtors' Schedule of the closing balances which totalled £25 586.83 (net of credit balances).

Unfortunately both the accountant and the book-keeper had been careless, and in addition to the errors which the accountant had made in the control account above, it was subsequently discovered that:

(1) in an individual debtor's account, a debt previously written off but now recovered (£161.20) had been correctly credited and redebited but the corresponding debit had not been posted in the control account;
(2) discounts allowed had been correctly posted to individual debtor's accounts but had been under-added by £100 in the memorandum column in the combined bank and cash book;
(3) allowances to customers shown in the control account included sums totalling £341.27 which had not been posted to individual debtors' accounts;
(4) a cheque for £2 567.10 received from a customer had been posted to his account as £2 576.10;
(5) the credit side of one debtor's account had been over-added by £10 prior to the derivation of the closing balance;
(6) a closing credit balance of £63.27 on one debtor's account had been included in the Debtors' Schedule among the debit balances;
(7) the purchase ledger contras, representing the settlement by contra transfer of amounts owed to credit suppliers, had not been posted to individual debtors' accounts at all;
(8) the balance on one debtor's account, £571.02, had been completely omitted from the Debtors' Schedule.

Required:
Identify and effect the adjustments to the Sales ledger control account and Debtors' Schedule, as appropriate, so that the net balances agree at 30 November 19_3.

(16 marks)

Chartered Association of Certified Accountants

Solutions

4.1 (a)

SLCA A–J

		£			£
May	19_5		May	19_5	
1	Balance b/d	12 903		Bank	9 652
	Sales	18 470		Bad debts	500
31	Balance c/d	150	31	Balance c/d	∴ 21 371
		31 523			31 523
June	19_5		June	19_5	
1	Balance b/d	21 371	1	Balance b/d	150

SLCA K–N

		£			£
May	19_5		May	19_5	
1	Balance b/d	14 520	1	Balance b/d	194
	Sales	19 300		Bank	21 500
				Sales returns	1 306
			31	Balance c/d	∴ 10 820
		33 820			33 820
June	19_5				
1	Balance b/d	10 820			

SLCA 0–S

		£			£
May	19_5		May	19_5	
1	Balance b/d	8 300	1	Balance b/d	150
	Sales	6 400		Bank	7 200
	Cheques dishonoured	200			
31	Balance c/d	200	31	Balance c/d	∴ 7 750
		15 100			15 100
June	19_5		June	19_5	
1	Balance	7 750	1	Balance b/d	200

SLCA T–Z

		£			£
May	19_5		May	19_5	
1	Balance b/d	14 600		Bank	18 400
	Sales	7 100		Sales returns	175
			31	Balance c/d	∴ 3 125
		21 700			21 700
June	19_5				
1	Balance b/d	3 125			

(b) There are several possible reasons for this, including:
(1) casting error in list of individual debtor balances by £1 000
(2) sales over-debited in an individual account by £1 000
(3) bank under-credited in an individual account by £1 000
(4) incorrect balance extracted from an individual account

(c) The double entry for this contra entry is:
Dr P. Parker, purchase ledger £400
Cr P. Parker, sales ledger £400
The net effect is that P. Parker has a remaining balance of £200 in the sales ledger.

(d) Advantages of splitting the sales into alphabetical sections:
(i) keeps physical size of each sales ledger manageable
(ii) by having an independent check for each part of the ledger errors take less time to locate than if there were just one sales ledger
(iii) if more than one sales clerk is employed it makes sense to have more than one sales ledger so that each can work on his/her book all of the time. This reduces time wastage by staff.

4.3 (a)

J. JOHNSTONE

Sales ledger control account

October		£	October		£
1	Balance b/f	8 600	1	Balance b/f	290
	Credit sales	11 710		Cash received	7 150
				Discounts allowed	1 210
				Sales returns	160
				Bad debts	470
31	Balance c/f	120	31	Balance c/f	11 150
		20 430			20 430
November			November		
1	Balance b/f	11 150	1	Balance b/f	120
	(1) Credit sale	130		(2) SDB overcast	360
				(4) M. Leigh PLCA ¢	520
1	Balance c/f	120	1	Balance c/f	10 400
		11 400			11 400
1	Balance b/f	10 400	1	Balance b/f	120

(b) *Schedule of adjustments to the sales ledger balances*

	£	£
Draft total of debit balances in Sales Ledger		10 000
Add (1) Credit sale, T. Wright	130	
(3) Transposition error, D. Noble	270	400
Corrected debit total, agreed to SLCA		£10 400

Note Cash sales and provision for doubtful debts are not entered in the individual debtor accounts, and therefore do not feature in the control.

CHAPTER 5

Incomplete Records

While most large and medium-sized businesses maintain a separate clerical function which operates a full double-entry bookkeeping system, a lot of small businesses do not. With most sole traders, for example, the books are kept by the owner or his wife. Employing an independent bookkeeper may not be justified by the size of the business, nor may the owners be able to afford one. The task has to be somehow fitted in with all the countless other tasks involved in running one's own business. It is frequently done in the evenings, when they are tired. As a result the recording is *incomplete* because they have not devoted sufficient *time* to it and probably also because they are not conversant with the techniques of double-entry. At the end of the financial year they would take their records to an accountant. The accountant has to play the role of a detective, having to work out missing items by deductions from information supplied. The techniques available to him are looked at in this chapter. From these deductions and information supplied, the final accounts can be prepared.

Remuneration for work of this kind forms a substantial part of the fee income of small firms of accountants in the High Street since most of their clients are also small businesses. In contrast the bulk of the work of large accounting firms is the auditing of accounts of companies before they are published, but even large firms have some small clients. Their work is usually performed in a specialist division of the firm.

Jobs on incomplete records tend to be of two types:

(1) those where the client has maintained records but in *single-entry* form, often in just a Cash Book. In these cases what is incomplete is not so much the records as the *system of recording*. The accountant posts the items from the Cash Book to ledger accounts, which he himself constructs, thereby converting the single-entry to double-entry. The year-end adjustments are then put through in respect of accruals, prepayments, and provisions. These are then used as the basis from which to prepare the year-end final accounts.

(2) jobs in which the client has not followed even a single-entry system. The recording has probably not been based on any system at all and is patchy. Here the accountant has very little to go on and is *not* able to prepare a normal set of final accounts. All he can do is to estimate profit for the year, as the *difference between the opening and closing capital values* of the business.

Examination questions tend to be of type 1, mainly because they are a good test of double-entry principles and involve application of several key accounting concepts. The only principle tested in (2) is the accounting equation Assets = Capital — Liabilities. We shall look first at the approach and techniques required to answer type 1 questions, then type 2 questions.

Type 1 — Single Entry Systems

Questions provide information on:

assets and liabilities at the start of the financial year
receipts and payments during the year
some of the assets and liabilities at the end of the year

From this you are required to prepare a set of year-end final accounts. In examinations it is not necessary to construct a full set of ledger accounts before preparing the final accounts. There is simply not enough time, nor does it indicate knowledge of additional principles. Your main aim is to prepare the final accounts. For this, the following techniques can be used:

Technique	*To Find*
1. Accounting ratios	Sales or cost of goods sold
2. Balancing figures in ledger accounts	Purchases, sales, expenses
3. Reconstructing the Cash Book	Cash drawings
4. Application of Capital = Assets − Liabilities equation	Opening capital profit, drawings

Let us look at each in turn.

1. Accounting Ratios

A clue to the figure for sales or cost of goods sold is often given in the form of the *mark-up* applied to cost of goods or the *margin* achieved on sales. Mark-up is the amount of profit added to cost, while margin is profit in relation to the selling price.

Question

Take this cost structure:
Cost + Profit = Selling price
£4 + £1 = £5
What is (a) mark-up?
(b) margin?

Answer

(a) Mark-up $= \frac{\text{Profit}}{\text{Cost}} = \frac{1}{4}$ or 25%

(b) Margin $= \frac{\text{Profit}}{\text{Price}} = \frac{1}{5}$ or 20%

Being both measurements of profitability we can expect them to be linked. They are. This is how:

When mark-up is $\frac{1}{4}$, margin is $\frac{1}{4 + 1} = \frac{1}{5}$

When mark-up is $\frac{2}{7}$, margin is $\frac{2}{7 + 2} = \frac{2}{9}$

You should know and be able to apply this relationship in questions because examiners often give the cost of goods sold and profit margin. What good is this? one might think. Since margin is a proportion of sales and sales is not given, profit cannot be found! Well — the mark-up can be deduced from the margin. Since cost is given and mark-up is now known, profit *can* be found after all. This simple technique has helped many a student unlock the trading account.

Question

Given: Cost of goods sold £1 000
Gross profit on sales 20%

Required: A Trading account

Answer

Since margin is $\frac{1}{5}$, mark-up must be $\frac{1}{4}$
i.e. Cost + Profit = Selling price
£4 + £1 = £5
Sales value of goods sold = £1 000 × $1\frac{1}{4}$
= £1 250

Trading account

	£
Sales	1 250
Less cost of goods sold	1 000
Gross profit	250

This technique can also be used to prepare the trading account when sales and mark-up is given.

2. Balancing Figures in Ledger Accounts

If no information is given on mark-up or margin, purchases and sales will have to be calculated through the change in creditors and debtors position. Taking debtors as the example, a business will know the value of debtors at the start of the financial year (from last year's balance sheet), debtors at the year-end and amounts received from debtors during the year (from the cash book or bank statements). From this it is possible to deduce the value of sales during the year as follows:

	£
Total received during the year	9 600
Less amounts received in respect of sales made last year	1 000
	8 600
Add sales made this year for which payment has not yet been received	1 400
Sales made to debtors in this year	10 000

Sales can also be deduced by constructing a ledger account for total debtors.

Total Debtors

1 Jan. 19_2 Bal b/f	1 000	Bank – cheques received	9 600
Sales (bal. fig.)	∴ 10 000	31 Dec. 19_2 Bal c/f	1 400
	11 000		11 000

In fact the second approach is better because examiners often prefer workings to be shown in the form of accounts.

Be careful

(a) The figure for sales deduced in this way represents *Credit* sales only. If a business has also made *Cash* sales during the year these have to be added to credit sales to arrive at total sales.

(b) If there are any discounts allowed, bad debts, or contras (set-offs) in the question, these have to be included in the account before arriving at the balancing figure.

We know that the figure of cash paid for an expense is not necessarily the charge for the year. It has to be adjusted for any accruals or prepayments. This is best done by constructing the ledger account and finding the charge as a balancing figure.

Illustration

	£
Wages paid during year	4 850
Outstanding 1 Jan. 19_2	200
Outstanding 31 Dec. 19_2	350
Charge for the year	?

Wages

Bank – wages paid	4 850	1 Jan. 19_2 Balance b/f	200
31 Dec. 19_2 Bal c/f	350	31 Dec. 19_2 P & L ∴	5 000
	5 200		5 200

3. Constructing the Cash Book

If a Cash Book has not been maintained by the client the accountant will prepare one from bank statements and cheque stubs retained. In questions you may have to construct a Cash Book from information on receipts and payments during the year. The figure for *cash drawings* is sometimes not given. This is because proprietors of small businesses are notoriously bad at recording the amount of cash withdrawn for private purposes throughout the year. The amount then has to be deduced as a balancing figure in the cash column of the Cash Book. Examiners sometimes also do not give the figure for closing cash or bank, although this is easily found in practice — simply by counting the amount of cash and looking at the bank statement.

Illustration

Given:

	£
Opening balance, 1 Jan 19_2:	
Cash	100
Bank	2 000
Cash sales during the year	1 400
Cheques received from debtors	7 500
Cheques paid to suppliers	6 000
Cash paid to suppliers	50
Cash paid for expenses	300
Cheques paid for expenses	2 500
Closing balance, 31 Dec. 19_2:	
Cash	150
Bank	not given

Required:

Cash drawings	?
Closing bank balance	?

Solution

Cash Book

	Cash	*Bank*		*Cash*	*Bank*
	£	£		£	£
1 Jan. 19_2 Bals b/f	100	2 000	Creditors	50	6 000
Cash sales	1 400		Expenses	300	2 500
Debtors		7 500	*Drawings*	∴ 1 000	
			31 Dec. 19_2 *Bals c/f*	150	∴ 1 000
	1 500	9 500		1 500	9 500

Be careful with *drawings*. The cash book reveals the amount of *cash* drawings only. If the proprietor used some of business *stock* for personal purposes during the year this has also to be reflected in the final accounts — by adding to the figure for drawings (*dr*) and subtracting from purchases (*cr*).

The fourth technique commonly required to answer questions is the main one needed to solve problems where the records are not even in single-entry (the type 2 client). As such, it is looked at in the section on type 2 questions below.

A common difficulty with questions on incomplete records is that in the mass of information supplied one does not know just where to *start*. You might find it helpful to follow the steps laid out below.

(1) put down on paper the format of the trading account and insert the figures given (easy)
(2) deduce the missing figures, using techniques 1 and/or 2 (not as easy, workings needed)
(3) determine gross profit
(4) perform workings for profit and loss account using technique 2 (not difficult). Be sure to leave some space below the trading account for the profit and loss account
(5) prepare the profit and loss account
(6) deduce the figure for drawings using technique 3, if required
(7) calculate opening capital using technique 4, described below
(8) finally, prepare the year-end balance sheet.

Type 2 Questions

Since no records of transactions have been maintained it is not possible to construct ledger accounts and thus not possible to close them off to a trading and profit and loss account. All that can be estimated is profit made during the year, using technique 4.

4. Capital = Assets − Liabilities

By looking at the various assets and liabilities at the start and end of the year, it is possible to prepare a statement of affairs or balance sheet at the start and end of the year. The increase in capital value of the business must represent profit for the year. Of course, a decrease represents a loss. The principle is that capital at end of year = Capital at start + Additional capital introduced during the year + Profit (− Loss) − Drawings.

Illustration

Given:	1 Jan. 19_2	31 Dec. 19_2
	£000	*£000*
Fixed assets	50	50
Current assets	25	30
Current liabilities	20	20

	1 Jan. 19_2	31 Dec. 19_2
	£000	*£000*
During the year:		
Drawings		10
Additional capital introduced		7
Required:		
Opening capital		?
Profit for the year		?
Closing capital		?

Solution

First find opening capital, by drawing up a

Statement of affairs as at 1 Jan. 19_2

	£000	*£000*
Fixed assets		50
Current assets	25	
Less Current liabilities	20	5
Net assets (= Capital)		55

Next, prepare a similar

Statement of affairs as at 31 Dec. 19_2

	£000	*£000*
Fixed assets		50
Current assets	30	
Less Current liabilities	20	10
Net assets		60
Financed by:		
Capital, 1 Jan. 19_2 (from above)		55
Add additional capital introduced		7
		62
Add *profit* (bal. fig. 70 – 62)		∴ 8
		70
Less drawings		10
Capital, 31 Dec. 19_2 (= Net assets)		60

Having found closing capital of £60 000 we work backwards to find the amount of profit for the year.

A Limitation

A limitation of deducing missing figures as balancing items is that its correctness depends on the correctness of the rest of the account or statement. Thus if in the above example we had forgotten to include the additional capital introduced of £7 000, our profit figure would have been out by £7 000. It is advisable therefore to read any question *very carefully* and make sure that you have included all items relevant to an account or statement before striking out the balancing item.

A Final Word

Although incomplete records are not an easy topic, successfully writing the answers to a question can be most satisfying as you shall not doubt experience for yourself when, starting with a mass of haphazard information you manage to deduce missing items one by one to finish with a complete set of final accounts and a balance sheet that balances. The techniques required do need a lot of practice, perhaps more so than for other topics, and I have included a generous selection of past examination questions for you to attempt. Remember that the more you do at home the quicker you will be able to do them in an examination.

If a question seems too difficult because of the amount of information or the manner in which the information is presented, make things easier for yourself by drawing up a pro-forma trading and profit and loss account, putting in the figures already given, then tackling each missing figure one by one as you work your way down the account — in other words, follows steps 1–8 outlined above. Apart from helping to organize your thoughts on paper it will show the examiner that you have approached the question correctly and this in itself will earn you some marks. Finally, remember to *reference* your workings to their place in the final accounts.

Questions

5.1 Sally who trades as a photographer does not keep complete accounting records, but is able to provide the following details for the year to 30 November 19_5:

Summary of the bank account:

	£	£
Fees received		18 620
Sale of old camera		40
		18 660
Deduct:		
Cash withdrawn from bank	2 900	
New camera purchased	180	
Paid to creditors	1 250	
Rent and rates of office (13 months)	1 950	
Personal cheques	8 560	
Wages of assistants	2 900	
	17 740	
Opening bank overdraft	120	17 860
Closing balance		£ 800

Notes:

(1) Two cheques had not been presented for payment at the year-end:

Kadok Limited (trade purchases)	£19
Sally's 19_4 Income tax	£120

Neither of these cheques are included in the above summary.

(2) Part of the cash withdrawn from the bank was used to pay for advertising (£300) and photographic materials (£250), the remainder being used for private purposes by Sally.

(3) The camera sold during the year had a 'book value' of £70 at the date of sale.

Other opening and closing balances are as follows:

	1 December 19_4	*30 November 19_5*
	£	£
Stock of materials	409	450
Trade creditors	640	430
Debtors	590	630*
Wages owed	40	60
Rent and rates prepaid	—	(1 month)
Photographic equipment (at valuation)	600	500

* £60 of this total is considered doubtful.

Required:
Prepare trading and profit and loss accounts for the year ending 30 November 19_5 and a balance sheet as at that date.

(24 marks)

Advanced level Accounting, London

5.2* Austin Allegro is a sole trader buying and selling used cars. He has not kept a complete set of records and has asked you to prepare appropriate financial statements for the year ended 31st December 19_4.

Below is a summary of his bank account for the year:

	£		£
Cash sales paid in	9 800	Balance b/f at 1/1/19_4	200
Receipts from Debtors	23 890	Payments to Trade Creditors	13 590
Life Insurance Maturity	2 145	Purchase of fixed assets	3 940
Additional Capital Investment	2 000	Sundry Expenses paid	640
		Rent paid	1 500
		Wages paid by cheque	8 740
		Insurance paid on firm	748
		Drawings (for living)	8 470
		Balance c/f at 31/12/19_4	7
	37 835		37 835

The following additional information is also available:

(a) Valuations of assets and liabilities:

	31/12/_3	31/12/_4
	£	£
Creditors for stock	1 750	1 450
Creditors for sundry expenses	200	335
Fixed Assets	5 960 (Net)	8 910 (Net)
Prepaid Rent	250	—
Rent payable	—	375
Wages payable	370	240
Debtors	4 010	5 275
Stocks of used vehicles	19 040	24 035

(b) The Life Insurance maturity came from a policy he had taken out on his wife ten years previously — he had paid all premiums privately. It was paid in by mistake — there is no intention to use it as extra capital.

(c) Depreciation had been charged at 10% on all fixed assets and had been reflected in the accounts.

(d) Discounts received from stock creditors amounted to £500 and discounts allowed to debtors amounted to £625.

(e) Towards the end of December there had been a slump in the market for used cars and it was felt that the net realizable value of his stock at 31 December 19_4 was £13,250.

Using the above information you are required to prepare a Profit and Loss Account for the year ended 31st December 19_4 together with a Balance Sheet as at that date.

(20 marks)

Institute of Chartered Accountants, Foundation

5.3 Ben is an ex-regular soldier who retired from the army on 1 October 19_8 and started a car-hire firm with a gratuity of £2 500 and no other assets or liabilities.

On 30 September 19_1 he borrowed £20 000 from his brother-in-law so that he could expand his business. Just before the receipt of the money from his brother-in-law, Ben owned a fleet of cars valued at £35 000 and stocks of spares of £470. His customers owed him £1 860 and his bank balance was £2 190. Deposits received in advance from prospective hirers amounted to £250 and he owed £2 110 to various suppliers.

On 30 September 19_3 the Inland Revenue became aware of the existence of the business and required to be informed of the profits or losses from the date of Ben's discharge from the army.

At 30 September 19_3 the fleet of cars was valued at £55 000 and stocks at £2 100 while debtors stood at £5 630. There was a bank overdraft of £1 190, deposits of £350 and creditors of £6 300.

Ben has kept no books of account but estimates that his drawings from the business were £80 per week from 1 October 19_8 to 30 September 19_1 and £250 per week from 1 October 19_1 to 30 September 19_3.

Required:

(a) Calculate the apparent profit up to 30 September 19_1
(b) Calculate the profit or loss from 1 October 19_1 to 30 September 19_3
(c) State whether it would have made any difference if Ben claimed to have won £10 000 at a race-track during 19_2 and used it in the business.

(13 marks)

Institute of Chartered Accountants, Foundation

5.4 Dorothy has been trading as the 'Smash Hit' music shop for several years but has never kept full accounting records. A summary of the business bank account for the year ended 31 October 19_6 is given below.

	£		£
Opening balance	700	Paid to suppliers	23 600
Cash banked (see note 1)	42 900	Rent and rates	1 500
Closing balance	1 400	Light and heat	2 200
		Advertising	950
		Wages of assistants	5 530
		Drawings	10 300
		Sundry expenses	920
	45 000		45 000

Details of assets and liabilities (other than the bank balance) at the start and end of the financial year are as follows:

	1 November 19_5	31 October 19_6
	£	£
Debtors	218	(see note 2)
Creditors	3 750	4 950
Advertising prepaid	—	600
Advertising accrued	250	—
Stocks at cost	6 120	(see note 3)
Shop fixtures	10 620	(see note 4)

Notes:

(1) All takings were banked, with the exception of £830 which had been used to purchase new furniture for Dorothy's house.
(2) Closing debtors were equivalent to one week's sales. One quarter of this total is considered 'doubtful' and should be provided for. Assume that the shop was open for fifty weeks in the year.
(3) Closing stock valued at selling price was £10 395. Average mark-up on cost price was 75%.
(4) Shop fixtures are to be depreciated by the 'straight line' method over a five-year period. By 31 October 19_6, the fixtures had been owned for exactly two years.

Required:
Prepare appropriate financial statements for Dorothy's business for the year ended 31 October 19_6.

(25 marks)

Advanced level Accounting, London

5.5 S. Olsen, a wholesaler, did not keep proper books of account. The following information on his business was available on 31 March 19_4:

	£		£
long term loan	10 000	premises	50 000
motor vehicles	16 500	stock	12 500
trade debtors	23 650	trade creditors	14 500
balance & bank	10 500	cash in hand	3 400
fixtures & fittings	12 000	accrued general expenses	450

The balance at bank above included private investment income of his wife. This income arose from an interim dividend of 5% and a final dividend of 11% on 10 000 ordinary shares of 50p each.

The following information for the year ended 31 March 19_5 was extracted from the cash book:

	Cash	*Bank*		*Cash*	*Bank*
	£	£		£	£
Opening balances	3 400	10 500	Cash purchases		26 500
			Drawings		7 700
Receipts from trade debtors (see Notes 2 & 3)		138 500	Payments to creditors		74 800
			Salaries and wages	1 500	4 500
			Heating and lighting		1 500
			Motor vehicle expenses	180	4 020
			General expenses	270	2 230
			Receipts from trade debtors banked	138 500	

Additional information:
(1) Discounts received during the year amounted to £1 100.
(2) Olsen calculates his selling price by adding 25% profit on cost. All the goods sold in the year were sold at this mark-up except for £6 400 of the opening stock, which was marked up by $12\frac{1}{2}$ % only.
(3) All receipts from trade debtors were entered in the cash account, but the total amount received has not been recorded properly. The figure for bankings has been ascertained from bank statements.
(4) Depreciation to be provided: motor vehicles 20% of book value
fixtures & fittings 10% of book value
(5) £1 000 salaries and wages were owing at 31 March 19_5.
(6) Interest at 11% per annum on the long term loan is to be provided for.
(7) Other balances at 31 March 19_5 were: closing stock £15 700
trade creditors £19 300
trade debtors £11 000

Required:
(a) A trading and profit and loss account for the year ended 31 March 19_5. (10 marks)
(b) A balance sheet as at 31 March 19_5. (9 marks)

(19 marks)

Advanced Level Accounting, AEB

5.6* Blenkinsopp, a retailer who does not keep proper books of account, provided the following summarized financial information on his activities for the year ended 31 March 19_6:

	Cash £	Bank £		Cash £	Bank £
Balances 1 April 19_5	600	4 500	Drawings	2 000	9 000
Government stock interest		250	Shop takings banked	46 500	
Shop takings (including receipts from credit sales)	56 600	46 500	Purchase of micro-computer for stock control		3 600
			Rent and rates		1 000
Sales proceeds of government stock held privately		3 000	Advertising	150	100
			Wages and salaries	5 000	
			Lighting and heating		350
			Repairs to computer printer	100	
			Creditors for goods	1 100	28 900
			Motor vehicle expenses	80	600

Additional information:

(1) Other balances as at 1 April 19_5:

	£
Freehold premises	35 000
Fixtures & fittings	6 500
Rent owing	250
Motor vehicle	7 000
Trade creditors	12 000
Trade debtors	10 800
Finance company loan — long term	15 000
Stock	7 850

(2) At 31 March 19_6:

Advertising paid in advance	50
Wages and salaries owing	180
Trade debtors	8 000
Stock	14 000
Trade creditors	6 700

(3) During the year Blenkinsopp took £600 of goods at cost from the shop for his own use.

(4) Depreciation:

Motor vehicles and fixtures and fittings are to be depreciated at 20% per annum on a reducing balance basis.

Blenkinsopp was advised to write the micro-computer off on an equal instalment basis over 3 years. It was purchased on 1 April 19_5 and it was anticipated that it would have no residual value.

(5) The rate of interest applicable to the long term loan was 9% per annum. No interest had been paid for the current financial year.

Required:

(a) A trading and profit and loss account for the year ended 31 March 1986. (10 marks)

(b) The balance sheet as at 31 March 1986. (9 marks)

(19 marks)

Advanced level Accounting, AEB

5.7 Jean Smith, who retails wooden ornaments, has been so busy since she commenced business on 1 April 19_5 that she has neglected to keep adequate accounting records. Jean's opening capital consisted of her life savings of £15 000 which she used to open a business bank account. The transactions in this bank account during the year ended 31 March 19_6 are summarized from the bank account at the top of the next page.

	£
Receipts:	
Loan from John Peacock, uncle	10 000
Takings	42 000
Payments:	
Purchases of goods for resale	26 400
Electricity for period to 31 December 19_5	760
Rent of premises for 15 months to 30 June 19_6	3 500
Rates of premises for the year ended 31 March 19_6	1 200
Wages of assistants	14 700
Purchase of van, 1 October 19_5	7 600
Purchase of holiday caravan for Jean Smith's private use	8 500
Van licence and insurance, payments covering a year	250

According to the bank account, the balance in hand on 31 March 19_6 was £4,090 in Jean Smith's favour.

Whilst the intention was to bank all takings intact, it now transpires that, in addition to cash drawings, the following payments were made out of takings before bankings:

	£
Van running expenses	890
Postage, stationery and other sundry expenses	355

On 31 March 19_6, takings of £640 awaited banking: this was done on 1 April 19_6. It has been discovered that amounts paid into the bank of £340 on 29 March 19_6 were not credited to Jean's bank account until 2 April 19_6 and a cheque of £120, drawn on 28 March 19_6 for purchases was not paid until 10 April 19_6. The normal rate of gross profit on the goods sold by Jean Smith is 50% on sales. However, during the year a purchase of ornamental gold fish costing £600 proved to be unpopular with customers and therefore the entire stock bought had to be sold at cost price.

Interest at the rate of 5% per annum is payable on each anniversary of the loan from John Peacock on 1 January 19_6.

Depreciation is to be provided on the van on the straight line basis: it is estimated that the van will be disposed of after five years' use for £100.

The stock of goods for resale at 31 March 19_6 has been valued at cost at £1 900.

Creditors for purchases at 31 March 19_6 amounted to £880 and electricity charges accrued due to that date were £180.

Trade debtors at 31 March 19_6 totalled £2 300.

Required:
Prepare a trading and profit and loss account for the year ended 31 March 19_6 and a balance sheet as at that date.

(25 Marks)

Association of Accounting Technicians, Intermediate

5.8* Using the information given below concerning PJN Limited, you are required to show in vertical and columnar form for internal use only and not for publication:

(a) manufacturing, trading, profit and loss, and appropriation accounts for the year ended 31st December, 19_3;
(b) a balance sheet as at 31st December, 19_3.

The balance sheet of PJN Limited as at 31st December, 19_2, was as follows:

	£	£	£
Fixed assets at cost		1 800 000	
less Depreciation provision		410 000	1 390 000

Current assets:			
Material stocks		135 000	
Work-in-progress		41 000	
Finished goods stocks		290 000	
Debtors	580 000		
less Bad debts provision	29 000	551 000	
Prepayments:			
Administration expenses		1 100	
Distribution costs		100	
Cash at bank		41 800	
		1 060 000	
Less Current liabilities:			
Creditors for materials	196 000		
Accruals: Wages	3 000		
Administration expenses	2 700		
Distribution costs	1 900		
Taxation	246 400		
Proposed dividend	90 000	540 000	520 000
			£1 910 000
Ordinary shares of £1 each fully paid			1 000 000
Retained profit			910 000
			£1 910 000

A summary of the company's bank account for the year ended 31st December, 19_3 was as follows:

	£	£
Balance at 31st December, 19_2		41 800
Receipts: Debtors		3 960 000
		4 001 800
Payments: Creditors for materials	1 211 000	
Wages	498 000	
Manufacturing overhead	757 000	
Administration expenses	581 100	
Distribution costs	360 300	
Fixed assets purchased on 30th June, 19_3	200 000	
Taxation	246 400	
Dividends	140 000	3 993 800
Balance at 31st December, 19_3		£8 000

Other information is as follows:

(1) Stocks at 31st December 19_3 were:

	£
Materials	150 000
Work-in-progress	40 000
Finished goods	300 000

(2) Prepayments and accruals at 31st December, 19_3 were:

	Prepayments £	Accruals £
Wages		5 000
Administration expenses	1 500	3 000
Distribution costs	500	2 000

(3) Bad debts amounting to £20 000 were written off against the provision during the year.

(4) The bad debts provision at the year-end is to be made equal to 5% of the year-end debtors, and any increase or decrease is to be regarded as distribution costs.

(5) At 31st December, 19_3, debtors amounted to £600 000 and creditors for materials to £200 000.
(6) The company's policy is to depreciate its fixed assets at the rate of 10% per annum on cost on a strict time basis. The depreciation charge for the year is to be divided between manufacturing, administration and distribution in the ratio of 8:1:1.
(7) No discounts were received from suppliers or allowed to customers during the year.
(8) No debtors or creditors accounts were set-off by contra during the year.
(9) Provision is to be made for taxation at the rate of 40% and for this purpose the figure of net profit for the year may be used.
(10) Provision is to be made for a proposed final dividend of 10 pence per share.
(11) Advance corporation tax and value added tax are to be ignored.

(40 marks)

Chartered Institute of Management Accountants

(Attempt this question only when you have studied Manufacturing accounts and Company accounts)

Solutions

5.1

SALLY

Trading and Profit and Loss Account for the year ended 30 November 19_5

	£	£
Fees (W_1)		18 660
Less cost of materials used		
Opening stock materials	409	
Purchases (W_2)	1 309	
	1 718	
Less closing stock materials	450	1 268
Gross profit		17 392
Less Expenses		
Loss on sale of camera	30	
Wages (W_3)	2 920	
Rent and rates (W_4)	1 800	
Advertising	300	
Depreciation on photographic equipment (W_5)	210	
Provision for doubtful debts	60	5 320
Net profit		£12 072

Workings

W_1 *Fees control*

1 Dec. 19_4 Bal b/d	590	Bank		18 620
Fees receivable	∴ 18 660	30 Nov. 19_5	Bal c/d	630
	19 250			19 250

W_2 *Creditors — PLCA*

Unpresented cheque	19	1 Dec. 19_4	Bal b/d	640
Bank	1 250	*Purchases*		∴ 1 309
Cash	250			
30 Nov. 19_5 Bal c/d	430			
	1 949			1 949

W_3 *Wages*

Bank	2 900	1 Dec. 19_4	Bal b/d		40
30 Nov. 19_5 Bal c/d	60	30 Nov. 19_5	*P&L*		∴ 2 920
	2 960				2 960

W_4 *Rent and rates*

Bank	1 950	30 Nov. 19_5	*P&L*	∴ 1 800
		30 Nov. 19_5	Bal c/d	150
	1 950			1 950

W_5 *Photographic equipment*

1 Dec. 19_4	600	Disposal		70
Bank — new camera	180	30 Nov. 19_5	*Depreciation*	∴ 210
		30 Nov. 19_5	Bal c/d	500
	780			780

The depreciation charge has been ascertained by the revaluation method.

To find opening capital we need to prepare a

Statement of affairs as at 1 December 19_4

	£	£	£
Fixed assets			
Photographic equipment			600
Current assets			
Stock		409	
Debtors		590	
		999	
Less Current liabilities			
Trade creditors	640		
Wages owing	40		
Bank overdraft	120	800	199
Net assets (= Capital)			£799

W_6 Drawings.

Cash (2900 − 300 − 250)	2 350
Cheques	8 560
Income tax*	120
Total	11 030

* The income tax a sole trader is liable to is a private, not business expense. Indeed some of the tax may relate to other forms of income such as interest, dividends and rent. Since Sally has paid the tax from the business bank account this amounts to a drawing.

We can now prepare the year-end balance sheet.

SALLY

Balance Sheet as at 30 November 19_5

	£	£	£
Fixed assets			
Photographic equipment			500
Current assets			
Stock		450	
Debtors	630		
Less provision for doubtful debts	60	570	
Rent and rates prepaid		150	
Bank (800 − 120 − 19)		661	
		1 831	

	£	£	£
Less Current liabilities			
Trade creditors	430		
Wages owing	60	490	
			1 341
Net assets			£1 841
Financed by:			
Capital			799
Add profit			12 072
			12 871
Less drawings (W_6)			11 030
Capital employed			£1 841

5.3 This is a typical type 2 question, where no system of recording has been maintained — not even single entry. Income statements cannot be prepared and profit has to be deduced from successive balance sheets.

(a)

BEN

Statement of affairs as at 30 September 19_1

	£	£	£
Fixed assets			
Cars			35 000
Current assets			
Stocks of spares		470	
Trade debtors		1 860	
Bank		2 190	
		4 520	
Less Current liabilities			
Deposits in advance	250		
Trade creditors	2 110	2 360	2 160
Net assets			£37 160
Financed by:			
Initial capital, 1 Oct. 19_8			2 500
Profit, 1 Oct. 19_8 to 30 Sept. 19_1			∴ 47 140
			49 640
Less drawings (£80 × 52) × 3 years			12 480
Capital employed, 30 Sept. 19_1			£37 160

(b)

BEN

Statement of affairs as at 30 September 19_3

	£	£	£
Fixed assets			
Cars			55 000
Current assets			
Stocks		2 100	
Debtors		5 630	
		7 730	
Less Current liabilities			
Deposits in advance	350		
Creditors	6 300		
Bank overdraft	1 190	7 840	110
Net assets			£54 890

Capital, 30 Sept. 19_1	37 160
Profit, 1 Oct. 19_1 to 30 Sept. 19_3	∴43 730
	80 890
Less drawings (£250 × 52) × 2 years	26 000
Capital employed, 30 Sept. 19_3	£54 890

(c) BEN

Statement of affairs as at 30 September 19_3

	£
Capital, 1 Oct. 19_1	37 160
Add new capital introduced	10 000
	47 160
Add *Profit* (bal. fig.)	33 730
	80 890
Less drawings	26 000
Capital employed, 30 Sept. 19_3	£54 890

Yes. Profit would be reduced by £10 000.

5.4 Most items in the trading account are not given and must be deduced first.

Workings

W_1 *To determine Sales*

	£
Takings banked	42 900
Takings not banked — drawings	830
	43 730
Less takings for last year's sales	(218)
49 weeks' sales	43 512
Closing debtors — 1 week's sales (43 512 × $\frac{1}{49}$)	888
Sales for the year	44 400

W_2 *To determine Purchases*

Total creditors

Bank — paid		23 600	1 Nov. 19_5	Bal b/f	3 750
31 Oct 19_6	Bal c/f	4 950	*Purchases*		∴24 800
		28 550			28 550

W_3 Closing stock = £10 395 × $\frac{100}{175}$ = £5 940

THE 'SMASH HIT' MUSIC SHOP

Trading and Profit and Loss Account for the year ended 31 October 19_6

	£	£
Sales (W_1)		44 400
Less cost of goods sold		
Opening stock	6 120	
Purchases (W_2)	24 800	
	30 920	
Less closing stock (W_3)	5 940	24 980
Gross profit		19 420
Less Expenses		
Rent and rates	1 500	
Light and heat	2 200	
Advertising (W_4)	100	
Wages of assistants	5 530	
Sundry expenses	920	
Provision for doubtful debts (888 × $\frac{1}{4}$)	222	
Depreciation on fixtures (W_5)	2 655	13 127
Net profit		£6 293

Working

Advertising

W_4

Bank — paid	950	1 Nov. 19_5	Bal b/f	200
		31 Oct. 19_5	*P&L*	∴ 100
		31 Oct. 19_5	Bal c/f	600
	950			950

W_5 By 1 November 19_5 shop fixtures had been depreciated for 1 year at 20% of cost

$\therefore$ Cost was £10 620 $\times \frac{100}{80}$ = £13 275

Depreciation charge for year = £13 275 × 20%
= £ 2 655

To find opening capital:

Statement of affairs as at 1 November 19_5

	£	£	£
Fixed asset			
Fixtures, at book value			10 620
Current assets			
Stock		6 120	
Debtors		218	
Bank		700	
		7 038	
Less Current liabilities			
Creditors	3 750		
Advertising accrued	250	4 000	3 038
Net assets (= Capital)			£13 658

We can now prepare Dorothy's year-end balance sheet.

THE 'SMASH HIT' MUSIC SHOP

Balance Sheet as at 31 October 19_6

	£	£	£
Fixed asset			
Fixtures, at cost			13 275
Less accumulated depreciation			5 310
			7 965
Current assets			
Stock		5 940	
Debtors	888		
Less provision for doubtful debts	222	666	
Advertising prepaid		600	
		7 206	
Less Current liabilities			
Creditors	4 950		
Bank overdraft	1 400	6 350	
Working capital			856
Net assets			£8 821
Financed by:			
Capital, 1 November 19_5			13 658
Add profit for the year			6 293
			19 951
Less drawings (10 300 + 830)			11 130
Capital employed			£8 821

5.5 (a)

S. OLSEN

Trading and Profit and Loss Account for the year ended 31 March 19_5

	£	£
Sales (W_2)		129 200
Less cost of goods sold		
Opening stock	12 500	
Purchases (W_1)	107 200	
	119 700	
Less closing stock	15 700	104 000
Gross profit		25 200
Discounts received		1 100
		26 300
Less Expenses		
Salaries and wages	7 000	
Heating and lighting	1 500	
Motor vehicle expenses	4 200	
General expenses (W_3)	2 050	
Depreciation on motor vehicles (16 500 × 20%)	3 300	
Depreciation on fixtures and fittings (12 000 × 10%)	1 200	
Loan interest (10 000 × 11%)	1 100	20 350
Net profit		£5 950

Workings

W_1 *Total Creditors — PLCA*

Bank	74 800	1 April 19_4	Bal b/f	14 500
Discounts received	1 100		*Credit purchases*	∴ 80 700
31 March 19_5 Bal c/f	19 300			
	95 200			95 200

Credit purchases (from above)	80 700
Cash purchases	26 500
Total purchases, to Trading account	107 200

W_2

	Cost	*Profit*	*Sales*
Sold at $12\frac{1}{2}$% mark-up	6 400	800	7 200
Sold at 25% mark-up	97 600	24 400	122 000
	104 000	25 200	129 200

W_3 *General expenses*

Cash	270	1.4.19_4	Bal b/f	450
Bank	2 230	31.3.19_5	*P&L*	∴ 2 050
	2 500			2 500

(b) To find opening capital:

Balance Sheet as at 31 March 19_4

Fixed assets	£	£	£
Premises			50 000
Motor vehicles			16 500
Fixtures and fittings			12 000
			78 500
Current assets			
Stock		12 500	
Trade debtors		23 650	
Bank		10 500	
Cash		3 400	
		50 050	

Less Current liabilities	£	£	£
Trade creditors	14 500		
General expenses owing	450		
Wife's income owing (W_4)	800	15 750	34 300
Net assets			112 800
Financed by:			
Capital owned			∴ 102 800
Long-term loan			10 000
Capital employed			112 800

W_4 Interim dividend 5 000 × 5%	250
Final dividend 5 000 × 11%	550
	800

It is now necessary to reconstruct the Cash Book to find the closing cash and bank balances.

W_5 *Total Debtors — SLCA*

1 April 19_4	Bal b/f	23 650	*Cash received*		∴ 141 850
Sales (W_2)		129 200	31 March 19_5	Bal c/f	11 000
		152 850			152 850

Cash Book

	Cash	Bank		Cash	Bank
	£	£		£	£
1.4.19_4 Bals b/f	3 400	10 500	Cash purchases		26 500
Debtors (W_5)	141 850		Drawings		7 700
Banked ¢		138 500	Creditors		74 800
			Salaries and wages	1 500	4 500
			Heating and lighting		1 500
			Motor expenses	180	4 020
			General expenses	270	2 230
			Banked ¢	138 500	
			31.3.19_5 *Bals c/f*	∴ 4 800	∴ 27 750
	145 250	149 000		145 250	149 000

We are now ready to prepare the year-end balance sheet.

S. OLSEN

Balance Sheet as at 31 March 19_5

Fixed assets	£	£	£
Premises			50 000
Motor vehicles			13 200
Fixtures and fittings			10 800
			74 000
Current assets			
Stock		15 700	
Trade debtors		11 000	
Bank		27 750	
Cash		4 800	
		59 250	
Less Current liabilities			
Trade creditors	19 300		
Salaries and wages owing	1 000		
Loan interest accrued	1 100		
Wife's income owing	800	22 200	
Working capital			37 050
Net assets			£111 050

Financed by:	£	£	£
Capital (derived)			102 800
Add profit			5 950
			108 750
Less drawings			7 700
Capital owned			101 050
Long-term loan			10 000
Capital employed			£111 050

5.7 An interesting question. The Trading Account is quite testing. Be careful with determination of cash sales. Also, watch the dates very closely.

JEAN SMITH

Trading and Profit and Loss Account for the year ended 31 March 19_6

	£	£
Sales (W_1)		50 400
Less cost of goods sold		
Purchases	27 400	
Less closing stock	1 900	25 500
Gross profit		24 900
Less Expenses		
Electricity (760 + 180)	940	
Rent (3 500 $\times \frac{12}{15}$)	2 800	
Rates	1 200	
Wages	14 700	
Van licence and insurance (250 $\times \frac{6}{12}$)	125	
Van running expenses	890	
Postages, stationery and other sundry expenses	355	
Depreciation on van (W_2)	750	
Loan interest (£10 000 $\times$ 5% $\times \frac{3}{12}$)	125	21 885
Net profit		£3 015

Workings

W_1 *Determination of Sales*

	£
Purchases (26 400 + 120 + 880)	27 400
Excluding goldfish	(600)
	26 800
Less closing stock	1 900
	24 900
Mark-up at 100%	24 900
Sales value	49 800
Sale of goldfish at cost	600
Total sales	50 400

W_2 Annual depreciation on van $= \frac{7\,600 - 100}{5} = £1\,500$

Since date of purchase is given it is assumed that depreciation is charged on a monthly basis.

1 Oct. 19_5 to 31 March 19_6 = 6 months.

Depreciation charge $= £1\,500 \times \frac{6}{12} = £750.$

Workings for balance sheet

We are not given the amount of cash drawings, so it is necessary to reconstruct the Cash Book and deduce it as a balancing figure.

Cash Book

		Cash £	Bank £		Cash £	Bank £
1 April 19_5	Capital		15 000	Creditors (26 400 + 120)		26 520
1 Jan. 19_6	Loan		10 000	Electricity		760
Takings banked ¢			42 340	Takings banked ¢	42 340	
Cash sales (W_3)		48 100		Rent		3 500
				Rates		1 200
				Wages		14 700
				1 Oct. 19_5 Van		7 600
				Caravan		8 500
				Motor vehicle expenses		250
				Motor vehicle expenses	890	
				Postages, stationery, etc.	355	
				Drawings	∴ 3 875	
				31 March 19_6 Bals. c/d	640	4 310(W_4)
		48 100	67 340		48 100	67 340

W_3	Sales during the year	50 400
	Less debtors outstanding at year-end	2 300
	Cash received from sales	48 100
W_4	Balance as per bank statement	4 090
	Add lodgement not yet credited	340
		4 430
	Less unpresented cheque	120
	Balance as per Cash Book	4 310

JEAN SMITH

Balance Sheet as at 31 March 19_6

	£	£	£
Fixed asset			
Van, at cost			7 600
Less depreciation			750
			6 850
Current assets			
Stocks		1 900	
Debtors		2 300	
Rent prepaid		700	
Van licence and insurance prepaid		125	
Bank (W_4)		4 310	
Cash		640	
		9 975	
Less Current liabilities			
Trade creditors	880		
Electricity accrued	180		
Loan interest accrued	125	1 185	8 790
Net assets			£15 640
Financed by:			
Capital			15 000
Add profit			3 015
			18 015
Less drawings (3 875 cash + 8 500 caravan)			12 375
Capital owned			5 640
Long-term loan			10 000
Capital employed			£15 640

CHAPTER 6

Correction of Errors

Given that in the course of a year thousands, sometimes millions of separate transactions have to be entered in the books it is perhaps not surprising that some errors are made. A tired bookkeeper, temporary loss of concentration, working in times of extra pressure, a mislaid invoice — all of these can, and in practice do, lead to incorrect entries being made in the books. Bookkeepers can try to be conscientious in trying to prevent errors but no system is fool-proof since even the best bookkeeper in the world is subject to the occasional human error, and the best computer to computer error. When an error is located it has to be corrected by first making a note of the adjustment required in the *journal*, then putting through the double-entry in the ledger(s).

Types of Errors

What are the nature of these errors? Well — they can be of many types but it is possible to classify them into a few groups. Some errors are more difficult to detect than others. A bookkeeper will not be easily alerted to errors which debit and credit accounts of the same amount since the trial balance prepared to 'check' the books will balance. Herein lies a major weakness of the trial balance — if it balances, this does not *in itself* prove that the books have been correctly written up. There are certain errors which are not picked up by the trial balance. These are as follows:

Name	*Nature of error*	*Example*
1. Error of Omission	A transaction is completely omitted from the books.	A purchase of goods is not recorded because the purchase invoice has been mislaid.
2. Error of Commission	A purchase (sale) is entered in the wrong creditor (debtor) account.	A sale of goods to J. Tyler is posted to J. Taylor's account.
3. Error of Principle	An item is entered in a completely wrong class of account.	A purchase of a fixed asset is posted to purchases account.
4. Error of Original Entry	A wrong account is entered in a book of original entry and this figure is then used for posting to the ledger(s).	A sales clerk in a hurry reads an invoice of £10 000 as £1 000 and enters this figure in his sales day book.

Let us move on now to those errors which *are* picked up by trial balance extraction. With these, both entries have been made on the same side, or the amounts entered on the two sides are different. For example, on the sale of goods to Jay Ltd. for £320 Jay Ltd.'s account is debited with the correct amount but sales account is credited with £230. (This is called a transposition error.) While a difference in trial balance totals alerts the bookkeeper to errors within the books, it does not tell him *where* the errors are. For this he has to check the entries made until they are found.

Consider a trial balance with the following totals.

	Dr	*Cr*
Totals	£97 500	£86 200

There is a material discrepancy and the bookkeeper has to go through the books. On first check he will be able to identify some but probably not all of the errors. Let us say that he is able to reduce the discrepancy to

	Dr	*Cr*
Totals	£92 100	£92 000

There is still a discrepancy but it is no longer material. At this point the bookkeeper has to make a decision — does he spend more time trying to locate those errors which did not reveal themselves easily or does he accept the small discrepancy and attend to current work to prevent a backlog building up in the books? He will probably attend to current work. The problem is that as the trial balance stands the balance sheet will not balance.

Suspense Accounts

To overcome this problem a *suspense account* is opened and the difference inserted into it to 'force' the trial balance to balance.

	Dr	*Cr*
	£	*£*
Totals	92 100	92 000
Suspense		100
	92 100	92 100

The accountant can now prepare the final accounts. In the balance sheet the suspense account will be shown as a current liability. A suspense account with a debit balance would be shown as a current asset.

If, at a later date, any of the remaining errors are found the correction can be made with suspense, thereby reducing its balance.

Example

The transposition error mentioned above (£320 for £230) is found after the final accounts have been prepared. The sales account has been understated by £90. To correct it.

Dr Suspense	£90	
Cr Sales		£90

This reduces the balance on suspense to just £10.

Note that even if all the postings to an account are made correctly the balance extracted from it will still be wrong if there is an error in:
(1) addition (casting), or
(2) a balance brought forward at the start of the year
In this case the trial balance will fail to agree.

Correction of Errors

This should be done in three mental stages:
(1) Work out what double-entry *actually took place*
(2) Determine what *should have taken place*
(3) Adjust the relevant accounts to eliminate the error.

Always ask yourself whether one or two accounts are in error. If only one account is in error it is double-entried with suspense; if two, they are double-entried with each other.

Illustration — Two accounts in error

A purchase of machinery, £5 000, is debited to purchases account.

	£	£
Stage 1 What took place		
Dr Purchases	5 000	
Cr Bank		5 000
Stage 2 What should have taken place		
Dr Machinery	5 000	
Cr Bank		5 000
Stage 3 Correction		
Dr Machinery	5 000	
Cr Purchases		5 000

Illustration — One account in error

A purchase of goods on credit from Blake for £8 000 is debited to purchases account as £800.

	£	£
Stage 1 What took place		
Dr Purchases	800	
Cr Blake		8 000
Stage 2, What should have taken place		
Dr Purchases	8 000	
Cr Blake		8 000
Stage 3 Correction		
Dr Purchases	7 200	
Cr Suspense		7 200

It is not necessary for you to write down all three steps on paper — do them in your head. The correcting entry (stage 3) is first noted in the journal with a narrative explaining it before being posted to the ledger.

Examination Questions

Examination questions on this topic usually give you an incorrect trial balance or balance sheet followed by a list of errors, and ask you to:

(1) correct them showing the required journal entries
(2) show the suspense account
(3) re-calculate profit for the year
(4) draw up a revised trial balance or balance sheet.

Some questions ask for just one or two of the above. Long questions ask for all four. To do (3) and (4), mark in pencil alongside each journal entry whether it affects the trading account, profit and loss account, or balance sheet. An amendment to purchases, sales, or stock will affect the trading account (gross profit). An amendment to an expense or miscellaneous income will affect the profit and loss account (net profit). A change in an asset, liability, or capital affects the balance sheet. Performing this exercise will reduce the amount of thinking you need to do and things you need to keep in your head when drawing up your statement of corrected profit and balance sheet.

Questions

6.1 At the completion of the financial year ended 30 April 19_4, the trial balance of Rock Ltd failed to agree and the difference was recorded in a suspense account. The company does not maintain control accounts.

The following information has been subsequently discovered prior to the preparation of the final accounts:

(1) The purchase of a secondhand delivery van costing £1 500 has been debited to the motor vehicle expenses account.
(2) No entry has been made in the accounts to record the theft of £250 cash from the business by a dishonest former employee. The cash will not be recovered.
(3) The total of the discount allowed column in the cash book has been overcast by £187.
(4) The receipt of £289 from Hand, a customer, has been correctly entered in the cash book but has been debited to Hand's account in the sales ledger as £298.
(5) Although the return of goods, sold for £45, from Brown, a customer, has been correctly entered in the returns inwards account not entry has been made in Brown's account in the sales ledger.

Required:

(a) Journal entries correcting each of the five errors given above. Narratives are not required. (5 marks)
(b) A suspense account showing clearly the original discrepancy on the trial balance. (5 marks)

(10 marks)

Advanced level Accounting, AEB

6.2 The draft accounts of a company for the year ended 31 December 19_4, showed a gross profit of £140 000 and a net profit before taxation amounting to £90 000. These figures are higher than in previous years. Attached to the accounts is a note stating that errors had been made in the preparation of the figures.

An investigation revealed the following:

(1) In previous years the stocks had been valued on a FIFO (First in, First out) basis, but the stock at 31 December 19_4 had been valued incorrectly on a LIFO (Last in, First out) basis. Prices had been rising steadily throughout the year, and the difference between the two stock values at the year-end was £6 000.
(2) Cash totalling £4 000 had been stolen from the company's premises during the year. No record had been made of this theft; there was no possibility of recovery; and the loss had not been insured.
(3) No provision had been made for the audit fee, estimated at £1 000.
(4) In order to allow for the effect of inflation on the value of the premises, £20 000 had been added to the net profit (premises account debited and the profit and loss account credited).
(5) A sales contract worth £8 000 had been negotiated prior to the year-end, but not signed until 3 January 19_5. The amount had been included in the sales total for the year to 31 December 19_4. The goods relating to this contract were not to be sent to the customer until February 19_5.
(6) An invoice for £2,000 goods received from a supplier had been totalled incorrectly at £200. The £200 had been posted to both the personal and nominal ledgers.

You are required to make:

(a) Journal entries, including appropriate narratives, to correct items (1), (2) and (3) above. (8 marks)
(b) A calculation of the effect of items (1)-(6) above on the original gross profit calculation and the original net profit calculation. (16 marks)

(24 marks)

Advanced level Accounting, London

6.3* Jackson Printing Company Limited, a small private company, has produced its unaudited balance sheet as at 31 March 19_4.

	£	£	£
Fixed Assets			
Tangible Assets:			
Freehold land and buildings			60 000
Plant and machinery		40 000	
Accumulated depreciation		18 000	22 000
Motor vans		25 000	
Accumulated depreciation		11 000	14 000
			96 000
Current Assets:			
Stocks		10 000	
Debtors		14 000	
Cash		1 200	
		25 200	
Current Liabilities — amounts falling due within one year:			
Creditors	10 000		
Bank	6 000	16 000	9 200
			105 200
Equity and Reserves:			
Called up shares			75 000
Retained profits			30 200
			105 200

In the course of your audit you find that:

(1) During the year a motor van was sold for £1 100. The van was bought four years ago at a cost of £10 000 and had been depreciated to £2 000. Proceeds were included in sales and no other entries had been made.

(2) The land and buildings had been revalued by a surveyor at freehold land £20 000 and buildings at £50 000. The directors wish to incorporate these new values in the balance sheet and to depreciate the buildings at 2% per annum.

(3) A debtor, owing the company £1 000, is unlikely to pay and should be written off.

Required:

(a) journal entries to adjust the balance sheet as at 31 March 19_4 for items referred to above (supporting narrative is not required), and

(b) a balance sheet as at 31 March 19_4, after the adjustments as in (1) above.

(16 marks)

Institute of Chartered Accountants, Foundation

6.4 After the draft accounts had been prepared for the financial year ended 31 December 19_3 the treasurer of an amateur football club discovered a batch of vouchers which had fallen down behind his desk, none of which had been processed.

The vouchers related to the following matters:

(1) an invoice date 23 January 19_4 from Patchems Medical Supplies for a new first aid kit for the club's trainer. The kit had cost £21.96 and had been supplied on 5 January 19_4;

(2) an invoice dated 11 January 19_4 from Sports Equipment (1978) Ltd. for £36.70, being the cost of a new goal net, corner flags and linesmen's flags, delivered to the club on 20 December 19_3;

(3) a cheque counterfoil, dated 15 December 19_3, for £15, being the fee for a match away from home to be played on 4 February 19_4;
(4) a cheque counterfoil, dated 5 January 19_4, for £20 being the fee for a match away from home to be played on 18 February 19_4;
(5) an invoice dated 6 January 19_4 for £328.85 for work carried out at the club's home ground during November 19_3 by Plumbing Services. The work consisted of the installation of two extra shower baths in the changing rooms (£268.30) and sundry repairs and renovations (£60.55);
(6) a cheque counterfoil dated 17 January 19_4 for £32.62 being the wages of the part-time groundsman, £11.21 of which had been earned up to 31 December 19_3.

Other information:
The club depreciates its equipment at the rate of 20% per annum on a straight-line basis on gross cost at the year-end.

Required:
(a) Journalize such of the above transactions as affect the 19_3 final accounts. (11 marks)
(b) State the individual items in the draft balance sheet affected by the journal entries in (a) and the respective amounts by which they would increase or decrease. (5 marks)

(16 marks)

Chartered Association of Certified Accountants

6.5* The draft final accounts of RST Ltd for the year ended 30 April 19_5 showed a net profit for the year after tax of £78 263.

During the subsequent audit, the following errors and omissions were discovered. At the draft stage a Suspense account had been opened to record the net difference.

(1) Trade debtors were shown as £55 210. However,
  (i) bad debts of £610 had not been written off,
  (ii) the existing provision for doubtful debtors, £1 300, should have been adjusted to 2% of debtors,
  (iii) a provision of 2% for discounts on debtors should have been raised.
(2) Rates of £491 which had been prepaid at 30 April 19_4 had not been brought down on the rates account as an opening balance.
(3) A vehicle held as a fixed asset, which had originally cost £8 100 and for which £5 280 had been provided as depreciation, had been sold for £1 350. The proceeds had been correctly debited to Bank but had been credited to Sales. No transfers had been made to Disposals account.
(4) Credit purchases of £1 762 had been correctly debited to Purchases account but had been credited to the supplier's account as £1 672.
(5) A piece of equipment costing £9 800 and acquired on 1 May 19_4 for use in the business had been debited to Purchases account. (The company depreciates equipment at 20% per annum on cost.)
(6) Items valued at £2 171 had been completely omitted from the closing stock figure.
(7) At 30 April 19_5 an accrual of £543 for electricity charges and an insurance prepayment of £162 had been omitted.
(8) The credit side of the wages account had been under-added by £100 before the balance on the account had been determined.

Required:
(a) prepare a statement correcting the draft net profit after tax (13 marks)
(b) post and balance the Suspense account. *(Note: The opening balance of this account has not been given and must be derived)* (4 marks)

(17 marks)

Chartered Association of Certified Accountants

Solutions

6.1 (a)

ROCK LTD.
The Journal

	Dr	*Cr*
	£	*£*
(1) Motor vehicles	1 500	
Motor vehicle expenses		1 500
(2) Loss by theft	250	
Cash		250
The theft, being an expense, should be written off to this year's P & L Account		
(3) Suspense	187	
Discounts allowed		187
Error involving one account only. The double-entry is therefore with suspense.		
(4) There are two errors here — transposition and posting to the wrong side of an account.		
Suspense	298	
Hand, debtor		298
To correct posting to wrong side		
Suspense	289	
Hand, debtor		289
Entry now made as it should have been		
(5) Suspense	45	
Brown, debtor		45

(b)

Suspense

	£		£
(3) Discount allowed	187	*Balance b/f* (bal. fig.)	819
(4) Hand, debtor	298		
(4) Hand, debtor	289		
(5) Brown, debtor	45		
	819		819

Original discrepancy on the trial balance was that the debit side exceeded the credit side by £819.

6.2 (a)

The Journal

	Dr	*Cr*
	£	*£*
(1) Stock	6 000	
Trading		6 000
Being adjustment to stock valuation		
(2) Profit and loss	4 000	
Cash		4 000
Being theft of cash		
(3) Profit and loss	1 000	
Provision for audit fee		1 000
Being provision for audit fee		

(b) You can adapt either a horizontal or vertical format for the profit correction. Both approaches are illustrated on the following page.

Corrected Trading and Profit and Loss Account
for the year ended 31 December 19_4

	£		£
(5) Sales written back	8 000	Draft gross profit b/f	140 000
(6) ↑ Purchases	1 800	(i) ↑ Closing stock valuation	6 000
Gross profit c/f	136 200		
	146 000		146 000
Reduction in gross profit	3 800	Draft net profit b/f	90 000
(2) Cash stolen	4 000		
(3) Audit fee	1 000		
(4) ↑ Premises written back	20 000		
Net profit c/f	61 200		
	90 000		90 000

Additional Notes

(4) The appreciation in premises is an increase in the *capital base* of the business, and not this year's profit. We need to take it out of profit and loss and credit the gain to *revaluation reserve*.

Correcting entry —		
Dr Profit and loss	20 000	
Cr Revaluation reserve		20 000

(5) Application of realization concept

(6) Correcting entry —

Dr Purchases	1 800	
Cr Creditors		1 800

Statement of corrected profit — vertical format

	£	£
Gross profit as per draft accounts		140 000
Add (1) ↑ Closing stock valuation		6 000
		146 000
Less (5) Sales written back	8 000	
(6) ↑ Purchases	1 800	9 800
Adjusted gross profit		136 200
Net profit as per draft accounts		90 000
Less Reduction in gross profit	3 800	
(2) Cash stolen	4 000	
(3) Audit fee	1 000	
(4) ↑ Premises written back	20 000	28 800
Adjusted net profit		£61 200

6.4 It is best to do both parts of the question *together*, taking each of the items in turn.

(a) *The Journal*	*Dr* £	*Cr* £	(b) *Effect on balance sheet*	£
(1) No effect on 19_3 accounts				
(2) Equipment	36.70		FA Equipment	36.70
Creditors		36.70	CL Creditors	36.70
Being purchase of equipment on 20 December				
I & E	7.34		Accumulated fund	(7.34)
Provision for depreciation — equipment		7.34	FA Equipment	(7.34)
Being depreciation on new equipment				
(3) Prepayment	15.00		CA Prepayment	15.00
Bank		15.00	CA Bank	(15.00)
Being a 19_4 match fee paid in advance				
(4) No effect on 19_3 accounts				

The Journal	*Dr*	*Cr*	(b) *Effect on balance sheet*	
	£	£		£
(5) Equipment	268.30		FA Equipment	268.30
Repairs	60.55		Accumulated fund	(60.55)
Creditors		328.85	CL Creditors	328.85
Being liability for work carried out in November				
I & E	53.66		Accumulated fund	(53.66)
Provision for depreciation — equipment		53.66	FA Equipment	(53.66)
Being depreciation on new showers				
(6) Wages	11.21		Accumulated fund	(11.21)
Accruals		11.21	CL Accrual	11.21
Being liability for December wages				

Items 1 and 4 will be treated in the 19_4 accounts.

For part (b) it is possible to draw up the following optional statement of effect on the balance sheet.

Net effect on Balance Sheet

	Ref.	£	£	£
Fixed assets				
Equipment	2			36.70
	2			(7.34)
	5			268.30
	5			(53.66)
				244.00
Current assets				
Prepayment	3		15.00	
Bank	3		(15.00)	
			—	
Less Current liabilities				
Creditors	2	36.70		
	5	328.85		
		365.55		
Accrual	6	11.21		
			(376.76)	(376.76)
Net assets				£(132.76)
Financed by:				
Accumulated fund	2			(7.34)
	5			(60.55)
	5			(53.66)
	6			(11.21)
				£(132.76)

CHAPTER 7

Club Accounts

Non-trading, non-profit-making organizations such as clubs and societies do not keep accounts in the same way as a business. The accounting function is often performed on a voluntary basis by the person elected as Treasurer of the club. It is unlikely that he will be versed in the principles of double-entry bookkeeping so it is not surprising to learn that most clubs keep financial records in single entry. Often the treasurer is pre-occupied with just the Cash Book. From this he prepares at the end of the year a summary of cash movements during the year in the form of a receipts and payments account.

Receipts and Payments Account

The emphasis here is on liquidity rather than profitability — a club, if it is to survive, must find sufficient funds to finance its activities, and this account shows how it is doing on this front.

Example

THE AMATEUR MUSICAL SOCIETY

Receipts and Payments Account for the year ended 31 December 19__1

Receipts	£	*Payments*	£
1 Jan. Bank balance b/f	300	Committee members' expenses	300
Subscriptions received	2 000	Rent of hall	800
Donations received	300	Light and heat	200
Sale of concert tickets	400	Concert expenses	300
		Purchase of piano	1 000
		31 Dec. Balance c/f	400
	3 000		3 000
1 Jan. Balance b/f	400		

A lot of small clubs present their final accounts in this simple format due to the limitations of the treasurer.

Doing this has two disadvantages:

(1) the receipts and payments account does not take account of *non-cash items* such as depreciation, accruals and prepayments, and the distinction between capital and revenue

(2) a balance sheet cannot be prepared from it — there is too little information.

Income and Expenditure Account

If the receipts and payments account is adjusted to incorporate the items in (1) above we would end up with an income statement. The larger clubs and those with treasurers with an accounting background do this — it is called an Income and Expenditure Account. An excess of income over expenditure is called a *surplus*, not profit.

The conversion of the receipts and payments account into an income and expenditure account is commonly asked for in questions. The most difficult part of the conversion is usually working out subscriptions receivable (which needs crediting to the income and expenditure account) from subscriptions received — this is a test of the accruals concept. It is unlikely that all members pay their dues on time. In addition, some may pay in advance. To work out the correct transfer to the income statement it is best to construct a ledger account to reflect all accruals and prepayments, then deduce the amount receivable as a balancing figure.

In addition to its main activity a club may organize the occasional one-off event such as an Annual Party for members or a raffle. Running a bar for a profit is another common side-activity. With these it is a good idea to show all income and expenditure connected with an activity *together* in the account, indicating the profit or loss on it. Alternatively, the account could contain a single figure of profit or loss on the activity, details being shown underneath by way of note. With the bar a separate *bar trading account* should be prepared first, and the profit transferred to the main income and expenditure account.

Balance Sheet

The larger clubs, which have assets to their name such as property, equipment, and a bank balance, would probably want to prepare a balance sheet. The structure here is no different from the balance sheet of a business. The only difference is in terminology — instead of capital the word *accumulated fund* is used. A surplus of income over expenditure is added to the fund, a deficit deducted. The figure for the fund then shows changes in the value of the club.

In the balance sheet remember to include unpaid subscriptions receivable as a current asset and subscriptions received in advance as a current liability.

Examination Questions

Examination questions on this topic usually give a summary of cash movements during the year (in effect, the receipts and payments account) with additional information on accruals, prepayments, and depreciation. From this you have to prepare the income and expenditure account and balance sheet. A number of figures are often not given. They have to be deduced as balancing figures by constructing the appropriate ledger accounts. Thus, if the figure for bar purchases is omitted it can be found by preparing the bar creditors control account. The opening value of accumulated fund usually isn't given either. This can be deduced by preparing a balance sheet at the start of the year. Questions on club accounts are often similar in nature to those on incomplete records.

Let us now look at a worked example of a typical question. The question selected is from a recent examination paper of the GCE Advanced level in Accounting, of the Associated Examining Board (AEB).

Worked Example

The Greenfields Tennis Club has been established for many years but recently its financial position has declined. The treasurer of the club has prepared the following receipts and payments account for the year ended 30 September 19_4.

		£			£
19_3			19_4		
1 October	Balance b/d	6 740	30 September	Affiliation to County Tennis Association	250
19_4				Purchase of tennis balls	180
30 September	Sales of tennis balls	260		Dance expenses	650
	Dance receipts	390		Wages	2 400
	Sale of fixtures	180		General expenses	2 680
	Subscriptions	4 310		Balance c/d	5 720
		11 880			11 880
19_4					
1 October	Balance b/d	5 720			

The following information is also available.

	30 September 19_3	30 September 19_4
	£	£
Pavilion	6 000	6 000
Stock of tennis balls	30	20
Fixtures and equipment	2 400	2 000
Subscriptions in advance	40	60
General expenses owing	70	110

Required:
(a) The income and expenditure account for the year ended 30 September 19_4 of the Greenfields Tennis Club.
(b) A balance sheet as at 30 September 19_4 of the Greenfields Tennis Club.

Solution

(a) GREENFIELDS TENNIS CLUB

Tennis Balls Trading Account for the year ended 30 September 19_4

	£	£
Sales		260
Less cost of balls sold		
Opening stocks	30	
Purchases	180	
	210	
Less closing stock	20	190
Profit, to income & expenditure account		70

Income and Expenditure Account for the year ended 30 September 19_4

	£	£	£
Income			
Subscriptions (W_1)			4 290
Profit on sale of balls			70
			4 360
Less Expenditure			
Affiliation to CTA		250	
Dance receipts	390		
Less expenses	(650)		
Loss on dance		260	
Wages		2 400	
General expenses (W_2)		2 720	
Depreciation on fixtures and equipment (W_2)		220	5 850
Deficit of income over expenditure			£(1 490)

Workings

W_1 *Subscriptions*

30 Sept. 19_4	*I & E*	∴ 4 290	1 Oct. 19_3	Bal b/f	40
30 Sept. 19_4	Bal c/f	60	Bank		4 310
		4 350			4 350

W_2 *General expenses*

Bank		2 680	1 Oct. 19_3	Bal b/f	70
30 Sept. 19_4	Bal c/f	110	30 Sept. 19_4	*I & E*	∴ 2 720
		2 790			2 790

W_3 It is necessary to find the depreciation on fixtures as a balancing figure, using the revaluation method.

Fixtures — net

1 Oct 19_3	Bal b/f	2 400	Bank — disposals *		180
			30 Sept. 19_4	Depreciation	∴ 220
			30 Sept. 19_4	Bal c/f	2 000
		2 400			2 400

* In the absence of any information, it is assumed that fixtures were sold at net book value.

(b) Since we are not given the opening value of accumulated fund it is necessary to *derive* it as a balancing figure in the opening balance sheet.

GREENFIELDS TENNIS CLUB

Balance Sheets as at:

30 September 19_3 £	£	£		30 September 19_4 £	£	£
			Fixed assets			
		6 000	Pavilion			6 000
		2 400	Fixtures and equipment			2 000
		8 400				8 000
			Current assets			
	30		Stock of tennis balls		20	
	6 740		Bank		5 720	
	6 770				5 740	
			Less Current liabilities			
40			Subscriptions prepaid	60		
70	110	6 660	General expenses owing	110	170	5 570
		£15 060	*Net assets*			£13 570
			Financed by:			
			Accumulated fund (derived)			15 060
			Less deficit for the year			(1 490)
		∴ £15 060				£13 570

Life Membership

Some clubs offer life membership for one large lump-sum payment. Let us take the example of a club which offers permanent membership for the payment of £50. When a member takes up the offer the income is received all in one year but the consideration is to be discharged over several years. Should we credit *all* of the £50 to that year's income and expenditure account? No — that would contravene the accruals (matching) concept. The club should estimate how many years on average a life member is likely to use the club. People do not stay in one place all of their lives — they move on after an average of about 10 years. Assuming the life member uses the club for that length of time the £50 should first be credited to a life membership account. Annual transfers of

$$\frac{£50}{10 \text{ years}} = £5$$

should be made from this to the income and expenditure account.

The account would look like this:

Life membership account

		£			£
31 Dec. 19_1	I & E	5	1 Jan. 19_1	Cash	50
31 Dec. 19_1	Bal c/f	45			
		50			50
31 Dec. 19_2	I & E	5	1 Jan. 19_2	Bal b/f	45
31 Dec. 19_2	Bal c/f	40			
		45			45
31 Dec. 19_3	I & E	5	1 Jan. 19_3	Bal b/f	40
31 Dec. 19_3	Bal c/f	35			
		40			40

. . . . and so on for 10 years, by which time the balance on the account is reduced to nil.

While there is a credit balance on the life membership account it is shown in the balance sheet as a *long-term liability* — to provide the amenities of the club to the life member for no payment. It is rather like a payment received in advance.

There is no one correct figure for the number of years for the transfer. This will vary with the experience of the individual club. Examination questions usually state the number of years used by the club in question. See question 7.4.

Questions

7.1* The Happy Wanderers Rambling Club is a non-profit making organization catering for the leisure pursuits of those interested in walking, hiking and rambling, each admitted member agreeing to pay a membership fee of £10 per annum on 1st January each year. In addition, fees are also charged for each outing/excursion. The club has a small clubhouse which serves as headquarters and also houses a bar and kitchen for light refreshments and snacks.

Below is a summary of the Cash/Bank book as maintained by the Treasurer:

Cash/Bank Book details — Year ended 31st December 19_2

	£		£
Balance at 1/1/_2	300	Wages — bar staff	200
Receipts from members:		Rent and rates	400
annual fees for 19_2	450	Insurance	80
annual fees for 19_1	30	Lighting and heating	110
annual fees for 19_3	10	Equipment and fittings:	
outings and excursions	490	purchase and repairs	140
Bar and snack takings	1 030	Creditors — bar & snack purchases	500
		Telephone, postage and stationery	85
		Magazines and periodicals	76
		Balance at 31st December 19_2	719
	2 310		2 310

The above details represent the only accounting records which have been maintained apart from the following information:

(1) the following sundry balances were applicable as at the start and end of the year:

	1st January 19_2	*31st December 19_2*
Creditors for bar and snack purchases	40	110
Prepayments: rent and rates	100	—
insurance	—	20
Accruals: rent and rates	—	75
insurance	15	—
telephone, postage and stationery	—	15
lighting and heating	—	15
wages — bar staff	20	25

(2) the record of members' annual fees revealed the following:
as at 1st January 19_2, 4 members had not paid their fees for 19_1
as at 31st December 19_2, 5 members had not paid their fees for 19_2, whilst 1 member had paid in advance for 19_3.

The annual fee had been set in 19_9 and had not changed since that date. It is the policy of the Club to write off as bad debts any annual fees outstanding for two years or over.

(3) certain members owed a total of £15 for outings and excursions as at 31st December 19_2.

(4) equipment and fittings had a book value at 1st January 19_2 of £1 200 with £800 depreciation having been provided to that date. All equipment and fittings are depreciated at a rate of 10% per annum on cost.

(5) the £140 spent on purchases and repairs of equipment and fittings included £40 for repairs. It is Club policy to charge a full year's depreciation in the year of acquisition.

(6) bar stock held at 1st January 19_2 had all been purchased on 1st December 19_1 at a cost of £30. At 31st December 19_2 stock on hand had cost £60.

Using the information and details above you are required to prepare:
(a) an Income and Expenditure Account for the year ended 31st December 19_2, and
(b) a Balance Sheet as at 31st December 19_2.
Your workings should show clearly the value of the Club's Accumulated Fund at 1st January 19_2.

(25 marks)

Institute of Chartered Accountants, Foundation

7.2 A summary of the Xanadu Accounting Association's cash book for the year to 31 March 19_4 was as follows:

	Dr		*Cr*
	£		*£*
Subscriptions re 19_2/3	600	Balance b/f	2 500
Subscriptions re 19_3/4	6 800	Printing costs	1 100
Donations received	3 400	Publicity expenses	5 800
Competition receipts	810	Competition prizes	700
Balance c/f	540	Rent of rooms	350
		Purchase of loudspeakers	500
		Sundry expenses	1 200
	12 150		12 150

The association's treasurer provides the following information:

(1)

	1 April 19_3	31 March 19_4
	£	£
Subscriptions due from members	600	500
Rent paid in advance	—	50
Stock of competition prizes	—	70
Stock of printing inks and paper	120	200

(2) Fixed assets on 1 April 19_3 comprised a printing machine with a book value of £700. The association has a policy of depreciating all fixed assets at 20% on the reducing balance method.

(3) 'Publicity expenses' are analysed as follows:

	£
Advertising campaign (lasting three years from 1 April 19_3)	4 200
Deposit on the purchase of new printing machine (the machine will not be delivered until October 19_4)	1 000
Cost of renovating old motor coach (The coach had been donated by a member on 1 September 19_3)	2 000
	7 200
Less Grant from World Xanadian Headquarters towards publicity expenses	1 400
	£5 800

Prepare the Income and Expenditure account for the year to 31 March 19_4. (A balance sheet is not required.)

(10 marks)

Advanced level Accounting, London, part-question

7.3 As treasurer of your local tennis club you have just prepared a draft Receipts and Payments account, which is reproduced below.

The club committee decides, however, that it wishes its financial statements for 19_3 and subsequent years to be in the form of an Income and Expenditure account accompanied by a balance sheet and requests you to amend the 19_3 account accordingly.

Receipts and Payments account for the year ended 31st December, 19_3

	£
Receipts:	
Cash in hand at 1st January, 19_3	100
Cash at bank at 1st January, 19_3: Current account	1 160
Deposit account	2 000
Member's subscriptions: 19_2	620
19_3	8 220
19_4	125
Interest on deposit account	85
Entry fees for club championship	210
Tickets sold for annual dinner/dance	420
Bank overdraft at 31st December, 19_3	4 000
	16 940
Payments:	
Groundsman's wages	4 000
Purchase of equipment (on 30th June, 19_3)	8 000
Rent for year to 30th September, 19_3	2 000
Rates for year to 31st March, 19_4	1 800
Cost of annual dinner/dance	500
Secretarial expenses	400
Prizes for club championship	90
Miscellaneous expenses	100
Cash in hand at 31st December, 19_3	50
	16 940

Additional information:

(1) At 31st December, 19_3, £700 was outstanding for members' subscriptions for 19_3.

(2) During 19_2, £230 was received in respect of members' subscriptions for 19_3.

(3) The cost of equipment purchased in previous years was:

	£
30th June, 19_2 (11 years ago)	5 000
1st January, 19_7	1 000
30th September, 19_1	1 000

(4) The committee decides that equipment should be depreciated at the rate of 10% per annum on cost.

(5) Rent has been at the rate of £2 000 per annum for the last two years and is not expected to change in the immediate future.

(6) Rates of £750 for the six months to 31st March, 19_3 were paid on 2nd November, 19_2.

(7) Interest of £250 on the bank overdraft had accrued at 31st December, 19_3.

(8) Taxation is to be ignored.

You are required to prepare:

(a) the club's Income and Expenditure account for the year ended 31st December, 19_3; and

(b) its balance sheets as at 31st December, 19_2, and as at 31st December, 19_3.

(35 marks)

Chartered Institute of Management Accountants

7.4* On 2 November 19_3, the Treasurer of the Olympiad Athletics Club died. The financial year of the club, which had been formed to provide training facilities for both field and track event athletes, had ended two days previously on 31 October 19_3. An extraordinary general meeting was convened for the purpose of appointing a new treasurer whose task it would be to prepare the annual accounts for that financial year.

An enthusiastic club member, Guy Rowppe, was duly appointed but, having only an elementary knowledge of book-keeping, soon found himself in difficulty.

He sought your assistance which you agreed to give. During your conversation he said, 'The previous treasurer maintained a Cash and Bank account. I have summarised the detailed entries into what I think you call a Receipts and Payments Account, and have rounded the figures to the nearest £1.'

At this point he supplied you with a copy of the following document:

OLYMPIAD ATHLETICS CLUB

Receipts and Payments Accounts for 12 months ended 31 October 19_3

Note No.	*Receipts*	*Cash* £	*Bank* £	*Note No.*	*Payments*	*Cash* £	*Bank* £
	Balances b/d	73	—		Balance b/d	—	105
	Membership fees:			(4)	Insurance premiums paid to brokers		580
(1)	entrance	80	170	(7)	Payments to suppliers of sporting requisites		5 270
(1)	annual subscriptions	215	4 465	(5)	Wages of groundsman		3 600
(2)	life membership		530	(8)	Postages and telephones		692
(3)	Training ground fees	454	7 206	(9)	Stationery		629
	Insurance:				World-wide Athletics Club affiliation fee		50
(4)	premiums		638	(10)	Rates of training ground		846
(4)	commissions		53		Upkeep of training ground		1 200
(11)	Interest received from investments		626		Transfers to bank	700	
(12)	Sale of office furniture		370	(11)	Purchase of investments		5 600
(6)	Sale of sporting requisites		8 774	(11)	Short term deposits		3 000
	Advertising revenue		603		Balances c/d	122	2 563
	Transfers from cash		700				
		£822	£24 135			£822	£24 135
	Balances b/d	122	2 563				

After you had perused the above account, Guy Rowppe explained the numbered items, as follows:

(1) On admittance to membership of the club, new members pay an initial entrance fee together with their annual subscription. At 31 October 19_2, annual subscriptions of £70 had been paid in advance and £180 was owing but unpaid; of this latter amount, £40 related to members who left during the current year and is now no longer recoverable. The figures at 31 October 19_3 are £100 subscriptions in advance and £230 in arrear. The policy of the club is to take credit for subscriptions when due and to write off irrecoverable amounts as they arise.

(2) As an alternative to paying annual subscriptions, members can at any time opt to pay a lump sum which gives them membership for life without further payment. Amounts so received are held in suspense in a Life Membership Fund account and then credited to Income and Expenditure Account in equal instalments over 10 years; the first such transfer takes place in the year in which the lump sum is received. On 31 October 19_2 the credit balance on the Life Membership Fund Account was £4 720, of which £850 was credited as income for year ended 31 October 19_3.

(3) The club has a permanent training ground. Non-members can use the facilities on payment of a fee. In order to guarantee a particular facility, advance booking is allowed. Advance booking fees received before 31 October 19_3 in respect of 19_4 total £470. The corresponding amount paid up to 31 October 19_2 in advance of 19_3 was £325. Members can use the facilities free of charge.

(4) Club members can take out insurances through the club at advantageous rates. Initially, premiums are paid by members to the club. Subsequently, the club pays the premiums to an insurance broker and receives commission. At 31 October 19_2 premiums received but not yet paid over to the broker amounted to £102 and commissions due but not yet received were £11. The corresponding amounts at 31 October 19_3 are £160 and £13 respectively.

(5) The groundsman is employed for the six months April to September only. He is then paid a retaining fee to secure his services for the following year. At 31 October 19_2 the groundsman had been paid a retainer (£250) for 19_3. Included in the Wages figure (£3,600) is the retainer (£300) for 19_4.

(6) Sporting requisites are sold only on cash terms. There are therefore no debtors for these items.

(7) On 31 October 19_2 sums owed to suppliers of sporting requisites totalled £163; the corresponding figure on 31 October 19_3 was £202. Stock of unsold sporting requisites on 31 October 19_2 was £811 and on 31 October 19_3, was £927. In arriving at this latter figure, the sum of £137, representing damaged and unsaleable stock at cost price, had been excluded.

(8) Postage stamps unused at 31 October 19_3, totalled £4.

(9) Stock of stationery on 31 October 19_2 and 19_3 was £55 and £36 respectively.

(10) Rates are payable to the District Council in two instalments (in advance) each year. £360 had been paid on 1 October 19_2, £390 on 1 April 19_3 and £456 on 1 October 19_3.

(11) The club receives interest on investments bought a number of years ago at a cost of £7 400 (current valuation £7 550). At the end of October 19_3, the club had acquired further investments which cost £5 600 (current valuation £5 600) and at the same time placed £3 000 in a short-term deposit account.

(12) The written down value of the furniture which had been sold during the year was £350; it had originally cost £800.

Other Matters:
Initially, the training ground had been acquired freehold* from a farmer at an inclusive cost of £4 000. Subsequently, the club had some timber buildings erected to provide various facilities for members. The total cost of these buildings was £35 000; depreciation is calculated at the rate of 10% per annum on a straight line basis. At 31 October 19_2, the provision for depreciation account had a balance of £9 400.

At 31 October 19_2, the furniture and equipment etc. was recorded in the club's books as £7 900 (cost) against which there was a provision for depreciation of £4 150 (calculated on the same basis as for buildings). Apart from the disposal referred to in note (12) (above) there had been no other disposals or acquisitions during the year.

Required:
Prepare the club's Income and Expenditure Account for year ended 31 October 19_3 and the Balance Sheet at that date.
All workings must be shown.

(32 marks)

* Freehold land is land held in perpetuity.

Chartered Association of Certified Accountants.

Solutions

7.2 An interesting short question testing not only club accounts but also the accruals concept and the distinction between capital and revenue.

XANADU ACCOUNTING ASSOCIATION

Income and Expenditure Account for the year ended 31 March 19_4

	£	£
Income		
Subscriptions (W_1)		7 300
Donations		3 400
Profit on competitions (W_2)		180
		10 880
Less Expenditure		
Printing costs (W_3)	1 020	
Publicity expenses (W_4)	2 000	
Rent of rooms	300	
Sundry expenses	1 200	
Depreciation on equipment (W_5)	240	4 760
Surplus of income over expenditure		£6 120

Workings

W_1 *Subscriptions*

1 April 19_3	Bal b/d	600	Cash		600
			Cash		6 800
31 March 19_4	*I & E*	∴ 7 300	31 March 19_4	Bal c/d	500
		7 900			7 900

W_2 *Competitions*

Receipts		810
Cost of prizes	700	
Less closing stock	70	630
Profit, to income and expenditure account		180

W3 *Printing*

1 April 19_3	Stock b/f	120	31 March 19_4	*I & E*	1 020
Cash		1 100	31 March 19_4	Stock c/f	200
		1 220			1 220

W4 *Publicity expenses*

Advertising *	1 400
Coach renovation	2 000
	3 400
Less grant	1 400
Charge, to income and expenditure account	2 000

* Since the benefit of the advertising campaign is expected to be felt over three years, it should be charged to income and expenditure account also over three years — application of the accruals concept. By the same reasoning, since the new printing machine will not be delivered until next year, the deposit on it should not be charged to this year's account.

W5 *Fixed assets*

Printing machine — net book value at 1 April 19_3	700
Add purchase of loudspeakers	500
Net book value at 31 March 19_4	1 200
Depreciation @ 20% of 1200	240

7.3 A long question, the two key testing points being depreciation on equipment and the ability to infer information on accruals and prepayments not only at the year-end but also at the end of *last* year.

(a) TENNIS CLUB

Income and Expenditure Account for the year ended 31 December 19_3

Income	£	£	£
Subscriptions (W1)			9 150
Entry fees for club championship		210	
Less cost of prizes		90	
Profit			120
Bank interest received			85
Less Expenditure			9 355
Groundsman's wages		4 000	
Rent (W2)		2 000	
Rates (W3)		1 725	
Annual dinner/dance:			
Sale of tickets	420		
Less cost	500		
Loss		80	
Secretarial expenses		400	
Miscellaneous expenses		100	
Depreciation on equipment (W4)		600	
Bank interest		250	9 155
Surplus of income over expenditure			£ 200

Workings *Subscriptions*

W1

1 Jan. 19_3	Bal b/f *	620	1 Jan. 19_3	Bal b/f		230
			Bank — for	19_2		620
				19_3		8 220
31 Dec. 19_3	*I & E*	∴ 9 150		19_4		125
31 Dec. 19_3	Bal c/f	125	31 Dec. 19_3	Bal c/f		700
		9 895				9 895
1 Jan. 19_4	Bal b/f	700	1 Jan. 19_4	Bal b/f		125

W_2

		Rent			
Bank		2 000	1 Jan. 19_3	Bal b/f	500
31 Dec. 19_3	Bal c/f (2 000 × $\frac{3}{12}$)	500	31 Dec. 19_3	*I & E*	∴ 2 000
		2 500			2 500

W_3

		Rates			
1 Jan. 19_3	Bal b/f (750 × $\frac{3}{6}$)	375	31 Dec. 19_3	Bal c/f (1800 × $\frac{3}{12}$)	450
Bank		1 800	31 Dec. 19_3	*I & E*	∴ 1 725
		2 175			2 175

W_4 *Fixed assets*

Since in part (b) of the question we need to construct balance sheets at the start and end of the year it is necessary to find, for equipment, the:

accumulated depreciation up to 31 December 19_2
charge for the year
accumulated depreciation up to 31 December 19_3

Since the exact dates of purchase are given it is assumed that depreciation is charged on a monthly basis.

Date of purchase	*Years held up to 31 Dec. 19_2*	*Cost*	*Annual dep'n @ 10%*	*Acc. dep'n up to 31 Dec 19_2*	*Charge for 19_3*	*Acc. dep'n up to 31 Dec. 19_3*
		£	£	£	£	£
30 June 19_2	10½	5 000	500	5 000	—	5 000
1 Jan. 19_7	6	1 000	100	600	100	700
30 Sept. 19_1	1¼	1 000	100	125	100	225
30 June 19_3	0	8 000	800	0	400	400
		15 000		5 725	600	6 325

(b)

TENNIS CLUB

Balance Sheet as at

31 December 19_2 £	£	£		*31 December 19_3* £	£	£
			Fixed assets			
		7 000	Equipment — at cost			15 000
		5 725	Less accumulated depreciation			6 325
		1 275	Net book value			8 675
			Current assets			
	620		Debtors for subscriptions		700	
	375		Rates prepaid		450	
	2 000		Bank — deposit account		—	
	1 160		— current account		—	
	100		Cash		50	
	4 255				1 200	
			Less Current liabilities			
230			Subscriptions prepaid	125		
500			Rent accrued	500		
—			Bank interest accrued	250		
—	730	3 525	Bank overdraft	4 000	4 875	(3 675)
		£4 800	*Net assets*			£5 000
			Financed by:			
			Accumulated fund (derived)			4 800
			Add surplus for the year			200
		∴ £4 800				£5 000

CHAPTER 8

Partnership Accounts

A partnership exists when two or more persons carry on business in common with a view to profit. It is the natural extension to the simple sole trader type of business. The agreement between partners is usually written down in a formal *deed of partnership*. This document covers, among others, the following matters:

(1) The *amount of capital* to be contributed by each partner
(2) The *profit (loss) sharing ratio*
(3) *Interest on capital.* The reward for risk-taking is profit and the greater the amount of capital risked by each partner (partnerships do not have the safeguard of limited liability) the greater is the return to him
(4) *Interest to be charged on drawings.* This is to discourage partners from taking out more from the partnership at any one time than they really need
(5) *Salaries.* Where a partner works harder than the others he may be allowed a salary for his additional investment in Time into the partnership. (This is in contrast to the return on capital, which is profit.)

An *oral agreement* which can be substantiated by figures in past final accounts may also be upheld. In addition an *implied agreement* may be held to exist again by looking at past accounts e.g. the profit-sharing ratio may be gauged by looking at past distributions of profit. If no agreement — written, oral, or implied — can be found to exist the terms of the *Partnership Act 1890* apply. Section 24 of this act provides that profits and losses are to be shared equally, no interest is to be allowed on capitals or charged on drawings, no salaries are payable to any partner and that a loan made by a partner is to receive interest at 5 per cent a year.

All the techniques of bookkeeping and accounting relevant to sole traders apply equally to partnerships, but the latter has one added complication. In the case of a sole trader the capital is wholly owned by one man; in partnerships accounts are needed to show the financial relationship between one partner and:
(1) the other partners
(2) the business as a whole.
This is done with the use of *appropriation, capital* and *current accounts.* We shall look at each in turn.

The Appropriation Account

The function of the appropriation account is to effect the agreement laid out in the formal deed regarding the sharing of profit (loss), interest on capital and drawings, and salaries. It is the tail end of the income statement, prepared just after the profit and loss account. The horizontal format looks as follows:

Pro-forma

Appropriation account

	£		£
Interest on capital		Net profit b/f	x
A	x	Interest on drawings	
B	x	A	x
Salary, A	x	B	x
Share of profit			
A	x		
B	x		
	£x		£x

The share of profit attributable to each partner is the final calculation — after all other appropriations have been made.

Be careful with the calculation of interest on drawings. Charge only for the months of the year for which the money was drawn.

Example

A and B agree an interest rate on drawings of 10 per cent, to encourage each partner to withdraw funds as little and as late as possible. In the financial year 1 January to 31 December B withdraws £600 on 1 April and a further £600 on 31 August. What is his interest charge?

	£
£600 for 9 months, $600 \times \frac{9}{12} \times 10\% =$	45
£600 for 4 months, $600 \times \frac{4}{12} \times 10\% =$	20
Total interest charge	65

It is not simply £1 200 × 10% = £120.

The Capital Account

The capital account shows the amount of *long-term* resources put into the business by each partner. Usually there is little movement in the account. It needs to be adjusted only if:

(1) A partner brings in more long-term resources or withdraws some of existing capital.
Example — B decides to hand over to the partnership his motor car, valued at £10 000. B's capital amount should be increased thus:
Dr Motor vehicles £10 000
Cr Capital, B £10 000

(2) An existing partner retires or a new partner is admitted. This situation is looked at later in the chapter.

The Current Account

This shows the amount of *short-term* funds contributed by each partner. The double-entry is with appropriation account. Whereas interest on capital, salary, and profit share were debited to appropriation each partner's current account is credited with these. Similarly, interest on drawings is debited. The actual amount of drawings is also debited since drawings reduce the amount of short-term funds contributed.

Pro-forma

Current account — A

	£		£
Drawings	x	1 Jan Bal b/d	x
Interest on drawings	x	Interest on capital	x
		Salary	x
31 Dec. Bal c/d	x	Share of profit	x
	£x		£x
		1 Jan. Bal b/d	x

The withdrawal of *any asset*, not just cash, is a drawing.

Example

If A takes business stock costing £400 for his personal use, he denies the business the chance to earn money on this and his current account should reflect this. The double entry is

Dr Current account, A	£400	
Cr Stock (or Purchases)		£400

A *debit* balance on a current account indicates that the partner has withdrawn more than his entitlement from interest on capital, salary and share of profit. This may happen where, for example, profits are lower than was expected or where the business has suffered a loss.

Loan by a Partner

If a partner wishes to *lend* money to the partnership this is a liability, not capital. In addition, since payment of loan interest is a mandatory business expense it is charged against profits in the profit and loss account. This contrasts with interest on partners' capital which is an *appropriation* of profit.

Appropriation Account — Vertical Format

The appropriation account has been shown above in horizontal format to emphasize that it is a double-entry with partners' current accounts. Where the profit and loss account is shown in a vertical form, the appropriation also should be, for consistency of presentation. The vertical format looks as follows:

Pro-forma

Appropriation account

	£		£
Net profit b/f			x
Add interest on drawings			
A	x		
B	x		x
		(*k*)	x
Less interest on capital			
A	x		
B	x		x
			x
Less salary — A			x
		(*l*)	x
Share of profit			
A	x		
B	x	(*m*)	x

Item *k* represents the total income available for appropriation. Item *l* represents the balance of profits remaining after all appropriations have been made. It is shared amongst the partners in the agreed profit-sharing ratio in the final part of the account. Item *m*, representing total profits shared, is equal to *l*.

Private Ledger

Since matters contained in the capital, current, and drawings accounts are of a confidential nature, they are usually kept in a separate book trusted to one of the partners to keep in a safe place. This book is called the *Private Ledger*.

Admission and Retirement

Partnerships are an inherently unstable form of business organization. Differences in opinion, a loss of trust, desire for change, death of a partner, retirement — all of these can lead to break-up of a partnership. This may well be followed by admission of a new partner to replace the person leaving. Technically, when this happens the old partnership ceases to exist and a new contract is drawn up by the new partners. In this there are two complications — *goodwill* and *revaluation of assets*. We need to look at each in turn.

Goodwill

Successful businesses have a reputation linked to their name. They also have an established group of loyal customers. Think of the reputation and loyalty attached to such names as Rolls-Royce, Jaguar, Coca-Cola, and Marks and Spencer. This intangible asset is known as *goodwill*. There is no account for goodwill in the books because:
(1) it has been acquired over time and not specifically *bought* like other assets
(2) it is difficulty to quantify in money terms.
Maintaining an account for goodwill in the books would thus contravene the basic principle of historic cost accounting.

When a person makes an application to join a partnership he has to pay a sum of money for the benefit of sharing in the profit and part-owning the business assets. Since goodwill is also an asset he can expect to have to pay a certain amount for this as well. Similarly when an existing partner retires from a successful business he will expect some payment for goodwill as consideration for giving up his share of the business to the remaining partners. In these circumstances it is necessary to put a figure on this intangible asset. This is no easy task. A number of methods are used in practice but all are arbitrary and subject to criticism. We do not need to consider the various methods of goodwill valuation, since the method to be followed is usually specified in questions. We are more concerned with how goodwill, when raised, is recorded in the books.

Bookkeeping Entries

A goodwill account is opened in the private ledger with the following double-entry:

Dr Goodwill
Cr Capital accounts of *original* partners in *original* profit-sharing ratio

This credits the existing partners with the goodwill they have built up over the years. The account is usually opened just for the day of admission or retirement. It is closed by:

Dr Capital accounts of *new* partners in *new* profit-sharing ratio
Cr Goodwill

This leads to the incoming partner sharing in the goodwill write-off. In this way he is effectively charged an element for it.

Example

A and B are in partnership sharing profits and losses equally, the balance on the capital accounts being £20 000 each. C is admitted as a partner, all three partners now having an equal one-third share. The goodwill of the business at the time of C's admission is valued at £30 000. C introduces £20 000 cash into the firm. The way this would be recorded in the capital accounts is shown on the following page.

Capital accounts

	A	B	C		A	B	C
	£	£	£		£	£	£
				Balances b/f	20 000	20 000	
Goodwill Out	10 000	10 000	10 000	Goodwill In	15 000	15 000	
Balances c/f	25 000	25 000	10 000	Cash			20 000
	35 000	35 000	20 000		35 000	35 000	20 000
				Balances b/f	25 000	25 000	10 000

The goodwill is:
(1) initially credited to A and B in the ratio $\frac{1}{2} : \frac{1}{2}$

(2) written off by A, B, and C in the ratio $\frac{1}{3} : \frac{1}{3} : \frac{1}{3}$

The existing partners' balance has increased by £5 000 each even though they have not introduced any additional capital. At the same time C's balance is £10 000 *less* than the amount of cash introduced by him. What has happened is this: since C is acquiring $\frac{1}{3}$ of the business he has to pay for $\frac{1}{3}$ of the goodwill. This amounts to £30 000 $\times \frac{1}{3} =$ £10 000. Since the original partners are giving up a share of the business they need to be compensated by the new partner. A and B share profits equally, so the £10 000 goodwill payment is split equally between them. End result:

A's capital increases by	£5 000
B's capital increases by	£5 000
C's capital decreases by	£10 000

An alternative method of accounting for goodwill is to enter only the consideration payable by the new to the existing partners in the ledger. The amount of goodwill payable is calculated first. Next the amount receivable by each existing partner is determined by looking at the profit-sharing ratio. The capital accounts under this method would look as follows:

Capital accounts

	A	B	C		A	B	C
	£	£	£		£	£	£
				Balances b/f	20 000	20 000	
Goodwill paid			10 000	Goodwill received	5 000	5 000	
Balances c/f	25 000	25 000	10 000	Cash			20 000
	25 000	25 000	20 000		25 000	25 000	20 000
				Balances b/f	25 000	25 000	10 000

Both methods produce the same final balance on each account. The first method is a little simpler and quicker to apply and is the one I have adopted in my answers to questions.

Revaluation of Assets

Historic cost accounting requires assets to be stated at cost less accumulated depreciation. In practice the underlying market value of an asset often does not correspond to its book value. Freehold land for example is usually worth more than original cost because of appreciation. An outgoing partner is usually paid his share of the business on the date of leaving. The assets (and liabilities) should therefore be revalued to their true values on that date so that he may be paid a fair sum. This is done in a *Revaluation Account*. Assets which are worth more than book value are brought up to current value by debiting the asset account and crediting revaluation with the amount of the increase. For assets worth *less* than book value the opposite entry takes place. A surplus on revaluation is credited to the *original* partners in the *original* profit-sharing ratio. In this way the outgoing partner is credited with his share of any increase in asset values. Conversely a deficit is debited to capital so that he pays for a share of the reduction in asset values. The format of the account is as follows:

Pro-forma

Revaluation account

	£		£
Assets decreased in value		*Assets increased in value*	
Furniture and fittings	x	Freehold land	x
Motor vehicles	x		
Stock	x		
Increase in provisions	x		
Surplus to capital accounts:			
A $\frac{1}{2}$	x		
B $\frac{1}{2}$	x		
	£x		£x

If the remaining partners do not wish to adopt the revalued amounts for the accounts they can continue using historic costs by writing back the revaluation surplus thus:

Dr Capital accounts of remaining partners in *new* profit-sharing ratio
Cr (*Dr*) Asset accounts with the amounts of the increase (decrease)

Conceptually this is similar to the goodwill entries above. In fact, in cases where both the revalued assets and goodwill are to be written out of the books or both retained in the books the adjustment for goodwill can be performed *within the revaluation account*. It is not necessary to open a separate account for goodwill since its treatment is exactly the same as the other assets.

It is sometimes the case that the outgoing partner takes with him a business asset e.g. a motor car. The double-entry for this is

Dr Capital account
Cr Asset account

with the revalued amount. The increase or decrease from book value of the asset taken over should be included in the revaluation account.

Outgoing partners do not usually demand full payment of the amount owing to them on the date of leaving. The balance owing is transferred from capital to a *Loan account*. In the balance sheet of the remaining partners this is shown as a liability.

Questions

8.1 Dawn, Edith, and Mandy are in partnership as Recreational Suppliers, sharing residual profits and losses in the ratio of 5:2:3 respectively. At 1 November 19_2 their capital and current account balances were:

	Capital Account	*Current Account*
	£	£
Dawn	8 000	580 (credit)
Edith	10 000	350 (debit)
Mandy	12 000	210 (credit)

By agreement, partners are entitled to interest on capital at the rate of 5% per annum.

On 1 May 19_3, by mutual agreement, Dawn increased her capital by paying a further £2 000 into the partnership bank account, whilst Edith reduced her capital to £6 000 but left her withdrawn capital in the partnership as a loan bearing interest at 5% per annum.

Partners are allowed to withdraw from current accounts at any time during the financial year but are charged interest on the amounts involved. Details of drawings made and interest chargeable in respect of each partner for the financial year ended 31 October 19_3 are:

	Drawings	*Interest on Drawings*
	£	£
Dawn	2 400	90
Edith	1 800	30
Mandy	3 000	25

Edith is remunerated, for her participation in the running of the partnership, by an annual salary of £2 500.

The trading profit (before interest) of Recreational Suppliers for the year ended 31 October 19_3 was £19 905.

Required:
For the year ended 31 October 19_3
(a) Prepare the profit and loss appropriation account for the partnership. (8 marks)
(b) Post to and balance the capital and current accounts of the individual partners. (9 marks)
(17 marks)

Chartered Association of Certified Accountants

8.2 On 1 January Year 4, Door and Porto were in partnership sharing profits in the proportions: Door 2/3, Porto 1/3. The credit balances on their capital accounts on that date were Door £40 000 and Porto £25 000.

On 1 April Year 4, Window was admitted as a partner and paid in £9 000. The profit sharing proportions then became: Door 2/5, Porto 2/5, Window 1/5.

On 1 September Year 4, Ventura was admitted as a partner and paid in £6 000. The profit sharing proportions then became: Door 3/10, Porto 3/10, Window 2/10, Ventura 2/10.

Goodwill was valued throughout Year 4 at £30 000, it remained unrecorded and adjustments with respect thereto were to be made through the partners' capital accounts.

Simple interest at 1% per month is allowed on the balances on partners' capital accounts after making adjustments for goodwill but before either debiting drawings or crediting profit shares.

The net profit for the year ended 31 December Year 4 was £110 000 (before charging interest on partners' capitals). Because of the seasonal nature of the business, it was agreed that the net profit per month in August and September was three times the net profit per month in January, February, March and April, and that the net profit per month in May, June, July, October, November, and December was twice the net profit per month in January, February, March and April.

Required:
(a) Calculate the balances on partners' Capital Accounts after the admission of Ventura but before crediting either interest or profit shares. (7 marks)
(b) Show the division of the net profit for Year 4 between the periods (i) January to March; (ii) April to August; (iii) September to December. (7 marks)
(c) Show the allocation of your profit figures from (b) above between the partners. (8 marks)
(22 marks)

London Chamber of Commerce and Industry, Higher

8.3 Parks, Langridge, and Sheppard were in partnership sharing profits and losses: Parks one-half, Langridge one-third and Sheppard one-sixth.

The firms' summarized Balance Sheet as on 31 March 19_5 was as follows:

	£	£		£	£
Capital:					
Parks	24 000		Freehold Land and Buildings		16 000
Langridge	12 000		Plant and Machinery		6 000
Sheppard	8 000	44 000	Motor car		2 400
Loan—Parks		4 000	Stock		11 200
Creditors		8 000	Debtors	12 000	
			Less Provision for Doubtful debts	1 200	10 800
			Balance at Bank		9 600
		£56 000			£56 000

Parks retired on 31 March 19_5 to commence business on his own account and Langridge and Sheppard continued in partnership, sharing profits in the ratio: Langridge two-thirds, Sheppard one-third.

It was agreed that Parks should take over certain plant and machinery valued at £1 500 and one of the firm's cars at its book value of £1 000.

It was further agreed that the following adjustments should be made in the Balance Sheet as on 31 March 19_5:

(1) Freehold land and buildings should be revalued at £20 000 and plant and machinery, inclusive of that taken over by Parks, at £5 000.
(2) The provision for doubtful debts should be increased by £300.
(3) A provision of £500 included in creditors for a possible claim for damages was no longer required.
(4) The stock should be reduced by £800 for obsolete and damaged items.

In accordance with the terms of the partnership agreement, the total value of goodwill on 31 March 19_5 was agreed at £30 000. Since Parks intended to retain certain of the customers it was agreed that the value of the proportion of the goodwill to be purchased by him was £6 000. Langridge and Sheppard decided that goodwill should not appear in the books of the new partnership as an asset, the necessary adjustments being made through the partners' Capital Accounts. Pending the introduction of further cash capital by the continuing partners, the amount owing to Parks was agreed to be left on loan account.

Required:

(a) the Revaluation Account;
(b) the partners' Capital Accounts in columnar form of the old and new firm, recording these transactions;
(c) the opening Balance Sheet of the new firm. (21 marks)
(d) What is the reasoning behind the adjustments made for goodwill? (4 marks)

(25 marks)

Institute of Chartered Accountants, Foundation

8.4* A, B, and C are in partnership, sharing profits and losses in the ratio 7:3:2 respectively. The summarized balance sheet of the partnership as at 30 November 19_3 was as follows:

	£		£
Capital accounts:		*Fixed assets:*	
A	26 000	Plant and vehicle	30 000
B	20 000	*Current assets:*	
C	15 000	Stock	20 000

Current liabilities:	£		£
		Debtors	12 000
Creditors	8 000	Bank	7 000
	69 000		69 000

On 1 December 19_3 C retired from the partnership. The following matters were agreed:

(1) The car owned by the partnership would be transferred to C at its book value of £2 000.
(2) The remaining fixed assets, which remain in the partnership, would be valued at £32 000.
(3) Stock would be valued at £21 000, Debtors at £11 500, and Goodwill was agreed at £5 000.
(4) £1 000 cash would be paid immediately to C, the balance due to him to remain as a loan to the partnership.

C's retirement was followed immediately by the admission of D to the partnership.

As her capital, D transferred to the partnership her existing business assets and liabilities as follows:

	£
Fixtures and fittings	12 000
Stocks	5 000
Debtors	3 000
Creditors	1 000

D's business was valued at £21 000 for the purpose of its transfer to the partnership. A, B, and D are to share profits and losses in the ratio 5:4:2 respectively.

A goodwill account is to be maintained to record all relevant transfers of goodwill between A, B, and C, and A, B, and D respectively.

Required:

(a) Prepare the capital accounts of A, B, C, and D recording the transactions of 1 December 19_3, and bringing down the balances on that date. (12 marks)
(b) Prepare the partnership balance sheet as at 1 December 19_3 immediately after all the above transactions have taken place. (7 marks)
(c) Explain the meaning of 'goodwill'. (6 marks)

(25 marks)

Advanced level Accounting, London

8.5* Proudie, Slope and Thorne were in partnership sharing profits and losses in the ratio 3:1:1. The draft balance sheet of the partnership as at 31 May 19_6 is shown below:

	£000 *Cost*	*£000* *Depreciation*	*£000* *Net Book Value*
Fixed assets			
Land and buildings	200	40	160
Furniture	30	18	12
Motor vehicles	60	40	20
	290	98	192
Current assets			
Stocks		23	
Trade debtors	42		
Less: Provision for doubtful debts	1	41	
Prepayments		2	
Cash		10	
		76	

	£000 Cost	£000 Depreciation	£000 Net Book Value
Less: Current liabilities			
Trade creditors	15		
Accruals	3	18	58
			£250
Financed by:			
Capital accounts			
Proudie		100	
Slope		60	
Thorne		40	200
Current accounts			
Proudie		24	
Slope		10	
Thorne		8	42
			242
Loan			
Proudie			8
			£250

Additional Information:

(1) Proudie decided to retire on 31 May 19_6. However, Slope and Thorne agreed to form a new partnership out of the old one, as from 1 June 19_6. They agreed to share profits and losses in the same ratio as in the old partnership.

(2) Upon the dissolution of the old partnership, it was agreed that the following adjustments were to be made to the partnership balance sheet as at 31 May 19_6:
   (i) Land and buildings were to be revalued at £200 000;
   (ii) Furniture was to be revalued at £5 000;
   (iii) Proudie agreed to take over one of the motor vehicles at a value of £4 000, the remaining motor vehicles being revalued at £10 000;
   (iv) Stocks were to be written down by £5 000.
   (v) A bad debt of £2 000 was to be written off, and the provision for doubtful debts was then to be adjusted so that it represented 5% of the then outstanding trade debtors as at 31 May 19_6;
   (vi) A further accrual of £3 000 for office expenses was to be made;
   (vii) Professional charges relating to the dissolution were estimated to be £1 000.

(3) It has not been the practice of the partners to carry goodwill in the books of the partnership, but on the retirement of a partner it had been agreed that goodwill should be taken into account. Goodwill was to be valued at an amount equal to the average annual profits of the three years expiring on the retirement. For the purpose of including goodwill in the dissolution arrangement when Proudie retired, the net profits for the last three years were as follows:

	£000
Year to 31 May 19_4	130
Year to 31 May 19_5	150
Year to 31 May 19_6	181

The net profit for the year to 31 May 19_6 had been calculated before any of the items listed in (2) above were taken into account. The net profit was only to be adjusted for items listed in (2iv), (2v) and (2vi) above.

(4) Goodwill is not to be carried in the books of the new partnership.

(5) It was agreed that Proudie's old loan of £8 000 should be repaid to him on 31 May 19_6, but any further amount owing to him as a result of the dissolution of the partnership should be left as a long-term loan in the books of the new partnership.

(6) The partners' current accounts were to be closed and any balances on them as at 31 May 19_6 were to be transferred to their respective capital accounts.

Required:

(a) Prepare the revaluation account as at 31 May 19_6. (12 marks)

(b) Prepare the partners' capital accounts as at the date of disolution of the partnership, and bring down any balances on them in the books of the new partnership. (9 marks)

(c) Prepare Slope and Thorne's balance sheet as at 1 June 19_6. (4 marks)

(25 marks)

Association of Accounting Technicians, Final

8.6* A and B are in partnership sharing profits and losses in the ratio 3:2. Their last balance sheet as at 31 December 19_4 was as follows:

	£	£		£	£
Capital accounts			*Fixed assets*		
A	16 000		Machinery	10 000	
B	12 000	28 000	Vehicles	8 000	18 000
Current accounts			*Current assets*		
A	3 000		Stock	30 000	
B	2 000	5 000	Debtors	22 000	52 000
Current liabilities					
Bank overdraft	23 000				
Creditors	14 000	37 000			
		70 000			70 000

The partnership has been profitable over many years and although profitability has been maintained, recently the firm has suffered from cash flow problems. In addition to the cash flow problems, the partnership needs to reinvest in fixed assets at a cost of £42 000. Profits have been £40 000 per annum over the last three years and it is anticipated that the same level of profit will continue during the present year. Profit accrues evenly throughout the year.

A and B are considering two alternative methods of raising the necessary funds from 1 July 19_5.

(1) To purchase the fixed assets on hire purchase over a period of three years. The hire purchase agreement provides for 36 equal instalments of £1 500. (It can be assumed that interest is applied evenly over the three years.) In addition a long-term loan of £30 000 is available from a finance company at 15% interest with only the interest being repayable over the first two years.

(2) To accept into the partnership a new partner C on the following terms from 1 July 19_5.

That C will bring into the partnership £60 000 cash as capital.

That the partners will be entitled to interest at a rate of 15% per year on fixed capital.

That A and B will be entitled to a salary of £3 200 per annum and £2 000 per annum respectively.

That the balance of profits and losses will be shared equally between the partners.

Required:

(a) A forecast profit and loss appropriation account for the year ending 31 December 19_5 assuming that alternative (1) is accepted showing clearly the adjusted net profit figure prior to appropriation. (8 marks)

(b) A forecast profit and loss appropriation account for the year ending 31 December 19_5 assuming that alternative (2) is accepted. (12 marks)

(20 marks)

Advanced level Accounting, AEB

8.7 Thorn and Snail are in partnership manufacturing and distributing two products, Product A and Product B. The following information is available for Year 4:

		Product A	*Product B*
Cost per unit:	Raw Materials	£7	£6
	Direct labour	£18	£20
	Variable Overhead	£2	£4
Selling prices:	Sales to Public	£42	£45
	Sales to Agents	£38	£40
Units manufactured		5 000	11 000
Units sold:	Sales to Public	2 300	6 500
	Sales to Agents	2 500	4 500
Units in stocks on 1 January		482	902
Costs per unit of stocks on 1 January		£25	£30
Stock shortage on 31 December		—	3
Advertising costs		£6 964	£8 410

Fixed Overheads £60 000. Partners' drawings: Thorn £39 217; Snail £30 783. Partners' capitals on 1 January: Thorn £140 000; Snail £120 000. Additional capital introduced by Snail on 1 July: £20 000. Sundry net assets other than stocks on 31 December: £294 616.

There were no raw materials or partly manufactured goods in stock either at the beginning or at the end of Year 4. Finished units are valued on a first in first out basis at their raw material, direct labour and variable overhead costs.

The partnership agreement provides for:-

(1) Interest on partners' capital at 7% per year.
(2) Thorn to receive as commission 5% of the net profit on Product A (before charging fixed overheads) and Snail to receive as commission 4% of the net profit on Product B (before charging fixed overheads).
(3) The balance of profits (or losses) to be divided between Thorn and Snail in the ratio of 11:9.

Required:

(a) Prepare a Trading, Profit and Loss, and Appropriation Account of the partnership for the year ended 31 December Year 4. (20 marks)

(b) Prepare the Balance Sheet of the partnership at 31 December Year 4. (4 marks)

(24 marks)

London Chamber of Commerce and Industry, Higher

(Attempt this question only when you know Manufacturing accounts and basic costing.)

Solutions

8.1 (a)

Appropriation Account

31 Oct. 19_3	£	31 Oct. 19_3	£
Salary — Edith	2 500	Net profit b/f (W_1)	19 805
Interest on capital		Interest on drawings	
Dawn (W_2)	450	Dawn	90
Edith (W_3)	400	Edith	30
Mandy	600	Mandy	25
Share of profit			
Dawn 5	8 000		
Edith 2	3 200		
Mandy 3	4 800		
	19 950		19 950

Workings

W_1 Loan interest 1 May–31 Oct. = £4 000 × 5% × $\frac{6}{12}$ = 100

The loan interest is a *charge against profit*, and not an appropriation of it. The trading profit b/f is therefore reduced from £19 905 to £19 805.

W_2 Interest on capital — Dawn

Initial capital	£8 000 × 5%	400
Additional capital	£2 000 × 5% × $\frac{6}{12}$	50
		450

W_3 Interest on capital — Edith

1 Nov. 19_2 to 31 Apr. 19_3	£10 000 × 5% × $\frac{6}{12}$	250
1 May 19_3 to 31 Oct. 19_3	£ 6 000 × 5% × $\frac{6}{12}$	150
		400

(b)

Private Ledger

Capital accounts

		Dawn £	Edith £	Mandy £			Dawn £	Edith £	Mandy £
1 May 19_3	Loan		4 000		1 Nov. 19_2	Bals b/f	8 000	10 000	12 000
31 Oct. 19_3	Bals c/f	10 000	6 000	12 000	1 May 19_3	Bank	2 000		
		10 000	10 000	12 000			10 000	10 000	12 000
					1 Nov 19_3	Bals b/f	10 000	6 000	12 000

Current accounts

	Dawn £	Edith £	Mandy £		Dawn £	Edith £	Mandy £
1 Nov. 19_2 Bal b/f		350		1 Nov. 19_2 Bals b/f	580		210
31 Oct. 19_3:				31 Oct. 19_3:			
Drawings	2 400	1 800	3 000	Salary		2 500	
Interest on drawings	90	30	25	Interest on capital	450	400	600
Balances c/f	6 540	3 920	2 585	Profit	8 000	3 200	4 800
	9 030	6 100	5 610		9 030	6 100	5 610
				1 Nov. 19_3 Bals b/f	6 540	3 920	2 585

8.2 (a)

Capital accounts

		Door £000	*Porto* £000	*Window* £000	*Ventura* £000			*Door* £000	*Porto* £000	*Window* £000	*Ventura* £000
Year 4						Year 4					
						1 Jan.	Bals b/f	40	25		
1 Apr.	Goodwill out	12	12	6		1 Apr.	Bank			9	
1 Apr.	Bals c/f	48	23	3		1 Apr.	Goodwill in	20	10		
		60	35	9				60	35	9	
						1 Apr.	Bals b/f	48	23	3	
1 Sept.	Goodwill out	9	9	6	6	1 Sept.	Bank				6
1 Sept.	Bals c/f	51	26	3		1 Sept.	Goodwill in	12	12	6	
		60	35	9	6			60	35	9	6
						1 Sept.	Bals b/f	51	26	3	

(b) This part is more a test of Arithmetic than Accounting.

Month	*Relative share of profit*	*Profit* £000		*Periodic profit* £000
January	1	5		
February	1	5		
March	1	5	(i)	15
April	1	5		
May	2	10		
June	2	10		
July	2	10		
August	3	15	(ii)	50
September	3	15		
October	2	10		
November	2	10		
December	2	10	(iii)	45
	22	110		110

(c) It is best to show the allocation of profit by means of an appropriation account.

Appropriation account

Year 4	£	*Year 4*	£
Interest on capital		Net profit	
Door £40 000 × 1% × 3	1 200	January to March	15 000
Porto £25 000 × 1% × 3	750		
Share of profit			
Door $\frac{2}{3}$	8 700		
Porto $\frac{1}{3}$	4 350		
	15 000		15 000
Interest on capital		Net profit	
Door £48 000 × 1% × 5	2 400	April to August	50 000
Porto £23 000 × 1% × 5	1 150		
Window £ 3 000 × 1% × 5	150		
Share of profit			
Door $\frac{2}{5}$	18 520		
Porto $\frac{2}{5}$	18 520		
Window $\frac{1}{5}$	9 260		
	50 000		50 000

		£		£
Interest on capital			Net profit	
Door	£51 000 × 1% × 4	2 040	September to December	45 000
Porto	£26 000 × 1% × 4	1 040		
Window	£ 3 000 × 1% × 4	120		
Share of profit				
Door	$\frac{3}{10}$	12 540		
Porto	$\frac{3}{10}$	12 540		
Window	$\frac{2}{10}$	8 360		
Ventura	$\frac{2}{10}$	8 360		
		45 000		45 000

8.3 (a)

Revaluation account

31 March 19_5		£	31 March 19_5	£
Plant and machinery		1 000	Land and buildings	4 000
Increase in provision for doubtful debts		300	Decrease in provision for creditors	500
Stock		800		
Revaluation surplus to:				
Parks	$\frac{1}{2}$	1 200		
Langridge	$\frac{1}{3}$	800		
Sheppard	$\frac{1}{6}$	400		
		4 500		4 500

(b)

Capital accounts

	Parks £	*Langridge* £	*Sheppard* £		*Parks* £	*Langridge* £	*Sheppard* £
31 March 19_5				31 March 19_5			
Plant and machinery	1 500			Balances b/f	24 000	12 000	8 000
Motor car	1 000			Revaluation surplus	1 200	800	400
Goodwill out *	6 000	16 000	8 000	Goodwill in	15 000	10 000	5 000
Loan	31 700						
Balances c/f		6 800	5 400				
	40 200	22 800	13 400		40 200	22 800	13 400
				1 April 19_5			
				Balances b/f		6 800	5 400

*		
Goodwill to be written out		30 000
Charged to Parks		6 000
Balance to be written out		24 000
Charged to:		
Langridge	$\frac{2}{3}$	16 000
Sheppard	$\frac{1}{3}$	8 000

(c)

LANGRIDGE AND SHEPPARD

Balance sheet as at 31 March 19_5

	£	£	£
Fixed assets			
Freehold land and buildings			20 000
Plant and machinery (5 000 − 1 500)			3 500
Motor cars (2 400 − 1 000)			1 400
			24 900
Current assets			
Stock		10 400	
Debtors	12 000		
Less provision for doubtful debts	1 500	10 500	
Bank		9 600	
		30 500	

	£	£	£
Less Current liabilities			
Creditors		7 500	
Working capital			23 000
Net assets			£47 900
Financed by:			
Capital — Langridge			6 800
Sheppard			5 400
			12 200
Loan from Parks (4 000 + 31 700)			35 700
Capital employed			£47 900

(d) See text.

8.7 (a)

THORN AND SNAIL

Trading, Profit and Loss and Appropriation account for the year ended 31 December Year 4

	Product A		*Product B*	
	£	£	£	£
Sales — to public		96 600		292 500
— to agents		95 000		180 000
		191 600		472 500
Less cost of goods sold				
Opening stock	12 050		27 060	
Manufacturing cost (W_1)	135 000		330 000	
	147 050		357 060	
Less closing stock (W_2)	18 414	128 636	26 970	330 090
Gross profit		62 964		142 410
Advertising costs		6 964		8 410
Contribution c/f		56 000		134 000

		Total
	£	£
Contribution b/f (56 000 + 134 000)		190 000
Fixed overhead		60 000
Net profit		130 000
Less interest on capital		
Thorn	9 800	
Snail (W_3)	9 100	18 900
		111 100
Less commission		
Thorn	2 800	
Snail	5 360	8 160
		102 940
Share of profit		
Thorn 11	56 617	
Snail 9	46 323	102 940

Workings

W_1 *Computation of manufacturing cost*

	Product A		Product B	
	Unit	Total	Unit	Total
	£	£	£	£
Raw materials	7	35 000	6	66 000
Direct labour	18	90 000	20	220 000
Prime cost	25	125 000	26	286 000
Variable overhead	2	10 000	4	44 000
Manufacturing cost	27	135 000	30	330 000

W_2 *Computation of closing stock*

	A	B
Opening stock units	482	902
Units manufactured	5 000	11 000
Available for sale	5 482	11 902
Less sold	4 800	11 000
	682	902
Less stock loss	—	3
Closing stock, units	682	899
	@£27	@£30
Valuation	£18 414	£26 970

W_3 *Interest on capital, Snail*

		£
Existing capital	£120 000 × 7%	8 400
Additional capital	£ 20 000 × 7% × $\frac{6}{12}$	700
		9 100

(b) *Working for balance sheet*

Current accounts

	Thorn	Snail		Thorn	Snail
31 Dec. Year 4	£	£	31 Dec. Year 4	£	£
Drawings	39 217	30 783	Interest on capital	9 800	9 100
			Commission	2 800	5 360
Balances c/f	30 000	30 000	Share of profit	56 617	46 323
	69 217	60 783		69 217	60 783
			1 Jan. Year 5		
			Balances b/f	30 000	30 000

THORN AND SNAIL

Balance Sheet as at 31 December Year 4

	£	£
Sundry net assets		294 616
Stocks (18 414 + 26 970)		45 384
Net assets		£340 000
Financed by:		
Capital accounts		
Thorn	140 000	
Snail	140 000	280 000
Current accounts		
Thorn	30 000	
Snail	30 000	60 000
		£340 000

CHAPTER 9

Departmental Accounts

Businesses which are divided into divisions dealing with different goods find it useful to know not only the result of the business as a whole but also the performance of each division. This applies equally whether the business is a manufacturer, wholesaler, or retailer. In this way management is able to identify the most profitable sections of the business and those sections that are not so profitable or loss-making.

To generate this additional information the bookkeeping for purchases and sales has to be modified. What is needed is for each purchase and sale to be analysed into the relevant division. From this it is possible to prepare an analysed trading account showing the gross profit on each division.

Example

A clothes retailer has three departments — menswear, ladieswear and footwear. It might arrange its purchase and sales day books as follows:

Date	*Supplier/ Customer*	*Invoice number*	*Total* £	*Menswear* £	*Ladieswear* £	*Footwear* £

Certain problems arise in the profit and loss account because while the split between departments of items in the trading account is obvious, the *apportionment* of expenses between departments is not so obvious. For example, it is almost impossible to identify the exact proportion of the administration expense, light and heat, and managerial salaries attributable to each department. Usually occupancy costs such as rent and rates and light and heat are apportioned by relative floor space while administration expenses are related to sales, but such bases are arbitrary. In some cases there is more than one acceptable basis. Examination questions usually state the basis to be followed. We will meet the problem of expense apportionment again in Chapter 16, Overhead absorption costing.

If an expense requires adjustment due to an accrual or prepayment, perform the adjustment *before* apportioning it to the various departments.

Contribution

An alternative approach is to make no attempt to try and apportion general business overheads to individual departments. Instead, only costs *directly* related to each department are charged against its revenue. This reveals the *contribution* provided by each department towards the general overheads. Total contribution less overheads gives net profit of the business as a whole. This approach is more useful for *managerial decision-making*. When deciding whether or not to shut down a department for example it is better to see whether it is contributing to the business' general overheads than if it is showing an accounting profit after it has been charged with overheads which are not directly attributable to it and *which would continue to be incurred even if the department was closed.* The significance of contribution is considered more fully in Chapter 19, Absorption and Marginal costing and Chapter 20, Decision-making and Relevant costs.

Questions

9.1* Andrew and Susannah are the joint owners of a store which is divided into three departments:
Clothing (C), Electrical goods (E), and Furniture (F). The following balances have been extracted from the books as at 30 Nov. 19_3:

		Dr	Cr
		£	£
Purchases	(C)	49 580	
	(E)	44 630	
	(F)	42 500	
Wages	(C)	16 200	
	(E)	12 050	
	(F)	10 000	
General office salaries		12 000	
Rent and rates		3 800	
Buildings insurance		700	
Repairs to premises		170	
Lighting and heating		1 070	
Sales	(C)		81 750
	(E)		79 300
	(F)		62 100
Telephone		740	
Sundry expenses		4 500	
Opening stocks	(C)	7 500	
	(E)	6 250	
	(F)	4 800	

Notes

(1) Closing stocks are: (C) 19 700, (E) 10 800, (F) 12 400.

(2) There is an accrued expense of £200 in respect of light and heat at 30 November 19_3.

(3) General office salaries and sundry expenses are to be divided equally between the departments. Other expenses are to be divided according to floor areas, as follows:
(C) six-tenths; (E) three-tenths; (F) one-tenth

(4) Andrew and Susannah share profits in the proportion 3:2 respectively. The partnership agreement provides for interest on their capitals at 5% per annum. The capital accounts are as follows:

	Andrew	Susannah
	£	£
Opening balances 1 December 19_2	12 000	10 000
Capital introduced 1 June 19_3	4 000	—
	16 000	10 000

Required:

(a) Prepare the departmental trading and profit and loss accounts (in columnar form) for the year to 30 November 19_3. (12 marks)

(b) Prepare the partnership appropriation account for the year to 30 November 19_3. (5 marks)

(c) The owners of the store are considering whether or not to open a cafe in the store. Preliminary budgets indicate that a loss of £10 000 may occur in the first year of operation.
What other factors may influence the owners when deciding whether or not to open the cafe? (8 marks)

(25 marks)

Advanced Level Accounting, London

9.2 The managing director of PZT Limited, a company owning three cinemas, has complained that the form of presentation of the company's profit and loss account for the year ended 31st December, 19_3, given below, does not tell him where the loss has been incurred and is of little use for management purposes.

You are required to redesign the profit and loss account so that his objections will be overcome.

	£	£
Sale of tickets		539 800
Sale of ice creams etc		37 000
		576 800
Less: Hire of films	107 960	
Salaries: Managers	36 000	
Projectionists	30 000	
Ticket salesgirls	12 000	
Usherettes	36 000	
Ice cream salesgirls	12 000	
General cinema costs	180 000	
Cost of ice-cream	18 500	
Head office costs	160 000	592 460
Trading loss		£(15 660)

You are given the following information:

(1) The three cinemas are the Astoria, Plaza, and Regal. Each is a large old cinema which has now been sub-divided into three smaller units, called studios, showing different films.

(2) Each cinema employs:
A manager.
A projectionist who is responsible for the showing of the films in all three studios.
A ticket salesgirl, who sells tickets for all three studios.
An usherette for each of the studios.
An ice-cream etc., salesgirl covering all studios. It is not possible to record the sales made in any one studio.

(3) Films are hired at a cost of 20% of the takings for that film.

(4) Sales of tickets for the year were as follows:

Cinema	*Studio*	£
Astoria	1	50 000
	2	4 800
	3	25 000
Plaza	1	60 000
	2	40 000
	3	30 000
Regal	1	150 000
	2	100 000
	3	80 000

(5) Individual annual salaries are as follows:

	£
Cinema manager	12 000
Projectionist	10 000
Ticket salesgirls	4 000
Usherette	4 000
Ice cream salesgirl	4 000

(6) Sales of ice cream etc, were as follows:

	£
Astoria	7 000
Plaza	10 000
Regal	20 000

These items are sold in all cinemas at a mark-up of 100% on cost.

(7) General cinema costs were as follows:

	£
Astoria	30 000
Plaza	50 000
Regal	100 000

(20 marks)

Chartered Institute of Management Accountants

9.3 Here is the trial balance at 31st December, 19_5, after the manufacturing account has been completed, of a company manufacturing and selling two products, X and Y:

	Dr *£000*	*Cr* *£000*
Ordinary shares of 25 pence each, fully paid		3 000
Retained profit at 31st December, 19_4		1 900
Fixed assets at cost	4 000	
Depreciation provision at 31st December, 19_5		1 000
Depreciation charge for year: Administration	40	
Distribution	40	
Materials stock at 31st December, 19_5	700	
Work-in-progress at 31st December, 19_5:		
Product X	100	
Product Y	50	
Finished goods stock at 31st December, 19_4:		
Product X	200	
Product Y	940	
Debtors	900	
Bad debts provision		40
Manufacturing overhead prepaid at 31st December, 19_5	10	
Cash at bank and in hand	695	
Creditors		250
Manufacturing overhead accrued at 31st December, 19_5		50
Sales: Product X		6 000
Product Y		4 000
Cost of finished goods manufactured during 19_5:		
Department A	5 200	
Department B	960	
Administration expenses	1 010	
Distribution costs	1 395	
	16 240	16 240

You are given the following information:

(1) Both products pass through two manufacturing departments, A and B. The costs of these departments are to be allocated to the products in the following ratios:

	Departments A	B
Product X	8	5
Product Y	5	1

(2) The values of stocks of finished goods at 31st Decmber, 19_5 were £600 000 for product X and £500 000 for product Y.

(3) Prepaid and accrued expenses at 31st December, 19_5 were:

	Prepaid	*Accrued*
	£000	£000
Administration expenses	60	210
Distribution costs	30	90

(4) The bad debts provision is to be made equal to 5% of the debtors, and the increase or decrease is to be treated as a distribution cost.

(5) Quantities manufactured and sold of each product during 19_5 were:

	Products	
	X	Y
	units	units
Manufactured	10 000	5 000
Sold	9 000	6 000

(6) Administration expenses, including the proportion of depreciation, are to be divided between the products in the ratio of quantities manufactured.

(7) Distribution costs including the proportion of depreciation and the change in the bad debts provision, are to be divided between the products in the ratio of quantities sold.

Required:
Prepare, in vertical and columnar form for internal use, a trading and profit and loss account for the year ended 31st December, 19_5, showing the amount of pre-tax profit made by each product; **(20 marks)**

Chartered Institute of Management Accountants, part-question

9.4 Ray Dyo, Harry Ull, and Val Vez are in partnership, trading under the name of Radtel Services, as radio and television suppliers and repairers, sharing profits and losses in the ratio one half, one third, and one sixth, respectively. Val Vez works full-time in the business with responsibility for general administration for which she receives a partnership salary of £4 000 per annum.

All partners receive interest on capital at 5% per annum and interest on any loans made to the firm, also at 5% per annum.

It has also been agreed that Val Vez should receive not less than £4 000 per annum in addition to her salary. Any deficiency between this guaranteed figure and her actual aggregate of interest on capital, plus residual profit (or less residual loss) less interest on drawings, is to be borne by Dyo and Ull in the ratio in which they share profits and losses; such deficiency can be recouped by Dyo and Ull at the earliest opportunity during the next two consecutive years provided that Val Vez does not receive less than the guaranteed minimum described above. During the year ended 30 September 19_3, Dyo and Ull had jointly contributed a deficiency of £1 500.

Radtel Services rents two sets of premises — one, a workshop where repairs are carried out, the other, a shop from which radio and television sets are sold. The offices are situated above the shop and are accounted for as part of the shop.

The workshop and shop are regarded as separate departments and managed, respectively, by Phuges and Sokkitt who are each remunerated by a basic salary plus a commission of one ninth of their departments' profits *after* charging their commission.

The trial balance of the firm on 30 September 19_4 is given on the following page.

	£	£
Stocks at 1 October 19_3:		
shop (radio and television sets)	19 750	
workshop (spares, components etc.)	8 470	
Purchases:		
radio and television sets	155 430	
spares, components etc.	72 100	
Turnover:		
sales of radio and television sets		232 600
repair charges		127 000
Wages and salaries (employees):		
shop and offices	54 640	
workshop	18 210	
Prepaid expenses (at 30 September 19_4)	640	
Accrued expenses (at 30 September 19_4)		3 160
Provision for doubtful debts at 1 October 19_3		920
Rent and rates:		
shop and offices	7 710	
workshop	8 450	
Stationery, telephones, insurance:		
shop and offices	2 980	
workshop	1 020	
Heating and lighting:		
shop and offices	4 640	
workshop	3 950	
Debtors	4 460	
Creditors		15 260
Bank	48 540	
Cash	960	
Other general expenses:		
shop and offices	3 030	
workshop	2 830	
Depreciation:		
shop and offices (including vehicles)	2 400	
workshop	2 580	
Shop fittings (cost)	17 060	
Workshop tools and equipment (cost)	55 340	
Vehicles (cost)	27 210	
Discount received:		
shop		420
workshop		390
Bank loan (repayable in 19_8)		15 000
Loan from Harry Ull		10 000
Capital Accounts:		
R. Dyo		40 000
H. Ull		40 000
V. Vez		20 000
Current Accounts (after drawings have been debited):		
R. Dyo	290	
H. Ull		1 040
V. Vez		920
Loan interest:		
bank loan	2 400	
loan from H. Ull	500	
Provision for depreciation:		
shop fittings		3 190
workshops tools and equipment		10 020
vehicles		5 670
	£525 590	£525 590

The following matters are to be taken into account:
(1) Managers' commissions.
(2) Partnership salary (Vez).
(3) Interest on partners' capital accounts (these have not altered during the year).
(4) Interest on partners' drawings; Dyo £70; Ull £30; Vez £20.
(5) Closing stocks: shop £31 080, workshop £10 220.
(6) Provision for doubtful debts at 30 September 19_4, £540.
(7) Residual profits/losses.
N.B. Loan interest and the movement in the provision for bad debts are regarded as 'shop' items.

Required:
(a) Prepare columnar departmental trading and profit and loss accounts and a partnership appropriation account for the year ended 30 September 19_4 and the partnership balance sheet at that date. (21 marks)
(b) Complete the posting of the partners' current accounts for the year. (4 marks)
(25 marks)

Chartered Association of Certified Accountants

9.5 Diversify Ltd. carry on two substantially different forms of business activity. The accounts sections has been asked to submit a breakdown of sales and profit between the two different classes of business for inclusion in the final published accounts. The information has been drawn up as follows:

	Activity A	*Activity B*	*Total*
	£	£	£
Sales	750 000	560 000	1 310 000
Net Profit	85 000	74 000	159 000

Required:
(a) An explanation of the advantages which can accrue to the business from such a breakdown. (6 marks)
(b) An explanation of the problems which may be encountered by a business which seeks to obtain separate figures for the profit or loss accruing from each of its different activities. (10 marks)
(16 marks)

Advanced Level Accounting, AEB

Solutions

9.2 It is necessary to break down the results so as to show the contribution from each studio to cinema costs and the contribution from each cinema to Head Office costs.

PZT LIMITED

Profit and Loss Account for the year ended 31st December 19_3

Cinema		*Astoria*		
Studio	1	2	3	Total
	£	£	£	£
Sale of tickets	50 000	4 800	25 000	79 800
Less Studio costs				
Hire of films	10 000	960	5 000	15 960
Usherette salaries	4 000	4 000	4 000	12 000
	14 000	4 960	9 000	27 960

Contribution to cinema costs	36 000	(160)	16 000	51 840
*Contribution from ice-cream sales**				(500)
				51 340
Less Cinema costs				
Salaries: Managers				12 000
Projectionists				10 000
Ticket salesgirls				4 000
General cinema costs				30 000
				56 000
Contribution to Head office costs				(4 660)

Cinema		*Plaza*		
Studio	1	2	3	Total
	£	£	£	£
Sale of tickets	60 000	40 000	30 000	130 000
Less Studio costs				
Hire of films	12 000	8 000	6 000	26 000
Usherette salaries	4 000	4 000	4 000	12 000
	16 000	12 000	10 000	38 000
Contribution to cinema costs	44 000	28 000	20 000	92 000
*Contribution from ice-cream sales**				1 000
				93 000
Less Cinema costs				
Salaries: Managers				12 000
Projectionists				10 000
Ticket salesgirls				4 000
General cinema costs				50 000
				76 000
Contribution to Head office costs				17 000

Cinema		*Regal*			*Total*
Studio	1	2	3	Total	of 3 cinemas
	£	£	£	£	£
Sale of tickets	150 000	100 000	80 000	330 000	539 800
Less Studio costs					
Hire of films	30 000	20 000	16 000	66 000	107 960
Usherette salaries	4 000	4 000	4 000	12 000	36 000
	34 000	24 000	20 000	78 000	143 960
Contribution to cinema costs	116 000	76 000	60 000	252 000	395 840
*Contribution from ice-cream sales**				6 000	6 500
				258 000	402 340
Less Cinema costs					
Salaries: Managers				12 000	36 000
Projectionists				10 000	30 000
Ticket salesgirls				4 000	12 000
General cinema costs				100 000	180 000
				126 000	258 000

	£	£
Contribution to Head office costs	132 000	144 340
Less Head office costs		160 000
Trading Loss		£(15 660)

* *Note to the Account*
Contribution from ice-cream sales

	Astoria £	*Plaza* £	*Regal* £	*Total* £
Sales	7 000	10 000	20 000	37 000
Less Costs				
Purchase of ice-creams	3 500	5 000	10 000	18 500
Salesgirls	4 000	4 000	4 000	12 000
	7 500	9 000	14 000	30 500
Contribution	(500)	1 000	6 000	6 500

From the above we can see that the Plaza and Regal cinemas are profitable. It is only *Astoria* which is unprofitable. Even here Studios 1 and 3 have made money for the company. Only Studio 2 showed a loss — due to the small number of films hired and shown. Management should find out the *reason* for the low turnover of Studio 2 before making a decision. Was it due, for example, to the fact that it was showing only specialist low-demand films (like foreign films or arts films) or was it due to the studio being shut down for repairs for part of the year? It *is* an old cinema.

9.3 *Trading and Profit and Loss Account for the year ended 31st December 19 5*

	X £000	Y £000	*Total* £000
Sales	6 000	4 000	10 000
Less cost of goods sold			
Opening stock of finished goods	200	940	1 140
Manufacturing cost b/f (W_1)	4 000	2 160	6 160
	4 200	3 100	7 300
Less closing stock, finished goods	600	500	1 100
	3 600	2 600	6 200
Gross profit	2 400	1 400	3 800
Less Expenses			
Distribution costs (W_2)	900	600	1 500
Administration expenses (W_3)	800	400	1 200
	1 700	1 000	2 700
Net profit	700	400	1 100

Workings
W_1 *Manufacturing cost*

Department	*X*		*£000*	*Y*		*£000*
A	$5\,200 \times \frac{8}{13}$	=	3 200	$5\,200 \times \frac{5}{13}$	=	2 000
B	$960 \times \frac{5}{6}$	=	800	$960 \times \frac{1}{6}$	=	160
Total			4 000			2 160

W_2 *Distribution costs*

	£000
Depreciation	40
Distribution costs	1 395
Add accrued costs	90
Increase in bad debts provision*	5
	1 530
Less costs prepaid	30
	1 500
* Required provision 900 × 5% =	45
Existing provision	40
Additional provision required	5

Charged to good X £1 500 × $\frac{9}{15}$ = £900
Y £1 500 × $\frac{6}{15}$ = £600

W_3 *Administration expenses*

	£000
Depreciation	40
Administration expenses	1 010
Add accrued expenses	210
	1 260
Less expenses prepaid	60
	1 200

Charged to good X £1 200 × $\frac{10}{15}$ = £800

Y £1 200 × $\frac{5}{15}$ = £400

CHAPTER 10

Company Accounts

Companies differ from sole traders and partnerships in three main respects:
(1) there is no limit to their membership and number of owners — they are therefore larger in size
(2) they are a separate legal identity — their owners therefore enjoy the protection of *limited liability*
(3) there is a separation of ownership from control.

From an accounting standpoint the principles you learnt in bookkeeping and the preparation of accounts of sole traders and partnerships also apply to companies. The differences lie in:
(1) *presentation* of the final accounts — these have to conform to statutory requirements and Statements of Standard Accounting Practice (SSAPs)
(2) how profit is appropriated
(3) the capital and reserves section of the balance sheet, reflecting the different sources of finance.

One of the features of sole traders and partnerships is that the owners have *day-to-day control* over their business. Companies are owned by the people who provide its capital, called shareholders or members, of which there may be many, in some cases millions. It would be impractical for all them to attempt to run the company. Fortunately, they do not want to. Most shareholders invest to share in a company's profits, and are happy to leave its running to the 'experts'. A *Board of Directors* is appointed for this, composed of specialists in marketing, production, finance, etc, and are given the responsibility of running the company, for which they are paid a salary. The profits of the company, calculated *after* payment of the salaries, are distributed as *dividend* to the shareholders.

The directors therefore have *stewardship* of the company on behalf of the members. To ensure that they carry out their duties honestly and in the interests of the members whom they serve, the law requires them to make public the financial affairs of the company once a year in an Annual Report. The minimum information to be contained in this Report is contained in the provisions of the *UK Companies Acts*, of which there have been several since the first one in 1844. In this way the law affords protection to the shareholders. Examination questions on company accounts usually ask for preparation of the final accounts in a form suitable for publication to shareholders. A knowledge of the main aspects of the presentation and disclosure requirements of the Companies Acts is therefore required. Detailed provisions of the acts is not required until study at professional level.

Private and Public Companies

Companies may be either private or public. While public companies can sell their shares to the public at large, through national advertising, private companies can do so only by finding a private buyer. Private companies tend to be family businesses which have been incorporated into a company to enjoy the benefit of limited liability. It is not uncommon for there to be only two directors, the minimum number necessary to form a company. If they wish to expand they must personally find additional people willing to invest in their business, such as friends and relatives. In contrast, public companies can advertise to the public at large for finance. As a result they find it much easier to expand and become large organizations, such as British Telecom, Shell, and the Ford Motor Company to name a few. The shares of the larger public companies are *quoted* (listed) on the Stock Exchange, a market-place for second-hand securities. A lot of these companies are multi-nationals i.e. operating in more than one country.

A further difference between the two types of company is in their name. Private companies must include the word limited in their name, or Ltd. for short; public companies the letters plc or PLC, which is an abbreviation of public limited company.

The Annual Report

In addition to the final accounts, being the Profit and Loss Account and Balance Sheet, the Report contains six other items — Notes to the Accounts, the Directors' Report, Auditors' Report, Chairman's Statement, Funds Flow Statement, and a Statistical section.

A brief description of each of these follows.

Notes to the Accounts

The disclosure requirements of the Companies Acts may be shown either on the face of the accounts or in the form of Notes appended thereto. Most companies present only aggregates of figures on the face of the accounts. Details and breakdowns are shown in the Notes. For example, while the balance sheet contains just one figure for tangible fixed assets, a breakdown of this total figure by types of asset, their historic cost, depreciation and acquisitions and disposals during the year are contained in the Notes. In this way the main accounts are kept short and simple, and the reader who is interested in detail is directed to the Notes.

Directors' Report

This must contain, among others, the following information:

(1) a fair review of the development of the company during the financial year and of its position at the year-end
(2) proposed dividends for the year and transfers to reserves
(3) particulars of the Directors such as their names, remuneration, holdings in the company's shares, and changes in the composition of the Board during the year
(4) significant post-balance sheet events, progress in the field of research and development, and likely future development of the company.

Companies with over 250 employees must include staff details such as the number of employees, total bill for wages and salaries, social security, and other pension costs. This is usually presented in the Director's Report or Notes.

Auditors' Report

Once the accounts have been prepared internally they must be checked or audited by an independent firm of professional accountants. This is to safeguard shareholders that their trustees are not conspiring to present a false picture of the company or perhaps covering-up a misappropriation of funds diverted for personal use. It is the duty of the auditors to check that the accounts give a *'true and fair'* view of the affairs of the company. Figures they are not happy with are discussed with the company's own accountants and directors, and often changed. If they are unable to persuade the directors to change the figures in dispute and feel that as a result of this the accounts fail to give a true and fair view they may *qualify* their report, i.e. not certify that the accounts give a true and fair view, explaining their reasons for doing this.

The legal requirement of the annual audit is a powerful deterrent against foul play by directors and an effective safeguard to shareholders' interests.

Chairman's Statement

Companies tend to include a statement from the Chairman in their Annual Report, although this is not legally required. The statement is a light-hearted general comment on the performance of the business over the year, both as a whole and by product group and geographical area. It is also a chance for comments on *non-financial factors* not covered in the accounts, such as changes in the environment in which the company is operating and the state of industrial and customer relations.

Statistical Section

Most companies present a statistical section in their report, although this again is not a legal requirement. In this, they take the opportunity to:

(1) present recent *trends* (typically over the past 5 years) in sales, profits and other key variables by means of graphs
(2) analyse the performance of the year under review by means of presentation devices like *pie-charts* and *bar-charts*. A common feature of annual reports is

a pie-chart to show distribution of the trading profit as between taxation, dividend to shareholders, retention, and other claimants (if any). Bar-charts are often used to show a breakdown of turnover by class of business and geographical area.

The reason for the popularity of this section is that most shareholders are non-accountants who are happier at looking at charts and diagrams than tables of figures and accounts.

You will not be able to be asked to prepare directors' reports, auditors' reports, chairman's statements or statistical sections in examination questions.

Funds Flow Statement

This statement, also called the Statement of Source and Application of Funds, seeks to link the profit and loss account to the balance sheet and this year's balance sheet to last year's. It has only recently become established as a feature of company accounts and is now recommended by SSAP 10. You may well be asked to prepare and comment on such statements in examinations. The whole of the next chapter is devoted to them.

Let us now look at the two main statements in the annual report — the Profit and Loss Account and Balance Sheet. The law requires that the accounts presented to shareholders give a 'true and fair' view of the financial affairs of the company. It also requires that the fundamental concepts of accounting are followed, i.e. going concern, accruals, consistency, and prudence. Any departure from a concept should be mentioned in the accounts stating the reasons for the departure.

Profit and Loss Account

The law lays down four alternative formats in which the profit and loss account is to be presented. At this stage it is sufficient for you to know just one. The natural choice is to use that which is most frequently used in practice and expected by examiners — Format 1. The other three formats are in fact not often used, either in practice or in examinations.

Format 1 is presented below. The numbers on the left-hand side will be used to explain the items after the account.

Pro-forma

Profit and Loss Account

		Note	£	£
(1)	Turnover			x
(2)	Cost of sales			(x)
	Gross profit			x
(3)	Distribution costs		(x)	
(3)	Administration expenses		(x)	(x)
(4)	Trading profit			x
(5)	Other operating income			x
				x
(6)	Income from shares in group companies		x	
(6)	Income from shares in related companies		x	
(6)	Income from other fixed asset investments		x	
(7)	Other interest receivable and similar income		x	x
				x
(8)	Amounts written off investments		(x)	

(9)	Interest payable and similar charges	(x)	(x)
	Profit or loss on ordinary activities before taxation		x
	Tax on profit or loss on ordinary activities		(x)
	Profit or loss on ordinary activities after taxation.		x
(10)	Extraordinary income	x	
(10)	Extraordinary charges	(x)	
(10)	Extraordinary profit or loss	x	
(10)	Tax on extraordinary profit or loss	(x)	x
			x
	Other taxes not shown under the above items		(x)
	Profit or loss for the financial year		x
	Transfers to Reserves	(x)	
(11)	Dividends paid and proposed	(x)	(x)
(12)	Retained profit for the year		£x

Explanation of the Items

(1) *Turnover.* This is to be shown exclusive of VAT. An analysis of turnover and profit is required for substantially different classes of business and for substantially different geographical areas e.g. Europe, Asia, North America.

(2) *Cost of sales.* Manufacturing concerns are *not* required to disclose details of production costs.

(3) *Expenses.* It is not necessary to show the amounts of all the many different types of expenses — most shareholders are not interested in such detail. Instead they may be grouped into two broad classes — *distribution costs* and *administration expenses.* The totals of these two groups are shown in the account. In questions it is advisable to calculate the totals separately in workings, then reference them to the entry in the account. The net of discounts allowed and discounts received should be shown as an administration expense.

(4) *Trading profit.* The law requires the amount charged in respect of certain items to be disclosed. These are *depreciation, hire of plant and machinery, directors' remuneration,* and *auditors' remuneration.* In practice companies usually include this information in the notes to the accounts.

(5) *Other operating income.* This consists of income arising outside the normal trading activity, such as rents receivable from sub-let of premises and profit on sale of fixed assets.

(6) *Income from shares receivable.* It is common for public companies to acquire holdings in other companies for a wide variety of reasons. In later studies you will meet the topic of *group accounts* or *consolidated accounts* which deal with the aggregation of results of a holding company with subsidiaries into one set of group accounts. For our purposes we need to know the distinction between income from group companies, related companies, and fixed asset investments. The income in question is *dividends.* Companies in which the holding or parent company has a controlling interest i.e. *over 50 per cent* of the equity shares, are known as group companies. If the holding is less than 50 per cent but *over 20 per cent* it is a related company. Holdings of *less than 20 per cent* are known as fixed asset investments.
Dividends can also be receivable from *short-term* holdings of shares purchased in times of excess liquidity.

(7) *Other interest receivable and similar income.* At times of excessive cash, companies not only buy shares but also lend some of the surplus, for

example to the government by acquiring treasury bills. These short-term loans attract interest. Details of the loans made have to be disclosed.

(8) *Amounts written off investments.* These represent reductions in the market value of the above investments.

(9) *Interest payable and similar charges.* This represents interest on bank loans and overdrafts and debenture interest. Details are required.

(10) *Extraordinary items* As the name suggests, this represents gains or losses arising from events *outside the ordinary trading activities of the company.* They are one-off items which are not expected to recur. An example would be the loss sustained by a multi-national company by the nationalization of a branch in a foreign country. Examination questions at this level usually state when an item is to be treated as extraodinary. The nature of an extraordinary item has to be disclosed.

(11) *Dividends.* This total figure includes both preference and ordinary dividend, both interim dividend paid and final dividend proposed. The split as between ordinary and preference, interim and final dividend has to be shown.

(12) *Retained profit.* This figure, representing undistributed profit for the year, is to be added to the retained profit at the beginning of the year to arrive at the final balance to be carried forward to next year, which is shown in the balance sheet.

The Balance Sheet

There are two allowable formats for the balance sheet, one horizontal and one vertical. Most companies in the UK now use format 1, being the vertical style of presentation, and this is also the one preferred by examiners. It is presented below. Again the numbers on the left-hand side will be used to explain the items after the balance sheet.

Pro-forma

Balance Sheet

		Note	£	£
(1)	Called-up share capital not paid			x
(2)	*Fixed assets*			
(3)	Intangible assets		x	
(4)	Tangible assets		x	
(5)	Investments		x	x
(6)	*Current assets*			
(7)	Stock		x	
(8)	Debtors		x	
(9)	Investments		x	
	Cash at Bank and in Hand		x	
			x	
(10)	*Creditors:* amounts falling due within one year		(x)	
(11)	Net current assets (liabilities)			x
	Total assets less current liabilities			x
(12)	*Creditors:* amounts falling due after more than one year		(x)	
(13)	Provisions for liabilities and charges		(x)	(x)
				£x

	Capital and Reserves	£
(14)	Called-up share capital	x
(15)	Share premium	x
(16)	Revaluation reserve	x
(17)	Other reserves	x
(18)	Profit and loss account	x
		£x

The total of capital and reserves is known as *Shareholders' Funds* or *Owners' Equity*. To find capital employed we need to add to this long-term liabilities (item 12). The upper half of the balance sheet minus item 12 represents *Net Assets*. Of course, capital employed is equal to net assets.

Explanation of the Items

(1) *Called-up share capital not paid.* This represents monies owing from shareholders for shares issued and called for but still unpaid. In effect they represent debtors. It is permissible for the item to be aggregated with the figure for debtors in current assets.

(2) *Fixed assets.* These are long-term assets held not primarily for resale but for use in the business. Usually only the aggregates of the three different classes of asset are shown in the balance sheet. Details are shown in the Notes. These must contain, for each type of asset within each class:
- the cost of the asset at the beginning and end of the financial year
- acquisitions and disposals during the year
- details of any depreciation, including charge for the year, the effect of disposals on depreciation and accumulated depreciation to date
- the method of depreciation used and useful lives/depreciation rates adopted.

The last point is usually shown in the Statement of Accounting Policies, to be found at the beginning of the notes to the accounts.

(3) *Intangible assets.* These are *non-physical* assets which cannot be seen or touched such as *goodwill* and *patents.* The concept of historic cost dictates that only those assets which have been bought at a cost may be shown in the accounts — at the cost of purchase. Therefore with goodwill only that which has been *paid for* in acquiring another business may be included in the balance sheet. The 'real' goodwill of a company, which has been built up through trading is *not* to be shown, as it has not been paid for. It can be seen then that the balance sheet figure of net assets may not represent a company's true value.

(4) *Tangible assets.* These are *physical* assets such as land and buildings, plant and machinery and motor vehicles.

(5) *Investments.* These represent shares in group companies held on a long-term basis. They are to be stated at the *lower of cost and market value.* Details are required.

(6) *Current assets.* These are short-term liquid assets expected to be converted into cash within the next twelve months.

(7) *Stocks.* Most companies show the aggregate figure for stock on the face of the balance sheet. The split between the different categories viz. raw materials, work-in-progress, and finished goods, is shown by way of note. The policy of valuing stock at the lower of cost and net realizable value should be mentioned in the statement of accounting policies.

(8) *Debtors.* Again only the aggregate figure is shown on the balance sheet itself. The individual amounts of trade debtors and prepayments are disclosed in the Notes. Debtors are split between amounts due within one year and amounts due after more than one year.

(9) *Investments.* These are *short-term* investments such as treasury bills. The disclosure requirements are similar to those for long-term investments.

(10) *Creditors: amounts falling due within one year.* These consist of trade creditors, bank overdraft, taxes owing, dividends payable, and other *current* liabilities.

(11) *Net current assets (liabilities).* This represents the *working capital* of the company at the balance sheet date.

(12) *Creditors: amounts falling due after more than one year.* These consist of debentures, bank loans, and other *long-term* obligations.

(13) *Provisions for liabilities and charges.* The concept of prudence requires companies to make provision for possible losses as soon as they become foreseeable. The provision is to be deducted from assets. The reason for making a provision should be stated.

(14) *Share capital.* The *authorized* share capital of a company represents the *maximum* it can issue to the public, divided into the different classes of share — ordinary, preference, cumulative preference. That part of the authorized capital which has actually been issued is known as the *issued* share capital. Only the amount of issued share capital which has been paid for is shown in the balance sheet. The notes disclose the authorized share capital and the amounts issued by type of share, number issued and nominal value.

(15) *Share premium.* When a company first sets up, each share is given a nominal or par value — this is usually the issue price of the new shares. If it does well and wishes to expand later, it may, if it has acquired goodwill and the shares are in demand, be able to sell at a price *higher* than nominal value. Monies received in excess of the nominal price are shown in a separate account, called share premium. The figure for share capital (item 14) then represents the nominal value of shares issued.

(16) *Revaluation reserve.* Freehold land is one fixed asset that is not subject to depreciation. Fixity of supply combined with an ever-increasing demand causes the value of most land to rise with time. If current market values move completely out of touch with historic cost as stated in the accounts such that the balance sheet ceases to give a true and fair view of asset values it is permissible to depart from historic cost. The figure for land can be updated by the creation of a revaluation reserve, the double-entry being:

Dr Freehold land
Cr Revaluation reserve

Since the gain benefits the owners of the company, the shareholders, the reserve is shown as part of shareholders' funds.

Both share premium and revaluation reserve are known as *capital reserves,* because they are *non-distributable.* Reserves that can be distributed as future dividend to shareholders are known as *revenue reserves.* Capital reserves can be utilized in only a limited number of ways, as stated in the Companies Acts, for example in financing a bonus issue of shares (see later).

(17) *Other reserves.* These may be either revenue reserves such as *general reserve* or capital reserves such as *capital redemption reserve* (defined later).

(18) *Profit and loss account.* This represents the retained, undistributed profits from this and previous years to be carried forward to next year. It can be used to pay part of next year's dividend, and is therefore a revenue reserve.

In the Notes it is necessary to show, for each reserve, the balance at the start of the year, additions during the year and balance at end of the year.

Note that capital reserves are shown before revenue reserves.

Statement of Accounting Policies

The law requires companies to disclose in their Annual Report the accounting policies used in subjective areas where there is more than one basis of treatment. These include:

(1) basis of accounting i.e. whether historic cost, current cost, or current purchasing power
(2) basis of depreciation i.e. whether straight-line, reducing-balance, or other method
(3) stock valuation, whether at cost, market value, or net realizable value
(4) research and development
(5) goodwill
(6) basis of consolidation (for group companies)
(7) any others relevant to the nature of the business

The statement is usually to be found as the first note in the Notes to the Accounts.

Freedom of Disclosure

The law lays down only the *minimum* amount of information that a company must disclose. They are free to disclose more than this of they so wish. In fact, with the development of *social responsibility accounting,* the trend is towards the disclosure of more and more information to the public, both of a financial and non-financial nature.

Examination Questions

If a question does not specifically ask for preparation of the accounts in accordance with statute you do not need to follow the precise rules on presentation and disclosure requirements. The examiner is testing merely whether you can prepare a set of final accounts from a list of balances with additional information and adjustments. If a question specifically mentions the Companies Acts then you need to present the accounts as required by law and prepare a full set of Notes to the Accounts. Failure to do this will lose you marks, even if the figures in the accounts are all correct. In addition to the figures examiners look out for what you have and have not disclosed, and how you have disclosed it.

You are unlikely in questions to be given all the information that is required to be disclosed. In such cases show what you can from the information — you can do no more than this. Some questions accept this limitation by asking for presentation 'in so far as the available information permits'. For some strange reason questions often fail to give information on the split between administration and distribution of common expenses such as wages and general expenses. In such cases it is usually best to assume that they are to be apportioned equally, stating the assumption made in your answer.

It is a requirement that companies show *previous year's figures* for all items in the Annual Report. This is to help the reader get an idea of the trend of events over the past year. Examination questions rarely provide prior-year figures, so you can ignore this requirement in your answers.

Miscellaneous Company Matters

Rights Issue

Public companies usually raise additional capital by offering shares to the public at large. The *costs* of a new share issue, in professional fees to the merchant bank handling the issue, publicity and advertising, can be quite high. One way to reduce this is by a rights issue. Under this *existing shareholders* are given the right to buy so many shares, for example one for every five held. The offer price is usually pitched slightly *below* the existing market price, a discount the company can afford to make in view of the issue cost savings. Of course, an existing shareholder does not have to take up his rights to buy the additional shares — he can sell them to a third party, at a profit.

Bonus Issue

Reserves represent monies attributable to shareholders but retained within the company to finance future activities and growth. If reserves increase beyond the level thought to be needed by the directors they can be *capitalized* by issuing shares to existing shareholders free of charge, on a pro-rata basis. Unlike a rights issue no additional money is received. Share certificates however, *are* issued.

Redemption

Monies received from issuing debentures and redeemable shares have to be *repaid* by a certain date, stated at the time of issue. This act of repayment is known as redemption. Companies Act requires that when *shares* are redeemed an equal amount is transferred from revenue reserves to a *capital redemption reserve* which is not distributable to shareholders. The reason for this requirement is to maintain the capital of the company. Companies are not allowed to reduce the amount of capital except in certain special cases (you will meet the topic of Reduction of Capital at professional level). The maintenance of capital is for the *protection of creditors*. If a company is in difficulty and capital is paid back to shareholders, this would be wrong since creditors have first claim on the assets in the event of a winding-up. The transfer to capital redemption reserve is usually made in the appropriation account. The double-entry is:

Dr P & L appropriation
    Cr Capital redemption reserve

The redemption reserve is then included under 'other reserves' in the balance sheet and details of it shown in the notes to the accounts. See question 10.4.

The above requirement does not apply to the redemption (repayment) of *debentures* — debentures are long-term loans and not part of a company's capital.

Questions

10.1* **(a)** The following balances have been extracted from the books of Safed Limited as at 30 September 19_4:

	£
Creditors	6 300
Sales	80 000
Land at cost	18 000
Buildings at cost	38 000
Furniture and fittings at cost	22 000
Bank (credit balance)	6 000
Depreciation: buildings	6 000
furniture and fittings	10 000
Discounts received	1 764
Unappropriated profit at 1 October 19_3	2 000
Provision for doubtful debts	816
Goodwill	16 400
Cash in hand	232
Stock at 1 October 19_3	14 248
Interim dividend on preference shares	600
Rates	2 124
Wages and Salaries	8 000
Insurance	1 896
Returns inward	372
General expenses	436
Debtors	12 640
Purchases	43 856
Debenture interest	400
Bad Debts	676
5% Debentures	16 000
6% £1 Preference Shares	20 000
£1 Ordinary Shares	20 000
General Reserve	10 000
Share Premium	1 000

Additional information:

(1) Stock on hand at 30 September 19_4 was £15 546
(2) Insurance paid in advance: £100.
(3) Wages owing: £280.
(4) Depreciation is to be provided at 10% on cost of buildings, and at 20% on the written down value of furniture and fittings.
(5) Provision for doubtful debts is to be reduced to 5% of debtors.
(6) Debenture interest outstanding of £400.
(7) The directors propose to pay a 5% Ordinary Dividend and the final Preference Dividend, and to transfer £8 000 to General Reserve.

Required:
The Profit and Loss Account for the year ended 30 September 1984 and a Balance Sheet as at that date, in accordance with the Companies Acts, in so far as the available information permits. (17 marks)

(b) Examine the accounts you have prepared in (a) and then answer the questions below:

(i) How did the Share Premium Account arise?
(ii) How could the goodwill acount have arisen?
(iii) Which of the reserves are capital reserves and which are revenue reserves, and what, in principle, is the difference between the two? (8 marks)

(25 marks)

Institute of Chartered Accountants, Foundation

10.2 Pebble plc is a wholesaling company whose balances at 31 December Year 3 included the following:

	£000
Undistributed profits brought forward from Year 2	2 778
Sales	10 200
Purchases	6 131
Carriage Inwards	21
Return Inwards	120
Return Outwards	117
Stock (1 January Year 3)	380
Goodwill	33
Rents receivable	4
General distribution costs	171
Administration wages and salaries	17
Salesmen's salaries and warehouse wages	16
Other administrative costs	88
Income from investments	19
Profit on sale of land	100

Notes:

(1) The item 'income from investments' included £12 000 from shares in group companies, with the balance from related companies.
(2) The profit on sale of land is considered to be an extraordinary item.
(3) Stock at 31 December was valued at £335 000.
(4) Accumulated provisions for depreciation of delivery vehicles and of office equipment are to be increased by £13 000 and £18 000 respectively.
(5) The goodwill arose on the takeover of a business which has proved to be unprofitable. Accordingly it has been decided to write it off.

Required:
Prepare as far as the given information permits, the company's Profit and Loss Account for the year ended 31 December Year 3, in a form suitable for distribution to its shareholders. Give only the minimum information required by the Companies Act 1981.

Note: Ignore taxation

(18 marks)

London Chamber of Commerce and Industry, Higher

10.3* Sagunto Ltd has an authorised capital of 1.5 million £1 ordinary shares, of which 1 million have been issued as fully paid.

The following information was extracted from the accounts for the year ended 30 September 19_6.

	£	*£*		*£*
Freehold premises at cost		250 000	Purchases	430 000
Carriage inwards		13 500	Returns inward	18 000
Sales		750 000	Returns outward	25 000
Stock 1 Oct 19_5		80 000	Directors' remuneration	20 000
Wages and salaries:			Auditors' fees	2 500
Administration	20 000		General administrative expenses	9 000
Distribution	40 000	60 000		
			Discounts allowed	2 500
Motor vehicle running costs		11 000	Retained earnings (Cr. Bal 1 Oct 19_5)	260 000

Additional information:

(1) The closing stock was valued at £90 000 cost.

(2) The ordinary share dividends for the year were:

Interim	3% Already paid
Final	8% Proposed.

(3) The directors decided to transfer £100 000 to General Reserve.

(4) Expenses in arrear at 30 September 19_6 were:

	£
Motor vehicle running costs	1 100
Salaries and wages: distribution staff	3 000

(5) Expenses paid in advance at 30 September 19_6 were:

	£
General administrative expenses	1 500

(6) The liability for the corporation tax for the year ended 30 September 19_6 had been agreed at £95 000.

(7) The company depreciated freehold premises at 4% per annum on cost. Aggregate depreciation to 30 September 19_5 was £40 000.

(8) On 1 October 19_5 the company's assets included:

	£
Motor vehicles at cost	40 000
Depreciation to date	16 000

Depreciation is provided at 20% per annum on a reducing balance basis.

The above figures include a motor vehicle which cost £8 000, and which had been in company ownership for exactly two years. It was sold for £2 500 on 1 October 19_5. There were no other purchases or sales of vehicles during the year.

(9) The company's motor vehicles were used by staff as follows

Distribution staff	30 000 miles per annum
Administration staff	10 000 miles per annum

Required:

(a) The trading and profit and loss account for the year ended 30 September 19_6. (13 marks)

(b) The appropriation account for the year ended 30 September 19_6. (4 marks)

(c) From your answer to (a) above, list those items which the company would be required to include in its published accounts under the Companies Act 1948-85. (8 marks)

(25 marks)

Advanced Level Acounting, AEB

10.4 Brampton Ltd. has an authorised share capital of 100 000 ordinary shares of £1 each and 16 000 8% redeemable preference shares of £1 each. The company's trial balance as at 30 April 19_6 was as follows:

	£	£
Ordinary share capital, fully paid		80 000
Share premium account		20 000
Plant and machinery at cost	76 000	
Motor lorries at cost	114 000	
Debtors and creditors	88 960	50 740
10% Debentures		18 000
Purchases and sales	326 978	466 668
General expenses	17 040	
Bad debts	4 800	
Stock at 1 May 19_5	15 400	
Debenture interest for half year to 31 October 19_5	900	
Discounts received		3 280
Bank	72 170	
Salaries	31 420	
Insurance	2 600	
Directors' fees	32 000	
Provisions for depreciation:		
Plant and machinery		60 000
Motor lorries		52 400
Interim preference dividend (see note 4)	640	
Profit and loss account, 1 May 19_5		30 760
Provision for doubtful debts, 1 May 19_5		1 060
	782 908	782 908

Notes:

(1) At 30 April 19_6:
  (a) Insurance, £420 was prepaid.
  (b) Doubtful debts totalled £900.
  (c) Stock totalled £16 500.
  (d) A corporation tax provision of £7 000 is to be made.
  (e) The directors propose to pay dividend of 10% to the ordinary shareholders.

(2) Depreciation is to be calculated on fixed assets at 20% on the reducing balance basis.

(3) The debenture interest for the second half of the year is to be accrued.

(4) £16 000 8% redeemable preference shares were redeemed at par value on 1 November 19_5. No new shares were issued by the company during the year.

Required:
Trading and profit and loss accounts for the year to 30 April 19_6, and a balance sheet as at that date, prepared in a vertical style. **(25 marks)**

Advanced Level Accounting, London

10.5 Leaf PLC is a company which manufactures and delivers artificial plants and flowers to shops and offices. The following balances stood in the books at 30 June 19_7:

	£000
Turnover	2 000
Purchase of raw materials	380
Factory wages	400
Factory overheads	205
Hire of plant	42

	£000
Motor vehicle running expenses	20
Warehouse wages	80
Office salaries	35
Rent and rates	23
General administrative expenses	10
Directors' emoluments	12
Auditors' remuneration	8
Rent from sub-let of premises	25
Compensation paid (see Note 1)	50
Corporation tax paid	140
Bank	5
Investment in Green Ltd	300
Investment in Twig plc	250
Dividend received from Green Ltd	20
Dividend received from Twig plc	30
UK government stocks (short-term)	20
Interest received from stock	5
Fixed assets, at cost:	
freehold premises	710
plant and equipment	600
motor vehicles	250
fixtures and fittings	100
Provision for depreciation, 1 July 19_6:	
plant and equipment	240
motor vehicles	100
fixtures and fittings	20
Stocks at 1 July 19_6:	
raw materials	35
work-in-progress	20
finished goods	140
Trade debtors	40
Trade creditors	30
10% Debentures, 31 December 19_9	800
Issued share capital	
10% preference shares of £1 each	200
ordinary shares	400
Interim dividend paid: preference	10
ordinary	60
Profit and loss account	200

Additional information:

(1) During one of its deliveries to a department store a large plant was accidentally dropped from the first floor to the shopping area below. It landed on a customer's head causing internal head injuries. The company agreed to pay £50 000 as compensation. The directors have decided to treat this as an extraordinary loss.
The saving in tax as a result of the decrease in profit is £20 000.

(2) The directors propose to pay a final dividend of 10% to the ordinary shareholders.

(3) Fixed assets are depreciated by the straight-line method, using the following percentages:

plant and equipment	10 per cent
motor vehicles	20 per cent
fixtures and fittings	10 per cent

(4) During the year:
- motor vehicles costing £80 000 were sold for £35 000. Accumulated depreciation on them was £50 000
- additional fixtures and fittings were purchased at a cost of £20 000.

(5) Stock at the year-end consisted of:

	£000
raw materials	15
work-in-progress	15
finished goods	50

(6) At the year-end:
rent and rates prepaid amount to £3 000
£2 000 has been prepaid for hire of plant
£5 000 of office salaries remain outstanding
corporation tax of £10 000 is still owing

(7) Leaf PLC holds 300 000 ordinary shares of £1 each in Green Ltd., which represents 35 per cent of the equity, and 500 000 preference shares of £0.50 in Twig plc, which represents 7 per cent of the preference shares. The current market value of the investment in Green Ltd. is £370 000, in Twig plc 200 000.

(8) At the year-end £15 000 ordinary dividend remained owing from Green Ltd.

(9) The authorized share capital of the company is £200 000 10 per cent preference shares of £1 each and 600 000 ordinary shares of £1 each.

(10) The directors have decided to create a general reserve of £100 000.

You are required to prepare the final accounts of Leaf PLC for the year ended 30 June 19_7 in accordance with the Companies Acts 1948–85, in so far as the available information permits. **(40 marks)**

Author's Question

Solutions

10.2

PEBBLE PLC

Profit and Loss Account for the year ended 31 December Year 3

	Notes	*£000*	*£000*
Turnover (W_1)	(1)		10 080
Cost of sales (W_2)			(6 080)
Gross profit			4 000
Distribution costs (W_3)		(200)	
Administration costs (W_4)		(123)	(323)
Trading profit	(2)		3 677
Other operating income			4
		•	3 681
Income from shares in group companies		12	
Income from shares in related companies		7	19
			3 700
Amounts written off investments	(3)		(33)
Profit on ordinary activities before taxation			3 667
Extraordinary income	(4)		100
Profit for the financial year before taxation			£3 767

Workings

	£000
W_1 Sales	10 200
Less returns inwards	120
Turnover	10 080

		£
W_2 *Cost of sales*		
Opening stock		380
Purchases	6 131	
Less return outwards	117	6 014
Carriage inwards		21
		6 415
Less closing stock		335
Cost of sales		6 080
W_3 *Distribution costs*		
Salesmen's salaries and warehouse wages		16
General distribution costs		171
Depreciation on delivery vehicles		13
Total		200
W_4 *Administration costs*		
Administrative wages and salaries		17
Other administrative costs		88
Depreciation on office equipment		18
Total		123

Notes to the Account

(1) *Turnover*
Turnover is exclusive of VAT.

(2) *Trading profit*
Trading profit is stated after charging £31 000 for depreciation.

(3) Amounts written off investments
This represents Goodwill which arose on the takeover of a business which has since proved to be unprofitable. Accordingly, the Directors have decided to write it off.

(4) *Extraordinary income*
This arose through the sale of land at a profit.

10.4 The answer to this question does not have to conform the Companies Acts. Nevertheless, I have prepared the accounts with the acts in mind.

BRAMPTON LTD

Profit and Loss Account for the year ended 30 April 19_6

	Notes	£	£
Turnover	(2)		466 668
Cost of sales (W_1)			(325 878)
Gross profit			140 790
Distribution costs (W_2)		(39 750)	
Administration expenses (W_3)		(59 770)	(99 520)
Trading profit	(3)		41 270
Interest payable and similar charges	(4)		(1 800)
Profit on ordinary activities before taxation			39 470
Provision for taxation			(7 000)
Profit on ordinary activities after taxation			32 470
Profit for the financial year			
Transfers to reserve	(12)	(16 000)	
Dividends paid and proposed	(5)	(8 640)	(24 640)
Retained profit for the year			£7 830

Workings

			£
W_1	*Cost of sales*		
	Opening stock		15 400
	Purchases		326 978
			342 378
	Less closing stock		16 500
	Cost of sales		325 878
W_2	*Distribution costs* *		
	General expenses $(\frac{17\ 040}{2})$		8 520
	Salaries $(\frac{31\ 420}{2})$		15 710
	Depreciation on plant		3 200
	Depreciation on motor lorries		12 320
	Total		39 750

* In the absence of any information I have apportioned wages and salaries and general expenses equally between distribution costs and administration expenses.

W_3	*Administration expenses*		
	General expenses		8 520
	Salaries		15 710
	Bad debts		4 800
	Insurance (2 600 − 420)		2 180
	Directors' fees		32 000
			63 210
	Discounts received	3 280	
	Reduction in provision for doubtful debts (1 060 − 900)	160	
			(3 440)
	Total		59 770

BRAMPTON LTD

Balance Sheet as at 30 April 19_6

	Notes	£	£
Fixed assets			
Tangible assets	(6)		62 080
Current assets			
Stock	(7)	16 500	
Debtors	(8)	88 480	
Cash at Bank		72 170	
		177 150	
Creditors: Amounts falling due within one year	(9)	(66 640)	
Net current assets			110 510
Total assets less current liabilities			172 590
Creditors: Amounts falling due after more than one year	(10)		(18 000)
			£154 590
Capital and reserves			
Called-up share capital	(11)		80 000
Share premium	(12)		20 000
Other reserves	(12)		16 000
Profit and loss account	(12)		38 590
			£154 590

Notes to the Accounts

(1) *Accounting Policies*

(a) *Basis of accounting* — The accounts are prepared under the historical cost system.

(b) *Depreciation* — Depreciation on fixed assets is provided on a reducing-balance basis at 20 per cent.
(c) *Stock* — Stock is valued at the lower of cost and net realizable value.

(2) *Turnover*
Turnover is exclusive of VAT.

(3) *Trading profit*
Trading profit is stated after charging:

	£
Depreciation	15 520
Director's fees	32 000

(4) *Interest payable and similar charges*
Interest payable is on 10% Debentures.

(5) *Dividends*

	£
Preference — interim dividend paid	640
Ordinary — final dividend proposed	8 000
	8 640

(6) *Tangible assets*

	Plant and machinery	*Motor lorries*	*Total*
	£	£	£
Cost at 1 May 19_5	76 000	114 000	190 000
at 30 April 19_6	76 000	114 000	190 000
Accumulated depreciation			
At 1 May 19_5	60 000	52 400	112 400
Charge for the year	3 200	12 320	15 520
At 30 April 19_6	63 200	64 720	127 920
Net book value			
At 1 May 19_5	16 000	61 600	77 600
At 30 April 19_6	12 800	49 280	62 080

(7) *Stock*
Stock consists of goods for resale.

(8) *Debtors*
Debtors comprise amounts falling due within one year as follows:

	£
Trade debtors	88 060
Prepayments	420
	88 480

(9) *Creditors: Amounts falling due within one year*

	£
Trade creditors	50 740
Debenture interest	900
Proposed dividend	8 000
Provision for tax	7 000
	66 640

(10) *Creditors: Amounts falling due after more than one year*
This consists of 10% Debentures repayable in ?

(11) *Called-up share capital*

	Authorized	*Issued*
	£	£
8 % redeemable preference shares of £1 each	16 000	—
Ordinary shares of £1 each	100 000	80 000
	116 000	80 000

On 1 November 19_5 16 000 8% redeemable preference shares of £1 each were redeemed at par value.

(12) *Reserves*	*Share premium*	*Capital redemption reserve*	*Profit and loss account*
	£	£	£
At 1 May 19_5	20 000	—	30 760
Transfers from profit and loss account	—	16 000	7 830
At 30 April 19_6	20 000	16 000	38 590

The capital redemption reserve was created on redemption of the preference shares, to maintain the company's capital.

10.5

LEAF PLC

Profit and Loss Account for the year ended 30 June 19_7

	Notes	*£000*	*£000*
Turnover	(2)		2 000
Cost of sales (W_1)			(1 200)
Gross profit			800
Distribution costs (W_2)		(150)	
Administration expenses (W_3)		(100)	(250)
Trading profit	(3)		550
Other operating income (W_4)			30
			580
Income from shares in related companies	(4)	35	
Income from other fixed asset investments		30	
Other interest receivable and similar income	(5)	5	70
			650
Amounts written off investments		(50)	
Interest payable and similar charges	(6)	(80)	(130)
Profit on ordinary activities before taxation			520
Tax on profit on ordinary activities			(170)
Profit on ordinary activities after taxation			350
Extraordinary charge	(7)	(50)	
Tax on extraordinary charge		20	(30)
Profit for the financial year			320
Transfer to Reserve	(17)	(100)	
Dividends paid to proposed	(8)	(120)	(220)
Retained profit for the year			£100

Workings

W_1 *Cost of sales*	*£000*	*£000*
Opening stock raw materials		35
Purchases		380
		415
Less closing stock materials		15
Cost of materials consumed		400
Factory wages		400
Prime cost		800
Factory overheads	205	
Hire of plant (42 − 2)	40	
Depreciation on plant	60	305
		1 105
Opening work-in-progress		20
		1 125
Less closing work-in-progress		15
Production cost		1 110

	£000
Opening stock finished goods	140
Add Production cost	1 110
	1 250
Less closing stock finished goods	50
Cost of sales	1 200

Information on costs of production are not required to be published.

W_2 *Distribution costs*

Motor vehicle running expenses	20
Depreciation on motor vehicles	50
Warehouse wages	80
Total	150

W_3 *Administration expenses*

Office salaries (35 + 5)	40
Rent and rates (23 − 3)	20
General administrative expenses	10
Depreciation on fixtures and fittings	10
Directors' emoluments	12
Auditors' remuneration	8
Total	100

W_4 *Other operating income*

Rent from sub-let of premises	25
Profit on sale of motor vehicles 35 − (80 − 50)	5
	30

LEAF PLC

Balance Sheet as at 30 June 19_7

	Notes	*£000*	*£000*
Fixed assets			
Tangible assets	(9)		1 230
Investments (W_5)	(10)		500
			1 730
Current assets			
Stocks	(11)	80	
Debtors	(12)	60	
Investments	(13)	20	
Cash at Bank and in Hand		5	
		165	
Creditors: Amounts falling due within one year	(14)	(95)	
Net current assets			70
Total assets less current liabilities			1 800
Creditors: Amounts falling due after more than one year	(15)		(800)
			£1 000
Capital and reserves			
Called-up share capital	(16)		600
General reserve	(17)		100
Profit and loss account	(17)		300
			£1 000

Working

W_5 Green Ltd — lower of cost and market value	300
Twig plc — lower of cost and market value	200
	500

Notes to the Accounts

(1) *Accounting policies*

(a) *Basis of accounting* — The accounts are prepared under the historical cost convention.

(b) *Depreciation* — Depreciation is provided to write off the cost of fixed assets on a straight-line basis over the following estimated useful lives:

plant and equipment	10 years
motor vehicles	5 years
fixtures and fittings	10 years

No depreciation is provided on freehold premises.

(c) *Stocks* — Stocks are valued at the lower of cost and net realizable value.

(2) *Turnover*

Turnover is exclusive of VAT

(3) *Trading profit*

Trading profit is stated after charging:

	£000
Depreciation	120
Hire of plant	40
Directors' emoluments	12
Auditors' remuneration	8

(4) *Income from shares in related companies*

This consists of dividends receivable from Leaf PLC's holding of 35 per cent of the ordinary shares of Green Ltd.

(Note that it is not necessary to show details of investments where the holding is less than 10 per cent of the ordinary share capital.)

(5) *Other interest receivable and similar income*

This consists of interest receivable from holdings of UK government stock.

(6) *Interest payable and similar charges*

This consists of interest payable on 10 per cent Debentures.

(7) *Extraordinary charge*

This resulted from an injury to a member of the public from a falling plant for which £50 000 compensation was paid.

(8) *Dividends*

		£000
Preference —	interim dividend paid	10
	final dividend proposed	10
Ordinary —	interim dividend paid	60
	final dividend proposed	40
		120

(9) *Tangible assets*

	Freehold premises	*Plant*	*Motor vehicles*	*Fixtures and fittings*	*Total*
	£000	*£000*	*£000*	*£000*	*£000*
Cost at 1.7.19_6	710	600	330	80	1 720
Additions	—	—	—	20	20
Disposals	—	—	(80)	—	(80)
Cost at 30.6.19_7	710	600	250	100	1 660

	Freehold premises £000	Plant £000	Motor vehicles £000	Fixtures and fittings £000	Total £000
Depreciation					
At 1.7.19_6	—	240	100	20	360
Charge for the year	—	60	50	10	120
Disposals	—	—	(50)	—	(50)
At 30.6.19_7	—	300	100	30	430
Net book value					
At 1.7.19_6	710	360	230	60	1 360
At 30.6.19_7	710	300	150	70	1 230

(10) *Investments*

Leaf plc hold 300 000 £1 ordinary shares in Green Ltd, which represents 35 per cent of its equity. The current market value of the investment is £370 000.

(11) *Stocks*

	£000
Raw materials	15
Work-in-progress	15
Finished goods	50
	80

(12) *Debtors*

Debtors comprise amounts falling due within one year as follows:

	£000
Trade debtors	40
Prepayments	5
Dividend receivable from Green Ltd	15
	60

(13) *Short-term investments*

These consist of UK government stock, cost £20 000.

(14) *Creditors: Amounts falling due within one year*

	£000
Trade creditors	30
Accrued expenses	5
Taxation owing	10
Proposed dividend	50
	95

(15) *Creditors: Amounts falling due after more than one year*

This consists of 10% Debentures repayable on 31 December 19_9.

(16) *Called-up share capital*

	Authorized £000	Issued £000
10% preference shares of £1 each	200	200
Ordinary shares of £1 each	600	400
	800	600

(17) *Reserves*

	General reserves £000	Profit and loss account £000
At 1.7.19_6	—	200
Transfers from profit and loss account	100	100
At 30.6.19_7	100	300

CHAPTER 11

Funds Flow Analysis

So far we have looked at two types of financial statements — the income statement (trading and profit loss account) and balance sheet. The first shows the profit or loss on a year's trading, the second the financial position of the business at the year-end. Because the balance sheet is prepared only once a year some of the figures may be quite different from the previous balance sheet. The income statement cannot explain the changes. For this a further statement is needed — the funds flow statement or statement of source and application of funds, which is the link between two successive balance sheets.

The statement is prepared in two stages. The first half notes the changes between the two balance sheets and classifies them as being either a *source of additional funds* for the year or an *application* of funds. Sources of funds generated from internal operations are shown first. The chief of these is *profit* made during the year adjusted for items not involving the movement of funds, such as *depreciation.* External sources follow. These are mainly long-term capital items such as the issue of shares and debentures and the sale of fixed assets. From total sources (internal plus external) is deducted applications, such as the purchase of fixed assets, repayment of loans and the payment of tax and dividends. The result is a net inflow or outflow of funds. A net inflow of long-term capital would go towards financing additional short-term or *working capital.* The second half of the statement analyses the change in working capital between the two balance sheets to find out which elements have benefited — stocks, debtors, creditors, and cash — and by how much. The net funds inflow, calculated in the first half of the statement, is thus balanced by the net increase in working capital calculated in the lower half. Of course, a net funds outflow depletes working capital by the same amount.

The income statement focuses on profit, and in so doing attempts to match revenues receivable in a period to costs attributable to that period. It does not compare revenues *received* to costs *incurred.* Thus mere book items such as depreciation (representing the share of capital costs allocated to a period) and the profit or loss on sale of fixed assets, which do not involve the movement of funds, are included. In addition, the account does not include any capital items since these are attributable to the income and expenditure of several accounting periods. Thus the purchase and sale of fixed assets and the raising and repayment of long-term finance get left out. In contrast, the funds flow statement focuses on *cash,* not profit. It therefore *excludes* non-cash items such as depreciation and *includes* capital items involving the movement of cash, such as the purchase and sale of fixed assets and changes in long-term finance. In so doing the funds flow statement provides a broader, more complete picture of the financial events of a business over the course of a year than the profit and loss account.

It is useful to have a statement focusing on cash rather than profit, because profitability alone does not guarantee survival (as we shall see in the next chapter). *Liquidity,* ensuring that a business has sufficient cash and near-cash resources to meet current commitments, is just as important. Many a business has failed because of poor management of cash and working capital.

Questions on this topic usually present two successive balance sheets along with an extract of relevant information from the profit and loss account. From this you are required to prepare a funds flow statement. Let us now look at the format of the statement. The guidelines to its preparation are contained in SSAP10, Statements of Source and Application of Funds, which recommends that all companies include one in their Annual Report.

Pro-forma

Statement of Source and Application of Funds

	£	£	£
Source of funds			
Profit before tax			x
Adjustment for items not involving the movement of funds:			
Depreciation		x	
Profit on sale of fixed assets		(x)	x
Total generated from operations			x
Funds from other sources			
Proceeds from sale of fixed assets		x	
Issue of shares for cash		x	x
			x
Application of funds			
Tax paid		x	
Dividend paid		x	
Purchase of fixed assets		x	
Repayment of loan		x	x
			£A
Increase/(decrease) in working capital			
Increase in stocks		x	
Increase in debtors		x	
Decrease in creditors		x	
Movement in net liquid funds:			
Increase in cash	x		
Decrease in short-term investments	(x)	x	£B

It is not possible to include all possible sources and applications — only the main ones have been included. In addition the changes in working capital may be the opposites. If stocks had decreased for example, this would be shown as a negative figure.

In the first half of the statement total sources minus total applications gives £A, the net funds flow. If sources exceed applications there has been a net inflow of funds and £A is positive. This then goes to finance the working capital of the business and the lower half of the statement shows how. £B = £A. If £(A) is negative some of the applications must have been financed by draining working capital. To what extent each item has been drained in then shown in the lower half.

Some explanation of the items in the statement is now needed.

Source of Funds

Profit before tax — This is the starting point of the statement. If, in a question, the figure is not given it has to be worked out by a process of deduction by looking at the two balance sheets. First, the difference between the two profit and loss account balances is struck. To this we have to add back the tax charge (not tax paid) for the year. The profit figure in the balance sheet is net of appropriations made out of distributable profit for the year. We therefore have also to add back the appropriations made such as dividends paid and proposed and transfers to reserves. The resulting figure will be the net profit before tax. This is illustrated in the worked example later.

Non-cash items — Since the statement is concerned with funds rather than accounting profit it is necessary to adjust the profit figure for those items appearing in the profit and loss account not involving the movement of funds.

Depreciation is the main item — as explained in Chapter 3 a provision for depreciation does not involve an outflow of money from the business. It has therefore to be added back to profit.

A *profit or loss on sale of a fixed asset* also does not involve a movement of funds, for similar reasons. A profit or loss on a sale implies an over- or under-provision for depreciation, which as we have seen does not involve an outflow of funds. If a profit has been credited to the income statement it needs to be eliminated by now reducing the profit figure. If a loss has been charged the profit figure needs adding to by the amount of loss. The cash inflow from the disposal is the sale price — this is shown as a source of funds.

Questions do not usually give all the necessary information on fixed assets and depreciation. The techniques you learnt in incomplete records come in handy here. The missing items can be deduced as balancing figures by reconstructing the ledger accounts. Remember to reference your workings to the main statement.

Application of funds

Applications reduce the cash resources of a business. The amount of tax and dividend paid during the year (usually in respect of last year) is sometimes not given in questions — they then have to be deduced as balancing figures by re-constructing the ledger accounts.

Increase/(decrease) in working capital

In the lower half of the statement, the movement in working capital is analysed. Since this is to balance the upper half a source of funds is now shown as a negative, an application as a positive. An increase in an asset, such as stock, is an *application* of funds since additional money had to be spent on it. A reduction in an asset is a *source* since money released from that asset is now available for use elsewhere in the business. An increase in a liability is a source — more funds have been loaned to the business. A decrease in a liability is an application since it represents repayment of a debt.

SSAP 10 recommends that the movement in liquid funds is shown as the last item. Since short-term investments are acquired to take advantage of a temporary period of surplus cash balances and can be quickly converted back to cash when the need arises they are classed as being liquid funds.

Let us now look at a worked example of a typical question on this topic. The question selected is from a recent examination paper of the Chartered Association of Certified Accountants.

Worked Example

The balance sheets of SAF Ltd were as shown below.

During the year ended 31 March 19_6 the company had

(a) sold plant with a written down value of £25 800 for £22 400

(b) made a profit before tax of £749 400 after charging depreciation of the following amounts:

	£
Buildings	4 000
Plant and machinery	110 200
Fixtures and equipment	28 100

Balance sheets as at 31 March

19_5 £	19_5 £		19_6 £	19_6 £
		Fixed assets		
		Tangible assets (at written down values)		
200 000		Land and buildings	196 000	
830 700		Plant and machinery	925 800	
182 400	1 213 100	Fixtures, fittings, tools and equipment	204 600	1 326 400
		Investments		
	10 800	Investments other than loans		72 000
		Current assets		
421 500		Stock	381 000	
134 600		Debtors	110 200	
89 200		Bank and cash	92 400	
645 300			583 600	
		Creditors: amounts due in less than one year		
—		Banks loans and overdrafts	77 300	
120 900		Trade creditors	9 400	
16 000		Bills of exchange payable	51 900	
		Other creditors		
157 300		Taxation	163 200	
175 000		Proposed dividends	190 500	
469 200			492 300	
	176 100	*Net current assets*		91 300
	1 400 000	*Total assets less current liabilities*		1 489 700
		Creditors: amounts due in more than one year		
	400 000	Debenture loans		150 000
		Provisions for liabilities and charges		
	56 000	Provision for legal damages and costs		—
		Capital and reserves		
	700 000	Called up share capital		700 000
	5 000	Share premium		5 000
	239 000	Profit and loss		634 700
	1 400 000			1 489 700

Note:
The amounts shown in 19_5 for taxation, proposed dividends and legal damages and costs were paid in the year ended 31 March 19_6 at the amounts stated.

Required:
(a) Prepare a Statement of Source and Application of Funds for SAF Ltd for the year ended 31 March 19_6.
(b) Comment briefly on the financial position of the company disclosed by your answer to (a).

Solution

1. The starting point is profit before tax . The figure is given in the question. If it had not been it would be possible to work it out, like this:

	£	£
Increase in retained profit (634 700 − 239 000)		395 700
Add back:		
Tax charge for the year	163 200	
Proposed dividends	190 500	353 700
Profit before tax		749 400

2. It is necessary to re-construct the ledger accounts for fixed assets to deduce the missing information.

W_1 *Plant and machinery — Net*

		£		£
1 April 19_5	Bal b/f	830 700	Disposal	25 800
Purchases		∴ 231 100	31 March 19_6	
			P & L — depreciation	110 200
			Bal c/f	925 800
		1 061 800		1 061 800

W_2 *Fixtures, etc — Net*

		£		£
1 April 19_5	Bal b/f	182 400	31 March 19_6	
Purchases		∴ 50 300	P & L — depreciation	28 100
			Bal c/f	204 600
		232 700		232 700

The amount of the cost of purchases in each case was not given, but has now been deduced. It is possible to work out missing figures by mental arithmetic but examiners often prefer workings to be in the form of accounts.

3. Note from the balance sheets that investments have been acquired during the year and some of the debentures have been redeemed.

4. We can now start preparing the actual statement.

SAF LTD

Statement of Source and Application of Funds for the year ended 31 March 19_6

Source of funds	£	£
Profit before tax		749 400
Adjustment for items not involving the the movement of funds:		
Depreciation (4 000 + 110 200 + 28 100)	142 300	
Loss on sale of plant (25 800 − 22 400)	3 400	145 700
Total generated from operations		895 100
Funds from other sources		
Sale of plant		22 400
		917 500
Application of funds		
Purchase of plant (W_1)	231 100	
Purchase of fixtures (W_2)	50 300	
Acquisition of investments (72 000 − 10 800)	61 200	
Tax paid	157 300	
Dividends paid	175 000	
Legal damages and costs paid	56 000	
Debentures redeemed (400 000 − 150 000)	250 000	980 900
		(63 400)

	£	£	£
Increase/(decrease) in working capital			
Decrease in stock		(40 500)	
Decrease in debtors		(24 400)	
Decrease in trade creditors		111 500	
Increase in bills of exchange payable		(35 900)	
Movement in net liquid funds:			
Increase in bank and cash	3 200		
Increase in bank loans	(77 300)	(74 100)	(63 400)

The changes in working capital simply represent the 19_6 balance minus the 19_5 balance.

The statement reveals that there has been a net *outflow* of funds of £63 400, caused partly by the redemption of debentures. This has resulted in an equivalent net decrease in working capital.

As a general rule total application of funds should not exceed total sources. A net ouflow of funds will necessitate it having to be financed by depleting reserves of working capital, and this can lead to liquidity and cash flow problems. Management should take the trouble to *budget* expected future business activities in advance to reveal periods of cash shortage and surplus. Where finance is needed for a major application such as purchase of a fixed asset or repayment of a loan, arrangements can then be made *in advance* for the raising of long-term capital. Long-term applications should not be financed from short-term (working) capital. A look at the technique of cash budgeting in deferred until Chapter 21, Budgeting and Budgetary Control.

The Funds Flow Statement — An Appraisal

The obvious value of a funds flow statement is that it provides a link between two successive balance sheets, but the benefits extend beyond this. The income statement shows the application to revenue expenses of the income generated from sales revenue. The funds flow statement shows how *all* funds, both revenue and capital, raised during the years have been applied to the business — to buy fixed assets, repay loans, pay tax, and dividends, and to increase the working capital. It also shows whether an increase or decrease in the amount of capital employed has been financed from long-term or short-term sources. The statement therefore gives a *more complete picture* of the financial events occuring over the past year than the income statement. In addition it reminds management of the importance of liquidity.

Businessmen sometimes mistakenly equate profits with cash. They are then puzzled by a worsening of the cash position in years of high profit. By focusing on funds rather than profit the statement helps to reconcile the apparent paradox. It might show for example that the reason for the worsening cash position was a purchase of fixed assets or repayment of a loan.

Funds flow analysis is usually conducted along with *ratio analysis* in interpreting the accounts of a business. Ratios are considered in the next chapter, after the questions on funds flow statements.

Questions

11.1 The balance sheets of Antipodean Enterprises at the end of two consecutive financial years, were:

Balance Sheets as at

31 December 19_2			*31 December 19_3*	
$	$		$	$
		Fixed assets as written down value		
38 000		Premises	37 000	
17 600		Equipment	45 800	
4 080	59 680	Cars	18 930	101 730
	17 000	*Investments (long term)*		25 000
		Current Assets		
27 500		Stocks	19 670	
14 410		Debtors and prepayments	11 960	
3 600		Short-term investments	4 800	
1 800		Cash and bank balances	700	
47 310			37 130	
		Current Liabilities		
20 950		Creditors and accruals	32 050	
—		Bank overdraft	28 200	
20 950			60 250	
	26 360	*Working Capital*		(23 120)
	$103 040	*Net Assets Employed*		$103 610
		Financed by:		
67 940		Opening capital	75 040	
4 000		Capital introduced/(withdrawn)	(6 500)	
15 300		Profit/(loss) for year	25 200	
(12 200)		Drawings	(15 130)	
	75 040	*Closing Capital*		78 610
		Long-term liability		
	28 000	Business development loan		25 000
	$103 040			$103 610

Profit for year ended 31 December 19_3 ($25 200) is after accounting for:

	$
Depreciation—premises	1 000
—equipment	3 000
—cars	3 000
Profit on disposal of equipment	430
Loss on disposal of cars	740

The written down value of the assets at date of disposal was:

	$
Equipment	5 200
Cars	2 010

Required:

(a) Prepare a Statement of Sources and Applications of Funds for Antipodean Enterprises for the year ended 31 December 19_3. (14 marks)

(b) Comment on the financial position of the business as revealed by your answer to (a) and by the balance sheet as at 31 December 19_3. (7 marks)

(21 marks)

Chartered Association of Certified Accountants

11.2* Albert Dejonge, a sole proprietor, received the following summarized balance sheets from his accountant for the years ended 31 December 19_4 and 31 December 19_5:

Balance Sheets as at 31 December

19_4		*19_5*
£		£
50 000	Capital	63 000
15 000	Net profit	25 000
65 000		88 000
9 000	Less drawings	12 000
56 000		76 000
20 000	Long term loan finance	25 000
7 500	Trade creditors	9 000
1 500	Expenses owing	1 000
£85 000		£111 000
	Assets	
24 000	Premises	31 000
19 000	Motor vehicles (Net book value)	21 000
17 000	Stock	35 300
16 000	Trade debtors	19 000
1 000	Expenses in advance	600
7 500	Balance at bank	3 000
500	Cash	1 100
£85 000		£111 000

Notes:

(1) There had been no purchases or sales of premises but the premises had been revalued at £31 000. Dejonge does not provide for depreciation on his premises.

(2) An additional motor vehicle was purchased on 1 January 19_5 at cost £6 000. There were no other sales or purchases of vehicles.

(3) During the latter part of 19_5, Dejonge had noted that his bank balance was falling and on 1 December 19_5 he arranged a bank overdraft facility with a limit of £10 000.

(4) At the end of December 19_5, after stock taking, £6 000 of stock had been destroyed by fire, and only £3 000 of the cost is to be recovered from the insurance company. No entries had been made in the accounts, and the closing stock figure had not been adjusted for the loss of the stock.

Dejonge told his accountant that he was very worried about his falling bank balance and he could not understand why this had happened when his profit for 19_5 was much better than 19_4.

Required

(a) A source and application of funds statement showing the change in working capital over the year. (14 marks)

(b) (i) Calculate suitable ratios and comment on Dejonge's liquidity position. Explain to him why liquid resources may fall despite an increase in trading profit. (7 marks)

(ii) Advise Dejonge whether it was financially necessary to secure the bank overdraft facility. (4 marks)

(25 marks)

Advanced Level Accounting, AEB

(Part (b) should be attempted after studying Ratio analysis and Interpretation of Accounts)

11.3* The following summarized information relates to Cliff Ltd

Profit and Loss Account Ended 31 December Year 5

	£000	£000
Turnover		456
Less Depreciation of machinery	18	
Other costs	450	468
		12
Profit on sale of machinery		4
Net loss		8

Balance Sheets as at 31 December

	Year 4 £000	Year 5 £000
Issued Ordinary £1 Shares	300	420
Share Premium	146	86
Property revaluation reserve	—	35
Profit & Loss Account	47	39
Trade creditors	23	37
Bank overdraft	3	—
	519	617
Freehold property at cost	130	12
Freehold property at revaluation	—	165
Machinery	37	42
Stocks	233	243
Debtors	119	117
Bank	—	38
	519	617

During Year 5 machinery with book value of £12 000 was sold and replaced by new machinery. No property was sold. No dividends were paid or proposed but shareholders all accepted a capitalization issue of 'one for five' and then subscribed in full for a rights issue of 'one for six' at par.

Required: A Statement of Source and Application of Funds for Year 5 in good style.

London Chamber of Commerce and Industry, Higher, part-question **(14 marks)**

11.4 The financial statements of Cantab Ltd. included the following balance sheet as at 31 May 19_6;

	£	£	£
Fixed Assets			
Land and buildings, at cost			740 000
Plant, at cost		612 000	
Less depreciation		145 000	467 000
			1 207 000
Current Assets			
Stock		710 000	
Debtors		596 000	
Bank		39 400	
		1 345 400	
Current Liabilities			
Creditors	843 000		
Taxation	146 000		
Dividend	150 000	1 139 000	206 400
			1 413 400
Share Capital			
Ordinary shares of £1 each, fully paid			500 000
Share premium account			50 000
Reserves: profit and loss account			863 400
			1 413 400

The directors of the company asked their accountant to produce an estimated statement of source and application of funds for the year to 31 May 19_7, and this is shown below:

	£	£
Source of Funds		
Net profit before taxation		69 000
Adjustment for items not involving the movement of funds:		
depreciation	38 000	
profit on sale of plant (note 1)	(4 000)	34 000
Total generated from operations		103 000
Other sources		
Issue of ordinary shares (note 2)	55 000	
Proceeds from sale of plant (note 1)	24 000	79 000
Total sources		182 000
Application of funds		
Dividend paid	150 000	
Taxation paid	146 000	
Purchase of plant	30 000	326 000
Net application of funds		(144 000)
Decrease in working capital		
Decrease in stock	(105 000)	
Increase in debtors	3 000	
Increase in creditors	(60 000)	
Movement in net liquid funds:		
Change in bank balance	18 000	(144 000)

Notes:
(1) This plant cost £80 000 in 19_2.
(2) In September 19_6, 50 000 shares are to be sold to existing shareholders as a 'rights' issue at a price of £1.10 each. In January 19_7, a 'bonus' issue of one for ten will be made. The bonus shares will be 'paid up' by means of an equivalent revaluation of land and buildings.
(3) The directors will propose a dividend of £175 000 at the end of the financial year.
(4) Taxation to be provided on the profit for the year to 31 May 19_7 is estimated at £20 000.

Required:
Prepare the estimated balance sheet of Cantab Ltd. as at 31 May 19_7.
Show your workings **(21 marks)**

Advanced Level Accounting, London

11.5* (a) From the following Balance Sheets prepare a Statement of Source and Application of Funds for Year 2. (18 marks)
(b) What conclusions do you draw from your Statement of Source and Application of Funds and what assumptions have you made? (7 marks)

Balance Sheets

	Year 1	*Year 2*		*Year 1*	*Year 2*
	£	£		£	£
Share Capital (£1 shares)	140 000	192 000	*Fixed Assets*		
Revaluation Reserve	20 000	—	Plant & Equipment		
General Reserve	24 000	34 000	(at cost)	102 800	140 600
Share Premium	—	8 000	*Less* depreciation	16 800	28 600
				86 000	112 000

	Year 1	Year 2		Year 1	Year 2
	£	£		£	£
Retained Earnings	19 000	27 000			
	203 000	261 000			
8% Debentures	40 000	50 000	Premises (valuation)	120 000	120 000
Current Liabilities			*Current Assets*		
Corporation tax	27 000	32 000	Stock	88 000	122 000
Creditors	46 000	55 000	Debtors	56 000	64 000
Dividends Proposed	21 000	30 000	Bank	—	10 000
Bank overdraft	13 000	—			
	350 000	428 000		350 000	428 000

Note: During Year 2 there was a bonus issue of 20 000 Shares of £1 each. **(25 marks)**

Institute of Chartered Accountants, Foundation

11.6 (a) It is common practice for companies to produce a Statement of Source and Application of Funds (Flow of Funds Statement) to be sent to shareholders, together with the profit and loss account and balance sheet.

How does such a statement help shareholders to analyse the company's financial performance? (12 marks)

(b) In the preparation of the Statement of Source and Application of Funds, and adjustment is made for items which appear in the accounts, but do not involve the movement of funds.
(1) Give an example of such an item.
(2) Explain briefly why this adjustment is made. (8 marks)
(20 marks)

Advanced Level Accounting, London

11.7 (a) Explain why a business which makes a substantial profit in a financial year may still be short of cash funds. (7 marks)
(b) Explain the meaning and uses of funds flow analysis. (8 marks)
(c) Give an example of the format of a funds flow statement which highlights the effect on working capital. Constituent elements should be named but figures need not be shown. (10 marks)
(25 marks)

Advanced level Accounting, AEB

Solutions

11.1 (a) *Workings*

W_1 *Equipment — Net*

1 Jan. 19_3	Bal b/f	17 600	Disposal		5 200
Purchase		∴ 36 400	31 Dec. 19_3	P & L — depreciation	3 000
			31 Dec. 19_3	Bal c/f	45 800
		54 000			54 000

W_2 *Cars — Net*

1 Jan.19_3	Bal b/f	4 080	Disposal		2 010
Purchase		∴ 19 860	31 Dec. 19_3	P & L — depreciation	3 000
			31 Dec. 19_3	Bal c/f	18 930
		23 940			23 940

ANTIPODEAN ENTERPRISES

Statement of Source and Application of Funds for the year ended 31 December 19_3

	$	$	$
Source of funds			
Profit before tax (given)			25 200
Adjustment for items not involving the movement of funds:			
Depreciation		7 000	
Profit on disposal of equipment		(430)	
Loss on disposal of cars		740	7 310
Total generated from operations			32 510
Funds from other sources			
Sale of equipment (5 200 + 430)		5 630	
Sale of cars (2 010 − 740)		1 270	6 900
			39 410
Application of funds			
Purchase of equipment (W_1)		36 400	
Purchase of cars (W_2)		19 860	
Acquisition of long-term investments		8 000	
Withdrawal of capital		6 500	
Drawings by owner(s)		15 130	
Repayment of long-term loan		3 000	88 890
			(49 480)
Increase/(decrease) in working capital			
Decrease in stocks		(7 830)	
Decrease in debtors		(2 450)	
Increase in creditors		(11 100)	
Movement in net liquid funds:			
Decrease in cash and bank	(1 100)		
Increase in bank overdraft	(28 200)		
Increase in short-term investments	1 200	(28 100)	(49 480)

(b) There have been substantial additions to fixed assets. It is good practice to finance long-term assets from long-term capital or borrowing. In this case we find that capital has been *withdrawn* during the year. In addition the long-term loan, instead of being increased, has actually been reduced. The fixed assets have, in fact, been financed by draining working capital. This is unwise. It has left the businesss dangerously *short of liquid funds.* In sharp contrast to 19_2 when working capital was a healthy $26 360 it is now a negative $23 120. The business does not have sufficient liquid funds to meet all its current commitments. The owner(s) have displayed poor financial management.

In order to overcome the liquidity crisis the investments, both short-term and long-term, should perhaps be converted to cash. This would boost the cash and bank balance to 700 + 4 800 + 25 000 = $30 500.

The owner(s) should also seriously consider introducing some additional capital, particularly as the business appears to be quite profitable. (Return on capital is currently $\frac{25\ 200}{103\ 610} \times 100 = 24.3\%$.)

11.4 *Workings*

W_1

Plant — at cost

1 April 19_6	Bal b/f	612 000	Disposal		80 000
Purchase		30 000	31 May 19_7	*Bal c/f*	562 000
		642 000			642 000

W₂

			Depreciation on plant			
Disposal		60 000	1 April 19_6	Bal b/f		145 000
31 May 19_7	*Bal c/f*	∴ 123 000	31 May 19_7	P & L — depreciation		38 000
		183 000				183 000

W₃

		Plant disposal	
Plant — at cost	80 000	*Depreciation*	∴ 60 000
P & L — profit on sale	4 000	Bank	24 000
	84 000		84 000

W₄

	Share Capital £000	*Share premium £000*
Balance at 1 April 19_6	500	50
Rights issue of 50 000 shares at £1.10 each	50	5
	550	55
Bonus issue (550 000 ÷ 10)	55	—
Estimated balance at 31 May 19_7	605	55

The revaluation reserve created on the land and buildings is thus £55 000

W₅

	£
Profit and loss account balance b/f	863 400
Add estimated profit before tax	69 000
	932 400
Less estimated tax	20 000
Profits available for distribution	912 400
Less proposed dividend	175 000
Profit and loss account balance c/f	737 400

CANTAB LTD

Estimated Balance Sheet as at 31 May 19__7

	£	£	£
Fixed assets			
Land and buildings, at valuation (740 000 + 55 000)			795 000
Plant, at cost (W_1)		562 000	
Less depreciation (W_2)		123 000	439 000
			1 234 000
Current assets			
Stock (710 000 − 105 000)		605 000	
Debtors (596 000 + 3 000)		599 000	
Bank (39 400 + 18 000)		57 400	
		1 261 400	
Less Current liabilities			
Creditors (843 000 + 60 000)	903 000		
Taxation	20 000		
Dividend	175 000	1 098 000	
Working capital			163 400
Net assets			£1 397 400
Financed by:			
Share capital — ordinary shares of £1 each (W_4)			605 000
Reserves			
Share premium account (W_4)		55 000	
Profit and loss account (W_5)		737 400	847 400
Capital employed			£1 397 400

CHAPTER 12

Ratio Analysis and the Interpretation of Accounts

So far we have been concerned mainly with the role of accounting as a technique of *recording* the performance of a business and on *reporting* this to its owners. While these are important functions they are not the only ones. In practice accountants are also expected to *evaluate* performance, inform management of underlying *trends*, and give advice on how unfavourable trends can be arrested and favourable trends further encouraged.

Useful though a set of accounts is, the figures in themselves do not tell the full story of a business. A key element in analysing performance is to study relationships between key variables that may be expected to be linked to one another, such as profit to sales, and sales to net assets. The chief tool for such analysis is Ratios. A ratio is simply the relationship between two variables. While telling us something additional about a business, a ratio, if it is to have real significance, has to be compared to a yardstick to determine whether it is good or bad. This yardstick is provided by comparison to previous years, competitors (inter-firm comparison), and budgets (expected performance). A few words on each follow.

Inter-firm comparison

Consider this information:

A Ltd.	Net profit	£10 000
B Ltd.	Net profit	£10 000

If you had to buy shares in one of the companies, which would you choose? At first sight it does not seem to matter — they are making equal profits. This is not to say however that they are equally *profitable*. What is really important is not the absolute amount of profit each is making so much as the amount of profit *in relation to capital employed*. We need information on this. You are told:

A Ltd.	Capital employed	£ 50 000
B Ltd.	Capital employed	£100 000

We can now compute a measure of profitability through a ratio.

$$\text{Return on capital employed} = \frac{\text{Net profit}}{\text{Capital}} \times 100$$

$$\text{For A Ltd} \quad \frac{10\,000}{50\,000} \times 100 = 20\%$$

$$\text{B Ltd,} \quad \frac{10\,000}{100\,000} \times 100 = 10\%$$

This simple calculation shows A to be the better investment. Investors in A are earning twice as much on their money as investors in B.

Because ratios are a relationship between two variables *within the same business*, they enable comparisons to be made between businesses, even though they may be of different sizes. Such comparisons are possible even between different countries. Thus the Ford Motor Company can make a direct comparison of the return on capital of its operations in the USA with operations in Europe, since both figures are expressed in a like manner — as a percentage.

Previous years

It is also of interest to learn how a business has done compared to previous years. Thus if A Ltd. achieved a return on capital of 15% last year, shareholders will be pleased with this years 20% return and management will concentrate on those policies which brought about the improvement.

Comparison over a longer time period e.g. the past 5 years, reveals trends of the direction a business is moving. These trends can be used to *forecast* future performance, in an exercise known as Budgeting.

Budget

A third yardstick is provided by comparing actual performance to expected or budgeted performance, revealing *variances* of both under- and over-achievement. The revealing of significant unfavourable variances can help management focus on those aspects of the business in most need of attention. A consideration of budgeting, variance analysis and performance evaluation is deferred until Chapters 21 and 22.

Different parties will be interested in different aspects of a business' performance. While the owners are interested most in profitability, bankers and creditors are interested in liquidity, potential shareholders in gearing and investment ratios. For this reason ratio analysis is usually separated into profitability, liquidity, working capital management, gearing, and investment ratios. We shall look at each in turn.

Profitability

The ultimate test of profitability is the amount of profit a business is earning for every £ of capital invested in it. This return on capital, or ROCE, should be compared to other returns in the same risk category, e.g. returns achieved by other firms in the same industry, to determine adequacy. Since capital employed is always equal to net assets this ratio is also known as the *return on net assets*. The profit figure taken to determine ROCE is usually *net profit before interest and tax*. Interest payable is excluded because its level is determined by the mix of finance between equity and debt, and not by the operating profitability of the business. Taxation is excluded because the amount of tax payable is felt to be determined by factors outside management's control — the rate of tax and levels of allowances are set by government. Not all accountants agree with this definition of profit. Some argue that good management will choose that mix of finance to minimize the cost of capital to the company and will arrange their financial affairs so as to minimize the tax liability to the government. The amount of these charges should therefore be included in the determination of ROCE for a more complete picture of efficiency.

What factors make for a high ROCE? Clearly the amount of profit on sales is important. This can be expressed as $\frac{\text{Net profit}}{\text{Sales}} \times 100$. The higher the figure the better. A high profit margin will not on its own however lead to a high ROCE. The *level of sales* is also important. A business holds assets not for the sake of it but to use the assets productively, by generating sales at a profit. The relationship between sales turnover and the asset base can therefore be expected to influence the ROCE. It can be measured as the asset turnover ratio, given by $\frac{\text{Sales}}{\text{Net assets}}$

Again the higher the figure the better. ROCE is in fact a product of the net profit on sales and asset turnover ratios.

$$\text{ROCE} = \underset{\text{on sales}}{\text{Net profit percentage}} \times \underset{\text{ratio}}{\text{Asset turnover}}$$

Illustration

Information regarding a business:

	£m
Net assets	200
Sales	400
Net profit	20

$$\text{Net profit on sales} = \frac{20}{400} \times 100 = 5\%$$

$$\text{Asset turnover} = \frac{400}{200} = 2$$

The above ratios indicate that for every £1 of asset the business is generating £2 of sales, and for every £1 of sales it is earning 5 pence in profit. For every £1 of asset it is therefore earning 5 pence × 2 = 10 pence in profit. The return on net assets should therefore be 10%. Let us see if this is so.

$$\text{ROCE} = \frac{20}{200} \times 100 = 10\%$$

$$\textit{or } 5\% \times 2 = 10\%$$

An inverse relationship usually exists between profit margin and asset turnover (stemming from the economist's downward-sloping demand curve). A business which increases price to improve its profit margin will suffer a drop in the volume of sales, especially if demand is price-elastic. In such a case the improvement in the profit margin may be offset by a worsening asset turnover leaving ROCE unchanged, or possibly even causing it to decline. The art of profit-maximization is to operate at that balance between the two ratios that produce the highest overall return on net assets.

Ratios can always be further analysed to their constituent parts. The reason for a decline in ROCE can for example, be analysed into whether it was caused by a reduced profit margin or by a lower asset turnover, or both. If the cause is a reduced profit margin this can be further investigated into *its* component parts. An important determinant of the net profit margin is the *gross profit margin*, given by $\frac{\text{Gross profit}}{\text{Sales}} \times 100$. A decline would be caused by either an increase in the cost of supplies or reduction in selling price. Net profit is also a function of the level of expenses and the accountant could compute *expense ratios*, being $\frac{\text{Item of expense}}{\text{Sales}} \times 100$, to try and identify which expenses are getting out of hand. Manufacturing concerns can in addition analyse their costs of production, as $\frac{\text{Direct material}}{\text{Sales}} \times 100$, $\frac{\text{Direct labour}}{\text{Sales}} \times 100$, $\frac{\text{Direct expenses}}{\text{Sales}} \times 100$ and $\frac{\text{Production overheads}}{\text{Sales}} \times 100$.

The asset turnover ratio similarly can be further investigated into its component parts, namely $\frac{\text{Sales}}{\text{Fixed assets}}$ and $\frac{\text{Sales}}{\text{Net current assets}}$. This might reveal for example that fixed assets are being underutilized because of surplus capacity. Management may then investigate just which assets are being underutilized by analysing $\frac{\text{Sales}}{\text{Fixed assets}}$ into $\frac{\text{Sales}}{\text{Plant}}$, $\frac{\text{Sales}}{\text{Buildings}}$ and $\frac{\text{Sales}}{\text{Vehicles}}$.
The question that should be asked is 'Are we using the assets productively and can we reduce the investment in any asset while maintaining the current level of activity?' A low sales to plant ratio could be attributable to machines lying idle because the production level does not warrant their use, or to frequent machine breakdowns. A low sales to buildings ratio could be caused by inefficient arrangement and layout of a factory, warehouse or office or simply by space lying unused. The number of vehicles may also be surplus to requirements.

Where over-investment is detected the surplus should be liquidated into cash and then used profitably by investing in assets really needed by the firm or by using it to finance working capital requirements. The significance of the component parts of the sales to net current assets ratio is considered in the section on working capital management later in this chapter.

Profitability analysis can be represented diagramatically as follows:

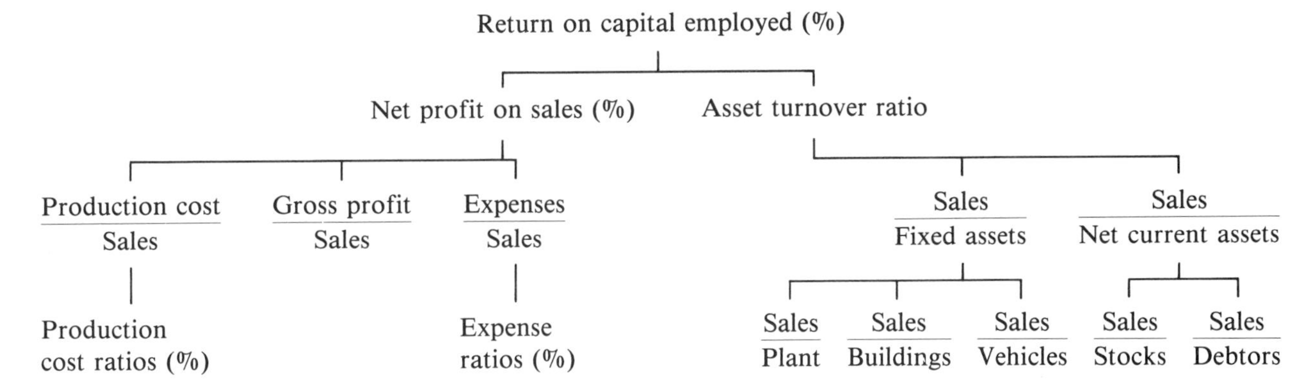

Liquidity/Solvency

These show the ability of a firm to meet commitments as they fall due. A firm should have sufficient liquid resources (cash and assets readily convertible into cash) to meet all current liabilities. Two ratios are commonly used as tests of liquidity — the *current ratio* and *acid-test ratio.*

The current ratio is simply Current assets/Current liabilities. As a general rule current assets should *always be equal* to current liabilities, a ratio of 1.5 or more assets to liabilities being considered safe. Certainly the ratio should never fall below 1. A firm whose current liabilities exceed liquid resources is not going to be popular with suppliers, bankers, and other creditors. If the ratio stays below 1 for long and creditors become increasingly impatient the firm may have to shut down — forced into closure by insolvency or bankruptcy. This is, unfortunately, not an uncommon occurrence — 7 out of every 10 new businesses close within one year of setting up. Of these, a large proportion fail not so much because of unprofitability as insolvency. A common cause of a negative working capital is *overtrading*. This is an attempt to finance too high a level of sales for the given size of business. The result is that the excessive investment in stock and debtors have to be financed by short-term credit — from suppliers and the bank. The danger of doing this is that a point may be reached when creditors are no longer prepared to support the business. The result is bankruptcy. This mistake is often made by inexperienced new businesses, the rapidly expanding small business, and those whose management pay insufficient attention to working capital. In the spate of closures during the high inflation and economic recession of the mid- to late seventies cash flow problems were as common a cause of business failure as unprofitability. It is only recently that businessmen have come to appreciate that profitability alone does not guarantee survival. Even a profitable firm can go under if it leaves itself short of liquid resources.

In businesses where stock is slow-moving it is wrong to count it as liquid assets. Consider the following balance sheet extract of Exclusive Ltd., a retailer of quality furniture.

	£000	*£000*
Current assets		
Stock		20
Debtors		6
Cash		4
		30

	£000	£000
Less Current liabilities		
Trade creditors	15	
Bank overdraft	5	20
Working capital		10

$$\text{Current ratio} = \frac{30\ 000}{20\ 000} = 1.5$$

The current ratio suggests a healthy liquidity position. However, assuming that it takes about 3 months on average for the shop to sell an expensive item of furniture should we count it as a liquid asset? No. An alternative test of liquidity is needed. This is provided by the acid-test ratio.

$$\frac{\text{Current assets — Stock}}{\text{Current liabilities}} = \frac{10\ 000}{20\ 000} = 0.5$$

This harsher but in this case more realistic test of liquidity tells us that the firm has left itself short of liquid assets. For every £1 of impending liability it has only 50 pence in liquid asset.

Simply holding stock does not guarantee quick conversion into cash and the acid-test ratio is a better test of solvency for businesses with slow-moving stock and firms suffering a slowdown in sales and being caught with a large amount of unwanted stock. As a general rule-of-thumb the acid test ratio *should not fall below 1.* In practice, however, a lot of firms operate dangerously below this level.

A technique often used in conjunction with ratios in analysing liquidity is funds flow analysis, the subject of the previous chapter.

The solvency position is determined largely by the quality of management of the working capital of a business. We look at this aspect of performance next.

Management of Working Capital

The aim here is to manage the various elements of the working capital cycle such that the minimum amount of finance is needed to sustain it. You will remember from Chapter 2 that the working capital cycle is the process of converting stocks ⟶ creditors ⟶ sales ⟶ debtors ⟶ cash ⟶ stocks ⟶ creditors ⟶ sales . . . and so on. The amount of finance needed to support the cycle is determined by

(1) the *length* of one complete cycle, and
(2) the *time-lag* between one part of the cycle and the next.

Policies should then be followed that reduce the cycle, for example giving preference to *cash customers* which reduces the cycle by the period of credit normally extended to debtors. In a lot of industries however trade is carried out on credit terms and in these cases management accepts the need to invest some amount in debtors and instead pursues policies to minimize this amount by speeding up the *debt collection period.* Stocks are not sold instantly. They are held in the warehouse or shop for a length of time before being sold. Some amount of money is then also needed to finance this idle stock. The quicker the rate of selling, the shorter is the period of stockholding and smaller the amount of capital tied up in stocks. The speed of selling can be measured by the *rate of stock turnover.* These measures of working capital management can be represented as:

Stocks ⟶ Creditors ⟶ Sales ⟶ Debtors ⟶ Cash

Rate of turnover (Stocks to Sales) — Debt collection period (Sales to Cash)

It is possible to conduct a numerical analysis of working capital management by calculating ratios for the above.

Rate of stock turnover

This indicates the number of times during one year that a batch of stock is completely sold and replaced with a fresh batch. A figure of 6 for example indicates 6 complete orders sold, meaning that each consignment was held on average for 2 months before being sold. The formula for the ratio is Cost of goods sold/Average stock. To find the exact value of average stock, stock levels would have to be recorded at the end of each trading day and added together at the end of the year, this figure then being divided by the number of trading days. Such an exercise is laborious, time-consuming, and expensive. Instead it is common to use a proxy for it by taking the *average of opening and closing stocks*. Although 'cheating' in this way does not give us the exact figure of average stock it is probably close enough not to affect the rate of turnover materially. Certainly it is the method you need to apply in examinations. All the information can be obtained from the trading account.

Illustration

	£000	*£000*
Sales		160
Less cost of goods sold		
Opening stock	15	
Purchases	130	
	145	
Less closing stock	25	120
Gross profit		40

$$\text{Rate of turnover} = \frac{120}{\frac{15 + 25}{2}} = 6$$

It is often useful to express the rate as the average number of days stocks are held before being sold. This is given by $\frac{365}{\text{Rate of turnover}}$. Thus for a business which has a rate of 9.125, stock holding period $= \frac{365}{9.125} = 40$ days.

There is no single ideal rate of turnover. It varies from firm to firm and industry to industry. Thus, while our furniture retailer might be happy with a rate of 6, this would never do for a greengrocer. He would need to replace stock every week, giving a rate of over 50. A newsagents would need a rate of 365. From a given position however, a *higher rate is preferable* since it implies an increase in selling activity, a decrease in average stockholding and hence a reduction in the amount of capital tied up in stock.

The rate of turnover can be increased simply by buying stock in smaller amounts but more frequently, thereby holding less in the warehouse at any one time. In addition to reducing the investment in stock this also incurs *lower storage and insurance costs*. The stock controller has to be careful though how far he goes down this road. If a low stock policy is taken too far there is the danger that the firm will be unable to respond to an unexpected increase in demand. Also, with no protection against interruptions from suppliers the *risk* of being caught out of stock, a *stock-out*, is increased. In addition, discounts on bulk-buying are lost. The art of stock control is to achieve the *optimum balance* between the conflicting forces calling for high and low stock levels — to hold that amount at which the total cost of stockholding, including the risk of a stock-out, is at its lowest.

Debt collection period

This measures the average number of days debtors take to pay by relating debtors at a particular date to the average value of credit sales per day. Alternatively it indicates the number of days of credit sales tied up in debtors. The formula expressed in days, is

$$\frac{\text{Trade debtors at balance sheet date}}{\text{Credit sales over the year} \div 365} \text{ or } \frac{\text{Debtors}}{\text{Credit sales}} \times 365$$

The period can be shortened by demanding quicker payment but this is often at the expense of reduced sales. The art of debt management is to achieve that balance between debtors and sales that will maximize the return on capital employed. Large firms employ specialist credit controllers to carry out this function. There are several possible causes of an unsatisfactory collection period. It could be that the procedure for chasing up slow payers is not being followed. A useful tool in this is the *aged debtors list*, which analyses debtors to the number of days each debt is outstanding. In this way the controller is alerted to those balances most in arrears. A second possible reason is that the setting of credit limits on customers have not been properly thought out. Each account in the sales ledger should then be examined and the credit limit revised downwards for the customers most in arrears. Another possible area of improvement is to review the policy on *cash discounts*. Offering larger cash discounts for quick payment should shorten the collection period, although this is at the expense of a lower profit margin.

Trade creditors

While a firm should try to give as little credit to customers as possible, it should *take* as much credit from suppliers as possible. It is useful to compute the average period of credit taken from the formula.

$$\frac{\text{Trade creditors at balance sheet date}}{\text{Credit purchases over the year}} \times 365$$

Thus, if a supplier gives 30 days to pay it is a good idea to take the full 30 days before paying. But if a cash discount is offered for quick payment the effective rate of interest on this should be computed. If it is above the rate the firm's cash is currently earning, the offer should be taken and the supplier paid early.

Cash

A final, and important, aspect of working capital is management of cash. The idea here is always to have some amount to finance day-to-day expenses such as wages, but not too much since holding cash does not earn interest and therefore incurs an opportunity cost. A formal exercise in *cash budgeting* is needed to reveal expected balances in the near future. Arrangements can then be made in advance for overdraft facilities in times when the business is expected to be short of cash and for short-term investments in times of expected cash surpluses. The nature of cash budgets and their preparation is looked at in Chapter 21, Budgeting and Budgetary Control.

Gearing

Companies finance their activities by either

(1) attracting *investment* in their equity shares, on which returns are variable depending on the level of profit
(2) *borrowing* from banks and the public by issuing debentures, on which they are committed to pay a fixed rate of interest.

The *gearing ratio* is a measure of the *proportion of the capital employed to which the company is committed to fixed return payments.* The formula is

$$\frac{\text{Long-term liabilities}}{\text{Capital employed}} \times 100$$

For the purpose of the ratio, preference shares are included under long-term liabilities since they command a fixed rate of return, though in the form of dividends and not interest.

Illustration

The following information relates to two companies.

	High Ltd	*Low Ltd*
Capital structure	*£000*	*£000*
Ordinary shares	15	60
10% Preference shares	15	—
8% Debentures	65	20
Reserves	5	20
Capital employed	100	100

The gearing ratio is given as follows:

High Ltd $\frac{80\ 000}{100\ 000} \times 100 = 80\%$

Low Ltd $\frac{20\ 000}{100\ 000} \times 100 = 20\%$

High Ltd with a large proportion of debt in its capital structure is said to be *high geared*. Low Ltd which has only limited fixed interest commitments is said to be *low geared*.

The gearing ratio is important because it affects the company's *cost of capital*, degree of *risk* in the capital structure, and *return to equity*. Borrowing is usually a cheaper source of finance than equity, not least because interest payments, being a normal business expense, are tax-deductible whereas dividends are not. Given this there is a temptation for companies to borrow heavily. Management has got to be careful however because a high proportion of debt introduces *risk* in the way the business is financed and makes it difficult for the company to raise further loans. After a certain level of borrowing is reached the benefit of cheap borrowing is more than offset by the cost in terms of increased financial risk in the capital structure, not only to lenders but also to investors (explained below). Just before this point is reached could be said to be the *optimum level of gearing* for a company. Unfortunately there is no single optimum level — this varies from firm to firm and industry to industry. The optimum cost of finance is a complex subject on which there is not unanimous agreement amongst accountants. You will meet the theoretical issues at degree and professional level.

The whole idea of a company borrowing money for say 8% is to earn a return greater than this, say 12%. The 4% profit then belongs to the owners of the company — the shareholders. It follows then that the greater the level of borrowing the higher the return to equity. In the above example, if both our companies earn 4% above the cost of borrowing, the earnings per share and return to equity will be much higher for the high geared company, High Ltd, because

(1) the *absolute* amount of profit is larger since it has borrowed more, and
(2) this larger profit is to be distributed amongst a *smaller* number of ordinary shareholders.

In bad years though, when the company makes a *loss* on borrowed funds, earning say only 6% on the 8% debentures, the earnings per share will fall more dramatically for High Ltd than Low Ltd, because

(1) the absolute amount of the loss is larger since it has borrowed more, and
(2) this larger loss is to be borne by a smaller number of shareholders.

Gearing thus works both ways. *Returns fluctuate violently for investors in high geared companies*, in line with whether return on capital employed has been above or below the cost of borrowing. For investors in low geared companies the fluctuations between good and bad years are less exagerated. This is an important consideration for a potential investor. If he wants the chance of large returns with the risk and excitement that goes with this he should buy ordinary shares in a high geared company. If he wants security he should look to a low geared company. See question 12.5.

Investment Ratios

In addition to gearing and profitability ratios *investors* will be interested in a number of additional ratios applicable to public limited companies. These include the *dividend yield*, *dividend cover*, *return on equity* and *earnings per share*. The *dividend yield* is the

$$\frac{\text{Ordinary dividend per share}}{\text{Market price per share}} \times 100$$

It represents to the shareholder the immediate return on his investment. The ratio does not include any profit attributable to equity but retained by the company. A low dividend yield does not in itself mean that a particular share is a bad investment. Dividend yield should be considered with *dividend cover* or the *pay-out ratio*. This is given by

$$\frac{\text{Profit attributable to equity}}{\text{Dividend}}$$

and shows the relationship between the maximum dividend the directors *could have declared* and what they did in fact declare. A high dividend cover implies a low dividend yield and substantial re-investment of profit in the company. This will hopefully increase future earnings. Potential shareholders may then look favourably on a low dividend yield and want to invest, to share in the future larger profits. The split of profit between dividends and retention is determined by the amount of dividends declared in the recent past (to which existing shareholders have become accustomed) and the amount of capital the company needs to finance its current and future operations. Retaining profit to finance investment is the cheapest source of finance but management has to be careful not to retain too much, as shareholders may be disappointed and sell leading to a fall in the share's market price. In addition such a policy may backfire in the future when the company needs to sell further shares.

Investment ratios which relate total equity earnings, whether they are distributed or not, to the value of the investment include the *return on equity* (ROE) and *earnings per share* (EPS).

$$\text{ROE} = \frac{\text{Profit attributable to equity}}{\text{Investment by equity}} \times 100$$

$$\text{EPS} = \frac{\text{Profit attributable to equity}}{\text{Number of ordinary shares issued}} \quad \text{(expressed as pence per share)}$$

Profit attributable to equity is given by profit after tax and interest less preference dividend (if any). These two ratios are often used by investors and potential investors in deciding whether the return on a particular company is sufficient for the level of risk taken.

A further ratio, often quoted in the financial press, is the *price-earnings ratio*. This is a measure of the relationship between earnings per share and market price.

$$\frac{\text{Market price per share}}{\text{Earnings per share}}$$

It represents the numbers of times current market price exceeds current earnings. Since market price changes everyday so does the ratio. The lower the figure the cheaper the company is as an investment in relation to its earnings potential.

Versatility

Although the above represent the more important ratios they are by no means the only ones. If one is interested in the relationship between two items not covered above he can easily 'invent' a ratio to meet his needs.

Example

Information regarding a major advertising campaign by a firm:

Increase in advertising expenditure	£10 000
Profit on resulting additional sales	£12 000

It is of interest to the firm to calculate the return obtained from the additional advertising. This can be done as:

$$\text{Return} = \frac{\text{Net benefit}}{\text{Cost}} \times 100$$

$$= \frac{£2\ 000}{£10\ 000} \times 100 = 20\%$$

Different Needs

As stated earlier in this chapter many different parties are interested in a set of accounts, and for different reasons. Potential creditors such as suppliers and banks will examine the liquidity ratios to estimate whether the business will be able to make payments as they fall due, while owners of a business are more interested in profitability. Potential shareholders are likely to be interested most in the gearing and investment ratios. A company considering a take-over bid of another company will probably conduct a detailed analysis of the potential acquisition involving *all* the ratios mentioned.

In addition, it is not only parties outside the business that are interested in a set of accounts. Insiders too are interested, that is, *management* and *workers*. In small single-product businesses, management may be content with calculating ratios for the business as a whole. In larger companies, in addition to ratios for the business as a whole, management will:

(1) in decentralized organizations, calculate ratios for each autonomous division, giving top management an idea of how each division and divisional manager is doing
(2) in group companies owning subsidiaries and related companies, calculate ratios for each company
(3) in multi-product companies, calculate ratios for each product group
(4) in multinationals, compare ratios for operations in different parts of the world.

Workers and trade union leaders will be interested in the profitability ratios and their comparison to previous years as a guide to their wage claims, and the liquidity ratios to assess the ability of the firm to meet these claims.

Limitations of Ratio Analysis

Users of ratios should be aware of the limitations of the technique to avoid the possibility of making false conclusions from them. There are several limitations:

(1) Ratios focus exclusively on proportions, completely ignoring absolute values. Because of this they are unable to reveal all significant changes in a business. This is easily illustrated with an example. The information on page 190 relates to Expansion Ltd.

	19_1	*19_2*
Net assets (capital employed)	£100 000	£200 000
Sales	£200 000	£400 000
Net profit	£ 20 000	£ 40 000
Net profit on sales	10%	10%
Asset turnover ratio	2	2
ROCE	20%	20%

Looking at the absolute figures it is clear that 19_2 was a year of considerable growth. The business experienced a large increase in the amount of capital employed. This was used to generate additional sales, producing increased profits. In contrast, the three *ratios* show no change. Because the variables have increased in the same proportion (each has doubled) the change has not shown up in the ratios.

(2) Without a proper understanding of the constituent elements of a ratio, a false picture may be obtained. A common miconception is that the profit margin and ROCE are the same. An improvement in ROCE is then taken to mean an increase in the profit margin. However, this need not be so. In fact, the profit margin may actually decline. Consider the following change for Expansion Ltd.

	19_1	19_2
Net profit on sales	10%	8%
Asset turnovers	2	3
ROCE	20%	24%

The improved return on capital, from 20% to 24% was caused by a *lower* profit margin. Price reductions boosted sales, leading to a higher asset turnover ratio. This has *more than offset* the reduced profit margin, and improved overall ROCE.

(3) The novice may also be misled by a ratio where changes take place in its constituent elements, but because they are in opposite directions and compensate one another, do not show up in the ratio. Expansion Ltd again:

	19_1	19_2
Net profit on sales	10%	5%
Asset turnover	2	4
ROCE	20%	20%

The unchanged ROCE from 19_1 to 19_2 hides the fact that a significant change has taken place in selling strategy — from high margins and moderate sales in 19_1 to low margins and volume sales in 19_2.

(4) While ratio analysis may be usefully conducted to analyse changes in a firm from one year to another, *inter-firm comparisons* should be made with caution. Only if the two firms follow identical accounting policies in subjective areas like depreciation and stock valuation will the comparison have any meaning.

(5) Ratios do not take into account the fact that the value of money changes with time. Comparison with previous years should then be made with care. The user should have an appreciation of the effect of inflation on a set of accounts.

(6) Accounts record only those aspects of a business which can be expressed in money terms. Calculating ratios from such accounts will therefore not give a complete picture of the business such as the atmosphere at the place of work, state of industrial relations and amount of goodwill.

For the above reasons ratios should be regarded only as *broad indicators* bringing to attention those aspects of a business that need further investigation. However they do not raise *all* the questions that need asking. In addition they do not provide answers to the questions raised — this has to be done by management and accountants.

Examination Questions

Examination questions on this topic are either
(1) closed, asking you to calculate a number of specific ratios followed by their interpretation, or
(2) open-ended, asking you to compare two businesses or the same business over time, in general terms.

The second type of question is probably more difficult since *you* have to decide which ratio to use. In this try and structure your answer by first stating that a business may be evaluated from several different standpoints depending on the user, then evaluate it from each standpoint — profitability, liquidity, and so on.

If a question requires you to analyse or interpret a set of accounts do just that. Do not stop at a mere calculation of the ratios. Comment on what the figures or change in figures *mean*, what could have brought them about and what management should *do* about them. This is proper analysis. Without it the answer is incomplete.

Questions

12.1* Lemon Ltd. and Pear Ltd. are retailers trading in similar goods, and situated in the same area. Their summarized Revenue Accounts and Balance Sheets relating to the last financial year are as follows:

Revenue Accounts

	Lemon	*Pear*		*Lemon*	*Pear*
	£000	*£000*		*£000*	*£000*
Opening Stock	30	10	Sales	200	200
Purchases	144	152	Closing Stock	36	8
Overhead Costs	46	31			
Net Profit	16	15			
	236	208		236	208

Balance Sheets

	Lemon	*Pear*		*Lemon*	*Pear*
	£000	*£000*		*£000*	*£000*
Issued Share Capital	100	100	Fixed Assets	128	120
Retained Profits	80	20	Stock	36	8
Bank Overdraft	—	2	Debtors	30	19
Trade Creditors	26	25	Bank	12	—
	206	147		206	147

Required:
(a) Calculate the following accounting ratios for both companies.
   (i) Current Ratio
   (ii) Liquidity (acid test) Ratio
   (iii) Rate of Stock Turnover
   (iv) Gross Profit Percentage of Sales
   (v) Net Profit Percentage of Sales
   (vi) Return on Capital Employed. (12 marks)
(b) As a customer using these two shops what differences would you expect to find between them? (6 marks)
(18 marks)

London Chamber of Commerce and Industry, Higher

12.2 John Smith has just completed his first year in business as a sole trader and has received the following draft set of accounts from his accountant.

JOHN SMITH

Trading and profit and loss account for year ended 31 October 19_4

	£	£
Sales		50 000
less: Cost of sales		32 000
Gross profit		18 000
less: General expenses	3 000	
Wages	4 000	
Rent and rates	5 000	
Depreciation	2 000	14 000
Net profit		4 000

Balance Sheet as at 31 October 19_4

	£	£	£
Fixed Assets			
Fixtures at cost		7 500	
less Depreciation		500	7 000
Motor van at cost		4 500	
less Depreciation		1 500	3 000
			10 000
Current Assets			
Stock	8 000		
Debtors	5 000		
Cash	6 000	19 000	
less: Current Liabilities			
Creditors		3 000	16 000
			26 000
Capital			
Opening balance		32 000	
plus: Net profit	4 000		
less: Drawings	10 000	(6 000)	26 000

John is anxious to compare his results with other businesses and a friend has given him the following information concerning Quicksale Ltd., a large retailer selling similar goods to John with several branches in the locality.

QUICKSALE LTD.

Trading and profit and loss account for year ended 31 October 19_4

	£	£
Sales		1 500 000
less: Cost of sales		1 350 000
Gross profit		150 000
less: General expenses	12 000	
Lease of motor vehicles	10 000	
Wages and salaries	35 000	
Rates	18 000	
Depreciation	15 000	90 000
Net profit		60 000

Balance Sheet as at 31 October 19_4

	£	£	£
Fixed Assets			
Premises at cost		210 000	
less Depreciation		35 000	175 000
Fixtures at cost		35 000	
less Depreciation		10 000	25 000
			200 000
Current Assets			
Stock	45 000		
Cash	50 000	95 000	
less: Current Liabilities			
Creditors		55 000	40 000
			240 000
Capital			
Called up share capital			150 000
Profit and loss account			90 000
			240 000

Required:

(a) Write a report comparing the performance of J. Smith and Quicksale Ltd. for the year ended 31 October 19_4, using relevant accounting ratios. (15 marks)

(b) Comment on the usefulness to J. Smith of the comparison between his business and Quicksale Ltd. (5 marks)

Advanced level Accounting, AEB **(20 marks)**

12.3 Martha is the accountant of a trading business. During the past year she produced interim accounts for the six months ended 30 November 19_5, and draft final accounts for the year ended 31 May 19_6, as follows:

	Interim Accounts	*Draft Final Accounts*
	£	£
Sales (all on credit terms)	140 000	336 000
Cost of sales (note 1)	42 000	112 000
Gross profit	98 000	224 000
Less expenses	56 000	168 000
Net profit	42 000	56 000
Fixed assets	70 000	63 000
Current assets (note 2)	42 000	71 000
Current liabilities (note 3)	(22 000)	(30 000)
	90 000	104 000
Share capital	30 000	30 000
Retained earnings	60 000	74 000
	90 000	104 000

Notes

(1) Average stock was £14 000 during the first six months.

(2) Current assets were:

	30 November 19_5	*31 May 19_6*
	£	£
Stock	16 000	25 000
Debtors	24 000	28 000
Bank	2 000	18 000
	42 000	71 000

(3) Current liabilities consisted entirely of trade creditors.

Martha informs you that the business leased additional premises from 1 December 19_5, and that sales arising therefrom totalled £70 000 for the six months to 31 May 19_6, with an average mark-up on cost prices of 150% being made on those goods.

Expenses relating to these additional premises totalled £21 000 for the period. Two-fifths of the closing stock of the business was located at these premises.

Prepare a report, using appropriate accounting ratios, to explain the changes in the financial situation of the business during the year ended 31 May 19_6.

(15 marks)

Advanced level Accounting, London

12.4 Bradwich PLC is a medium sized engineering company whose shares are listed on a major Stock Exchange.

It has recently applied to its bankers for a 7 year loan of £500 000 to finance a modernization and expansion programme.

Mr Whitehall, a recently retired civil servant, is contemplating investing £10 000 of his lump sum pension in the company's ordinary shares in order to provide both an income during his retirement and a legacy to his grandchildren after his death.

The bank and Mr Whitehall have each acquired copies of the company's most recent annual report and accounts.

Required:

(a) State, separately for each of the two parties, those aspects of the company's performance and financial position which would be of particular interest and relevance to their respective interests. (8 marks)

(b) State, separately for each of the two parties, the formula of four ratios which would assist in measuring or assessing the matters raised in your answer to (a).

(8 marks)
(16 marks)

Chartered Association of Certified Accountants

12.5 Three companies have the capital structures shown below.

Company	*A*	*B*	*C*
	£000	*£000*	*£000*
Ordinary shares	600	400	50
12% Debentures	—	200	550
	600	600	600

The return on capital employed was 20 per cent for each firm in 19_4, and in 19_5 was 10 per cent. Corporation tax in both years was assumed to be 55 per cent, and debenture interest is an allowable expense against corporation tax.

(a) Calculate the percentage return on the shareholders' capital for each company for 19_4 and 19_5. Assume that all profits are distributed.

(17 marks)

(b) Use your answer to explain the merits and the dangers of high gearing.

(8 marks)
(25 marks)

Advanced Level Accounting, London

12.6* The following information relates to two businesses in the same line of business for the year ended 30 April 19_4:

A. Fresco's Business £	£		*B. Pick's Business* £	£
	420 000	Sales	250 000	
	50 000	Average stock at cost	80 000	
	16 000	Drawings for the year	21 500	
	15 000	Selling and administration expenses	25 000	
	20%	Mark-up on cost	25%	
		Balance Sheets as at 30 April 19_4		
		Fixed assets		
	—	Land and buildings (At cost)	100 000	
	60 000	Plant and machinery (Net book value)	55 000	
	25 000	Motor vehicles (Net book value)	28 000	
	85 000			183 000
		Current assets		
30 000		Stock	60 000	
70 000		Trade debtors	35 000	
20 000		Balance at bank	—	
5 000	125 000	Cash	1 500	96 500
	210 000			279 500
		Financed by:		
	181 000	Capital account		203 500
		Current liabilities		
28 000		Trade creditors	46 000	
1 000		Accrued expenses	2 000	
—	29 000	Bank overdraft	28 000	76 000
	210 000			279 500

Notes:

(1) During the year Fresco had bought a motor vehicle for private use but it had been treated as a business vehicle. The cost of the vehicle was £10 000 and it had been depreciated by £2 500.

(2) Pick's works manager advised him that stock bought on 1 September 19_3 for £10 000, and included in the closing stock, was redundant and of no value. Pick decided to write off the stock; no entries had yet been made.

(3) Fresco owned the business's land and buildings but they had not previously been brought into account. His accountant advised him to record them in the business's books on a retrospective basis. The land and buildings were valued at £118 000 on 1 May 19_3.

N.B. Ignore depreciation on land and buildings.

Required:

(a) After making all the necessary adjustments for each separate business calculate:
  (i) the rate of stock turnover;
  (ii) the gross profit/sales and the net profit/sales ratios;
  (iii) the working capital ratio;
  (iv) the return on proprietor's capital employed calculated on the adjusted opening capital. (14 marks)

(b) As a potential buyer of one of the businesses, draft a short report indicating which business appears to be the more attractive investment. Include in your report any reservations you may have and use the results of your calculations to support your argument. (11 marks)

(25 marks)

Advanced Level Accounting, AEB

12.7* The directors of Dennis Limited cannot understand why, when shareholders' funds and sales show an increase over the previous year, net profit has declined. Also, they cannot understand why, even though profits have been made during the year, and the property revalued, there has been a substantial fall in the bank balance to a point where the company is now overdrawn as never before.

The company's accounts for 19_3, together with the figures for 19_2, are given below.

Profit statement for the year ended 31 December

	19_3	19_2
	£	£
Sales	780 000	650 000
Stock, 1 January	22 000	18 000
Purchases	647 800	524 000
	669 800	542 000
Less: Stock, 31 December	38 000	22 000
Cost of sales	631 800	520 000
Gross profit	148 200	130 000
Administrative expenses	93 600	71 500
Distribution costs	46 800	39 000
	140 400	110 500
Net profit for the year	7 800	19 500
Profit and loss account brought forward	9 500	2 500
	17 300	22 000
Transfer to general reserve		12 500
Profit and loss account carried forward	£17 300	£9 500

Balance Sheet at 31 December

	19_3		*19_2*	
	£	£	£	£
Fixed assets:				
Land and buildings — cost				60 000
valuation		80 000		
Plant and machinery — cost	45 000		40 000	
depreciation	25 000		20 000	
		20 000		20 000
		100 000		80 000
Current assets:				
Stock		38 000		22 000
Debtors		120 000		75 000
Bank		—		13 000
		158 000		110 000
Current liabilities:				
Trade creditors	62 500		60 500	
Bank overdraft	38 200		—	
		100 700		60 500
		57 300		49 500
		£157 300		£129 500
Capital and Reserves:				
Ordinary shares		120 000		100 000
Surplus arising on revaluation of land and buildings		20 000		—
General reserve		—		20 000
Retained profits		17 300		9 500
		£157 300		£129 500

Additional information:

(1) On 1 January 19_3 land and buildings were revalued at £80 000 — which had been the market value of this asset for the past 3 years.

(2) On 1 February 19_3 the company made a bonus issue of one ordinary share for each five held.

(3) All purchases and sales were credit transactions.

(4) During the year plant and machinery which had cost £10 000 (written down value £3 000) was sold for £1 500.

Required:

Prepare a report for the directors of Dennis Limited, which must contain:

(a) not more than eight ratios for comparing the year ended 31 December 19_3, with the year ended 31 December 19_2, together with brief comments about the significance of the information drawn from such ratios.

(b) a source and application of funds statement to illustrate the change in the bank balance during 19_3

Ignore taxation.

(25 marks)

Institute of Chartered Accountants, Foundation

12.8 Company financial statements, including profit and loss accounts, balance sheets and statements of source and application of funds, are used by a variety of individuals and institutions for a wide variety of purposes.

Required:

Specify six different types of users of financial statements and explain in each case the aspects of performance or position in which they are interested.

(16 marks)

Chartered Association of Certified Accountants

12.9 (a) Describe the way in which you would attempt to assess the short-term liquidity and financial stability of a company from its balance sheet. Illustrate your answer with quantitative examples and state the reservations you would have regarding your conclusions. (15 marks)

(b) What is the significance of the 'return on capital employed' ratio as an indication of the profitability of a business? What are the principal measurement problems encountered in computing this ratio from conventionally produced accounts? (10 marks)

(25 marks)

Advanced Level Accounting, AEB

12.10 (a) 'If a balance sheet shows a negative working capital position (i.e. current liabilities exceed current assets) then the business is certain to be in financial difficulties'.
Comment on this statement. (12 marks)

(b) A company has a current ratio of 1.5:1 whereas its quick assets ratio (acid test) is calculated at 0.8:1. What do these figures indicate about the composition and adequacy of the working capital? (8 marks)

(20 marks)

Advanced Level Accounting, London

12.11 Why is it important for a firm to control its working capital? How might a firm endeavour to exercise such control?

(20 marks)

Advanced Level Accounting, London

12.12 To what extent is ratio analysis useful as a tool of evaluating the performance of:

(a) a business from one year to another?

(b) different businesses?

(20 marks)

Author's Question

Solutions

12.2 (a) Before we can write the report it is necessary to make a few computations.

	John Smith *£ in 000s*	*Quicksale Ltd* *£ in 000s*
Profitability ratios		
Return on capital employed	$\frac{4}{26} \times 100 = 15.38\%$	$\frac{60}{240} \times 100 = 25\%$
Net profit percentage on sales	$\frac{4}{50} \times 100 = 8\%$	$\frac{60}{1500} \times 100 = 4\%$
Asset turnover	$\frac{50}{26} = 1.92$ times	$\frac{1500}{240} = 6.25$ times
Gross profit percentage on sales	$\frac{18}{50} \times 100 = 36\%$	$\frac{150}{1500} \times 100 = 10\%$
Liquidity ratios		
Current ratio	$\frac{19}{3} = 6.33$	$\frac{95}{55} = 1.73$
Acid test ratio	$\frac{11}{3} = 3.67$	$\frac{50}{55} = 0.91$
Working capital ratios		
Rate of stock turnover	$\frac{32}{8} = 4$ times	$\frac{1350}{45} = 30$ times
Average number of days stock held	$\frac{365}{4} = 91$ days	$\frac{365}{30} = 12$ days

Report comparing John Smith with Quicksale Ltd. for the year ended 31 October 19_4

It is convenient to divide the report in two — firstly in terms of profitability, then liquidity and working capital management.

Profitability

Smith's net profit on sales is twice that of Quicksale Ltd. This would suggest that prices are higher. Perhaps because of this, Quicksale is achieving a greater volume of sales in relation to net assets (6.25 times > 1.92 times) and a higher rate of turnover of goods (30 times > 4 times). The net result is that Quicksale is achieving a better return on net assets than Smith (25% > 15.38%). The comparison reveals different selling strategies in the two businesses — Quicksale is happy to work on low margins in order to gain volume sales while Smith is more concerned with the amount of profit on each sale, sacrificing his competitive position in terms of price to the customer. It may be wise for Smith to review his pricing policy.

Liquidity and working capital management

Neither business can be said to be suffering from liquidity problems. If anything Smith has *too much* working capital. Simply holding a lot of current assets does not yield a return and Smith should consider investing some of it in a profitable use.

As mentioned earlier Smith is holding stock for much longer than Quicksale — 3 months compared to a mere 12 days. Given that the two shops are selling similar goods this is worrying.

Quicksale works on a cash basis not allowing any credit. Smith on the other hand *is* allowing credit. Being a smaller shop it is able to offer this personal service, probably on an informal basis to regular customers.

(b) Smith just happened to acquire Quicksale Ltd's accounts through a friend of his and although the two businesses are in the same trade Smith must not read too much into a direct comparison, for four reasons:

(i) the two businesses are of significantly different *sizes*

(ii) they are *organized* differently, Quicksale Ltd being a company operating several shops while Smith is a sole trader in just one shop

(iii) Smith has *just set up* while Quicksale is a well-established business

(iv) Smith does not know what policies Quicksale has adopted in subjective areas such as depreciation and stock valuation. If they are different from Smith's we would not be comparing like with like.

To make a better comparison Smith would have to get access to a set of accounts of a similar sized retailer following identical accounting policies, preferably still in the process of establishing itself. Unfortunately, he will not find this easy since sole traders do not publish their accounts.

12.3 *Report on Martha's trading business*

It is useful to compare the first half performance of the original business to the second half performance of the original business plus additional activity resulting from the additional premises. To do this we have to *adjust* the second half's result to eliminate the business resulting from the additional premises.

All calculations are in £000.

Profitability ratios

	First half	*Second half*	*Additional business*
Gross profit on sales	$\frac{98}{140} \times 100 = 70\%$	$\frac{224 - 98 - 42}{336 - 140 - 70} \times 100 = \frac{84}{126} = 66\frac{2}{3}\%$	$\frac{42^*}{70} \times 100 = 60\%$ $^*70 \times \frac{150}{250} = 42$
Net profit on sales	$\frac{42}{140} \times 100 = 30\%$	$\frac{56 - 42 - 21}{336 - 140 - 70} \times 100 = \frac{(7)}{126} = \text{Loss}$	$\frac{42 - 21}{70} \times 100 = 30\%$

The gross profit percentage on sales seems very high, and remains so right throughout the year. While the rate of net profit for the first half and additional business is a healthy 30%, the second half of the year was run at a loss. It would be useful to construct expense ratios.

	First half	*Second half*	*Additional business*
Expense to sales ratio	$\frac{56}{140} \times 100 = 40\%$	$\frac{168 - 56 - 21}{126} \times 100 = \frac{91}{126} = 72\%$	$\frac{21}{70} \times 100 = 30\%$

The reason for the loss in the second half of the year was a sharp increase in expenses. Martha needs to calculate *individual ratios* for each item of expenditure to find the precise reason for the increase.

Note that the net profit on the additional business matches the high 30% of the first half, despite the lower gross profit margin. This is because expenses are lower — only 30% of sales compared to 40% in the first half.

	First half	*Second half*	*Additional business*
Rate of stock turnover	$\frac{42}{14} = 3$	$\frac{112 - 42 - 28}{\frac{16 + 15}{2}} = \frac{42}{15.5} = 2.7$	$\frac{28^*}{25 \times \frac{2}{5}} = \frac{28}{10} = 2.8$ $^*70 \times \frac{100}{250} = 28$
Average number of days stock held	$\frac{365}{3} = 122$ days	$\frac{365}{2.7} = 135$ days	$\frac{365}{2.8} = 130$ days

Stock is being held for a very long time before being sold. Figures for the industry norm would be useful. There was a slowing-down in the rate of turnover of the original business in the second half of the year.

We can also comment on the liquidity position in the first and second halves of the year.

	First half	*Second half*
Acid-test (quick) ratio	$\frac{26}{22} = 1.18$	$\frac{46}{30} = 1.53$

Stock is excluded from current assets since they were held for too long to be considered liquid. The second half of the year saw an improvement in the liquidity position. This was largely due to debts being collected sooner (by 5 days).

	First half	*Second half*
Average debt Collection period	$\frac{24}{140} \times 183 = 31$ days	$\frac{28}{336 - 140} \times 182 = 26$ days

Conclusion
The second half of the year shows a *deterioration* in the financial situation of the original business. This is worrying. Corrective action needs to be taken quickly in respect of the level of expenses and the rate of selling. The business resulting from the additional premises seems to be healthy, and generating a high rate of profit.

12.5 (a)

	Company		
	A *£000*	*B* *£000*	*C* *£000*
19_4			
Net profit (600 × 20%)	120	120	120
Debenture interest (B 200 × 12%)	—	24	
(C 550 × 12%)			66
	120	96	54
Corporation tax at 55%	66	52.8	29.7
Profit attributable to equity	54	43.2	24.3
Return on equity	$\frac{54}{600} \times 100 = 9\%$	$\frac{43.2}{400} \times 100 = 10.8\%$	$\frac{24.3}{50} \times 100 = 48.6\%$
19_5			
Net profit (600 × 10%)	60	60	60
Debenture interest (B 200 × 12%)	—	24	—
(C 550 × 12%)	—	—	66
	60	36	(6)

Corporation tax at 55%	33	19.8	—
Profit attributable to equity	27	16.2	—
Return on equity	$\frac{27}{600} \times 100$	$\frac{16.2}{400} \times 100$	$\frac{0}{50} \times 100$
	= 4.5%	= 4%	= 0%

(b) The figures illustrate the benefit of high gearing to shareholders when a profit is made on borrowed funds. In 19_4, when the return on capital employed is higher than the cost of borrowing, the shareholders in company C, the high geared company, earn by far the highest percentage return on their investment. For why this should be so, see text.

In 19_5, when return on capital is *less* than cost of borrowing, the opposite is true. The shareholders in C earn nothing. In contrast those in A, the low geared company, are not as badly affected. Again, for the reason for this, see text.

PART II
Cost Accounting

CHAPTER 13
Manufacturing Accounts

Accounting for manufacturing businesses is more complicated than for trading organizations because in addition to the buying and selling functions of the warehouse and offices the manufacturing function of the factory also has to be accounted for. This is done in the *Manufacturing Account*, which is a historic cost statement of all the costs incurred in production. Its purpose is to determine production cost.

Manufacturing accounts are a good starting point to our study of cost accounting because it is the main link between financial accounting and costing. The financial accountant is interested in the manufacturing account because it forms part of his year-end income statement, the cost acountant because it reveals the amounts of the various costs the factory has incurred over the past financial year.

Basic Layout

There are many costs involved in manufacture and the account lists these by type — in a particular order. A distinction is made between *direct costs* and *indirect costs.* Direct costs are those costs which can be attributed to individual units of production whereas indirect costs are overheads which cannot be traced to particular units. For example, the amount of wood used in the manufacture of a table is a direct cost. So is the labour cost of a machine operator since the amount of his wages embodied in each table can be ascertained by multiplying the amount of time spent by his wage rate. In contrast, labour of the factory supervisor or cleaner is indirect since their work covers *all* machines and *all* units of tables generally, making it difficult to allocate their cost to individual units.

Direct costs may be either direct material, direct labour, or direct expenses (such as salesmen's commission or royalty payable on units sold). The sum of direct costs gives us what is called *prime cost.* Adding indirect costs to this gives production cost. To arrive at total cost we need to add selling and distribution costs and administration expenses.

Statement of Costs

	£	£
Direct material		4
Direct labour		5
Direct expenses		1
Prime cost		10
Indirect factory overheads		5
Production cost		15
Selling and distribution cost	3	
Administration expenses	2	5
Total cost		20

The above is the basis of the layout of the manufacturing account. All that needs to be included is revenue from sales. Examination questions usually ask for the trading and profit and loss account to be prepared after the manufacturing account. In some questions a balance sheet is also asked for.

These three elements of the income statement can conveniently be regarded as:

Account	*Place*	*Activity*	*Costs*
Manufacturing account	Factory	Production	Production costs
Trading account	Warehouse	Buying and selling	Selling and distribution costs
Profit and loss account	Office	Administration	Administration expenses

Let us now look at a pro-forma of the income statement of a manufacturer.

Manufacturing, Trading, and Profit and Loss Account (Pro-forma)

	£	£	£
Raw materials			
Opening stock			x
Purchases			x
Carriage inwards			x
			x
Less closing stock			(x)
Cost of materials consumed			x
Manufacturing wages			x
Royalties			x
Prime cost			x
Factory overhead expenses			
Indirect labour		x	
Power		x	
Factory rent and rates		x	
Factory light and heat		x	
Depreciation of plant and machinery		x	x
			x
Add opening stock, work-in-progress			x
			x
Less closing stock, work-in-progress			(x)
Factory cost of finished production c/d			x
Sales			x
Less cost of goods sold			
Opening stock, finished goods		x	
Factory cost of finished production b/d		x	
		x	
Less closing stock, finished goods		(x)	x
Gross (warehouse) profit			x
Discounts received			x
			x
Selling and distribution costs			
Carriage outwards	x		
Depreciation on delivery vans	x		
Advertising	x		
Salesmen's salaries	x	x	
Administration expenses			
Office rent and rates	x		
Office light and heat	x		
General expenses	x		
Administrative salaries	x	x	
Financial costs			
Bank charges	x		
Interest payable	x	x	(x)
Net profit			£x

Points to Note:

(1) Whereas a trading firm has stocks of only finished goods, a manufacturing concern has 3 types of stock — raw materials, work-in-progress (representing partly-completed goods), and finished goods.

(2) Costs of production (direct costs plus share of overheads) are initially accumulated in a *work-in-progress account,* which is an *asset* account. On completion they are transferred to a finished goods account. At this point the costs of production embodied in them are still regarded as an asset. When they are sold they are expensed to the sales account, and written off at the year-end to trading account. Any stocks remaining at the year-end are shown in the balance sheet as a current asset.

(3) Cost of materials consumed is found by applying the *accruals concept* by adding material stocks bought last year but used this and subtracting closing stock, bought this year but not yet used.

(4) Since only goods *completed* are transferred to the warehouse it is necessary to make an adjustment for opening and closing works-in-progress.

(5) The year-end stock of finished goods is valued at total manufacturing cost i.e. it includes a share of factory overheads. In Chapter 19 we shall see that there is controversy about whether this should be done — in the Absorption v. Marginal costing debate.

(6) The factory and office share some common expenses, such as rent and rates, light and heat. These are *apportioned* on some logical basis such as area and wattage. Apportionment of overheads is considered in more detail in Chapter 16, Overhead Absorption Costing. Questions usually disclose the total of the expense in the trial balance. Instructions on the split are then given in the additional notes.

Factory Profit

Some firms charge out goods from factory to warehouse at an amount in *excess* of production cost. This is to give some credit to the efforts of the factory workforce and managers, at the same time charging the warehouse a more realistic amount for the goods it receives — after all, if it had to buy from outside it would have to pay more than just manufacturing cost. This factory profit is also known as *profit loading.*

The basic income statement above needs a few additional entries when this happens. Production costs of goods completed is no longer the last item on the manufacturing account. To this we have to add the profit loading to arrive at transfer price to the warehouse (trading account).

Since a business cannot recognize profit until a sale is made and goods delivered to the customer (the *realization concept*) we have a problem with year-end closing stock of finished goods since they include an element for factory profit. The profit has not yet been realized, so it is necessary to *reduce* the value of the stock by the amount of factory profit credited to it. This reduced value then appears in the balance sheet. The double-entry, in the first year of trading, is

Dr P & L

Cr Provision for unrealized profit.

If, in subsequent years, an *increase* is needed the double-entry is

Dr P & L

Cr Provision (with the increase)

If. however, a *decrease* is needed because closing stock is less than opening stock, the opposite entry is made

Dr Provision (with the decrease)

Cr P & L

This adjustment is shown at the end of the P & L account, as 'provision for unrealized profit'.

Illustration

The following information relates to the first two years of operations of Hurley Ltd.

Year ended	31.12._1	31.12._2
	£	£
Sales	15 000	19 000
Factory cost of finished production	10 000	12 000
Opening stock, finished goods	—	1 500
Closing stock, finished goods	1 500	1 100
Selling and distribution costs	800	900
Administration expenses	700	700

It is company policy to charge goods to the warehouse at factory cost + 25%.

Prepare, for both years:

(a) the ledger account — provision for unrealized profit

(b) the Trading and Profit and loss account

Answer

(a) *Provision for unrealised profit*

		£			£
31.12._1	Bal c/d	300	31.12._1	P & L (W_1)	300
31.12._2	P & L	∴ 80	1.1._2	Bal b/d	300
31.12._2	Bal c/d (W_2)	220			
		300			300

Workings

W_1 Provision 31.12._1 = £1 500 × $\frac{25}{125}$ or $\frac{1}{5}$ = 300

Be Careful. The provision is *not* £1 500 × 25%. If you are not sure why, see the mark-up margin rule in Chapter 5, Incomplete Records.

W_2 Provision 31.12._1 = £1 100 × $\frac{1}{5}$ = 220

(Note the similarity of this account with other provision accounts such as depreciation and doubtful debts.)

(b) HURLEY LTD

Trading and Profit and Loss Account for the years ended

	31.12._1		31.12._2	
	£	£	£	£
Sales		15 000		19 000
Less cost of goods sold				
Opening stock	—		1 500	
Factory cost + 25% mark-up b/f	12 500		15 000	
	12 500		16 500	
Less closing stock	1 500	11 000	1 100	15 400
Gross (warehouse) profit		4 000		3 600
Selling and distribution costs	800		900	
Administration expenses	700	1 500	700	1 600
		2 500		2 000
Provision for unrealized profit				
increase in		(300)		
decrease in				80
Net profit		£2 200		£2 080

An increase in the provision *reduces* profit, and vice-versa.

Bookkeeping Aspects of Costing

The bookkeeping entries necessary to prepare the year-end cost and income statements may be kept either:

(1) in a Cost Ledger separate from the financial accounts. Under this *interlocking system* it is possible to prepare a separate Costing Profit and Loss Account and necessary to reconcile the cost accounts to the financial accounts.

(2) with the financial ledgers. Under this *integrated system* it is not possible to prepare a separate Costing Profit and Loss Account and not necessary to reconcile the cost accounts to the financial accounts.

Integrated and interlocking accounts are not in the syllabus of most examinations at this level. If you are a student of the Chartered Association of Certified Accountants, Chartered Institute of Management Accountants, or Association of Accounting Technicians Final, you will need to refer to your course material or another book for coverage of this topic.

Questions

13.1 A company manufacturers and retails clothing.

You are required to group the costs which are listed below and numbered 1 to 20 into the following classifications (each cost is intended to belong to only one classification):

(i) direct materials
(ii) direct labour
(iii) direct expenses
(iv) indirect production overhead
(v) research and development costs
(vi) selling and distribution cost
(vii) administration costs
(viii) finance costs

1. lubricant for sewing machines
2. floppy disks for general office computer
3. maintenance contract for general office photocopying machine
4. telephone rental plus metered calls
5. interest on bank overdraft
6. Performing Rights Society charge for music broadcast throughout the factory
7. market research undertaken prior to a new product launch
8. wages of security guards for factory
9. carriage on purchases of basic raw material
10. royalty payable on number of units of product XY produced
11. road fund licences for delivery vehicles
12. parcels sent to customers
13. cost of advertising products on television
14. audit fees
15. chief accountant's salary
16. wages of operatives in the Cutting Department
17. cost of painting advertising slogans on delivery vans
18. wages of storekeepers in materials store
19. wages of fork lift truck drivers who handle raw materials
20. developing a new product in the laboratory

(10 marks)

Chartered Institute of Management Accountants

13.2* The following trial balance was extracted from the books of Bashmetal Limited, a manufacturing company, at 31 October 19_5:

	£	£
Share Capital (Authorised and Issued)		
Ordinary shares of 25p each		60 000
Profit and Loss Account, 1 November 19_4		18 550
Share Premium Account		5 000
6% Debentures		20 000
Debtors and Creditors	64 947	20 260
Opening Stocks: Raw materials	18 260	
Work-in-progress	12 480	
Finished goods	18 060	
Bank	38 400	
Factory buildings	42 000	
Plant and machinery	28 420	
Fixtures and fittings	9 600	
Provision for depreciation:		
Factory buildings		4 200
Plant and machinery		17 052
Fixtures and fittings		3 840
Production wages	71 940	
Raw materials purchased	49 770	
Bad debts written off	460	
Carriage inwards	190	
Carriage outwards	2 840	
Non-productive factory labour	21 450	
Light, heat and power	2 200	
Rent, rates and insurance	3 650	
Directors' salaries	41 205	
Audit fee	1 600	
Sales		300 000
Bank charges	1 400	
Advertising	1 200	
Debenture interest paid	600	
Administration expenses	18 230	
	448 902	448 902

Notes:

(1) Closing stocks are valued as follows:

	£
Raw materials	19 460
Work-in-progress	14 444
Finished goods	24 215

(2) Factory buildings are depreciated at 2% per annum. All other fixed assets are depreciated at 20% of cost.

(3) There were accruals at 31 October 19_5 as follows:

Advertising	£150
Carriage inwards	£90

(4) £150 of the rent, rates and insurance was paid in advance at 31 October 19_5.

(5) The rent, rates and insurance is to be split in the proportion $\frac{3}{5}$ factory, $\frac{2}{5}$ administration, and the light, heat and power is apportioned $\frac{1}{2}$ factory, $\frac{1}{4}$ administration and $\frac{1}{4}$ selling expenses.

(6) A Corporation tax provision of £30 000 is to be made, and the directors propose a dividend of 20%.

Required:
(a) Prepare the manufacturing, trading and profit and loss accounts of Bashmetal Limited for the year ended 31 October 19_5 (including an appropriation account). (22 marks)
(b) Prepare the balance sheet of the company as at 31 October 19_5. (8 marks)
Note: The above accounts and balance sheet need not be in a form suitable for publication.

Advanced Level Accounting, London **(30 marks)**

(Attempt this question only when you know Company accounts.)

13.3 The following balances as at 31 December 19_5 have been extracted from the books of William Speed, a small manufacturer:

	£
Stocks at 1 January 19_5: Raw materials	7 000
Work in progress	5 000
Finished goods	6 900
Purchases of raw materials	38 000
Direct labour	28 000
Factory overheads: Variable	16 000
Fixed	9 000
Administrative expenses: Rent and rates	19 000
Heat and light	6 000
Stationery and postages	2 000
Staff salaries	19 380
Sales	192 000
Plant and machinery: At cost	30 000
Provision for depreciation	12 000
Motor vehicles: At cost	16 000
Provision for depreciation	4 000
Creditors	5 500
Debtors	28 000
Drawings	11 500
Balance at Bank	16 600
Capital at 1 January 19_5	48 000
Provision for unrealised profit at 1 January 19_5	1 380
Motor vehicle running costs	4 500

Additional information:
(1) Stocks at 31 December 19_5 were as follows:

	£
Raw materials	9 000
Work in progress	8 000
Finished goods	10 350

(2) The factory output is transferred to the trading account at factory cost plus 25% for factory profit. The finished goods stock is valued on the basis of amounts transferred to the debit of the trading account.
(3) Depreciation is provided annually at the following percentages of the original cost of fixed assets held at the end of each financial year:

Plant and machinery	10%
Motor vehicles	25%

(4) Amounts accrued due at 31 December 19_5 for direct labour amounted to £3 000, and rent and rates prepaid at 31 December 19_5 to £2 000.

Required:
Prepare a manufacturing, trading and profit and loss account for the year ended 31 December 19_5 and a balance sheet as at that date.
Note: The prime cost and total factory cost should be clearly shown.

(25 marks)

Association of Accounting Technicians, Intermediate

13.4 William Boot owns a factory which manufactures waterproof footwear. The following is a summary of the transactions of the company during the financial year ending 31 May 19_4:

Value of opening stocks of raw materials:

Rubber	£16 225
Linings	£2 950
Glue	£325

Purchases of raw materials:

Rubber	£162 120
Linings	£14 025
Glue	£800

Factory expenses:

Wages of production workers, 6 300 man-hours at £3 per man-hour.
Hire of special moulds (a direct expense), £1 500.
Rent and Rates, £14 501 (three seventeenths of this total is for an office building).
Non-productive labour, £16 480.
Light, Heat and Power, £18 500. (This includes a payment of £700 which relates to the following year).
Depreciation is calculated at £2.50 per machine-hour. (Records show that six machines have been used for six hours per day for two-hundred-and-fifty days during the year.)
Sundry factory expenses, £9 400.

At 31 May 19_4 raw materials were:

Rubber	£30 880
Linings	£3 135
Glue	£150

Work in progress was valued at £24 500 at the start of the year and £35 302 at the end of the year.

47 500 pairs of boots were sold in the year for a total of £750 000. The opening stock of finished boots was valued at £40 000 (12 000 pairs) and the closing stock at £90 000 (27 000 pairs).

(a) You are required to prepare:
   (i) A manufacturing account and trading account for the year to 31 May 19_4. (24 marks)
   (ii) A calculation of the production cost of one pair of boots. (4 marks)
(b) A footwear retailer has offered Mr Boot a special order for 20 000 pairs. Mention two matters that should be considered before deciding whether to accept the order. (2 marks)

(30 marks)

Advanced Level Accounting, London

13.5 Mullett Ltd are a manufacturing company producing two separate products Bits and Togs. The following balances have been extracted from their accounting records on 31 August 19_1:

	£
Sales: Bits	240 000
Togs	180 000
Purchases of raw materials: Bits	63 000
Togs	42 000
Direct wages: Bits	60 000
Togs	20 000
Royalties: Togs	14 000
General factory expenses	21 000
Factory canteen costs	8 400

	£
Indirect factory labour	16 300
Rent and rates	6 275
Factory light and heat	4 300
Office light and heat	1 872
General office expenses	40 126
Delivery van expenses	9 000
Office salaries	27 450
Stocks 1 September 19_0:	
Raw materials: Bits	12 000
Togs	9 000
Work in progress: Bits	8 210
Togs	5 128
Finished goods: Bits	15 210
(at transfer price) Togs	11 347

The following information concerning the financial year ended 31 August 19_1 is also given:

(1) Prepayments at 31 August 19_1:
General office expenses £2 100

(2) Accruals at 31 August 19_1:

Factory light and heat	£300
Rent and rates	£600
Delivery van expenses	£421

(3) Stocks at 31 August 19_1:

		£
Raw materials	Bits	8 000
	Togs	11 000
Work in progress	Bits	9 320
	Togs	6 238
Finished goods	Bits	14 170
(at transfer price)	Togs	12 214

(4) Indirect labour includes £3 000 incurred on laying the foundations of a new factory extension and £500 on repainting the offices.

(5) Rent and rates are to be divided between the factory and offices in the ratio of 4:1.

(6) Canteen costs and indirect labour are to be divided between Bits and Togs in the proportion of the direct wages paid.

(7) Factory rent and rates and factory heat and light are to be divided between Bits and Togs in the ratio of 3:2.

(8) General factory expenses are to be divided between Bits and Togs in proportion to turnover.

(9) Finished goods manufactured during the year are transferred from the factory to the finished goods warehouse at the manufacturing cost of production plus 10 per cent.

Required:

(a) The manufacturing account for the year ended 31 August 19_1 showing clearly the factory cost and manufacturing profit for each product. (16 marks)

(b) The trading account for the year ended 31 August 19_1 showing clearly the gross profit for each product. (3 marks)

(c) The profit and loss account for the year ended 31 August 19_1. (4 marks)

(23 marks)

Advanced Level Accounting, AEB

13.6 The Harvest Manufacturing Company produces only one product. Because of their perishable nature, stocks of all kinds are maintained at very low levels and can be safely ignored for budgeting purposes. The profit for the year just completed has been calculated as shown on page 214.

		£000
Sales (2 000 units)		200
Material	varying in proportion to output	40
Labour	varying in proportion to output	60
Other Variable Manufacturing Expenses	varying in proportion to labour hours	30
Sales Commissions	2% of sales value	4
Fixed Expenses	same irrespective of output	16
Total expenses		150
Profit		50

Next year: material prices are expected to rise 5%; labour rates and other variable manufacturing expenses are expected to rise by 10% but sales commissions will be the same percentage and fixed expenses will remain the same. Harvest is currently considering three alternative strategies for next year:

(1) Make no changes in either selling price or product design and hope to sell at least as many units as last year.

(2) Increase selling price by 10% and hope volume does not drop by more than 5%.

(3) Redesign the product and increase the selling price by 15% and hope to increase volume by 10%. Different material would be used costing 5% less per pound (lb) than LAST YEAR; however 8% more material per unit of output would be required. As the work would be less skilled, wage rates would be 4% less per hour than wage rates paid LAST YEAR, but 25% more labour hours per unit of output would be needed. To handle the increased volume, £4 000 would have to be spent on rent for additional accommodation.

Required:

(a) Calculate the budgeted profit under each of the three alternative strategies being considered by Harvest for next year. (15 marks)

(b) Briefly suggest any other factors that should be considered by Harvest in selecting its strategy for next year. (4 marks)

(19 marks)

London Chamber of Commerce and Industry, Higher

13.7 The trial balance of YMB plc at 30th June, 19_5 was as follows:

	Dr £000	Cr £000
Ordinary shares of £0.25 each, fully paid		50 000
6% preference shares of £1.00 each, fully paid		2 000
Share premium		8 000
Retained profit at 30th June, 19_4		36 120
Freehold land and buildings at cost	15 000	
Plant and equipment at cost	80 000	
Motor vehicles at cost	10 000	
Depreciation provisions at 30th June, 19_4:		
freehold land and buildings		7 200
plant and equipment		12 500
motor vehicles		2 000
Stocks at 30th June, 19_4:		
materials	13 000	
work-in-progress	84	
finished products	9 376	
packaging materials	18	
Trade debtors	23 000	
Provision for bad debts		1 000
Cash at bank	2 000	

	Dr £000	Cr £000
Trade creditors		6 000
Sales		200 000
Purchases of materials	62 000	
Manufacturing wages	29 500	
Variable manufacturing overhead expenses	20 000	
Fixed manufacturing overhead expenses	34 895	
Variable distribution costs	2 702	
Fixed distribution costs	2 970	
Variable administration expenses	4 000	
Fixed administration expenses	14 155	
Preference dividend	120	
Interim ordinary dividend	2 000	
	324 820	324 820

You are given the following information:

(1) There were no additions to fixed assets during the year.

(2) Freehold land and buildings are to be depreciated at the rate of 2% per annum by the straight line method, assuming no residual value.

(3) Plant and equipment are to be depreciated at the rate of 10% per annum on cost.

(4) Motor vehicles are to be depreciated at the rate of 25% per annum by the diminishing (reducing) balance method.

(5) The annual depreciation charges are to be allocated as follows:

	Land and buildings	*Plant and equipment*	*Motor vehicles*
Fixed manufacturing overhead expenses	75%	80%	—
Fixed distribution costs	10%	5%	80%
Fixed administration expenses	15%	15%	20%

(6) The bad debts provision is to be increased by an amount equal to one per cent of sales. The item is to be regarded as variable distribution cost.

(7) Stocks at 30th June, 19_5, valued at full manufacturing cost where appropriate, were:

	£000
Materials	15 000
Work-in-progress	80
Finished products	10 900
Packaging materials (variable distribution costs)	20

(8) Prepayments and accruals at 30th June, 19_5 were:

	Prepayments £000	*Accruals* £000
Manufacturing wages	—	500
Fixed administration expenses	900	1 100
Variable distribution costs	100	400

(9) Provision is to be made for corporation tax at the rate of 50% of the net profit (advance corporation tax is to be ignored) and a final ordinary dividend of £0.02 per share.

You are required to prepare, for YMB plc's internal purposes, the following historic cost financial statements:

(a) a manufacturing, trading and profit and loss account, in vertical and columnar form, for the year ended 30th June, 19_5; (22 marks)

(b) a balance sheet, in vertical and columnar form, as at that date. (18 marks)

(40 marks)

Chartered Institute of Management Accountants

13.8* Phratepak plc is a company which specialises in the manufacture of crates used for the despatch of goods in bulk for the export market.

At 31 December 19_3 the following balances appeared in the company's books.

	Dr.	*Cr.*
	£	£
Fixed assets at cost:		
Premises	370 000	
Plant and machinery	264 000	
Tools, equipment etc.	123 600	
Vehicles	79 700	
Provisions for depreciation (at 1 January 19_3):		
Premises		21 400
Plant and machinery		119 300
Tools, equipment etc.		82 500
Vehicles		25 200
Purchases (*less* returns):		
Raw materials	236 150	
Consumable stores (used in manufacturing operations)	28 890	
Packing cases (*see Note 4*)	7 430	
Wages (*see Note 3*):		
Factory (operatives)	101 732	
Warehouse (storemen and drivers)	55 207	
Rates (*see Notes 2 and 3*)	62 200	
Heating and lighting (*see Notes 2 and 3*)	12 165	
Power (*see Notes 2 and 3*)	80 073	
Insurance (*see Notes 2 and 3*)	7 600	
Directors' fees	15 000	
Sales		876 863
Profit and loss account (at 1 January 19_3)		10 030
Ordinary share capital (£1.00 shares)		100 000
8% Preference share capital (£1.00 shares)		50 000
7% Debentures		500 000
Preference dividend paid	4 000	
Debenture interest paid	35 000	
Stocks at 1 January 19_3:		
Raw materials	48 080	
Consumable stores	1 482	
Work-in-progress (*see Note 6*)	27 930	
Finished goods	61 070	
Packing cases (*see Note 4*)	987	
Trade debtors	62 731	
Discount allowed	1 462	
Trade creditors		28 540
Discount received		639
Bank	34 165	
Cash	13 074	
Salaries (*see Note 3*):		
Factory (manager and supervisors)	28 019	
Warehouse (storekeepers etc.)	16 422	
Office	36 303	
	£1 814 472	£1 814 472

Notes at 31 December 19_3:

(1) Depreciation is to be provided on a straight line basis (one cost) at the following rates per annum.

	%
Premises	2
Plant and machinery	12.5
Tools, equipment etc.	10
Vehicles	20

(2) Expenses should be apportioned as follows:

	Factory	*Warehouse*	*Office*
	%	%	%
Rates	60	30	10
Power	80	15	5
Heating and lighting	75	15	10
Insurance	50	45	5
Depreciation for year:			
Premises	60	30	10
Plant and machinery	70	30	—
Tools and equipment	80	20	—
Vehicles	—	90	10

(3) Adjustment has not yet been made for Accruals:

	£
Heating and lighting	535
Power	2 927
Wages: Factory	6 145
Warehouse	1 980
Salaries: Factory	1 351
Warehouse	805
Office	781
Prepayments:	
Rates	10 600
Insurance	400

(4) Occasionally, when production facilities are fully committed, Phratepak has to buy in crates from another manufacturer in order to fulfil an urgent order.

(5) Stocks at 31 December 19_3:

	£
Raw materials	51 670
Consumable stores	2 007
Work-in-progress	16 420
Finished goods	43 407
Packing cases (*see Note 4*)	Nil

(6) Work-in-progress is valued at prime cost plus attributable manufacturing overheads.

(7) Corporation tax of £4 200 is to be provided. (*Hong Kong candidates read as Profits Tax*)

(8) The directors have proposed an ordinary dividend of 20p per share.

Required:
Prepare
(a) Manufacturing Account for year ended 31 December 19_3, (9 marks)
(b) Trading and Profit and Loss Accounts for year ended 31 December 19_3, and (16 marks)
(c) Balance Sheet as at 31 December 19_3. (9 marks)

N.B. (1) In the Profit and Loss Account, expenses should be classified under the two separate headings 'Warehouse expenses' and 'Other expenses'.
(2) All workings *must* be shown. **(34 marks)**

Chartered Association of Certified Accountants

Solutions

13.1

Expense no.		*Cost classification*
1	iv	indirect production overhead
2	vii	administration cost
3	vii	administration cost
4	vii	administration cost
5	viii	finance cost
6	iv	indirect production overhead
7	v	research cost *or* vi selling cost
8	iv	indirect production overhead
9	i	direct material
10	iii	direct expense
11	vi	selling and distribution cost
12	vi	selling and distribution cost
13	vi	selling and distribution cost
14	vii	administration cost
15	vii	administration cost
16	ii	direct labour
17	vi	selling and distribution cost
18	iv	indirect production overhead
19	iv	indirect production overhead
20	v	research and development cost

13.3

WILLIAM SPEED

Manufacturing, Trading and Profit and Loss Account for the year ended 31 December 19_5

	£	£	£
Raw materials			
Opening stock			7 000
Purchases			38 000
			45 000
Less closing stock			9 000
Cost of materials consumed			36 000
Direct labour (28 000 + 3 000)			31 000
Prime cost			67 000
Factory overheads			
Variables		16 000	
Fixed		9 000	
Depreciation on plant and machinery (30 000 × 10%)		3 000	28 000
			95 000
Add work-in-progress, 1 January 19_5			5 000
			100 000
Less work-in-progress, 31 December 19_5			8 000
Factory cost of goods completed			92 000
Add profit loading 25%			23 000
Transfer to warehouse (trading account) c/d			£115 000
Sales			192 000
Less cost of goods sold			
Opening stock finished goods		6 900	
Factory cost plus profit loading b/d		115 000	
		121 900	
Less closing stock finished goods		10 350	111 550
Gross profit			80 450
Factory profit			23 000
			103 450

	£	£	£
Distribution costs			
Depreciation on motor vehicles (16 000 × 25%)	4 000		
Motor vehicle running costs	4 500	8 500	
Administrative expenses			
Rent and rates (19 000 − 2 000)	17 000		
Light and heat	6 000		
Stationery and postages	2 000		
Staff salaries	19 380	44 380	52 880
			50 570
Increase in provision for unrealized profit*			690
Net profit			£49 880

* Provision balance b/f	1 380
Increase, to P & L	∴ 690
Balance c/f £10 350 × $\frac{25}{125}$ ($\frac{1}{5}$)	2 070

WILLIAM SPEED

Balance Sheet as at 31 December 19_5

	£ Cost	£ Dep'n	£ Net
Fixed assets			
Plant and machinery	30 000	15 000	15 000
Motor vehicles	16 000	8 000	8 000
	46 000	23 000	23 000
Current assets			
Stocks — raw materials		9 000	
work-in-progress		8 000	
finished goods	10 350		
less provision for unrealized profit (W_1)	2 070	8 280	
Debtors		28 000	
Prepayments		2 000	
Bank		16 600	
		71 880	
Less Current liabilities			
Creditors	5 500		
Accruals	3 000	8 500	
Working capital			63 380
Net assets			£86 380
Financed by:			
Capital			48 000
Add Profit			49 880
			97 880
Less drawings			11 500
Capital employed			£86 380

13.4 (a) (i)

WILLIAM BOOT

Manufacturing and Trading Account for the year ended 31 May 19_4

	£	£
Raw materials		
Opening stock		19 500
Purchases		176 945
		196 445
Less closing stock		34 165
Cost of materials consumed		162 280
Production wages		18 900
Hire of moulds		1 500
Prime cost		182 680
Factory overheads		
Rent and rates (£1 450 × $\frac{14}{17}$)	11 942	
Wages	16 480	
Light, heat and power	17 800	
Depreciation on machines (9 000 @ £2.50)	22 500	
Sundry expenses	9 400	78 122
		260 802
Add work-in-progress 1 June 19_3		24 500
		285 302
Less work-in-progress 31 May 19_4		35 302
Factory cost of boots completed c/d		£250 000
Sales		750 000
Less cost of boots sold		
Opening stock finished boots	40 000	
Factory cost b/d	250 000	
	290 000	
Less closing stock boots	90 000	200 000
Gross profit		£550 000

(ii)

Finished boots:	*Pairs*
Opening stock	12 000
Produced (bal.fig.) ∴	62 500
Available for sale	74 500
Closing stock	27 000
Boots sold	47 500

$$\text{Unit production cost} = \frac{\text{Total production cost}}{\text{Number of boots produced}} = \frac{£250\ 000}{62\ 500} = £4$$

(b) Factors to be considered would include:

(i) existence of sufficient spare capacity. 20 000 boots is a large order.

(ii) terms of contract — compare to profitability of existing business.

(iii) possibility of repeat orders?

13.6 A short but interesting question combining budgeting with manufacturing accounts. The question is as much a test of arithmetic as accounting.

(a) It is wise to first make a few calculations on unit costs.

	Last year		£	Next year Expected	£
Selling price	200 000 / 2 000	=	100		
Material cost	40 000 / 2 000	=	20	20 × 1.05	21
Labour cost	60 000 / 2 000	=	30	30 × 1.10	33
Other variable expenses	30 000 / 2 000	=	15	15 × 1.10	16.50

		Strategy 1 £	£
Sales	2 000 units @ £100		200 000
Less variable costs			
Material	2 000 units @ £21	42 000	
Labour	2 000 units @ £33	66 000	
Other manufacturing expenses	2 000 units @ £16.50	33 000	
Sales commissions	£200 000 × 2%	4 000	
			145 000
Contribution			55 000
Less fixed expenses			16 000
Profit			£39 000

		Strategy 2 £	£
Sales	1 900 units @ £110		209 000
Less variable costs			
Material	1 900 units @ £21	39 900	
Labour	1 900 units @ £33	62 700	
Other manufacturing expenses	1 900 units @ £16.50	31 350	
Sales commissions	£209 000 × 2%	4 180	
			138 130
Contribution			70 870
Less fixed expenses			16 000
Profit			£54 870

		Strategy 3 £	£
Sales	2 200 units @ £115		253 000
Less variable costs			
Material	2 200 units @ £20.52 (W_1)	45 144	
Labour	2 200 units @ £36 (W_2)	79 200	
Other manufacturing expenses	2 200 units @ £18.75 (W_3)	41 250	
Sales commissions	£253 000 × 2%	5 060	
			170 654
Contribution			82 346
Less fixed expenses	16 000 + 4 000 Rent		20 000
Profit			£62 346

W_1 20 × 0.95 × 1.08 = 20.52
W_2 30 × 0.96 × 1.25 = 36
W_3 15 × 1.25 = 18.75

(b) The Marketing Department would be advised to conduct some research to try and estimate the *price elasticity of demand* of its product since knowledge of whether demand is elastic (price-sensitive) or inelastic (price-insensitive) will determine the effect on volume of the price changes proposed in Strategies 2 and 3.

The Plant Manager should also be consulted to confirm whether there is sufficient *spare capacity* to handle the proposed increases in volume under Strategies 2 and 3.

13.7 Since the accounts are to be prepared for *internal* purposes the presentation and disclosure requirements of the Companies Acts do not have to be complied with.

(a) YMB PLC

Manufacturing, Trading and Profit and Loss Account for the year ended 30 June 19_5

	£000	*£000*	*£000*
Raw materials			
Opening stock			13 000
Purchases			62 000
			75 000
Less closing stock			15 000
Cost of materials consumed			60 000
Manufacturing wages			30 000
Prime cost			90 000
Factory overheads			
Variable expenses		20 000	
Fixed expenses		34 895	
Depreciation on land and buildings (W_1)		225	
Depreciation on plant and equipment (W_1)		6 400	61 520
			151 520
Add work-in-progress, 1 July 19_4			84
			151 604
Less work-in-progress, 30 June 19_5			80
Factory cost of finished production c/d			£151 524
Sales			200 000
Less cost of goods sold			
Opening stock of finished goods		9 376	
Factory cost of finished production b/d		151 524	
		160 900	
Less closing stock of finished goods		10 900	150 000
Gross profit			50 000
Distribution costs			
Variable (W_2)	3 000		
Fixed	2 970		
Depreciation on land (W_1)	30		
Depreciation on plant (W_1)	400		
Depreciation on motor vehicles (W_1)	1 600		
Provision for doubtful debts	2 000	10 000	
Administration expenses			
Variable	4 000		
Fixed (14 155 − 900 + 1 100)	14 355		
Depreciation on land (W_1)	45		
Depreciation on plant (W_1)	1 200		
Depreciation on motor vehicles (W_1)	400	20 000	30 000

	£000	£000	£000
Net profit			20 000
Less provision for corporation tax			10 000
Profit after tax			10 000
Retained profit b/f			36 120
Profits available for distribution			46 120
Less Appropriations			
Preference dividend paid		120	
Interim ordinary dividend paid		2 000	
Final ordinary dividend proposed		4 000	6 120
Retained profit c/f			£40 000

Workings

W_1 *Depreciation*

	Land £000	*Plant* £000	*Vehicles* £000
Manufacturing expenses	225	6 400	—
Distribution costs	30	400	1 600
Administration expenses	45	1 200	400
	300	8 000	2 000

W_2 *Variable distribution costs*

		£000			£000
1 June 19_4	Bal b/f — packing materials	18	30 June 19_5	*P & L*	∴ 3 000
	Bank	2 702	30 June 19_5	Bal c/f — packing materials	20
30 June 19_5	Bal c/f — accrued	400	30 June 19_5	Bal c/f — prepaid	100
		3 120			3 120

(b)

YMB PLC

Balance Sheet as at 30 June 19_5

	£000 *Cost*	£000 *Dep'n*	£000 *Net*
Fixed assets			
Freehold land and buildings	15 000	7 500	7 500
Plant and equipment	80 000	20 500	59 500
Motor vehicles	10 000	4 000	6 000
	105 000	32 000	73 000
Current assets			
Stocks — materials		15 000	
work-in-progress		80	
finished products		10 900	
packaging materials		20	
Trade debtors	23 000		
Less provision for doubtful debts	3 000	20 000	
Prepayments		1 000	
Cash at bank		2 000	
		49 000	
Less Current liabilities			
Trade creditors	6 000		
Accrued expenses	2 000		
Ordinary dividend proposed	4 000		
Provision for tax	10 000	22 000	
Working capital			27 000
Net assets			£100 000

Financed by:

	£000	*£000*
Ordinary shares of £0.25 each, fully paid		50 000
6% preference shares of £1.00 each, fully paid		2 000
		52 000
Reserves		
Share premium	8 000	
Retained profit	40 000	48 000
Capital employed		£100 000

CHAPTER 14

Cost Classification and Labour Costing

Costs can be classified in several different ways, according to the purpose for which the classification is required, i.e. whether it is to prepare the year-end final accounts, for decision-making, planning, performance evaluation or control.

In the previous chapter, Manufacturing Accounts, we met two ways in which the accountant classifies costs in order to prepare the year-end income statement. One was by *function* — according to the purpose they serve e.g. production cost, distribution cost, administration cost. The other was classification into *direct* and *indirect* costs, direct costs being those costs which can be attributed to individual units of production, indirect costs being those which cannot be traced to individual units. This classification was needed in order to distinguish between the prime cost of production and overheads.

A classification useful for decision-making and planning is in terms of *cost behaviour in relation to changes in the level of activity.* Activity may be measured as the level of output, number of hours worked, number of miles travelled, or number of clients seen, according to the nature of the business. *Fixed costs* do not change with the level of activity. This is because they accrue on a *time* basis rather than with activity level. Examples include rent and rates, interest on loans and executive salaries. *Variable costs* vary directly with activity level, examples being direct materials, direct labour and direct expenses (e.g. royalty payable per unit). The graph below illustrates the contrasting nature of fixed and variable costs.

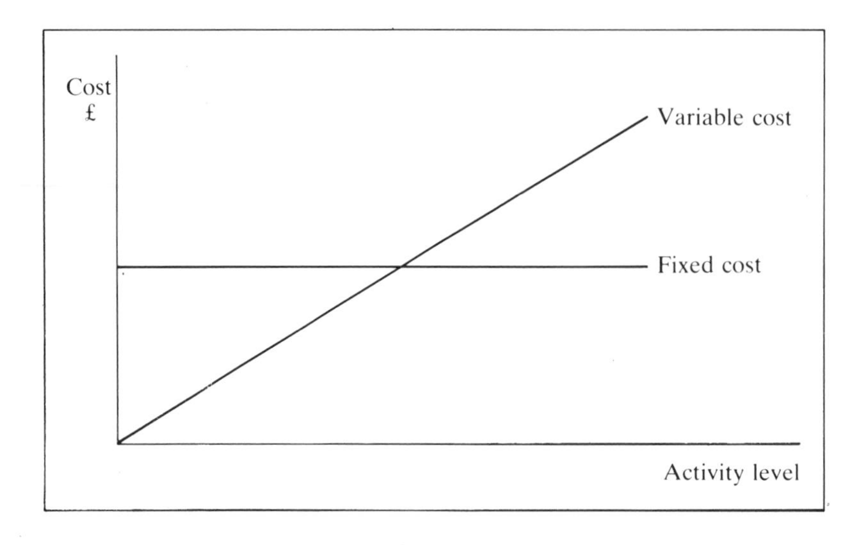

In addition, some costs are of a *semi-variable* nature. As the name implies these include both a fixed and variable component. For example the cost of electricity and telephone incur a standing charge which is fixed, but also a charge related to usage, which is variable. Thus the total bill rises with increased usage. The graph below illustrates this.

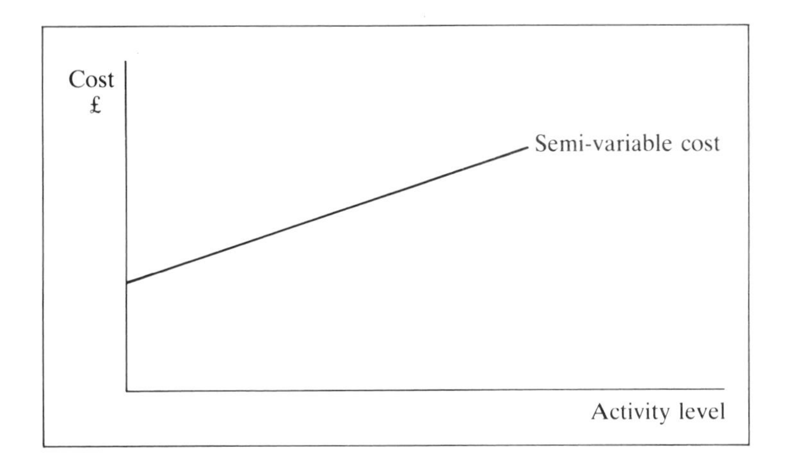

Semi-fixed costs are fixed over a limited range of output but once this limit is reached, increase as a 'lump' — because the expenditure is indivisible. For example, let us take a supervisor capable of supervising work up to 400 man hours a week. His weekly pay is £200. An activity level of 300 man hours necessitates employment of one supervisor. An increase to 350 hours does not change the cost — it is fixed over this range of activity. If man hours worked rises to 450 however, cost *does* change — by a lump to £400. (A second supervisor is needed.) In this case the cost has increased more than proportionately to the increase in activity level as is shown in the graph below.

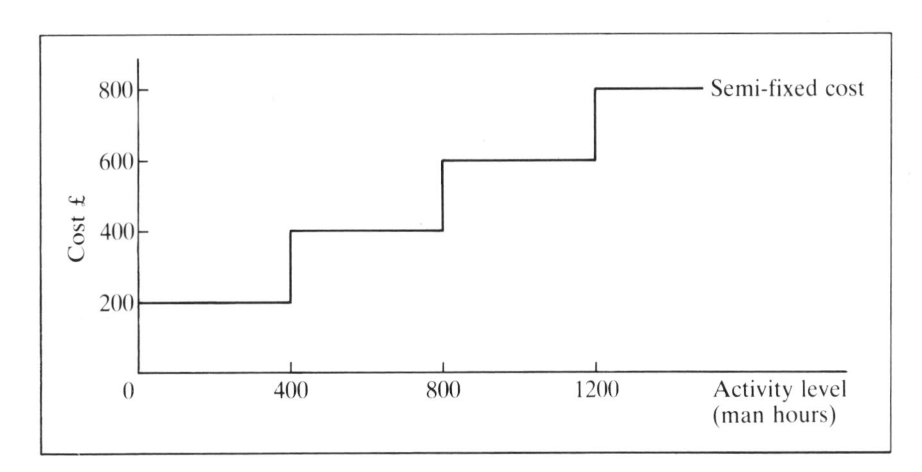

The cost line looks rather like a series of steps — for this reason semi-fixed costs are also known as *step costs*.

In addition to decision-making, the above classification (by cost behaviour with changes in activity level) is important to the process of budgetary control and variance analysis, as we shall see in Chapters 21 and 22. It is also an essential part of break-even analysis, considered in Chapter 23.

Another classification useful for decision-making is whether a cost is *relevant* or *irrelevant* to a future decision. For example, in choosing between two alternatives past or 'sunk' costs are irrelevant since their level cannot be affected by a future decision. So too are future *common* costs. The only relevant costs are the *future differential* costs i.e. those costs which are avoidable and which differ between the alternatives under consideration. Relevant costing and decision-making is looked at in Chapter 20.

Large organizations are often de-centralized into divisions, with divisional managers being responsible for the performance of their own division. Their performance is frequently monitored by top management using the techniques of *standard costing*, *budgeting*, and *variances*. In evaluating performance top management must be careful to classify costs into whether they are *controllable* or *non-controllable* by the person they are seeking to evaluate. Thus while the direct labour cost would be classified as a controllable cost, the head office overhead apportioned to the division would not. If a manager is blamed for an adverse variance on a cost which he cannot control, he is not likely to support and co-operate with the evaluation system. More on this in Chapter 22.

Cost Unit

A cost unit is simply a unit to which costs are related. The specific unit will vary from industry to industry. In steel-making the cost unit would be cost per ton of steel, in motor manufacture cost per car, in dairy farming cost per gallon of milk, in bottle-making cost per thousand bottles and in transport cost per mile travelled.

Determination of Unit Cost

One of the chief functions of the cost accountant is to determine unit cost. The financial accountant needs this information to *value stocks* and *determine gross profit*, the management accountant needs it for performance evaluation, control, decision-making and planning. The total cost of a unit can be split into:

	£
Direct materials	x
Direct labour	x
Direct expenses	x
Prime cost	x
Production overhead	x
Production cost	x
Administration, selling and distribution overhead	x
Total cost	x

There are several different methods of costing the amount of direct materials used in a unit — these are looked at in the next chapter. Determination of the unit overhead cost is no simple matter and is considered in the chapter following. In the remainder of this chapter we look at direct labour and direct expenses.

Labour

Our study of labour can be conveniently divided into labour remuneration schemes which look at the different methods of remunerating labour, and labour costing which is concerned with determination of the unit labour cost.

Remuneration Schemes

There are several alternative methods of remunerating labour each with a different associated cost. They may be classified into two broad types of payment — *time rate* and *piecework* (or piece-rate). Time rate remunerates labour on the basis of the amount of time worked, such as £ per hour, £ per week, or an annual salary. In contrast wages under piecework are a function of *output* rather than time — the worker is paid according to the number of 'pieces' he completes. Total earnings are number of pieces multiplied by the rate per piece. The advantage of piecework is that a direct incentive to effort is built into the remuneration system, but it should not be used in circumstances where the work is too important to be hurried, where quality of work is more important than quantity such as the company doctor and where output of the worker cannot be measured in pieces, such as the factory foreman and clerical/executive staff. Piecework is particularly suitable for *production workers* where an incentive system is needed to ensure that workers do not cheat on the job (which they are tempted to do more than non-production workers because of the boring and repetitive nature of the job). Also, with these workers it is usually possible to measure the number of pieces of work completed.

Some employers combine the two systems by operating a *bonus scheme*. Here the worker is on a fixed wage but has the chance to earn a bonus if he performs above a set standard. Bonus schemes are usually introduced to increase worker productivity. The most common type is the *premium bonus scheme*, in which the worker is paid a premium for time saved in completing a job in less than standard time. Several methods of calculating the premium are used, the two best known being the *Halsey* and the *Rowan* schemes. In the Halsey scheme the worker receives a fixed proportion of any time he saves in completing a job, the most common being 50%.

Illustration

An operator is given a job for which the time allowed is 5 hours. The wage rate is £8 an hour. He performs the task in 4 hours. What is his earning under the Halsey 50% bonus scheme?

$$\begin{aligned}\text{Earning} &= (4 \text{ hours} + 50\% \text{ of saving, 1 hour}) \times \text{wage rate} \\ &= (4 + \tfrac{1}{2}) \times £8 \\ &= £36\end{aligned}$$

With no bonus scheme in operation the amount payable is 4 hours @ £8 = £32. This is lower than under the bonus scheme but in its absence the worker would probably take the full 5 hours alloted for the job, thereby raising cost to 5 × £8 = £40. This is now *higher* than the incentive scheme.

Under the *Rowan* scheme the premium to be added to the basic pay is the *percentage the time saved is of the time allowed*. Using the above example, pay under Rowan would be calculated as follows:

$$\begin{aligned}\text{Percentage saving in time} &= \frac{\text{Time saved}}{\text{Time allowed}} \times 100 \\ &= \frac{1}{5} \times 100 \\ &= 20\%\end{aligned}$$

$$\begin{aligned}\text{Wage rate} &= \text{Standard} + 20\% \text{ Bonus} \\ &= £8 \quad + £1.60 \\ &= £9.60\end{aligned}$$

$$\begin{aligned}\text{Total earning} &= 4 \text{ hours @ } £9.60 \\ &= £38.40\end{aligned}$$

Where work is organized in teams/groups rather than individually a *group bonus scheme* may be employed. This rewards output by the group as a whole.

Other methods of remunerating labour include operation of *profit-sharing schemes* and providing *benefits in kind* i.e. non-financial rewards such as a company car and free lunch.

Labour Costing

This is concerned with determination of the unit labour cost. Direct wage cost can be determined by *time and motion studies* estimating the *standard time* needed for an operation. Standard time multiplied by wage rate for each operation gives the direct wage cost embodied in each unit. No attempt is made to calculate the unit *indirect* wage cost since this is by definition not traceable to individual units. Instead the cost is charged to the product as part of the unit overhead, determination of which is looked at in Chapter 16. The classification of a labour cost as being direct or indirect is sometimes not clear, as with idle-time due to a machine breakdown and overtime premiums. These are usually treated as overheads, but not in all circumstances. This complication is returned to in the section on job costing in Chapter 17.

Examination questions often ask for a calculation of the effect on a firm's costs of changing from one payment system to another — usually from time rate to a bonus system. The obvious benefit of the latter is increased productivity, but with this being rewarded with a bonus the labour cost per unit may not fall by much — in some cases it actually rises for a while. The real benefit of increased output to a firm is a *decrease in the unit overhead cost*. Since most overheads do not increase with output, an increase in output reduces the overhead cost per unit. Put another way, there is better utilization of fixed overheads. Operating a bonus scheme is thus beneficial to both employer and employee — the employee has the chance to increase his earnings and the employer benefits from a reduction in unit cost. See question 14.6.

Direct Expenses

Direct expenses are those costs other than material and labour which can be traced to particular cost units. If for example a firm is producing a good on licence, for a royalty payment of £1 for every unit sold, this £1 is a direct expense as it can be attributed to each unit sold. Another common direct expense is salesmen's commission since this is usually related to the number of units sold.

Questions

14.1 (a) Explain what you understand by the term 'cost behaviour', why it is important in the context of cost and management accounting, and what behaviour patterns may be encountered. (8 marks)

(b) What factors influence the behaviour of costs in response to changes in an organization's level of activity? (9 marks)

(17 marks)

Chartered Association of Certified Accountants

14.2 'Costs may be classified in different ways for different purposes.' Elucidate this statement.

(20 marks)

Author's Question

14.3 (a) 'The same cost may be classified in a variety of different ways for different purposes.'
Identify three different ways of classifying the wages of an employee and give an example of the purpose of each method of classification. (6 marks)

(b) Discuss the possible effects, on a company's costs, of changing the method of remunerating its direct workers from a time-rate to a piece-rate based scheme. (11 marks)

(17 marks)

Chartered Association of Certified Accountants

14.4 A manufacturer, who is about to set up in business, is considering either a day rate or a piece-rate system of paying employees. What factors should be considered before a decision is made?

(20 marks)

Advanced level Accounting, London

14.5* (a) Define the following terms:
(i) time rate
(ii) piecework
(iii) Halsey premium bonus scheme
(iv) Rowan premium bonus scheme (8 marks)

(b) The time allowed for a job is 12 hours, the rate of pay for it £7 per hour. Calculate the amount payable under the a. Halsey 50% and b. Rowan premium bonus schemes if the actual time take is:
(i) 11 hours
(ii) $9\frac{1}{2}$ hours (12 marks)

(20 marks)

Author's Question

14.6* The following information is available:

Normal working day	8 hours
Guaranteed rate of pay (on time basis)	£5.50 per hour
Standard time allowed to produce 1 unit	3 minutes
Piecework price	£0.10 per standard minute
Premium Bonus	75% of time saved, in addition to hourly pay

Required:
For the following levels of output produced in one day:
80 units
120 units
210 units
Calculate earnings based on:
(a) piecework, where earnings are guaranteed at 80% of time-based pay.
(b) premium bonus system.

(12 marks)

Association of Accounting Technicians, Final

14.7 A small company classifies all its production overheads of £2 400 per week as fixed. The company currently produces 150 components per week on a sub-contracting basis and has been asked by its major customer to increase its output. Management is reluctant to operate for more than the normal 40 hours each week but in an attempt to meet its customer's wishes decides to offer an incentive scheme to its four direct operators whose current rates of pay are as follows:

	Hourly rate
	£
G Ahmed	3.00
A Brown	3.00
D Choudery	4.00
G Spencer (working Foreman)	5.00

With the agreement of the employees, who are not members of a trade union, their basic hourly rates are to be reduced for a trial period of four weeks to those shown below but with each of them being given a bonus of £0.60 for every unit produced.

	Revised hourly rate
	£
G Ahmed	1.50
A Brown	1.50
D Choudery	2.50
G Spencer	3.50

After the first week of the trial period, production was 180 units. The production manager studied the results and believed the introduction of the bonus was too costly because the increase of 20% in production had increased labour costs by 32%. He is considering recommending changes to the newly-introduced scheme.

Required:

(a) calculate how the increase in labour cost of 32% was derived;

(b) comment on whether the production manager was correct in assuming that the bonus scheme was too costly, showing your supporting calculations. **(12 marks)**

Chartered Institute of Management Accountants

14.8 (a) With reference to wages systems, what is meant by:

(i) piece rates

(ii) time rates

(iii) standard hours?

(4 marks)

(b) Bath Ltd. has a payments scheme specifically designed for trainees. Under the scheme earnings are calculated as follows:

$$\text{Earnings} = \text{Rate per hour} \times \sqrt{(\text{Standard hours} \times \text{Clock hours})}$$

If the rate per hour is £3.60 and five standard hours are allowed for a job, show

(i) the earnings accruing if clock hours are seven;

(ii) how standard rates are earned when clock hours equal standard hours.

(2 marks)

(c) A firm's bonus scheme pays employees a bonus of 50 per cent of the time saved in completing a job. Harry Jones, a new employee, is confused because the basic pay for a job when no time is saved is greater than when four hours are saved.

Use the figures in the following table to resolve Harry's confusion:

Time allowed (Hours)	Time taken (Hours)	Rate per hour	Basic Pay	Bonus Pay	Total Pay
		£	£	£	£
8	8	4.50	36	—	36
8	4	4.50	18	9	27

(4 marks)

(d) What are the advantages and disadvantages to a firm of introducing a bonus system?

(5 marks)
(15 marks)

Advanced Level Accounting, London

14.9* You have been approached for your advice on the proposed introduction of an incentive scheme for the direct operatives in the final production department of a factory producing one standard product. This department, the Finishing Shop, employs 30 direct operatives all of whom are paid £3 per hour for a basic 40 hour week, with a guaranteed wage of £120 per week. When necessary, overtime is worked up to a maximum of 15 hours per week per operative and is paid at time rate plus one half. It is the opinion of the Personnel Manager that no more direct operatives could be recruited for this department.

An analysis of recent production returns from the Finishing Shop indicate that the current average output is approximately 6 units of the standard product per productive man hour. The Work Study Manager has conducted an appraisal of the working methods in the Finishing Shop and suggests that it would be reasonable to expect operatives to process 8 units of the product per man hour and that a piece work scheme be introduced in which the direct operatives are paid 55p for each unit processed. It is anticipated that, when necessary, operatives would continue to work overtime up to the previously specified limit, although as the operatives would be on piece work no premium would be paid.

Next year's budgeted production for the factory varies from a minimum of 7 000 units per week to a maximum of 12 000 units per week, with the most frequent budgeted weekly output being 9 600 units. The expected selling price of the product next year is £10 per unit and the budgeted variable production cost of the incomplete product passed into the Finishing Shop amounts to £8 per unit. Variable production overheads in the Finishing Shop, excluding the overtime premium of the direct operatives, are budgeted to be £0.48 per direct labour hour worked and it is considered that variable overheads do vary directly with productive hours worked. Direct material costs are not incurred by the Finishing Shop. The fixed overheads incurred by the factory amount in total to £9 000 per week.
Stocks of work in progress and finished goods are not carried.

Required:

(a) Calculate the effect on the company's budgeted weekly profits of the proposed incentive scheme in the Finishing Shop.
Calculations should be to the nearest £. (15 marks)

(b) Explain the reasons for the changes in the weekly budgeted profits caused by the proposed incentive scheme. (7 marks)

(22 marks)

Chartered Association of Certified Accountants

Solutions

14.7 (a) *Original cost* — 40 hours

	£
Ahmed	120
Brown	120
Choudery	160
Spencer	200
	600

New cost

	Basic	+	*Bonus**	=	*Total*
	£		£		£
Ahmed	60		108		168
Brown	60		108		168
Choudery	100		108		208
Spencer	140		108		248
					792

* 180 units × £0.60 = £108

$$\text{Percentage increase} = \frac{792 - 600}{600} \times 100 = 32\%$$

(b)

	Previous time-rate	Current incentive scheme
	£	£
Wages	600	792
Overhead	2 400	2 400
	3 000	3 192
Units of output	150	180
Cost per unit	$\frac{3\,000}{150} = £20$	$\frac{3\,192}{180} = £17.73$

The production manager was *not* correct in assuming that the bonus scheme was too costly. He failed to take account of the effect of the increased output on *unit overhead cost*. Since the overhead cost does not rise with output, the increase from 150 to 180 units has reduced the unit overhead cost. Although labour cost has risen in the new incentive scheme, this has been *more than offset* by the fall in unit overhead cost. As a result unit total cost has fallen — from £20 to £17.73.

14.8 (a) See text.

(b) (i) Earnings when clock hours are seven:
$3.60 \times \sqrt{(5 \times 7)}$
$= 3.60 \times 5.916 = £21.30$

(ii) Standard Earnings $= 3.60 \times \sqrt{(5 \times 5)}$
$= 3.60 \times 5 = £18$

Earnings when clock hours equal five:
$3.60 \times \sqrt{(5 \times 5)} = £18$

∴ when clock hours equal standard hours the standard rate of £18 is earned.

(c) The confusion can be resolved in two ways:

(i) What is really important is not total pay but the *hourly rate* of pay.

Time taken (hours)	*Total pay* £	*Hourly rate* £
8	36	$\frac{36}{8} = 4.50$
4	27	$\frac{27}{4} = 6.75$

The above calculation shows that when time is saved the rate of pay is higher, at £6.75.

(ii) The 4 hours saved on the job can be used to earn additional income *on another job*. Assuming Harry performs the next job also in 4 hours, his total pay in the 8 hours is 27 + 27 = £54. This compares with only £36 if he performs only one job in the 8 hours.

(d) Advantages of introducing a bonus system:

(i) workers are encouraged to increase output
(ii) the increase in output reduces the *unit* fixed cost
(iii) by keeping records of time spent on jobs by each worker, slow workers are easily identified

Disadvantages:

(i) workers may sacrifice quality and thoroughness of work for speed
(ii) calculating wages payable to each worker is made more complex and expensive.

CHAPTER 15

Material Costing and Stock Valuation

Valuing stock might at first seem to be a simple enough exercise but this is not the case for the reason that there are several alternative methods of valuation, each producing a different figure. The value placed on stock is of crucial importance, because:

(1) it affects the charge-out rate of materials issued from stores, and hence the unit *production cost*
(2) this affects the figure for cost of goods sold which in turn affects *gross profit*
(3) it affects the value of *net assets* in the balance sheet
(4) the closing stock of one year is carried forward as the opening stock of the next year. Any error in valuation therefore affects not only that year's profit figure but also the subsequent year's.

SSAP9: Stocks and Work-in-progress

Stocks remaining unsold should be valued at their cost and not their selling price. The specific recommendation of the accounting standard is for firms to value stock at the '*lower of cost and net realizable value*', in line with the concept of prudence. *Cost* is defined as that expenditure which has been incurred in bringing the product to its present location and condition. While for middlemen this is just cost of purchase plus transport costs, for manufacturers to cost of materials would be added conversion cost — on direct labour and overheads. (Note that this supports absorption, full costing as opposed to marginal, variable costing.) *Net realizable value* is selling price less costs of completion, selling, and distribution.

Since net realizable value is normally greater than cost, cost is the basis on which stocks are valued in most cases. Herein lies the problem — there is more than one interpretation of the meaning of cost. Three subjective areas can be identified:

(1) For manufactured goods, should cost be taken as direct materials, labour, and direct expenses or should an element of *overhead* be charged as well? This question is considered in Chapter 19, Absorption and Marginal Costing.
(2) If it is decided to use absorption costing, *on what basis* should fixed overheads be charged to individual stock units? The problem of allocation and apportionment of overheads is looked at in Chapter 16, Overhead Absorption Costing.
(3) In a period of changing prices should materials be issued from stores to production at the *latest* prices, *earlier* prices or an *average* price for the year? Further, should stock records be kept on a *periodic* or *perpetual* inventory basis? These questions are considered in this chapter.

Let us look at the question of the issue price of materials and valuation of closing stock with problem (3) in mind. There are three main methods of valuation — first in first out (FIFO), last in first out (LIFO), and average cost (AVCO) — each producing a different result. I shall first describe each method, then illustrate it with reference to the following information.

Winston is a dealer in automatic rice cookers. On 1 January he had 15 cookers in stock at cost £30 each. His activities in January are shown on the following page.

Purchases	Jan	4	30 @ £32	
		10	22 @ £34	
		20	20 @ £36	
Sales	Jan	6		35 @ £40
		25		40 @ £45

At 31 January Winston had 12 cookers remaining.

FIFO

As its name suggests this method assumes that the *goods first in are first out*. In other words the oldest goods on hand are the first to be issued. Consequently closing stock is valued at the *most recent purchase prices.*

For Winston the closing stock of 12 cookers is valued at £36 each, this being the price of the last batch of purchases — on 20 January.
Stock valuation, 12 @ £36 = £432.

LIFO

As the name again suggests this method assumes that the *goods last in are first out*. In other words the goods most recently received are issued first. Consequently, closing stock is valued at *purchase prices pertaining in the earlier part of the period.* LIFO calculations are more complicated than FIFO, because it is necessary to work out from which batch of purchases each individual batch of sales is made. Only in this way can closing stock be valued.

For Winston:

Date	*Purchases*	*Sales*	*Balance*	*£*	*£*
January					
1			15 @ £30		300
4	30 @ £32		15 @ £30	300	
			30 @ £32	960	1260
6		30 @ £32			
		5 @ £30	10 @ £30		300
10	22 @ £34		10 @ £30	300	
			22 @ £34	748	1048
20	20 @ £36		10 @ £30	300	
			22 @ £34	748	
			20 @ £36	720	1768
25		20 @ £36	10 @ £30	300	
		20 @ £34	2 @ £34	68	368

Stock valuation = £368

AVCO

The unit valuation under this method is *weighted average cost*. This is found by dividing the total purchase price of units by the number of units. This figure is then used to value closing stock.

For Winston:

	Date	*Units*	*£*
Opening stock	Jan 1	15 @ £30	300
Purchases	4	30 @ £32	960
	10	22 @ £34	748
	20	20 @ £36	720
		87	2728

$$\text{Unit cost} = \frac{£2728}{87} = £31.36 \text{ (to the nearest penny)}$$

Stock valuation = 12 units @ £31.36
= £376 (to the nearest £)

Comparison

Since the different methods produce different values of stock, gross profits also differ.

WINSTON

Trading account for January

	FIFO	LIFO	AVCO
	£	£	£
Sales	3 200	3 200	3 200
Opening stock	450	450	450
Purchases	2 728	2 728	2 728
	3 178	3 178	3 178
Less closing stock	432	368	376
Cost of goods sold	2 746	2 810	2 802
Gross profit	454	390	398

Note that:
(1) sales and purchases are the same under all three methods
(2) in a period of rising prices FIFO places the highest value on closing stock and consequently produces the highest gross profit. LIFO shows the lowest profit.

Of the three methods FIFO corresponds most closely to the physical flow of goods in businesses trading in perishable products but also in many businesses dealing in goods of a non-perishable nature. It is in fact the most popular method of stock valuation in the UK. The tax authorities do not accept LIFO as a basis for valuation — partly because it leads to lower reported profit. AVCO is suitable for businesses which have no definite policy on the issue of goods and for businesses trading in goods in liquid form, such as a petrol station.

Periodic v. Perpetual Inventory

Apart from deciding on the basis of stock valuation, businesses also have to decide whether to keep a constant running check on stock levels, known as perpetual inventory, or value stock only at the end of a period, periodic inventory. The decision depends largely on the size and type of business. A department store with thousands of different stock items, including many of small value, would probably not want to incur the cost of perpetual inventory, and settle instead for periodic inventory. In contrast, a manufacturing concern which needs to keep detailed costing records of the types and quantities of materials and components in stock at all times might use perpetual inventory. In this all purchases of materials would be recorded in a *Stores Ledger Account*, as would all issues to jobs. In this way the stock level of each item in store is known at all times. See question 15.2.

It should be said that in the current information revolution brought on by the application of computers to business, an increasing number of firms including even department stores and supermarkets are introducing perpetual inventory. Each stock item is printed with a code. When it is sold or issued, a scanner, usually a pen, identifies the code at the check-out point, cash desk or stores department so that an instant record is made of the fact that the item is no longer in stock. The computer can even be programmed to re-order stock when the re-order level has been reached.

The AVCO method described earlier assumed periodic inventory. Where perpetual inventory is used it is necessary to re-calculate weighted average cost *after each batch of purchases*. This figure is then the unit valuation at which subsequent stock is issued.

For Winston:

Date	*Purchases*	*Sales*	*Unit cost** £	*Units in stock*	*Value* £
Jan 1			30.00	15	450
4	30 @ £32		31.33	45	1 410
6		35 @ £31.33		10	313
10	22 @ £34		33.16	32	1 061
20	20 @ £36		34.25	52	1 781
25		40 @ £34.25		12	411

* to the nearest penny

In the above table, following a purchase, it is best to write in the new total value of stock first, then the number of units, leaving the unit cost (given by total value divided by number of units) as the final calculation. When a sale is made the number of units of stock remaining should be filled in first, this then multiplied by the unit cost to arrive at the new reduced total value of stock. Note how the unit valuation changes every time a fresh purchase is made.

Standard Cost

Some manufacturing concerns use standard cost, a pre-determined budgeted unit cost, as the basis for valuing stock. Standard costing is considered in Chapter 22.

Examination Questions

Examination questions on this topic usually give information on purchases and sales over a period of time and ask for a calculation of the value of closing stock under two or more methods. Workings need to be shown for LIFO and AVCO. Trading accounts are sometimes asked for.

Questions

15.1* On 1 January Year 6 the management of Florentine Ltd, retailers of electrical goods, decided to add home computers to their range. Initially this was to be on a temporary basis, and they required monthly trading statements to enable profitability to be measured. In the first 6 months, only one model was marketed. In each of these months, 200 units were bought and 180 units were sold, at the following prices:

	Purchase Price (per unit) £	*Selling Price (per unit)* £
January	200	300
February	180	270
March	160	250
April	160	240
May	150	220
June	140	200

Because of increasing competition no further computers were bought, and those remaining were sold in July for £190 each.

Required:
Prepare Trading Accounts (in columnar form) for each of the seven months January to July, using the FIFO (first in, first out) basis of stock valuation.

London Chamber of Commerce and Industry, Higher **(16 marks)**

15.2 An importer deals only in one commodity and has recorded the following transactions for the first six months of the year.

Purchases Date	*Quantity Purchased Units*	*Gross Invoice Value £*	*Quantity Discount*
February 1st	100	30 000	NIL
March 1st	200	60 000	2.5%
May 1st	300	90 000	5%

Sales Date	*Quantity Sold Units*	*Total Sales Value £*
February	75	30 000
May	350	175 000

There was an opening balance at January 1st of 50 units, valued at £12 500.

Required:
(a) Prepare the stores ledger for the six months using the perpetual inventory system and the FIFO method of pricing issues. (10 marks)
(b) Prepare a trading account to show the gross profit for the period, using the FIFO method of valuation. (2 marks)
(c) Prepare a trading account to show the gross profit for the period, using the LIFO method of valuation. (4 marks)

Association of Accounting Technicians, Final **(16 marks)**

15.3 An engineering company charges goods to production on the basis of the AVCO (Average Cost) perpetual inventory method. Details of the receipts and issues of splash cans for 19_3 were:

SPLASH CANS

Receipts		*Issues*	
10 January	20 @ £14.00	28 February	15
4 April	10 @ £14.00	8 May	6
2 June	12 @ £14.30	20 July	14
22 September	20 @ £15.10	11 October	18
9 November	14 @ £15.20	3 December	20

On 1 January 19_3 the stock of splash cans on hand comprised 7 cans with a total value of £96.60.

(a) Draft a statement as below to record receipts and issues:

	Goods		*Stocks*		
Date	*Received*	*Issued*	*Average Cost*	*Units Held*	*Total Value*

(12 marks)

(b) If at the end of the financial year, the company adopts the periodic method of valuing stocks what would have been the value of closing stock at 31 December 1983 using:
(i) AVCO (Average Cost).
(ii) FIFO (First in, First Out).
(iii) LIFO (Last in, First out)? (10 marks)

(c) Explain the reasons for the differences in stock valuations produced by each of the methods in (b) above. (8 marks)

(30 marks)

Advanced Level Accounting, London

15.4* A businessman started trading with a capital in cash of £6 000 which he placed in the business bank account at the outset.

His transactions, none of which were on credit, were as follows (in date sequence) for the first accounting period. All takings were banked immediately and all suppliers were paid by cheque. He traded in only one line of merchandise.

Purchases		*Sales*	
Quantity	*Price per unit*	*Quantity*	*Price per unit*
	£		£
1 200	1.00		
1 000	1.05		
		800	1.70
600	1.10		
		600	1.90
900	1.20		
		1 100	2.00
800	1.25		
		1 300	2.00
700	1.30		
		400	2.05

In addition he incurred expenses amounting to £1 740, of which he still owed £570 at the end of the period.

Required:

Prepare separately using both the FIFO (first in first out) and the LIFO (last in first out) methods of stock valuation:

(a) a statement of cost of sales for the period, and

(b) a balance sheet at the end of the period.

Note: workings are an integral part of the answer and must be shown **(18 marks)**

Chartered Association of Certified Accountants

15.5 (a) Explain clearly what is meant by the FIFO and LIFO methods of issuing stocks and the effect of each on stock valuations and profits of a firm in conditions of changing price levels. (10 marks)

(b) Illustrate your answer to (a) by reference to figures of opening and closing stock valuations related to annual purchases over three years in which prices and physical stock levels are rising. (15 marks)

(25 marks)

Advanced Level Accounting, AEB

15.6 Describe, and discuss the relative merits of, the various methods that may be used for pricing the issue of raw materials to production. **(17 marks)**

Chartered Association of Certified Accountants

15.7 A company has produced draft financial statements for the year ended 30 April 19_6 which show a net profit of £108 400. Stock valuations were included as follows:

	30 April 19_5	*30 April 19_6*
Stocks of raw materials (see note 1)	£36 000	£53 000
Stocks of work-in-progress (see note 2)	£59 000	£45 000
Stocks of finished goods (see note 3)	£71 000	£77 000
Quantity of finished goods in stock	14 200 units	15 400 units

Notes

(1) Raw materials consist of four separate stock items. The financial director has estimated the cost and 'net realisable value' of the four items at 30 April 19_6, as follows:

Stock item	*Cost*	*'Net realizable value'*
	£	£
1	15 000	6 000
2	10 000	15 000
3	12 000	18 000
4	10 000	14 000
	47 000	53 000

(2) The work-in-progress at 30 April 19_5, had been over-valued by 60%. No adjustment for this material error had been made in the draft accounts for the year ended 30 April 19_6.

(3) It is normal policy for the company to value its stocks of finished goods on 'first in first out' (FIFO) principles. However, the stock at 30 April 19_6, had been valued in error on 'last in first out' (LIFO) principles. The FIFO valuation per unit at the end of the financial year was 6% higher than at the start of the year.

Required:

(a) Prepare a statement showing the revised net profit of the company for the year ended 30 April 19_6, after taking into account any necessary amendments due to notes 1 to 3 above. (10 marks)

(b) The financial director states that fundamental accounting concepts should be abandoned if their use results in a failure to disclose a 'true and fair view' in the financial statements of a limited company. Comment on the financial director's statement. (5 marks)

(15 marks)

Advanced Level Accounting, London

Solutions

15.2 (a)

Stores Ledger Account

	Receipts			*Issues*			*Balance*		
Date	Quantity	Unit cost	Total cost	Quantity	Unit cost	Total cost	Quantity	Unit cost	Total cost
		£	£		£	£		£	£
1 January							50	250	12 500
1 February	100	300	30 000						
February				50	250	12 500			
				25	300	7 500	75	300	22 500
1 March	200	292.5*	58 500						
1 May	300	285*	85 500						
May				75	300	22 500			
				200	292.5	58 500			
				75	285	21 375	225	285	64 125
			174 000			122 375			

* *Determination of unit cost of receipts*

£ (60 000 × 0.975) ÷ 200 units = £292.5

£ (90 000 × 0.95) ÷ 300 units = £285

(b) ***Trading account for the six months 1 January–30 June***

	£	£
Sales		205 000
Less cost of goods sold		
Opening stock	12 500	
Purchases	174 000	
	186 500	
Less closing stock	64 125	
		122 375
Gross profit		£82 625

Note that the total of the issues column represents the cost of goods sold.

(c) It is first necessary to work out the closing stock valuation under LIFO.

Date	*Purchases*	*Sales*	*Balance*	£	£
1 Jan			50 @ £250		12 500
1 Feb	100 @ £300		50 @ £250	12 500	
			100 @ £300	30 000	42 500
Feb		75 @ £300	50 @ £250	12 500	
			25 @ £300	7 500	20 000
1 Mar	200 @ £292.5		50 @ £250	12 500	
			25 @ £300	7 500	
			200 @ £292.5	58 500	78 500
1 May	300 @ £285		50 @ £250	12 500	
			25 @ £300	7 500	
			200 @ £292.5	58 500	
			300 @ £285	85 500	164 000
May		300 @ £285	50 @ £250	12 500	
		50 @ £292.5	25 @ £300	7 500	
			150 @ £292.5	43 875	63 875

Trading account for the six months under LIFO

	£	£
Sales		205 000
Less cost of goods sold		
Opening stock	12 500	
Purchases	174 000	
	186 500	
Less closing stock	63 875	122 625
Gross profit		£82 375

15.3 (a) AVCO perpetual inventory

Date	*Goods Received*	*Goods Issued*	*Stocks Average cost** £	*Stocks Units held*	*Value* £
19_3					
1 January			13.80	7	96.60
10 January	20 @ £14.00		13.95	27	376.60
26 February		15 @ £13.95		12	167.40
4 April	10 @ £14.00		13.97	22	307.40
8 May		6 @ £13.97		16	223.52
2 June	12 @ £14.30		14.11	28	395.12
20 July		14 @ £14.11		14	197.54

22 September	20 @ £15.10		14.69	34	499.54
11 October		18 @ £14.69		16	235.04
9 November	14 @ £15.20		14.93	30	447.84
3 December		20 @ £14.93		10	149.30

* to the nearest penny

(b) (i) AVCO periodic inventory

	units	£
Opening stock	7 @ £13.80	96.60
Purchases:	20 @ £14.00	280.00
	10 @ £14.00	140.00
	12 @ £14.30	171.60
	20 @ £15.10	302.00
	14 @ £15.20	212.80
	83	1 203.00

$$\text{Unit average cost} = \frac{£1\ 203.00}{83}$$

= £14.49 (to the nearest penny)

Units available for issue	83
Less issues	73
Units of closing stock	∴ 10

Stock valuation = 10 units @ £14.49
= £144.90

(ii) FIFO
10 units @ £15.20 = £152.00

(iii) LIFO

Date	*Receipts*	*Issues*	*Balance*	£	£
1 Jan			7 @ £13.80		96.60
10 Jan	20 @ £14.00		7 @ £13.80	96.60	
			20 @ £14.00	280.00	376.60
26 Feb		15 @ £14.00	7 @ £13.80	96.60	
			5 @ £14.00	70.00	166.60
4 Apr	10 @ £14.00		7 @ £13.80	96.60	
			15 @ £14.00	210.00	306.60
8 May		6 @ £14.00	7 @ £13.80	96.60	
			9 @ £14.00	126.00	222.60
2 June	12 @ £14.30		7 @ £13.80	96.60	
			9 @ £14.00	126.00	
			12 @ £14.30	171.60	394.20
20 July		12 @ £14.30	7 @ £13.80	96.60	
		2 @ £14.00	7 @ £14.00	98.00	194.60
22 Sept	20 @ £15.10		7 @ £13.80	96.60	
			7 @ £14.00	98.00	
			20 @ £15.10	302.00	496.60
11 Oct		18 @ £15.10	7 @ £13.80	96.60	
			7 @ £14.00	98.00	
			2 @ £15.10	30.20	224.80
9 Nov	14 @ £15.20		7 @ £13.80	96.60	
			7 @ £14.00	98.00	
			2 @ £15.10	30.20	
			14 @ £15.20	212.80	437.60
3 Dec		14 @ £15.20			
		2 @ £15.10	7 @ £13.80	96.60	
		4 @ £14.00	3 @ £14.00	42.00	138.60

(c) *FIFO, LIFO and AVCO periodic*
19_3 was a year of rising prices. Consequently FIFO places a higher valuation of stock than LIFO (£152.00 compared to £138.60). This is because under FIFO the closing stock is valued at the *latest* prices, under LIFO at the *earlier* prices. The AVCO valuation being an average for the year is, as can be expected, in between the FIFO and LIFO valuations.

AVCO periodic v AVCO perpetual
Here the two stock figures are different because under perpetual inventory the stock valuation is affected *with each purchase*, whereas under periodic inventory the closing stock is determined by a *single* weighted average cost of purchase over the whole year. The perpetual inventory method gives a better reflection of the true cost of the stock in that it takes account of *all* price changes during the year. Under periodic inventory the stock figure is affected by the *average* price increase, and fails to take account of individual movements in price during the year.

15.7 (a) *Workings*

W_1 Stock should be valued not at net realizable value (nrv) but at the *lower of cost and nrv.*

Corrected stock valuation of raw materials:

Stock item	*Valuation*
1	6 000
2	10 000
3	12 000
4	10 000
	38 000

Draft valuation	53 000
Corrected valuation	38 000
Overvaluation	∴ 15 000

W_2 *Work-in-progress:*

Correct valuation	100
Overvaluation	60
Draft valuation	160

$$\text{Overvaluation} = £59\,000 \times \frac{60}{160} = £22\,125$$

W_3 Unit valuation 30 April 19_5 $= \dfrac{£71\,000}{14\,200} = £5$

19_6 $= £5 \times 1.06 = £5.30$

Total stock valuation 30 April 19_6	= 15 400 units @ £5.30
	= £81 620
Current LIFO valuation	£77 000
Undervaluation	£ 4 620

We can now prepare our

Statement of revised net profit

	£	£
Net profit as per draft accounts		108 400
Add Opening work-in-progress overvalued (W_2)	22 125	
Finished goods stock undervalued (W_3)	4 620	26 745
		135 145
Less Raw materials over-valued (W_1)		15 000
Revised net profit		120 145

(b) There are a number of fundamental accounting concepts which underlie a set of accounts. Having stood the test of time they are expected to be observed for reasons of *consistency* and because they make sense in themselves. Departure from such a concept can however be justified if adhering would fail to disclose a 'true and fair view' of the financial affairs of a business. The departure must however be agreed with the *auditors* of the company since, in the final analysis, it is they who have the responsibility of certifying the accounts to be 'true and fair'. Where a departure from an accepted concept takes place this must be noted in the accounts along with the reason for this.

CHAPTER 16

Overhead Absorption Costing

The overheads of a business are the *indirect* costs of running it — indirect material, indirect labour and indirect expenses. These are costs which cannot be charged directly to products and so must be charged indirectly to them, using the methods described in this chapter.

Overheads may be classified into 4 main groups:

(1) *Production overhead,* also known as factory overhead or works overhead. Examples are factory rent and rates, factory light and heat, power, depreciation of plant and buildings, and supervisors' salaries.

(2) *Administration overhead,* such as office rent and rates, office light and heat, clerical and executive salaries, stationery, postages, and telephone.

(3) *Selling overhead,* such as the cost of advertising, sales promotion, sales staff salaries, and research and development. Where research and development is a major item of expenditure it is classified as an overhead group on its own.

(4) *Distribution overhead.* These include warehouse costs, packaging, transport, and depreciation of delivery vans.

Overheads may be either:

fixed	e.g.	rent and rates, depreciation
variable	e.g.	power, salesmen's commissions
semi-fixed	e.g.	supervisors' salaries, or
semi-variable	e.g.	telephone, electricity

Cost Centre

If costs are to be effectively controlled it must be possible for management to trace them to that part of the organization incurring the cost. This is the cost centre. *A cost centre is an area of responsibility, such as a department, to which costs can be related for control purposes.* If the persons in the centre have *control* over the costs they can be made responsible for them. In this way the organization can be broken down into several different cost centres, with each centre manager being responsible for his own cost level. Cost can be of two types — production or service. Production centres are directly involved in production e.g. machining department. In contrast service cost centres exist to facilitate production e.g. maintenance and canteen.

Determination of Unit Cost

We know from Chapter 14 that one of the chief functions of the cost accountant is to determine unit production cost. This consists of direct labour, direct material, direct expenses and overheads. The question of deciding the issue price of materials was looked at in the previous chapter, labour and direct expenses in the chapter previous to that. It is now time to look at the fourth item of unit cost, overheads. Since overheads cannot be charged directly to cost units they must be shared between them on some equitable basis. This is done by first allocating and apportioning the overheads to cost centres, then absorbing them into cost units. It is possible to identify four separate stages in the calculation of overhead cost per unit:

Stage	*Procedure*
1	The various factory overhead costs are *allocated* or *apportioned* to the production and service cost centres.
2	The costs of the service centres are *re-apportioned* to the production centres.
3	Appropriate departmental *overhead absorption rates* are calculated.
4	The overhead costs are *absorbed* into cost units by applying the absorption rates to jobs passing through each centre.

Let us look in detail at each of the stages:

Stage 1 — Allocation and Apportionment

Those costs which are wholly identifiable with one cost centre are *allocated* to that centre. For example, the salary of a machine supervisor can be allocated to the machining department, the wages of a cook to the canteen. There are some overheads however which cannot be charged to just one centre, because the benefit of the expenditure is felt by several centres, e.g. rent and rates. The total has to be shared or *apportioned* over the cost centres on some equitable basis. With rent and rates since the charge is a function of area, relative areas covered by the cost centres is a fair basis of apportionment. Other occupancy costs such as light and heat should also be shared by floor space. With depreciation of fixed assets and insurance, book value might be the best basis. The cost of power and electricity should be related to usage. In some cases there is more than one possible fair basis of apportionment. Examiners do not usually state which basis to apply — you have to apply your common sense and judgement in each case.

Stage 2 — Re-apportionment

Since the beneficiaries of a service department are not actual products but production departments, their costs must be charged to those departments. In this there is again more than one method. The chosen one should be that which best reflects the relative benefits derived by the other departments. For example the total cost of operating a canteen could be charged on the basis of number of employees in each department, the cost of stores on the basis of value of materials or number of stores requisitions issued (note the scope for more than one basis). In some questions the relative benefits of a service department to other departments is given in percentages — these should then form the basis of your re-apportionment.

In some cases the benefit of a service department is felt by other service departments in addition to production departments. For example personnel benefits other service departments such as stores and maintenance as well as production departments. A difficulty arises here since the costs of a service department written off to other departments may be re-activated by being charged its share of costs of another service department from which it benefits. This charge must now be re-apportioned back to the user departments. In so doing another service department whose costs have been written off can be re-activated — and so on. This process can continue for a long time before it is complete. There are three methods of re-apportionment in such cases — the *repeated distribution method, specified order of closing,* and *algebraic solution* using simultaneous equations. If cross-charges are in the syllabus of your course it is sufficient at this level to know just one method. Repeated distribution would be the sensible choice since it is the simplest of the three. I have illustrated a solution to a problem on cross-charges using repeated distribution in question 16.5.

Allocations, apportionments and re-apportionments are usually shown in the form of an Overhead Analysis Sheet formatted like the pro-forma below.

Overhead Analysis Sheet

Item of expenditure	*Basis of allocation/ apportionment*	*Total*	*Production* *Machine*	*Assembly*	*Service* *Stores*	*Mainten-ance*
		£	£	£	£	£
Indirect wages	Actual	x	x	x	x	x
Rent and rates	Area	x	x	x	x	x
Light and heat	Area	x	x	x	x	x
Depreciation	Book value	x	x	x	x	x
Insurance	Book value	x	x	x	x	x
Power	Effective HP	x	x	x	x	x
	(i)	A	B	C	D	E
Re-apportionment:						
Stores	Value of materials issued		x	x	(D)	—
Maintenance	Percentages given		x	x	—	(E)
	(ii)	L	M	N	—	—

In the above pro-forma:

(1) Having allocated and apportioned the various expense items amongst the cost centres it is advisable for you to check that the total of B, C, D, and E in line (i) equals A — as it should do. This is to satisfy yourself that you have not made any arithmetical error before proceeding to the second stage.

(2) By line (ii) all the overheads have been apportioned to the production cost centres only. M therefore represents the total amount of overhead that has to be charged to jobs passing through the machine department, N through the assembly department. Again, it is advisable to do a quick check that M plus N does equal L.

(3) In listing your items of expense time will be saved if you group items to be shared on the same basis *together* then apportion their *total* to the cost centres instead of each individually. You can do this because the relative proportions for each expense are the same.

Stages 3 and 4 — Absorption

Now that the accountant knows the amount of overhead charged to each production cost centre it only remains for him to establish rates for their *recovery* through the jobs which pass through them. In this there is again more than one method — in fact there are six. Let us look at them, illustrating their calculation for the following information on a hypothetical company with just one production cost centre.

Income Statement

	£000	£000
Sales		700
Less cost of goods sold		
Direct material	200	
Direct labour	100	
Prime cost	300	
Production overhead	200	500
Gross profit		200

Direct labour hours worked	50 000
Machine hours worked	40 000
Number of units produced	25 000

(i) *Rate per direct labour hour*

Cost centre overheads/Cost centre direct labour hours

$$\frac{£200\ 000}{50\ 000} = £4 \text{ per direct labour hour}$$

For every hour of direct labour spent on a unit in the department it will be charged £4 as its share of overhead. This method is suitable where the departmental overhead incurred is related mainly to *time* and work is *labour-intensive* e.g. packing department.

The final stage (4) in overhead recovery is *application* of the absorption rate to jobs. Taking a product which has had £4 of direct material and £4 of direct labour spent on it and which has had $2\frac{1}{2}$ hours in the factory total unit cost would be:

	£
Direct material	4
Direct labour	4
Prime cost	8
Overhead, $2\frac{1}{2}$ hours @ £4	10
Unit production cost	18

(ii) *Percentage of direct labour cost*

Cost centre overheads/Cost centre direct labour cost × 100

$$\frac{£200\ 000}{£100\ 000} \times 100 = 200\%$$

Thus for every £1 of direct wage that a unit has spent on it, it is charged £2 of overhead. The implicit assumption in this method is that overheads are a function of direct wages rather than time. Jobs requiring skilled labour at high wage rates will therefore be charged a higher rate of overhead than jobs requiring unskilled labour at low wage rates. Is this fair? It would be if the overheads incurred were a function of direct wages. In reality however, most overheads are a function of *time* e.g. rent and rates, supervisors' salary. For this reason this method is not as sound as the first from a cost accounting point of view. It is however simpler to use since records do not have to be kept of the time spent by workers on each job, and would be the preferred method where wage rates within a department are uniform e.g. in an assembly department where all assemblers are paid a standard wage rate.

Note that since the different methods of overhead recovery are likely to produce different rates of absorption they will also produce different figures for unit cost. By this method for example:

	£
Direct material	4
Direct labour	4
Prime cost	8
Overhead, £4 × 200%	8
Unit production cost	16

Unit cost is £16 compared to £18 using the first method. If price is based on cost the different methods will then also produce different selling prices.

(iii) *Percentage of direct material cost*

Overheads/Direct material cost × 100

$$\frac{£200\ 000}{£200\ 000} \times 100 = 100\%$$

For every £1 of direct material spent on an unit, it is charged £1 of overhead. For our product overhead recovered is £4 × 100% = £4.

Although simple to apply, this method cannot really be recommended as it has no logical basis. A job requiring expensive material will be charged more overhead than a job requiring cheap material even though the overhead incurred on the two may be the same. The method fails to account for the different times spent on different jobs. A slow job taking twice as long as another but using the same value of material would be charged the same overhead. This is not likely to produce meaningful rates of absorption and as a consequence the unit costs computed may fail to reflect the true cost of each unit.

(iv) *Percentage of prime cost*

Overheads/Prime cost × 100

£200 000/£300 000 × 100 = $66\frac{2}{3}$%

For each of £1 of prime cost spent on an unit, it is charged £0.666˙ of overhead. For our product, overhead recovered is £8 × $66\frac{2}{3}$% = £5.33.

As prime cost consists of direct material and direct labour the disadvantages which apply to the percentage of direct material cost and percentage of direct labour cost also apply to this method. It is not one which can be recommended.

(v) *Rate per machine hour*

Overheads/Machine hours

$$\frac{£200\,000}{40\,000} = £5 \text{ per machine hour}$$

For our product, overhead recovered is $2\frac{1}{2}$ hours @ £5 = £12.50.

Where work is of a *capital-intensive* nature this is a good method to use. In the machining department for example, most of the overheads — depreciation, insurance, repairs, power — are related to time and use of the machines, so it seems fair to relate the recovery of the overheads also to time and use of the machines.

(vi) *Rate per unit of output*

Overheads/Units produced × 100

$$\frac{£200\,000}{25\,000} = £8 \text{ per unit}$$

For our product overhead recovered is £8.

This method is extremely simple and cheap to operate but is suitable only where the cost centre performs just one standard task for all units passing through it, and each unit takes up the *same amount of man and machine time* e.g. car bodies passing through the painting section of a factory. It is suitable for most of the cost centres of mass-production industries producing identical units in an identical fashion such as chemicals, steel manufacture, motor manufacture, and dairy farming.

Be Careful

Sometimes you have to cost jobs passing through more than one cost centre. Make sure you apply the correct absorption rate to the product in each centre.

Illustration

The cost accountant of a factory with two production departments has calculated the following overhead absorption rates:

	Machining	*Assembly*
	£	£
Rate per direct labour hour	8	3
Rate per machine hour	4	5
Rate per unit of output	7	6

The chosen rates are per machine hour for the machining department and per labour hour for assembly. How much overhead should be charged to a product spending 4 hours in machining followed by $1\frac{1}{2}$ hours in assembly?

Answer

Overhead charged:

Machining 4 hours @ £4	16.00
Assembly $1\frac{1}{2}$ hours @ £3	4.50
	£20.50

In some questions you are given more information than is necessary to perform the task set, as above. In these cases select only that cost data which is relevant.

The Blanket Absorption Rate

Since most factories are divided into several departments with products passing from one department to another, separate absorption rates are calculated for each department. A simplification of this would be to calculate just one rate for the factory as a whole.

Example

Total overheads of a factory	£750 000
Direct labour hours worked	250 000

Using the rate per direct labour hour

$$\text{Blanket overhead rate} = \frac{£750\ 000}{250\ 000} = £3$$

All units would be charged overhead £3 per direct labour hour regardless of the amount of time it spent in different departments.

Be careful of the distinction between the blanket overhead rate and the rate per unit of output — they are not the same. The latter calculates a separate rate based on units produced *independently for each cost centre.* A factory with three production cost centres would have three separate absorption rates. With the blanket rate there is no attempt to divide the factory into separate cost centres. In effect the whole of the factory is one large cost centre.

While blanket rates simplify the accounting for overheads they can only be used in certain conditions. If, as is the case in most industries, different departments incur different amounts of overhead and products spend unequal times in the different departments, a single absorption rate for the whole factory would not be appropriate. Jobs spending the bulk of their time in departments with large overheads should be charged proportionately *more* than those spending most of their time in departments with low overheads. In such a case calculating and applying separate departmental overhead rates, although more expensive to operate, would produce more meaningful results of unit cost. A blanket rate can be satisfactorily used *only when all products spend roughly the same amount of time in each department.*

The Need to Forecast

So far we have been relating actual overhead expenditure to actual activity in determining the absorption rate. In practice there are two difficulties of doing this:

1. It is necessary to wait until the end of a financial year before the totals of the variables are known. Thus for a company with its financial year running from 1 January to 31 December, goods produced in January and February cannot be fully costed until after December. This is impractical. The problem can be overcome by calculating the variables at more frequent intervals, say monthly, but if this is done a second problem is created.

2. Changes in activity level between months will change the absorption rate. Take a company which uses the rate per unit of output:

	January	*June*
Overhead incurred	£50 000	£45 000
Production	10 000 units	5 000 units
Absorption rate	£5	£9

This company experiences a slow-down in activity in summer, yet overheads being mostly fixed stay much the same. As a result the decrease in production *increases the absorption rate.* Units produced in January are changed £5 of overhead while identical units produced in June are charged £9. This leads to frequent changes in unit cost, selling price and/or gross profit. In these circumstances it is better to calculate the *average* absorption rate for the whole year by basing total *annual* overhead to annual activity levels. If we do this however, we are back to our first problem of having to wait until the end of the accounting year before rates can be established. *The dilemma is overcome by predetermining the rate by basing an annual estimated overhead expenditure to estimated levels of activity.* This information is generated from preparation of the annual budget, a subject-matter we consider in Chapter 21.

Under- and Over-absorption

It is most unlikely that actual levels of expenditure and activity will turn out to be exactly as budgeted. If they are not, there will be a discrepancy between the amount of overhead incurred and the amount absorbed into products (which is based on the budgeted rate).

Example

For a Machining Department cost centre:

Budgeted overheads	£200 000
Budgeted machine hours	40 000
Absorption rate per machine hour	£5

	Case A	*Case B*
Actual overhead incurred	£200 000	£180 000
Actual machine hours worked	30 000	40 000
Overhead absorbed	£150 000	£200 000

In Case A the budgeted number of machine hours has not been reached. As a result only £150 000 of the £200 000 overhead incurred has been charged to jobs — there is an *under-absorption* of £50 000. In B the activity forecast has been achieved but this time the overhead incurred is below plan. £200 000 has been charged to jobs even though only £180 000 has been incurred — there is an *over-absorption* of £20 000.

Under-absorption will occur if:
(1) actual activity is below budget, or
(2) actual overhead is above budget.

Over-absorption will occur if:
(1) actual activity is above budget, or
(2) actual overhead is below budget.

Further consideration of overhead variances is given in Chapter 22, Standard Costing and Variance Analysis.

The better the forecasting the smaller will be the amount of under- or over-absorption. Such incorrect amounts of overhead are not uncommon in practice. They can be avoided only if absorption rates are based on actual expenditure and activity levels but we have seen the two problems this can cause. Most firms choose to forecast the rate in their annual budget and accept the inevitable under/over-absorption. The question is — how should they be dealt with? The perfectionist might like to share the under/over recovery among all jobs worked over the year, but in practice this may prove to be too complicated and expensive an exercise. Another possible solution is to carry forward the discrepancy to the next accounting period, charging it to jobs produced then. This cannot however be justified on theoretical grounds — its effect would be to distort the unit cost of future products simply because of a forecasting error in the past. Instead most firms prefer to *write off the amount of the under/over absorption to that year's profit and loss account.* This is in fact the official recommendation of SSAP9, Stocks and work-in-progress. The ledger accounts would look as follows.

In the case of A:

Factory overheads

Incurred — Bank	200 000	Absorbed — WIP	150 000
		Under-absorption — P & L	50 000
	200 000		200 000

The under-absorption would be a *charge* to P & L.

In the case of B:

Factory Overheads

Incurred — Bank	180 000	Absorbed — WIP	200 000
Over-absorption — P & L	20 000		
	200 000		200 000

The over-absorption would be a miscellaneous *income* in P & L.
See question 16.4.

Non-manufacturing Overheads

A manufacturing concern will have not only a factory but also warehouse and offices. These also attract overhead expenses. A warehouse incurs *distribution costs* such as storage space, containers, and delivery vans. An office incurs *administration expenses* such as clerical and accountancy charges, managerial salaries, and office occupancy costs. It will also incur *selling costs* such as advertising and publicity, and possibly also research and development.

In this chapter we have looked so far at possible ways of absorbing production overheads to cost units. At the end of the day it is not sufficient for a business to recover just prime cost and production overhead. The administration, selling and distribution overheads have to be recovered as well. The question is — on what basis? Should their recovery be charged directly to products? Since there is no clear link between the manufacture of a product and an indirect non-manufacturing expense most firms do not attempt to charge them to individual cost units. Instead a selected mark-up is added to production cost to cover them.

Example

Let us take a factory manufacturing dining tables:

Per table	£
Direct material	80
Direct labour	40
Prime cost	120
Factory overhead	80
Production cost	200
Mark-up, 25%	50
Total cost	250
Profit	50
Selling price	300

In the year-end financial statements the factory overhead is shown in the *trading account* as part of the cost of goods sold while the non-manufacturing overhead is shown in the *profit and loss account* under expenses. Closing stocks therefore incorporate a share of the production overhead but not administration, selling and distribution overhead. (Whether part of the production overhead *should* be carried forward in closing stock to be charged in the following year is the topic of debate in Chapter 19, Absorption and Marginal Costing.)

Some firms boldly attempt to charge non-manufacturing overheads *directly* to cost units by using bases such as the number of staff in each cost centre for administrative expenses and sales value of each centre for selling costs. Such apportionments are very arbitrary however and often do not reflect the relationship between the chosen basis and incurring of the cost. For example, a popular high-value product may incur a low unit selling cost, because the quality of the product sells itself, while a not so popular low-value product may incur a higher unit selling cost. For this reason most firms to do not attempt to charge non-manufacturing overheads directly to products.

Questions

16.1 The Harlton Manufacturing Company uses job costing. The Company has four production departments and three service departments. Indirect labour and other indirect costs for a typical month have been allocated as shown:

HARLTON MANUFACTURING COMPANY

	Production Departments				*Service Departments*		
	Grinding	*Blending*	*Firing*	*Polishing*	*Personnel*	*Administration*	*Maintenance*
Indirect labour (£)	4 600	3 300	5 400	2 900	700	1 800	800
Other indirect costs (£)	1 400	1 200	2 800	1 600	500	300	1 200

The service departments' costs are allocated as follows:

	Grinding	*Blending*	*Firing*	*Polishing*	*Administration*	*Maintenance*
Personnel (%)	15	25	30	20	5	5
Administration (%)	10	30	40	15	—	5
Maintenance (%)	15	35	45	5	—	—

In the Grinding and Firing departments, job costing uses an overhead rate per machine hour; in Blending and Polishing, an overhead rate per direct labour hour is used.

Machine hours worked are 611 in Grinding, and 520 in Firing. Direct labour hours worked are 1,034 in Blending, and 431 in Polishing.

Required:

(a) Calculate the overhead recovery rates for each of the production departments. (20 marks)

(b) Use your answers to calculate the cost of job number 84/1 which incurs the following costs:

Grinding Department:	Direct materials cost	£120
	Direct labour hours at £2.40 per hour	14
	Machine hours	30
Then passed to Blending where		
	Direct materials cost	£97
	Direct labour hours at £2.60 per hour	18

(10 marks)

(30 marks)

Advanced Level Accounting, London

16.2* (a) Why is it necessary to *apportion* overheads to departments? How is this done in practice? (9 marks)

(b) A firm has three production departments and two service departments. Details of their costs for a month are shown below:

	Production Departments			*Service Departments*	
	A	B	C	G	H
	£	£	£	£	£
Indirect labour	10 000	8 000	4 000	3 000	2 000
Other overheads	6 000	5 000	3 000	1 500	1 000

It has been agreed to charge Department H's costs as follows: 45% to A; 35% to B; 15% to C; 5% to G. Department G's costs are to be charged: 55% to A; 25% to B; 20% to C. A and C recover overheads on the basis of direct labour hours, which are 885 for A and 537 for C; B recovers overheads on the basis of machine hours, which are 613.
Calculate the overhead recovery rate for the production department. (10 marks)

(c) Use your answer to explain how overheads are *absorbed* by production. (6 marks)
(25 marks)

Advanced Level Accounting, London

16.3* AC Limited is a small company which undertakes a variety of jobs.

Budgeted Profit and Loss Statement: year ending 31st December, 19_6

	£	£
Sales		750 000
Costs:		
Direct materials	100 000	
Direct wages	50 000	
Prime cost	150 000	
Fixed production overhead	300 000	
Production cost	450 000	
Selling, distribution and administration cost	160 000	610 000
Profit		£140 000

Budgeted data:

Labour hours for the year	25 000
Machine hours for the year	15 000
Number of jobs for the year	300

An enquiry has been received and the production department has produced estimates of the prime cost and hours required for job A57.

	£
Direct materials	250
Direct wages	200
Prime cost	£450
Labour hours required	80
Machine hours required	50

Required:

(a) calculate by different methods **six** overhead absorption rates; (6 marks)

(b) comment briefly on the suitability of each method calculated in (a); (8 marks)

(c) calculate cost estimates for job A57 using in turn each of the six overhead absorption rates calculated in (a). (6 marks)
(20 marks)

Chartered Institute of Management Accountants

16.4 A company is preparing overhead budgets and determining the apportionment of these overheads to products.

Cost centre expenses and related information have been budgeted as follows:

	Total	*Machine Shop A*	*Machine Shop B*	*Assembly*	*Canteen*	*Maintenance*
Indirect wages (£)	78 560	8 586	9 190	15 674	29 650	15 460
Consumable materials (incl. maintenance) (£)	16 900	6 400	8 700	1 200	600	—
Rent and rates (£)	16 700					
Buildings insurance (£)	2 400					
Power (£)	8 600					
Heat and light (£)	3 400					
Depreciation of machinery (£)	40 200					
Area (sq ft)	45 000	10 000	12 000	15 000	6 000	2 000
Value of machinery (£)	402 000	201 000	179 000	22 000	—	—
Power usage — technical estimates (%)	100	55	40	3	—	2
Direct labour (hours)	35 000	8 000	6 200	20 800	—	—
Machine usage (hours)	25 200	7 200	18 000	—	—	—

Required:

(a) Determine budgeted overhead absorption rates for each of the production departments, using bases of apportionment and absorption which you consider most appropriate from the information provided. (13 marks)

(b) On the assumption that actual activity was:

	Machine Shop A	*Machine Shop B*	*Assembly*
Direct labour hours	8 200	6 500	21 900
Machine usage hours	7 300	18 700	—

and total production overhead expenditure was £176 533, prepare the production overhead control account for the year (you are to assume that the company has a separate cost accounting system). (6 marks)

(c) Explain the meaning of the word 'control' in the title of the account prepared in answer to (b). (3 marks)

(22 marks)

Chartered Association of Certified Accountants

16.5 Shown below is an extract from next year's budget for a company manufacturing three different products in three production departments.

Product	*A*	*B*	*C*
Production	4 000 units	3 000 units	6 000 units
Direct Material Cost	£7 per unit	£4 per unit	£9 per unit
Direct Labour Requirements:	hours per unit	hours per unit	hours per unit
Cutting Department:			
Skilled operatives	3	5	2
Unskilled operatives	6	1	3
Machining Department	$\frac{1}{2}$	$\frac{1}{4}$	$\frac{1}{3}$
Pressing Department	2	3	4
Machine Hour Requirements:			
Machining Department	2	$1\frac{1}{2}$	$2\frac{1}{2}$

The skilled operatives employed in the Cutting Department are paid £4 per hour and the unskilled operatives are paid £2.50 per hour. All the operatives in the Machining and Pressing Departments are paid £3 per hour.

	Production Departments			Service Departments	
	Cutting	*Machining*	*Pressing*	*Engineering*	*Personnel*
Budgeted Total Overheads	£154 482	£64 316	£58 452	£56 000	£34 000
Service department costs are incurred for the benefit of other departments as follows:					
Engineering Services	20%	45%	25%	—	10%
Personnel Services	55%	10%	20%	15%	—

The company operates a full absorption costing system.

Required:

(a) Calculate, as equitably as possible, the total budgeted manufacturing cost of:
 (i) one completed unit of Product A, and
 (ii) one incomplete unit of Product B, which has been processed by the Cutting and Machining Departments but which has not yet been passed into the Pressing Department. (15 marks)

(b) At the end of the first month of the year for which the above budget was prepared the production overhead control account for the Machining Department showed a credit balance. Explain the possible reasons for that credit balance. (7 marks)

(22 marks)

Chartered Association of Certified Accountants

16.6 What difficulties arise in apportioning overheads to production, and how are these difficulties overcome? Give examples. **(20 marks)**

Advanced Level Accounting, London

16.7 (a) Outline the procedures and information required in order to establish a set of pre-determined production overhead absorption rates, for a company manufacturing a range of different products in a factory containing a number of production departments and several service departments. (12 marks)

(b) Critically examine the purpose of calculating overhead absorption rates. (5 marks)

(17 marks)

Chartered Association of Certified Accountants

16.8 (a) Outline briefly the process of charging indirect costs to cost units. (6 marks)

(b) What are the factors which should influence how the costs of internal services in an organization are passed on to the users of those services? Illustrate your answer. (11 marks)

(17 marks)

Chartered Association of Certified Accountants

Solutions

16.1 (a) It is first necessary to prepare an Overhead Analysis Sheet.

	Production				*Service*		
	Grinding	*Blending*	*Firing*	*Polishing*	*Personnel*	*Administration*	*Maintenance*
	£	£	£	£	£	£	£
Indirect labour	4 600	3 300	5 400	2 900	700	1 800	800
Other indirect costs	1 400	1 200	2 800	1 600	500	300	1 200
Re-apportionment:							
Personnel	180	300	360	240	(1 200)	60	60
Administration	216	648	864	324	—	(2 160)	108
Maintenance	325	759	976	108	—	—	(2 168)
Total overhead	6 721	6 207	10 400	5 172	—	—	—

We can now calculate the overhead absorption rates for jobs passing through the production departments.

Department	*Basis*	*Calculation*
Grinding	Machine hour rate	$\frac{£6\,721}{611}$ = £11 per machine hour
Firing	Machine hour rate	$\frac{£10\,400}{520}$ = £20 per machine hour
Blending	Direct labour hour rate	$\frac{£6\,207}{1\,034}$ = £6 per labour hour
Polishing	Direct labour hour rate	$\frac{£5\,172}{431}$ = £12 per labour hour

(b) *Job No. 84/1*

Department		£	£
Grinding	Direct materials		120.00
Grinding	Direct labour, 14 hours @ £2.40		33.60
Blending	Direct materials		97.00
Blending	Direct labour, 18 hours @ £2.60		46.80
Prime cost			297.40
Overheads absorbed:			
Grinding	30 machine hours @ £11	330.00	
Blending	18 direct labour hours @ £6	108.00	438.00
Total production cost			735.40

16.4 (a) It is first necessary to prepare an Overhead Analysis Sheet.

	Basis of apportionment		*Production*			*Service*	
Item		*Total*	*Machine Shop A*	*Machine Shop B*	*Assembly*	*Canteen*	*Maintenance*
		£	£	£	£	£	
Indirect wages	Actual	78 560	8 586	9 190	15 674	29 650	15 460
Consumable materials	Actual	16 900	6 400	8 700	1 200	600	—
Rent and rates	Area	16 700					
Insurance	Area	2 400	5 000	6 000	7 500	3 000	1 000
Heat and Light	Area	3 400					
Power	Usage	8 600	4 730	3 440	258	—	172
Depreciation of machinery	Value	40 200	20 100	17 900	2 200	—	—
		166 760	44 816	45 230	26 832	33 250	16 632

		£	£	£	£	£	
Re-apportionment:							
Maintenance	Machine usage		4 752	11 880	—	—	(16 632)
Canteen	Labour hours*		7 600	5 890	19 760	(33 250)	—
		166 760	57 168	63 000	46 592	—	—

* Ideally it would be best to use number of employees, but in the absence of this information I have used direct labour hours.

We can now calculate the overhead absorption rates for jobs passing through the production departments. I have chosen the following methods:

Department	*Method*	*Reason*
Machine Shop A	Machine hour rate	Capital-intensive
Machine Shop B	Machine hour rate	Capital-intensive
Assembly	Direct labour hour rate	Labour-intensive

Machine Shop A $\frac{£57\ 168}{7\ 200} = £7.94$ per machine hour

Machine Shop B $\frac{£63\ 000}{1\ 800} = £3.50$ per machine hour

Assembly $\frac{£46\ 592}{20\ 800} = £2.24$ per direct labour

(b) *Production Overhead Control*

	£		£
Overhead expenditure incurred	176 533	Overheads Absorbed:	
		Machine A, 7 300 hours @ £7.94	57 962
		Machine B, 18 700 hours @ £3.50	65 450
		Assembly, 21 900 hours @ £2.24	49 056
			172 468
		Under-absorbed — to P & L	4 065
	176 533		176 533

(c) The word 'control' suggests that it is a Total Account, not part of the double-entry system but representing the *aggregate* of entries in the cost ledger of overheads incurred and absorbed. The control account is useful as a *checking device.* The total of the individual accounts should be equal to the single entries in the control account. If they do not the cost clerk is alerted to errors in the cost ledger.

Control accounts are also used in financial accounting such as the sales ledger control account for the individual entries in the sales ledger and purchase ledger control account for the purchase ledger (see Chapter 4).

16.5 A comprehensive question on overhead absorption costing, and one which is longer than might at first seem.

(a) It is first necessary to apportion the service departments' overheads to the production overheads. Since the two service departments benefit each other in addition to the production departments the apportionment is made more complicated. I have used the *Repeated Distribution method.*

	Production departments			*Service departments*	
	Cutting	*Machining*	*Pressing*	*Engineering*	*Personnel*
	£	£	£	£	£
Budgeted total overheads	154 482	64 316	58 452	56 000	34 000
Re-apportionment of Services:					
Engineering	11 200	25 200	14 000	(56 000)	5 600
Personnel	21 780	3 960	7 920	5 940	(39 600)
Engineering	1 188	2 673	1 485	(5 940)	594
Personnel	326.7	59.4	118.8	89.1	(594)
Engineering	17.8	40.1	22.3	(89.1)	8.9
Personnel	4.9	0.9	1.8	1.3	(8.9)
Engineering	0.3	0.7	0.3	(1.3)	—
	188 999.7	96 250.1	82 000.2	—	—
Take as	£189 000	£96 250	£82 000		

Next we have to calculate overhead absorption rates for the three Production departments. I have chosen the following methods:

Department	*Type*	*Method*	*Reason*
Cutting	Labour-intensive	Direct labour hour rate	Since wage rates are not uniform
Machining	Capital-intensive	Machine hour rate	Since the overheads are related mainly to operation of the machines
Pressing	Labour-intensive	Direct wages* percentage	Since uniform wage rates apply

* The direct labour hour rate can also be used for the pressing department. I have shown the answer using this basis as well.

Cutting

Product	*Budgeted units*	*Hours per unit*	*Total labour hours*
A	4 000	9	36 000
B	3 000	6	18 000
C	6 000	5	30 000
			84 000

$$\text{Overhead absorption rate} = \frac{£189\,000}{84\,000} = £2.25 \text{ per labour hour}$$

Machining

Product	*Budgeted units*	*Hours per unit*	*Total machine hours*
A	4 000	2	8 000
B	3 000	$1\frac{1}{2}$	4 500
C	6 000	$2\frac{1}{2}$	15 000
			27 500

$$\text{Overhead absorption rate} = \frac{£96\,250}{27\,500} = £3.50 \text{ per machine hour}$$

Pressing

Product	*Budgeted units*	*Hours per unit*	*Total labour hours*	*× Wage rate*	*Total direct wages*
A	4 000	2	8 000	£3	£24 000
B	3 000	3	9 000	£3	£27 000
C	6 000	4	24 000	£3	£72 000
			41 000		£123 000

$$\text{Overhead absorption rate} = \frac{£82\,000}{123\,000} \times 100 = 66.66\% \text{ of direct wages}$$

$$\textit{or} \quad \frac{£82\,000}{41\,000} = £2 \text{ per direct labour hour}$$

We can now answer the question set

(i) *Unit of A Complete*

	Calculation	£	£
Direct material	Given		7.00
Direct labour			
Cutting department — skilled	3 hours @ £4	12.00	
— unskilled	6 hours @ £2.50	15.00	
Machining department	½ hour @ £3	1.50	
Pressing department	2 hours @ £3	6.00	34.50
Prime cost			41.50
Production overhead			
Cutting department	9 hours @ £2.25	20.25	
Machining department	2 hours @ £3.50	7.00	
Pressing department	£6 × 66.66%	4.00	
	(or 2 hours @ £2)		31.25
Total unit cost			£72.75

(ii) *Unit of B Incomplete*

	Calculation	£	£
Direct material	Given		4.00
Direct labour			
Cutting department — skilled	5 hours @ £4	20.00	
— unskilled	1 hour @ £2.50	2.50	
Machining department	¼ hour @ £3	75	23.25
Prime cost			27.25
Production overhead			
Cutting department	6 hours @£2.25	13.50	
Machining department	1½ hours @ £3.50	5.25	18.75
Total unit cost			£46.00

Since B has not yet been pressed it does not have to share in the recovery of the pressing department's overhead — yet.

(b) A credit balance on the production overhead control account implies an *over-absorption* of overheads. This is caused by either:
 (i) actual activity level being above budget, or
 (ii) actual overhead incurred being below budget.

A third possible reason is that the first month of the year is expected to be busier than the average month i.e. expected to produce *more than* $\frac{1}{12}$ of the annual output. In this case, the higher level of activity will absorb a greater amount of overhead, leading to over-absorption.

CHAPTER 17
Job and Contract Costing

Costing Systems

The nature of the costing system used will depend on the *nature of the production process* and *type of good or service being costed.* There are two broad types of costing; job costing and process costing.

Job costing is suitable where the jobs being worked on are *unique* i.e. not standard. Often they are being made to a specific order such as a custom-built car, a one-off special export order or a contract to build an office. Since each job, being different from the next, requires different amounts of labour, material, and overhead spent on it, a separate record of its cost needs to be kept. Where an individual job is a long-term contract spanning several accounting periods, the techniques of *contract costing* have to be employed.

In industries where *identical units* are produced in an identical fashion, usually by mass-production methods, *process costing* is more suitable. Since one unit of output is identical to the next and has incurred the same cost, it is not necessary to keep a record of the cost of each individual unit. Instead it is sufficient to calculate *average* cost by dividing the total cost of production by the number of units produced. Process costing is used in continuous flow, mass-production industries such as chemicals, oil-refining, flour-milling and motor manufacture.

Job and contract costing are looked at in this chapter, process costing in the next chapter.

Job Costing

The purpose of job costing is the *keeping of separate cost records for each individual job.* This is done on a *job order cost sheet* which records the material and labour used in a job with their charge-out rates. Allocated overheads are also entered on this sheet. The job is, in effect, a cost centre to which the various costs are charged. Job costing is an expensive system to operate and should only be used in circumstances where it is really needed.

Example

The following information relates to Job Q–2:

Direct materials. In Department A, 20 kilos of material K_2 were issued from stores at £5 per kilo. In addition 12 kilos of L_1 were issued in Department B at £4. Of this a quarter was returned to stores.

Direct labour

Department	*Hours worked*	*Hourly rate*
		£
A	10	11
B	8	9

Direct expense. A special piece of equipment was hired for 2 days for the job. The daily hire charge was £37.

Production overheads. These are charged to jobs at the rate of £6 per direct labour hour.

Non-manufacturing overheads. The company adds 20% to production cost to cover its selling, distribution and administration overhead.

Calculate the cost of Job Q-2.

Answer

Job order cost sheet
for Job No. Q-2

Direct materials					
Department	*Material*	*Quantity (kilos)*	*Issue price (£ per kilo)*	£	£
A	K_2	20	5	100	
B	L_1	9	4	36	136
Direct labour					
Department	*Hours worked*	*Hourly rate* £		£	
A	10	11		110	
B	8	9		72	182
Direct expense					
Hire of equipment (£37 × 2 days)					74
Prime cost					392
Production overhead					
18 direct labour hours @ £6 per hour					108
Production cost					500
Non-manufacturing overhead (500 × 20%)					100
Total cost of job					£600

Examination questions

Examination questions on job costing usually require the answer to be in the above format. Sometimes you may have to do some preliminary workings on the amount of material and direct labour hours chargeable to a job, the issue price of materials and/or the overhead absorption rates.

In some questions you have to apply your judgement on whether a cost incurred on a particular job should in fact be charged to that job. For example, if defects in work carried out on a job necessitate the spending of additional time and material on it, should the cost of this be charged to the customer of that job? Perhaps not — that would be unfair. Some amount of faulty work can be expected to occur in all factories due to machine or human error. The usual costing practice is to treat the resulting cost as an *overhead*, to be recovered by charging to *all* jobs. *Normal losses* of material are usually also treated as a production overhead. *Abnormal losses* however, being not expected in the normal course of production, should not be charged to any job but instead written off to profit and loss account as an expense for the period. Another situation that sometimes arises is *overtime* being worked on a job to complete it on schedule because of a machine breakdown, non-availability of material, or a strike in the factory. Should the overtime labour premium be charged to the job? Again, it would be unfair to the customer. The premium should be treated as a production overhead. Charging premiums for overtime can only be justified if the job has to be finished before the agreed date because of a *request from the customer for early completion*.

Usefulness

Keeping a separate record of the cost of individual jobs can be useful in a number of ways:

(1) *Pricing*. A common pricing policy is cost plus % mark-up.

(2) *Determination of profit*. Where the price for a job has been quoted before it is carried out, a record of how much the job costs to complete must be kept if we are to know the profit earned on the job.

(3) *Work-in-progress valuation*. Those jobs which are still in the process of completion on the last day of the financial year can be easily valued if individual cost records are kept.

(4) *Cost control*. Similar jobs can be expected to incur similar costs. By keeping a record of the cost of each job, those jobs which are costing more than they should can easily be identified, and corrective action taken.

Contract Costing

Where a job is a *long-term contract covering several accounting periods*, as is the case in civil engineering and shipbuilding, costing of the job becomes a little more complicated and the techniques of contract costing have to be employed. A double-entry contract account is maintained for each job. All direct costs incurred on the contract and overheads allocated to it are debited to the account, while income from the contract is credited to it. The contract account is, in effect, an individual profit and loss account, from which it is possible to determine the profit on each job.

The client usually makes *several payments during the lifetime of the contract*, the amount payable in each instalment being determined by a professional valuation of the partly-completed job by a firm of architects or surveyors. The client is often allowed to withhold some of the payment even after the contract has been completed, for a period of time — known as the *retention money*. This is to allow time for him to assess whether the job has been completed to his satisfaction. If it has not, the contractor has to make good any defects in the original work before being entitled to the retainer.

Recognition of Profit

While the *realization* concept states that profit should be regarded as earned *when goods are passed to the customer*, such an approach is unsuitable for jobs covering several accounting periods. Adherence to it would result in the income statement taking credit only for jobs completed during the year rather than the value of *all* work carried on during the year. Years in which a large number of jobs are completed would show a disproportionately higher profit compared to years in which the same amount of work is done but fewer contracts completed. To overcome this problem *SSAP 9 (stocks and work-in-progress)* allows a *proportion* of profit to be recognized on contracts still in progress provided that there is *reasonable certainty that the contract will be completed for the sum agreed*. This means that the contractor does not take all of a year's apparent profit (being value of architect's certificate less cost of certified work) to that year's profit and loss account. A fraction, usually $\frac{1}{3}$, is held back as the *apparent profit not yet recognized as earned*, as a contingency for additional expenditure becoming necessary on the contract, for example for faulty work. It is transferred to profit and loss account after sufficient time has elapsed during which it becomes clear that no further costs will be necessary on the contract. Meanwhile the amount is shown in the balance sheet under reserves.

Since the outcome of long-term contracts in their early stages are not known with reasonable certainty, no profit should be taken. SSAP 9 also recommends that if a loss on a contract is incurred in any one year the *whole* of the loss should be charged to that year's profit and loss account, i.e. as soon as it arises, in line with the concept of prudence. For an illustration of these three different treatments of profit/loss see question 17.4.

Contents of a Contract Account

Materials are debited to the account. They may either be purchased and received directly from suppliers or sent to the contract site from stores. At the end of a contract year closing stocks of material are carried down as a debit to the next contract period, to be charged then (in line with the accruals concept).

Direct labour costs are also debited to the account. Any outstanding wages at the year-end should also be debited and carried down as a credit balance of the next period.
(All direct expenses and allocated overheads are also debited to the account.)

Fixed assets used on a contract are initially charged to it by debiting the account. At the end of a period the reduced value of the assets is carried down as a credit balance, being a debit balance at the start of the next period. In this way it is ensured that each year is charged its fair share of depreciation.

Let us now look at an actual example of a contract account.

Example

Steel Contractors Ltd. started work on a two-year factory construction project on 1 April 19_5. Details of the contract for the first year are as follows:

	£000
Materials purchased and delivered to site	50
Materials issued from store	40
Materials returned to store	5
Site wages	100
Site direct expenses	35
Architect's fees	15
Paid to Cement Ltd. for work sub-contracted	75
Allocated overheads	120
Plant sent to site	250

On 31 March 19_6 materials on site cost £10 000 and there was £10 000 outstanding for wages. The value of the plant was estimated at £190 000.

The company received an architect's certificate for £600 000 in respect of work carried out to date. This amount was received at the end of the year less 10 per cent retention money. As a provision for the possibility of further expenditure becoming necessary on the work carried out so far the company takes credit for only two-thirds of the profit on work certified. Work costing £30 000 was not certified as being worthy of payment yet.

(a) Prepare the contract account for the year to 31 March 19_6.
(b) What is the value of the work-in-progress at the year-end?
(c) Show an extract of the year-end balance sheet relating to items on this contract.

Answer

(a)

Contract account

	£000		£000
Materials delivered to site	50	Materials returned to store	5
Materials from store	40		
Site wages	100		
Site direct expenses	35		
Architect's fees	15	31 March 19_6	
Paid to sub-contractor	75	Materials c/f	10
Allocated overheads	120	Plant c/f	190
Plant sent to site	250	Cost of work not certified c/f	30
Wages accrued c/f	10	Cost of work certified c/f	∴ 460
	695		695
Cost of work certified b/f	460	Architect's certificate	600
P & L a/c — profit taken*	84		
Profit not taken c/f	56		
	600		600
1 April 19_6		1 April 19_6	
Materials b/f	10	Wages accrued b/f	10
Plant b/f	190	Profit not taken b/f	56
Cost of work not certified b/f	30		

You will note that the contract account is divided into three sections. The purpose of the first (and longest) section is to establish the total cost incurred on the contract over the year. This is found as a balancing figure on the account. The year-end balances are carried forward to the third section, which then represents part of the future costs still to be incurred on the contract. The calculation of the amount of profit to be credited to this year's profit and loss account is performed in the second section. The apparent profit is reduced by:

(1) the contingency for additional expenditure becoming necessary on the building in the future, $\frac{1}{3}$, and
(2) the amount of the retainer, $\frac{1}{10}$.

$$\text{* Profit taken} = \text{Apparent profit} \times \tfrac{2}{3} \times \frac{\text{Cash received}}{\text{Value of work certified}}$$

$$= (600 - 460) \times \tfrac{2}{3} \times \tfrac{9}{10} = 84$$

In next year's account the profit taken will be reduced by £84 000, being the profit already taken this year.

(b) *Valuation of year-end work-in-progress*

	£000
Cost of work certified to date	460
Cost of work not certified	30
Add profit taken to date	84
	574
Less progress payments received $(600 \times \frac{9}{10})$	540
Work-in-progress	34

(c)

STEEL CONTRACTORS LTD

Balance Sheet extract as at 31 March 19_6

	£000	£000		£000
Fixed assets			Profit and loss account	
Plant at site	250		(profit taken)	84
Less depreciation	60	190	Reserves (profit not taken)	56
Current assets			*Current liabilities*	
Materials	10		Wages accrued	10
Work-in-progress	34			
Debtor (retention money)	60			

Questions

17.1* The process plant division of a group of companies has built a food packaging machine to a customer's requirements. A price of £49 000 had been quoted with the intention of achieving 25% profit on the selling price.

Customer:	Bond Foods Limited
Customer's Order No:	7206 dated 3rd February, 19_6
Job Order No:	1412
Date work started:	5th March, 19_6
Date job completed in factory:	29th April, 19_6
Date delivered:	2nd May, 19_6
Date commissioned:	6th May, 19_6

	March	*April*
	£	£
Materials used:		
Machining Dept.	2 900	700
Assembly Dept.	1 900	1 400
Direct wages rate per hour:		
Machining Dept.	4	4.40
Assembly Dept.	5	5.25
	Hours	Hours
Direct labour hours:		
Machining Dept.	200	100
Assembly Dept	50	500
Machine hours in		
Machining Dept.	350	180
Technical drawings		
(direct cost)	£2 115	

Production overhead is absorbed at the predetermined rate of £10 per direct labour hour in the Assembly Dept. and £15 per machine hour in the Machining Dept.

Commissioning costs, i.e. installation and initial running-in of the machine at the customer's site, were £750 and these are to be treated as a direct production cost.

Selling and general administration costs are charged to jobs at the rate of $33\frac{1}{3}$% of production cost.

Required:

(a) prepare a job order cost sheet and insert on it the information given above in such a way as to be useful to management; (16 marks)

(b) explain 'job costing' and 'batch costing'. (4 marks)

(20 marks)

Chartered Institute of Management Accountants

17.2 In order to identify the costs incurred in carrying out a range of work to customer specification in its factory, a company has a job costing system. This system identifies costs directly with a job where this is possible and reasonable. In addition, production overhead costs are absorbed into the cost of jobs at the end of each month, at an actual rate per direct labour hour for each of the two production departments.

One of the jobs carried out in the factory during the month just ended was Job No. 123. The following information has been collected relating specifically to this job:

400 kilos of Material Y were issued from stores to Department A. 76 direct labour hours were worked in Department A at a basic wage of £4.50 per hour. 6 of these hours were classified as overtime at a premium of 50%.

300 kilos of Material Z were issued from stores to Department B. Department B returned 30 kilos of Material Z to the storeroom being excess to requirements for the job.

110 direct labour hours were worked in Department B at a basic wage of £4.00 per hour. 30 of these hours were classified as overtime at a premium of 50%. All overtime worked in Department B in the month is a result of the request of a customer for early completion of another job which had been originally scheduled for completion in the month following.

Department B discovered defects in some of the work, which was returned to Department A for rectification. 3 labour hours were worked in Department A on rectification (these are additional to the 76 direct labour hours in Department A noted above). Such rectification is regarded as a normal part of the work carried out generally in the department.

Department B damaged 5 kilos of Material Z which then had to be disposed of. Such losses of material are not expected to occur.

Total costs incurred during the month on all jobs in the two production departments were as follows:

	Department A	*Department B*
	£	£
Direct materials issued from stores*	6 500	13 730
Direct materials returned to stores	135	275
Direct labour, at basic wage rate†	9 090	11 200
Indirect labour, at basic wage rate	2 420	2 960
Overtime premium	450	120
Lubricants and cleaning compounds	520	680
Maintenance	720	510
Other	1 200	2 150

Materials are priced at the end of each month on a weighted average basis. Relevant information of material stock movements during the month, for materials Y and Z, is as follows:

	Material Y	*Material Z*
Opening stock	1 050 kilos (value £529.75)	6 970 kilos (value £9,946.50)
Purchases	600 kilos at £0.50 per kilo 500 kilos at £0.50 per kilo 400 kilos at £0.52 per kilo	16 000 kilos at £1.46 per kilo
Issues from stores	1 430 kilos	8 100 kilos
Returns to stores	—	30 kilos

* This includes, in Department B, the scrapped Material Z. This was the only material scrapped in the month.

† All direct labour in Department A is paid a basic wage of £4.50 per hour, and in Department B £4.00 per hour. Department A direct labour includes a total of 20 hours spent on rectification work.

Required:

(a) Prepare a list of the costs that should be assigned to Job No. 123. Provide an explanation of your treatment of each item. (17 marks)

(b) Discuss briefly how information concerning the cost of individual jobs can be used. (5 marks)

(22 marks)

Chartered Association of Certified Accountants

17.3* XY Constructions Ltd is building an extension to a college operated by the Education Authority. Work on the college extension commenced on 1 April 19_1 and after one year, on 31 March 19_2, the data shown below were available.

You are required to:

(a) prepare the account for the contract for the year ended 31 March 19_2;

(b) show in relation to the contract an extract from the balance sheet as at 31 March 19_2.

	£000
During the year:	
Plant sent to site	100
Direct materials received at site	460
Direct wages incurred	350
Direct expenses incurred	45
Hire of tower crane	40
Indirect labour costs	70
Supervision salaries	42
Surveyors fees	8
Service costs	18
Hire of scaffolding	20
Overhead incurred on site	60
Head office expenses apportioned to contract	70
Cash received from the Education Authority	1 000
At 31 March 19_2	
Value of plant on site	75
Work certified, valued at	1 250
Cost of work not certified	250
Wages accrued	30
Service costs accrued	2
Materials unused on site	40

(17 marks)

Chartered Institute of Management Accountants

17.4 A construction company is currently undertaking three separate contracts and information relating to these contracts for the previous year, together with other relevant data, is shown below.

	Contract MNO £000s	*Contract PQR £000s*	*Contract STU £000s*	*Construction Services Dept. Overhead £000s*
Contract price	800	675	1 100	
Balances brought forward at beginning of year:				
Cost of work completed	—	190	370	—
Material on site	—	—	25	—
Written down value of plant and machinery	—	35	170	12
Wages accrued	—	2	—	—
Profit previously transferred to Profit/Loss/A/c	—	—	15	—
Transactions during year:				
Material delivered to sites	40	99	180	—
Wages paid	20	47	110	8
Payments to sub-contractors	—	—	35	—
Salaries and other costs	6	20	25	21
Written down value of plant:				
issued to sites	90	15	—	—
transferred from sites	—	8	—	—

Balances carried forward at the end of year:				
Material on site	8	—	—	—
Written down value of plant and machinery	70	—	110	5
Wages accrued	—	5	—	—
Pre-payments to sub-contractors	—	—	15	—
Value of work certified at end of year	90	390	950	—
Cost of work not certified at end of year	—	—	26	—

The cost of operating the Construction Services Department, which provides technical advice to each of the contracts, is apportioned over the contracts in proportion to wages incurred.

Contract STU is scheduled for handing over to the contractee in the near future and the site engineer estimates that the extra costs required to complete the contract, in addition to those tabulated above, will total £138 000. This amount includes an allowance for plant depreciation, construction services and for contingencies.

Required:

(a) Construct a cost account for each of the three contracts for the previous year and show the cost of the work completed at the year end. (9 marks)

(b) (i) Recommend how much profit or loss should be taken, for each contract, for the previous year. (7 marks)

(ii) Explain the reasons for each of your recommendations in (b)(i) above. (6 marks)

(22 marks)

Chartered Association of Certified Accountants

17.5 Fittapool commenced business on 1 May 19_2 with £5 000 cash, installing standard sized swimming pools which they purchased from Poolmake Ltd. In addition to purchasing the ready made pools, Fittapool subcontract the digging of the ground in preparation for the pool to Rentadigger. The direct costs for each pool are as follows:

	£
Purchase of pool from Poolmake Ltd	1 600
Payment to Rentadigger	900
Fitting costs	1 000
	3 500

Poolmake Ltd are paid in full and in advance for each pool which is ordered. Payment is made immediately a customer's order is received and the pool is delivered on site within two days. Rentadigger are paid immediately after the completion of the digging which is two weeks after the order has been placed by the customer. The fitting of the pool then takes a further two weeks and the costs involved in fitting are paid on completion of the installation.

The direct costs have remained unaltered throughout the two years but general overheads have risen from £14 000 in the first year ended 30 April 19_3 to £19 000 in the second year ended 30 April 19_4. There are no accruals or prepayments relating to general overheads at the end of either financial year. Customers pay a standard price of £5 000 per pool payable as shown on the following page.

	£
Deposit on placing order	1 000
Instalment on completion of digging	1 000
Final payment on completion of fitting	3 000
	5 000

During the year ended 30 April 19_3 sixteen orders were received and at 30 April 19_3 work on three pools was in progress; two being 40% complete and one being 60% complete. During the year ended 30 April 19_4 twenty orders were received and at 30 April 19_4 work on six pools was in progress; four being 40% complete and two being 60% complete.

At the end of each of the two years Fittapool had paid Poolmake Ltd for all of the pools on which work had commenced and, in addition, had paid Rentadigger for work done on those pools which were 60% complete. Fittapool have adopted the following policies in their accounts.

(1) Contracts are included as revenue on the completion of the contract.
(2) Work in progress is valued as a percentage of direct costs.

Required:

(a) Fittapool's revenue accounts for each of the years ended 30 April 19_3 and 30 April 19_4. (11 marks)

(b) Fittapool's balance sheet as at 30 April 19_3 and 30 April 19_4. (9 marks)

(c) State and explain two accounting conventions that are involved in arriving at a work in progress valuation. (5 marks)

(25 marks)

Advanced level Accounting, AEB

Solutions

17.2 (a) *Job No. 123*

		£	£
Direct materials			
Y 400 kilos	@ £0.505 (W_1)	202.00	
Z 265 kilos (W_3)	@ £1.45 (W_2)	384.25	586.25
Direct labour			
Dept A (W_4)	76 hours @ £4.50	342.00	
Dept B (W_5)	110 hours @ £4.00	440.00	782.00
Overheads			
Dept A	76 hours @ £2.70 (W_6)	205.20	
Dept B	110 hours @ £2.25 (W_6)	247.50	452.70
Total cost			1 820.95

Workings and Explanations

W_1 *Determination of issue price of Y*

	kilos	*per kilo*	£
Opening stock	1 050		529.75
Purchases:	600	0.50	300.00
	500	0.50	250.00
	400	0.52	208.00
	2 550		1 287.75

$$\text{Weighted average cost} = \frac{£1\ 287.75}{2\ 550} = £0.505 \text{ per kilo}$$

W_2 *Issue price of Z*

	kilos	*per kilo*	£
Opening stock	6 970		9 946.50
Purchase	16 000	1.46	23 360.00
	22 970		33 306.50

$$\text{Weighted average cost} = \frac{£33\ 306.50}{22\ 970} = £1.45 \text{ per kilo}$$

W_3 *Quantity of Z*

	kilos
Issued	300
Less returns	30
	270
Less damaged	5
Chargeable to job	265

Since the 5 kilos damaged in Department B were not expected, it would be unfair to charge the customer of job 123 £7.25 (5 kilos × £1.45) for the error in production. The loss is an *abnormal* one, and as such should not be charged to *any* job but written off to the year's profit and loss account.

Note. Even if the loss had not been unexpected i.e. a *normal loss*, it would still have been a little unfair to charge it *wholly* to job 123. A fairer treatment would be to count it as a *production overhead* and absorb it into *all* jobs.

W_4 *Direct labour hours, Dept. A*
A maximum of 76 hours (including 6 hours at overtime rate) plus 3 hours rectification work could be allocated to job 123. Since the overtime has arisen due to scheduling difficulties, machine breakdowns, or idle time, it would be unfair to charge all of the 50% overtime premium to the job. Instead it should be treated as a *production overhead* and the cost spread over *all* jobs worked in the department.

The 3 additional hours in Dept. A were necessitated by defects in the original work. It would therefore be unfair to charge the client for what was an error of production. Standard costing practice dictates that it be treated as an overhead.

The number of direct labour hours chargeable to the job is therefore 76 hours at the basic rate of £4.50.

W_5 *Direct labour hours, Dept. B*
110 hours, of which 30 hours were overtime, can be identified with the job. Since the overtime worked was as a result of re-scheduling necessitated by early completion of *another job* the 50% overtime premium should be charged *to that job*. The charge to this job is therefore 110 hours, all at the basic rate of £4.00.

W_6 *Overheads*
The method of overhead absorption applied by the factory is the rate per direct labour hour. To calculate the rate we must first find the total direct labour hours worked and total overhead incurred, for each department.

$$\text{Direct labour hours worked} = \frac{\text{Direct labour cost at basic rate}}{\text{Basic rate per hour}}$$

For Dept. A $\frac{£9\ 000^*}{£4.50}$ = 2 000 hours

* £9 090 − 20 rectification hours @ £4.50
= 9 090 − 90 = £9 000

For Dept. B $\frac{£11\ 200}{£4.00}$ = 2 800 hours

Item of overhead	*Dept. A*	*Dept. B*
	£	*£*
Rectification work	90	—
Indirect labour	2 420	2 960
Overtime premium	450	—*
Lubricants and cleaning compounds	520	680
Maintenance	720	510
Other	1 200	2 150
Total overhead	5 400	6 300

* The £120 overtime premium is to be charged directly to the job for which the customer requested early completion. It is therefore excluded from overheads.

The overhead absorption rates can now be calculated.

For Dept. A $\frac{£5\ 400}{2\ 000}$ = £2.70 per direct labour hour

For Dept. B $\frac{£6\ 300}{2\ 800}$ = £2.25 per direct labour hour

(b) Information regarding the cost of individual jobs can be used for pricing, determination of profit, work-in-progress valuation, and cost control. For explanations see text.

17.4 (a)

Contract Account

	MNO	*PQR*	*STU*		*MNO*	*PQR*	*STU*
	£000	*£000*	*£000*		*£000*	*£000*	*£000*
Cost of work b/f		190	370	Wages accrued b/f		2	
Materials b/f			25	Plant transferred		8	
Plant b/f		35	170				
Materials received	40	99	180				
Wages	20	47	110	Year-end balances:			
Paid to sub-contractor			35	Materials c/f	8		
Salaries	6	20	25	Plant c/f	70		110
Plant received	90	15		Prepayment c/f			15
Services overhead*	4	10	22	Work not certified c/f			26
Wages accrued c/f		5		Cost of work certified c/f	∴ 82	∴ 411	∴ 786
	160	421	937		160	421	937

(b) (i)	*MNO*	*PQR*	*STU*		*MNO*	*PQR*	*STU*
Cost of work certified b/f	82	411	786	Value of work certified	90	390	950
Profit taken previous periods			15	P & L a/c – loss taken		21	
P & L a/c – profit taken			114				
Profit not taken c/f	8		∴ 35				
	90	411	950		90	411	950
Materials b/f	8			Wages accrued b/f		5	
Plant b/f	70		110	Profit not taken b/f	8		35
Prepayment b/f			15				
Work not certified b/f			26				

Workings

* *Construction services dept. overhead*

Costs incurred	*£000*
Plant depreciation (12 − 5)	7
Wages	8
Salaries and other costs	21
Total	36

Contract	*Wages incurred* *£000*
MNO	20
PQR (47 − 2 + 5)	50
STU	110
	180

Apportionment of overhead

Contract	*£000*
MNO $36 \times \frac{20}{180} =$	4
PQR $36 \times \frac{50}{180} =$	10
STU $36 \times \frac{110}{180} =$	22
	36

(ii) *Contract MNO*

This contract has just started this year and seems to be in its early stages. Since the eventual outcome is not known with reasonable certainty it is prudent not to take credit for any of the £8 000 apparent profit yet.

Contract PQR

The *whole* of the £21 000 loss on this contract should be charged to this year's profit and loss account, in line with SSAP 9.

Contract STU

A lot of work has already been done on this contract — it is, in fact, nearing completion. Some credit can therefore be taken for work carried out this year.

The expected total profit on the contract can be found by:

	£000
Cost of work certified	786
Cost of work not certified	26
Estimated costs to completion	138
Total cost of contract	950
Contract price	1 100
Expected profit on contract	150

We can therefore take credit for

$$£150\,000 \times \frac{\text{Cash received* £950 000}}{\text{Contract price £1 100 000}}$$

= £129 545 (take as £129 000)

* In the absence of information about retention money it is assumed that full payment has been received for work certified to date.

Since £15 000 credit has already been taken in previous periods we can take 129 000 − 15 000 = £114 000 as profit earned this year.

It is not necessary in this case to reduce profit by a fraction to provide against future contingencies since an amount has *already been provided* for in the £138 000 estimated costs to completion.

Note
It is possible for a different profit figure to be taken for this contract — as long as the reasoning is sound and prudent and workings and assumptions are clearly explained.

17.5 A long list of workings is needed before the contract (revenue) accounts can be prepared.

Workings	19_3		19_4	
W_1 *Payments made*	*Pools*	£	*Pools*	£
To Poolmake Ltd.	16	25 600	20	32 000
To Rentadigger	14	12 600	18	16 200
For fitting	13	13 000	17	17 000
		51 200		65 200
W_2 *Income received*	*Pools*	£	*Pools*	£
As deposits	16	16 000	20	20 000
On completion of digging	13 + 1	14 000	2 + 14 + 2	18 000
On fitting of pool	13	39 000	3 + 14	51 000
		69 000		89 000

Note
Completion of digging represents $\frac{2 \text{ weeks}}{4 \text{ weeks}} \times 100 = 50\%$ of the work on a pool. Pools 40% complete are therefore still being dug and the £1000 instalment is *not yet receivable*. On the 60% completed pools digging has finished and fitting is in operation. The £1 000 instalment has therefore already been received, though not the £3 000 final payment.

W_3 *Income recognized as earned*	19_3		19_4	
	Pools	£	*Pools*	£
Completed pools	13	65 000	17	85 000

W_4 *Work-in-progress valuation*

	£
At 30 April 19_3	
2 at 40% of direct costs £3 500	2 800
1 at 60% of direct costs £3 500	2 100
	4 900
At 30 April 19_4	
4 at 40% of direct cost £3 500	5 600
2 at 60% of direct costs £3 500	4 200
	9 800

The revenue accounts can now be prepared.

(a)

FITTAPOOL

Revenue accounts for 19_3 and 19_4

Year ended 30 April 19_3	£		£
Purchase of pools	25 600		
Paid to Rentadigger	12 600		
Fitting costs	13 000	Work-in-progress c/f (W_4)	4 900
General overheads	14 000	Cost of work completed c/f	60 300
	65 200		65 200
Cost of work completed b/f	60 300	Income 19_3 (W_3)	65 000
P & L a/c — profit taken 19_3	4 700		
	65 000		65 000

Year ended 30 April 19_4	£		£
Work-in-progress b/f	4 900		
Purchase of pools	32 000		
Paid to Rentadigger	16 200		
Fitting costs	17 000	Work-in-progress c/f (W_4)	9 800
General overheads	19 000	Cost of work completed c/f	79 300
	89 100		89 100
Cost of work completed b/f	79 300	Income 19_4 (W_3)	85 000
P & L a/c — profit taken 19_4	5 700		
	85 000		85 000
1 May 19_4			
Work-in-progress b/f	9 800		

Workings for balance sheet

W_5 *Income not yet recognized as earned*

	19_3		19_4	
	Pools	£	*Pools*	£
Deposits — 40% complete	3	3 000	6	6 000
Instalment — 60% complete	1	1 000	2	2 000
		4 000		8 000

W_6

Bank

	£		£
1 May 19_2 Capital	5 000	Payments made (W_1)	51 200
Income received (W_2)	69 000	Overheads	14 000
		30 April 19_3 Bal c/f	8 800
	74 000		74 000
1 May 19_3 Bal b/f	8 800	Payments made (W_1)	65 200
Income received (W_2)	89 000	Overheads	19 000
		30 April 19_4 Bal c/f	13 600
	97 800		97 800
1 May 19_4 Bal b/f	13 600		

The balance sheets can now be prepared.

(b)

FITTAPOOL

Balance sheet as at 30 April 19_3

	£		£
Current assets		Capital	5 000
Work-in-progress (W_4)	4 900	Add profit	4 700
Bank (W_6)	8 800		9 700
		Reserve — income not yet recognized as earned (W_5)	4 000
	13 700		13 700

Balance sheet as at 30 April 19_4

	£		£
Current assets		Capital	9 700
Work-in-progress (W_4)	9 800	Add profit	5 700
Bank (W_6)	13 600		15 400
		Reserve — income not yet recognized as earned (W_5)	8 000
	23 400		23 400

(c) *Accounting conventions used in valuing work-in-progress:*
  (i) *Accruals* (*matching*) — Since the benefit of the costs incurred on the year-end partly-completed pools will be enjoyed *next year* when the pools are sold, the costs should also be charged to next year's revenue account. It is for this reason that the work-in-progress is carried forward as a debit to next year.
  (ii) *Prudence* — The pools are started at the *lower of cost and net realizable value.* Fittapool is not taking credit for any of the profit embodied in partly-completed pools until they are completed and the final payment has been received.

Note Another convention is Consistency in the method of work-in-progress valuation, which facilitates a year-to-year profit comparison.

CHAPTER 18

Process Costing

As was mentioned at the start of the last chapter, process costing is suitable for industries where production is in batches in a series of continuous operations or processes. In this situation it is impossible to identify the cost associated with each unit in a batch. Instead an *average* cost is computed as the total cost divided by number of units. This system needs less work than the maintenance of a job costing system. In the latter, costs have to be identified directly with jobs and this necessitates the keeping of timesheets by workers, records of jobs to which materials are issued, and the number of direct labour or machine hours spent on each job if overhead absorption is on that basis. The above tasks are not necessary in process costing since costs do *not* have to be analysed to individual units of output. Process costing is therefore a cheaper system to operate. The information it generates however is less precise, and, in certain situations, computation of average cost can produce misleading results.

The production process is divided into a number of separate processes or operations. Raw materials start in process 1, are transferred to process 2, and so on. The output of one process becomes the *input* of the next. An account is maintained for each process, to which the direct costs incurred and overheads allocated are debited. The sum is transferred to the next process thereby closing the account. The account of the second process starts with the costs brought forward from the first process. Costs incurred are again debited and the total transferred to the third process — and so on. As production proceeds therefore, there is an accumulation of costs from previous processes.

A record is kept of the number of units processed or volume in terms of weight. The total process cost divided by total units or weight gives the average cost.

Illustration

A good is manufactured in three distinct processes — 1, 2, and 3. 100 units are produced in the month of June, in which the following costs are incurred:

	Process		
	1	2	3
Direct material	£1 000	£1 500	£1 750
Direct labour	£2 000	£3 500	£3 250
Direct labour hours	100	200	150

Overheads of £4 500 are apportioned on the basis of direct labour hours.

Prepare the process accounts.

Answer

Process 1

	Unit cost	*Total*		*Unit cost*	*Total*
	£	*£*		*£*	*£*
Material	10	1 000			
Labour	20	2 000			
Overhead	10	1 000	To Process 2 c/f	40	4 000
	40	4 000		40	4 000

Process 2

	Unit cost	*Total*		*Unit cost*	*Total*
From Process 1 b/f	40	4 000			
Material	15	1 500			
Labour	35	3 500			
Overhead	20	2 000	To Process 3 c/f	110	11 000
	110	11 000		110	11 000

Process 3

	Unit cost	*Total*		*Unit cost*	*Total*
From Process 2 b/f	110	11 000			
Material	17.5	1 750			
Labour	32.5	3 250			
Overhead	15	1 500	To finished goods c/f	175	17 500
	175	17 500		175	17 500

The total cost of production of the 100 units is £17 500, giving an average cost of £175. These figures are transferred to the finished goods account, where they remain as an asset. When sold they are expensed to trading account.

Normal and Abnormal Losses

Certain losses occur in production as inputs move from one process to another. These are categorized into those which are expected (normal losses) and those not expected to occur under normal efficient working conditions (abnormal losses). The accounting treatment for the two is different. Losses which have no market value are known as *waste*, those which can be sold at a nominal price as *scrap*.

Normal losses are unavoidable in the normal course of production. Examples include loss through evaporation, chemical change, and remnants such as the leather lost in making a shoe, the diamond lost in cutting a ring. Where normal loss is expected the process account is credited with this amount, *regardless of the actual loss that takes place*. The debit is to a normal loss account. Deviations of actual loss from normal are accounted for in an abnormal loss or gain account. When the scrap is sold the normal loss account is credited, the debit being to cash, bank, or debtor. These entries are illustrated in an example later.

Abnormal losses result from errors in production such as carelessness, accidents, and the use of inferior quality material. Being not expected in the normal course of operations the costs incurred as a result are *not* charged to the product. Instead they are written out to an abnormal loss account by

Dr Abnormal loss
Cr Process account

The value attached to the loss is the full cost of good production. In questions it is often necessary to work out the normal cost of one unit as

$$\frac{\text{Total normal process cost} - \text{Normal scrap value}}{\text{Normal units processed}}$$

The value of the abnormal loss is given as units of abnormal loss × normal cost of one unit. If any of the abnormal loss is sold (for example as scrap) the double-entry is:

Dr Cash, bank, or debtor
Cr Abnormal loss

The balance on the abnormal loss account is written off to the costing profit and loss account. Abnormal losses are *not* included in the unit cost calculation. The process account shows the cost of production based on normal efficient working conditions. Any losses of an abnormal nature are not allowed to enter into cost calculations and stock valuation.

Abnormal gain
Where the loss from a process is *less* than expected an abnormal gain results. The normal cost of the gain (being units of gain × normal cost of 1 unit) is transferred to an abnormal gain account by

Dr Process account
Cr Abnormal gain

The gain is credited to the costing profit and loss account. In an abnormal gain the opportunity is lost of earning the scrap value on the expected loss which did not materialize. The account should therefore be reduced by this amount. The double-entry is:

Dr Abnormal gain
Cr Normal loss

with the scrap value of abnormal gain units. This in fact closes the normal loss account (see illustration below).

Illustration

A good is manufactured in two processes. 100 units are introduced into Process 2 at a cost of £440. £300 are spent in process 2. Normal loss is expected at 10 per cent of units introduced. These are sold for scrap at £2 each. Show the ledger accounts recording the above if the actual units produced in process 2 is:

(a) 80 units
(b) 95 units

Answer

(a)

Process 1

	Units	*Per unit* £	*Total* £		*Units*	*Per unit* £	*Total* £
Costs	100	4.40	440	To Process 2 c/f	100	4.40	440

Process 2

	Units	*Per unit* £	*Total* £		*Units*	*Per unit* £	*Total* £
From Process 1 b/f	100	4.40	440	Normal loss	10	2	20
Costs			300	Abnormal loss*	10	8	80
				To finished stock c/f	80	8	640
	100		740		100		740

$$* \text{ Normal cost of 1 unit} = \frac{£(440 + 300) - £20}{(100 \times 0.90) \text{ units}} = \frac{£720}{90} = £8$$

$$\text{Abnormal loss} = (80 - 90) \text{ units} \times £8 = £80$$

Normal loss

In Process 2	10	2	20	Bank	10	2	20

Abnormal loss

In Process 2	10	8	80	Bank	10	2	20
				Costing P & L			60
	10		80		10		80

Finished stock

From Process 2 b/f			640

Costing P & L

Abnormal loss			60

Bank

Normal loss	20	Process 1 — costs	440
Abnormal loss	20	Process 2 — costs	300

(b)

Process 1

	Units	Per unit £	Total £		Units	Per unit £	Total £
Costs	100	4.40	440	To Process 2 c/f	100	4.40	440

Process 2

	Units	Per unit £	Total £		Units	Per unit £	Total £
From Process 1 b/f	100	4.40	440				
Costs			300	Normal loss	10	2	20
Abnormal gain	5	8	40	To finished stock c/f	95	8	760
	105		780		105		780

Normal loss

	Units	Per unit £	Total £		Units	Per unit £	Total £
In Process 2	10	2	20	Bank	5	2	10
				Abnormal gain	5	2	10
	10		20		10		20

Abnormal gain

	Units	Per unit £	Total £		Units	Per unit £	Total £
Normal loss	5	2	10	In Process 2	5	8	40
Costing P & L			30				
	5		40		5		40

Finished stock

From Process 2 b/f	760		

Costing P & L

		Abnormal gain	30

Bank

		Process 1 — costs	440
		Process 2 — costs	300

So far the complications of work-in-progress have been ignored. Let us now bring them into our discussion. The accounting treatment of opening work-in-progress is different from that of closing work-in-progress.

Closing Work-in-progress

In practice when costs are calculated, perhaps at the end of a month, there are likely to be some units started but not yet complete. The implication of this is that unit cost cannot be calculated as total process cost divided by number of units. It is necessary to convert the incomplete units into their equivalent in terms of complete units. Thus 100 units which are 70 per cent complete are equivalent to 70 complete units. 70 is then the figure which is used in the unit cost computation.

Sometimes the various elements of cost may not all have been incurred up to the same percentage. For example material cost may be wholly incurred at the start of the process. Any work-in-progress at the end of the month therefore represents 100 per cent of the material cost. This may not be so for labour and overhead, which are usually incurred *throughout* the process. In these cases *separate* equivalent production units need to be calculated for each item of cost.

Example

Information relating to Process 1 for a period.

Units introduced	1 000
Units completed	800
Closing work-in-progress	200
Costs incurred:	
Material	£3 000
Labour	£2 300
Overhead	£1 800

The work-in-progress is 100% complete in respect of materials, 60% of labour and 50% of overheads.
What is the cost of the closing work-in-progress and the completed production transferred to process 2?

Answer

	Item of Cost		
	Material	*Labour*	*Overhead*
Cost incurred	£3 000	£2 300	£1 800
Completed units	800	800	800
Equivalent units in WIP	200	120	100
Total equivalent units	1 000	920	900
Unit cost	£3 000 / 1 000 = £3	£2 300 / 920 = £2.50	£1 800 / 900 = £2
WIP valuation	200 × £3 = £600	120 × £2.50 = £300	100 × £2 = £200

Total unit cost 3 + 2.50 + 2 = £7.50
Total WIP valuation 600 + 300 + 200 = £1 000

The value of completed production is 800 units × £7.50 = £6 000.

The process account would look as follows:

Process 1

	Units	*Per unit* £	*Total* £		*Units*	*Per unit* £	*Total* £
Material	1 000	3	3 000				
Labour			2 300	To process 2 c/f	800	7.50	6 000
Overhead			1 800	Closing WIP c/f	200		1 100
	1 000		7 100		1 000		7 100

The closing work-in-progress of this period is, of course, the opening work-in-progress of the next period.

Opening Work-in-progress

When opening works-in-progress exist, a decision has to be made on whether to allow the costs embodied in them to influence the current periods computation of unit cost (the *weighted average cost* method) or not (the *first in, first out* method). The difference between the two is best illustrated with an example.

Illustration

The following information applies to Process 2:

Costs embodied in opening work-in-progress, 400 units, $\frac{3}{4}$ complete:

Material	£800
Conversion costs	£900

Materials are added at the start of a process, conversion costs accrue evenly throughout.

In Process 2:

Units started	3 200
Material cost	£ 6 400
Conversion costs	£15 600
Closing work-in-progress	600, $\frac{1}{2}$ complete

What is the value of the closing work-in-progress and completed units?

Answer

We first have to find the number of units completed during the period.

	Units
Opening work-in-progress	400
Introduced in process	3 200
	3 600
Less closing work-in-progress	600
Completed in process	3 000

Using the Weighted Average Cost Method

	Material	*Conversion costs*
Opening WIP	800	900
Process 2 costs	6 400	15 600
Total cost	£7 200	£16 500
Completed units	3 000	3 000
Closing WIP equivalent units	600	300
Total equivalent units	3 600	3 300
Unit cost	$\frac{£7\ 200}{3\ 600}$ = £2	$\frac{£16\ 500}{3\ 300}$ = £5

Valuation of WIP:		£
Material	600 units × £2 =	1 200
Conversion costs	300 units × £5 =	1 500
		2 700

Valuation of completed units

3 000 units × £7 = 21 000

Note that:

Material +	Conversion costs	=	Completed units +	WIP
7 200 +	16 500	=	21 000	+ 2 700
	£23 700	=	£23 700	

In the above statement costs embodied in the opening work-in-progress have been merged with the costs incurred in the current process to give a figure for average unit cost. No attempt is made to separate the previous process costs (as reflected in the opening WIP £1 700) from the current process costs.

The process account looks as follows:

Process 2

	£		£
Opening WIP b/f	1 700		
Material	6 400	To finished goods c/f	21 000
Conversion costs	15 600	Closing WIP c/f	2 700
	23 700		23 700

Using the First In, First Out Method

This method assumes that the work-in-progress units being first in are also first out i.e. they are completed *before* any of the current process units. The whole of the closing work-in-progress is therefore valued at the unit cost of the *current* process only. The costs embodied in the opening work-in-progress do not enter into the calculation.

The statement of unit cost looks as follows:

	Material	*Conversion costs*
Process 2 costs	£6 400	£15 600
Units completed in process	3 000	3 000
Less opening WIP equivalent units	400	300
	2 600	2 700
Add closing WIP equivalent units	600	300
Total equivalent units in process 2	3 200	3 000
Unit cost	£6 400 / 3 200 = £2	£15 600 / 3 000 = £5.20

		£
Valuation of WIP:		
Material	600 units × £2	1 200
Conversion costs	300 units × £5.20	1 560
		2 760
Valuation of completed units:		
Opening WIP		1 700
Material	2 600 units × £2	5 200
Conversion costs	2 700 units × £5.20	14 040
		20 940

Note again that:

Material + Conversion costs	=	Completed units + WIP
7 200 + 16 500	=	20 940 + 2 760
£23 700	=	£23 700

The process account looks as follows:

Process 2

	£		£
Opening WIP b/f	1 700		
Material	6 400	To finished goods c/f	20 940
Conversion costs	15 600	Closing WIP c/f	2 760
	23 700		23 700

The decision on which method to use is determined by the nature of production in the process i.e whether the opening work-in-progress *is* the first to be completed or not. In processes where the opening work-in-progress is in liquid or gaseous form the average cost method is to be preferred since it is not possible to separate them from additional inputs introduced during the process.

Batch Costing

In some industries production of all units is not identical, ruling out process costing, yet not sufficiently different to justify the considerable costs of maintaining a job costing system. From a number of standard operations similar, though not identical, goods may be produced. In these cases batch costing may be used. Take, for example, a manufacturer of dining tables which produces cheap, standard, and quality versions of the same table. The production process may be standardized into several operations with the quality table passing through more operations than the cheap table, as shown in the table below:

Operation	*Average cost* £	*Cheap*	*Standard*	*Quality*
Preparation	30	✓	✓	✓
Assembly 1	50	✓	✓	✓
Assembly 2	40	✓	✓	✓
Varnishing	20	✓	✓	✓
Decoration by Hand	40			✓
Additional varnishing	30		✓	✓
Inspection	20	✓	✓	✓
Second inspection	15			✓
Packing	20	✓	✓	✓

By calculating the total cost of each operation it is possible to identify the average unit cost of it by dividing the total cost by the number of units in the batch. Hypothetical figures for these are shown above. The cost of a unit is simply the total of the average cost of each operation through which it passes. The final cost is of course an average cost of each unit of that type.

For our example:

	Table		
Operation	*Cheap* £	*Standard* £	*Quality* £
Preparation	30	30	30
Assembly 1	50	50	50
Assembly 2	40	40	40
Varnishing	20	20	20
Decoration by Hand			40
Additional varnishing		30	30
Inspection	20	20	20
Second inspection			15
Packing	20	20	20
Total cost	£180	£210	£265

Batch costing contains elements of both job and process costing. It resembles process costing in that the cost computed is an average per unit, job costing in that separate cost calculations have to be made for each order. Batch costing is used in a lot of *multi-product* industries where process costing cannot be used and where job costing is prohibitively expensive.

Questions

18.1 Cloudy plc manufactures a product called Day which passes through two processes; light and dark. The normal level of loss and the scrap value of any loss is as follows:

	Light Process	*Dark Process*
Normal loss as a percentage of total input	10%	5%
Scrap value per kg.	£3	£6

The actual data incurred for the month of May 19_3 was:

	Light Process	*Dark Process*
Output in kg.	850	1 075

Costs		
Direct materials introduced at the start of the process	1 000 kg at £3.3 per kg.	250 kg at £12 per kg.
Direct labour	£850	£1 500
Direct expenses	£750	£1 510

Production overhead is absorbed on the basis of direct wages. The budgeted overhead for the accounting year was £56 000 and the budgeted direct labour £28 000. There were no stocks of work in progress at the beginning or end of May.

Required:
Prepare the accounts for:
(a) Each of the processes, Light and Dark;
(b) Normal loss;
(c) Abnormal loss and/or gain.

(20 marks)

Institute of Chartered Accountants, Foundation

18.2* AB Chemicals Limited produces a compound by mixing certain ingredients within two separate processes. For a particular week the recorded costs were:

Process 1 — Material: 2 000 kilogrammes at £2 per kilogramme
Labour: £360
Process plant time: 24 hours at £200 per hour
Process 2 — Material: 3 100 kilogrammes at £6 per kilogramme
Labour: £240
Process plant time: 40 hours at £76.30 per hour

Indirect production overhead for the week amounted to £2 400 and is absorbed on the basis of labour cost.

Normal outputs are: Process 1 80% of input
Process 2 90% of input

Discarded materials have scrap values of £0.30 per kilogramme from Process 1 and £1.50 per kilogramme from Process 2. Assume that sales of scrap are made for cash during the week.

There was no work-in-progress at either the beginning or end of the week.

Output during the week was 1 400 kilogrammes from Process 1 and 4 200 kilogrammes from Process 2.

Required:
(a) show the accounts for:
(i) Process 1;
(ii) Process 2;
(iii) abnormal gain/loss;
(iv) profit and loss — relating to transactions in any of the above accounts;
(v) finished goods. (16 marks)

(b) explain, in relation to process costing, the concept of 'equivalent units' and give a simple example using your own figures. (4 marks)

(20 marks)

Chartered Institute of Management Accountants

18.3 On 1 March, 19_6, a company placed 30 000 units in production. All items produced were sold at £7.40 per item immediately on completion. Manufacture was performed in three successive processes, the costs of which were as shown at top of next page.

	Materials Used	*Direct Wages*	*Machine Hours*
	£	£	£
Process 1	11 395	20 550	59
Process 2	9 750	8 100	176
Process 3	1 950	13 035	117

Works overheads of £26 400 were allocated to production in the ratio of machine hours worked.

The process accounts were credited with normal scrap arisings, which were £370 for Process 1 and £204 for Process 2.

Separate accounts were kept for abnormal scrap and for rejects, details of which were:

Process 1: 900 items scrapped and sold for £800 cash.
Process 2: 2 100 items scrapped and sold for £2 500 cash.
Process 3: 1 000 items rejected and sold for cash at 60 per cent of normal prices.

Prepare:
(a) the process accounts for each process; (18 marks)
(b) the accounts to show: (1) abnormal loss and, (2) rejects after the completion of the production and the transactions involving scrap and rejects. (7 marks)
(25 marks)

Advanced level Accounting, London

18.4* A chemical company carries on production operations in two processes. Materials first pass through Process I, where a compound is produced. A loss in weight takes place at the start of processing. The following data, which can be assumed to be representative, relates to the month just ended:

Quantities (kilos)	
Material input	200 000
Opening work-in-process (half processed)	40 000
Work completed	160 000
Closing work-in-process (two-thirds processed)	30 000
Costs (£)	
Material input	75 000
Processing costs	96 000
Opening work-in-process — materials	20 000
— processing costs	12 000

Required:
Determine, using the average cost method, the cost per kilo of compound in Process I, and the value of both work completed and closing work-in-process for the month just ended. **(11 marks)**

Chartered Association of Certified Accountants, part-question

18.5 A manufacturing company makes a product by two processes and the data below relate to the second process for the month of April.

A work-in-progress balance of 1 200 units brought forward from March was valued, in cost, as follows:

	£
Direct materials, complete	10 800
Direct wages, 60% complete	6 840
Production overhead, 60% complete	7 200

During April, 4 000 units were transferred from the first process to the second process at a cost of £7.50 each, this input being treated as direct material within the second process.

Other costs incurred by the second process were:

	£
Additional direct materials	4 830
Direct wages	32 965
Production overhead	35 538

3 200 completed units were transferred to finished goods store. A loss of 520 units, being normal, occurred during the process. The average method of pricing is used.

Work-in-progress at the end of April consisted of 500 completed units awaiting transfer to the finished goods store and a balance of unfinished units which were complete as regards direct material and 50% complete as regards direct wages and production overhead.

Required:

(a) prepare for the month of April the account for the second process; (14 marks)

(b) present a statement for management setting out the:
   (i) cost per unit of the finished product, by element of cost and total;
   (ii) cost of production transferred to finished goods;
   (iii) cost of production of completed units awaiting transfer to finished goods;
   (iv) cost of uncompleted units in closing work-in-progress, by element of cost and in total. (6 marks)

(20 marks)

Chartered Institute of Management Accountants

Solutions

18.1

CLOUDY PLC

Light Process

	kg	*Per kg*	*Total*		*kg*	*Per kg*	*Total*
		£	£			£	£
Direct materials	1 000	3.30	3 300				
Direct labour			850	Normal loss	100	3	300
Direct expenses			750	Abnormal loss (W_2)	50	7	350
Production overhead (W_1)			1 700	To Dark Process c/f	850	7	5 950
	1 000		6 600		1 000		6 600

Normal loss — Light

In Light Process	100	3	300	Bank*	100	3	300

Abnormal loss — Light

In Light Process	50	7	350	Bank	50	3	150
				Costing P & L			200
	50	7	350		50		350

Workings

W_1 Overhead absorption rate $= \dfrac{£56\ 000}{28\ 000} =$ £2 per direct wage

Overhead absorbed:

Light process £850 × £2 = £1 700
Dark process £1 500 × £2 = £3 000

W_2 Normal cost of 1 unit $= \dfrac{£\,(3\,300 + 850 + 750 + 1\,700) - £300}{(1\,000 \times 0.90)\text{ kg.}}$

$= \dfrac{£6\,300}{900} = £7$

Abnormal loss $= (850 - 900)\text{ kg.} \times £7$
$= £350$

Dark Process

	kg	*Per kg* £	*Total* £		*kg*	*Per kg* £	*Total* £
From Light Process b/f	850	7	5 950				
Direct materials	250	12	3 000				
Direct labour			1 500				
Direct expenses			1 510				
Production overhead (W_1)			3 000	Normal loss	55	6	330
Abnormal gain (W_3)	30	14	420	To finished goods c/f	1 075	14	15 050
	1 130		15 380		1 130		15 380

Normal loss — Dark

In Dark process	55	6	330	Bank*	25	6	150
				Abnormal gain	30	6	180
	55		330		55		330

Abnormal gain — Dark

Normal loss	30	6	180	In Dark process	30	14	420
Costing P & L			240				
	30		420		30		420

Workings
W_3

Normal cost of 1 unit $= \dfrac{£\,(5\,950 + 3\,000 + 1\,500 + 1\,510 + 3\,000) - £330}{(1\,000 \times 0.95)\text{ kg.}}$

$= \dfrac{£14\,960 - £330}{1\,045} = £14$

Abnormal gain $= (1\,075 - 1\,045)\text{ kg.} \times £14$
$= £420$

* It has been assumed that all losses were sold, and cheques received, during the month. If payment has not been received by the end of the month bank should be replaced by *debtor.*

18.3 (a)

Process 1

	Units	*Per unit* £	*Total* £		*Units*	*Per unit* £	*Total* £
Materials	30 000		11 395	Normal loss	—		370
Direct wages			20 550	Abnormal loss (W_1)	900	1.20	1 080
Overheads, 26 400 × $\frac{59}{352}$			4 425	To process 2 c/f	29 100	1.20	34 920
	30 000		36 370		30 000		36 370

Process 2

	Units	*Per unit* £	*Total* £		*Units*	*Per unit* £	*Total* £
From Process 1 b/f	29 100	1.20	34 920				
Materials			9 750	Normal loss	—		204
Direct wages			8 100	Abnormal loss (W_2)	2 100	2.26	4 746
Overheads, 26 400 × $\frac{176}{352}$			13 200	To Process 3 c/f	27 000	2.26	61 020
	29 100		65 970		29 100		65 970

Process 3

	Units	*Per unit* £	*Total* £		*Units*	*Per unit* £	*Total* £
From Process 2 b/f	27 000	2.26	61 020				
Materials			1 950				
Direct wages			13 035	Rejects (W_3)	1 000	3.14	3 140
Overheads, 26 400 × $\frac{117}{352}$			8 775	Finished goods	26 000	3.14	81 640
	27 000		84 780		27 000		84 780

(b)

Abnormal loss

		£	£			£	£
From Process 1	900	1.20	1 080	Bank	900	0.88˙	800
				Costing P & L			280
	900		1 080		900		1 080
From Process 2	2 100	2.26	4 746	Bank	2 100	1.19	2 500
				Costing P & L			2 246
	2 100		4 746		2 100		4 746

Rejects

From Process 3	1 000	3.14	3 140	Cash (W_4)	1 000	4.44	4 440
Costing P & L			1 300				
	1 000		4 440		1 000		4 440

Workings

W_1 Normal cost of 1 unit, Process 1 $= \dfrac{£36\,370 - £370}{30\,000} = £1.20$

W_2 Normal cost of 1 unit, Process 2 $= \dfrac{£65\,970 - £204}{29\,100} = £2.26$

W_3 Normal cost of 1 unit, Process 3 $= \dfrac{£84\,780}{27\,000} = £3.14$

W_4 Sale price of rejects $= £7.40 \times 60\%$
$= £4.44$

18.5 (a)

Second Process

	Units	*Per unit* £	*Total* £		*Units*	*Per unit* £	*Total* £
Balances b/f:							
In WIP b/f							
Direct materials	1 200		10 800	Normal loss	520		
Direct wages			6 840	To finished goods (W_1)	3 200	29.45	94 240
Production overhead			7 200	Completed units not			
Finished goods b/f	4 000	7.50	30 000	yet transferred c/f	500	29.45	14 725
2nd Process Costs:				Closing WIP c/f:			
Direct materials			4 830	Direct materials	980	9.75	9 555
Direct wages			32 965	Direct wages (W_2)			4 655
Production overhead			35 538	Production overhead (W_3)			4 998
	5 200		128 173		5 200		128 173

Workings

W_1

	Direct materials	*Direct wages*	*Production overhead*
Opening WIP			
10 800 + 30 000 =	40 800	6 840	7 200
Second Process costs	4 830	32 965	35 538
Total cost	£45 630	£39 805	£42 738
Completed units	3 700	3 700	3 700
Closing WIP equivalent units*	980	490	490
Total equivalent units	4 680	4 190	4 190
Unit cost	$\dfrac{£45\,630}{4\,680}$ = £9.75	$\dfrac{£39\,805}{4\,190}$ = £9.50	$\dfrac{£42\,738}{4\,190}$ = £10.20

Total unit cost = 9.75 + 9.50 + 10.20
= £29.45

*			units
	WIP units b/f		1 200
	Finished units b/f		4 000
	Total units in process		5 200
	Normal loss	(520)	
	Completed units transferred	(3 200)	
	Not yet transferred	(500)	
	Total units accounted for		(4 220)
	Balance (= unfinished units)		980

W_2 Direct wages 490 units × £9.50 = £4 655
W_3 Production overhead 490 units × £10.20 = £4 998

(b) *Statement of Cost of Second Process*

			£
(i)	Cost per unit		
	Direct materials		9.75
	Direct wages		9.50
	Production overhead		10.20
	Total		29.45
(ii)	Cost of production transferred to finished goods		
	3 200 units × £29.45		94 240
(iii)	Cost of production awaiting transfer		
	500 units × £29.45		14 725
(iv)	Cost of closing work-in-progress		
	Direct materials	980 units × £9.75	9 555
	Direct wages	490 units × £9.50	4 655
	Production overhead	490 units × £10.20	4 998
	Total		19 208

CHAPTER 19

Absorption and Marginal Costing

In Chapter 16 we brought into the unit cost calculation *all* manufacturing costs, both variable and fixed, associated with a product. We saw the difficulties of trying to attach indirect overheads to products and the alternative means accountants use to resolve them. Such a system is called *absorption costing* or *full costing*. Since the mid 1930s, and increasingly in recent years, the case has been put forward for an alternative system of costing, in which only *variable* manufacturing costs are allocated to the product and included in the stock valuation. The fixed manufacturing overhead is treated as an expense for the period and wholly written off to the income statement, the same as the selling and distribution and administration overhead. They are not included in the stock valuation; there is no possibility of any of it being carried forward to next year. This system is known as *marginal, variable*, or *direct costing*.

The difference between the two systems lies in their interpretation of the *matching concept*. Absorption costing takes the view that all costs, including fixed overheads, are incurred for the benefit of the product and that the charge for overheads should therefore be made *when the product is sold*. Any unsold stocks remaining at the end of the year should be valued at full manufacturing cost and charged against profit in the subsequent year when it is sold. Proponents of marginal costing reply by saying that overheads tend to be related to *time* rather than production level, and quote rent and rates, supervisors' salaries, and insurance as examples. With these fixed costs it would make more sense to match their charge against profit *in the period in which their benefit is received.* They claim that it would be wrong to carry forward such costs to future years when the business knows that the full benefit of the payment has already been received by the year-end. All fixed costs should be written off to profit and loss and only *variable* production costs embodied in closing stocks carried forward.

In summary, absorption costing matches all production costs to the product while marginal (variable) costing matches only variable production costs to the product and fixed costs to time. This is the only difference between the two systems, but it is an important one both in principle and in the way it affects reported profit, as we shall see in this chapter.

Marginal Costing

Let us first look at this costing system. The figures below relate to the activities of a manufacturer for a year:

	£
Direct material	4 000
Direct wages	3 000
Factory overheads	1 000
Sales	10 000
Variable selling costs	500
Fixed selling costs	600
Fixed administrative expenses	900

Costs embodied in stocks:

	Opening	*Closing*
Direct material	600	1 100
Direct wages	400	900
Factory overheads	100	150
	1 100	2 150

An income statement prepared on a marginal costing basis would look as follows:

	£	£
Sales		10 000
Less variable cost of goods sold		
Opening stock (600 + 400)	1 000	
Variable production cost (4 000 + 3 000)	7 000	
	8 000	
Less closing stock (1 100 + 900)	2 000	
	6 000	
Variable selling costs	500	
Total variable cost		6 500
Contribution		3 500
Less fixed (period) costs		
Factory overheads	1 000	
Fixed selling costs	600	
Administrative expenses	900	
		2 500
Profit		£1 000

Note that:

(1) Stock is valued at variable cost only. Under absorption costing value of opening stock is £1 100, closing stock £2 150.

(2) Sales minus variable cost gives the *contribution* available to cover fixed costs.

(3) Profit is contribution less fixed costs.

Be Careful

A positive contribution does not necessarily mean a profit. If fixed costs are greater than contribution the firm will suffer a loss.

Example

	£	£
Contribution		3 500
Less fixed costs		
Factory overheads	2 000	
Fixed selling costs	1 200	
Administrative expenses	1 800	
		5 000
Loss		£(1 500)

Comparison

Let us now look at an example of comparative income statements under the two systems.

The following information relates to the Gnome Manufacturing Company Limited:

Per unit	£
Selling price	10
Direct material cost	2
Direct labour cost	1
Variable production overhead	1
Variable selling cost	0.5
Per month	
Fixed production overhead	2 500
Fixed selling costs	600
Fixed administrative expenses	900

There was an opening stock of 50 gnomes at the start of month 1. Fixed overheads embodied in this was £125. The budget forecast that production would be equal to sales, at 1 000 gnomes per month.

Actual results for the first three months are as follows:

	1	2	3
Production in units	1 000	1 100	900
Sales in units	1 000	900	1 100

The method of overhead absorption used by the company is the blanket rate per unit of planned output.

Required:

Comparative income statements under marginal costing and absorption costing.

THE GNOME MANUFACTURING COMPANY LTD.

Marginal cost income statement for months 1-3

	Month 1		*Month 2*		*Month 3*	
	£	£	£	£	£	£
Sales		10 000		9 000		11 000
Less *variable* cost of goods sold						
Opening stock	200 (W_1)		200		1 000	
Direct materials	2 000		2 200		1 800	
Direct labour	1 000		1 100		900	
Variable production overheads	1 000		1 100		900	
	4 200		4 600		4 600	
Less closing stock	200		1 000 (W_2)		200 (W_3)	
	4 000		3 600		4 400	
Variable selling costs	500	4 500	450	4 050	550	4 950
Contribution		5 500		4 950		6 050
Less fixed (period) costs						
Production overheads	2 500		2 500		2 500	
Selling costs	600		600		600	
Administrative expenses	900		900		900	
		4 000		4 000		4 000
Net profit		£1 500		£950		£2 050

Working

Stocks are valued throughout at *variable* cost only i.e. £4

W_1 50 gnomes at £4 each = £200
W_2 250 gnomes at £4 each = £1 000
W_3 50 gnomes at £4 each = £200

Note that variable selling costs are not included in the stock valuation — this includes only variable *production* costs.

And now under absorption costing.

THE GNOME MANUFACTURING COMPANY LTD.

Absorption costing income statement for months 1-3

	Month 1		*Month 2*		*Month 3*	
	£	£	£	£	£	£
Sales		10 000		9 000		11 000
Less cost of goods sold						
Opening stock	325 (W_4)		325		1 625	
Direct materials	2 000		2 200		1 800	
Direct labour	1 000		1 100		900	
Production overheads absorbed (W_5)	3 500		3 850		3 150	
	6 825		7 475		7 475	
Less closing stock	325		1 625 (W_6)		325	
	6 500		5 850		7 150	
Under (over) absorption adjustment (W_5)	—	6 500	(250)	5 600	250	7 400
Gross profit		3 500		3 400		3 600
Less non-manufacturing expenses						
Variable selling costs	500		450		550	
Fixed selling costs	600		600		600	
Administrative expenses	900	2 000	900	1 950	900	2 050
Net profit		£1 500		£1 450		£1 550

Workings

W_4 Stocks are now valued at *full* manufacturing cost i.e. 50 @ £4 variable cost + £125 fixed cost = £325

W_5 The chosen overhead absorption method is the blanket rate per unit of output

$$\text{Rate} = \frac{\text{Total planned production overhead}}{\text{Planned output}}$$

$$= \frac{\text{£2 500 fixed + £1 000 variable}}{\text{1 000 gnomes}} = \text{£3.50}$$

	Month 1		Month 2		Month 3	
Incurred	2 500 + 1 000 =	3 500	2 500 + 1 100 =	3 600	2 500 + 900 =	3 400
Absorbed	1 000 × 3.50 =	3 500	1 100 × 3.50 =	3 850	900 × 3.50 =	3 150
Under (over) absorption		—		(250)		250

W_6 *Valuation of closing stock*

There are two methods of finding the *unit* full cost.

Method 1

$$\text{Unit cost} = \frac{\text{Total production cost charged*}}{\text{Units produced}}$$

$$\text{Month 2,} \quad \frac{2\ 200 + 1\ 100 + 3\ 850}{1\ 100} = \text{£6.50}$$

$$\text{Month 3,} \quad \frac{1\ 800 + 900 + 3\ 150}{900} = \text{£6.50}$$

* Note that this is not production cost incurred; any under (over) absorption is included in the stock valuation.

Method 2

Unit costs:	£
Direct material	2.00
Direct labour	1.00
Production overhead	3.50
Total unit cost	6.50

Now, value of closing stock = 250 gnomes @ £6.50
= £1 625

Do follow the illustration through a second time if you did not understand it all in your first reading.

We can now use the illustration to make some observations on the two systems. Firstly, note that when:

Production = Sales	Month 1	Absorption cost profit = Marginal cost profit
Production > Sales	Month 2	Absorption cost profit > Marginal cost profit
Production < Sales	Month 3	Absorption cost profit < Marginal cost profit

Since the only difference between the two months is in the treatment of production overheads and valuation of stock the difference in profit can be reconciled through stock.

Consider month 2 when there is a build-up of stock. Absorption cost profit is higher than marginal cost profit by £500. This is because with the latter all the production overheads have been charged against profit while with the former part of it has been included in the large year-end stock valuation and *carried forward to the next month*. The charge for production overhead has effectively been *reduced*. This leads to the higher profit figure. A statement can be prepared to clarify the reconciliation:

	Closing stock		*Opening stock*		*Increase in stock*		*Profit*
	£		£		£		£
Absorption costing	1 625	–	325	=	1 300		1 450
Marginal costing	1 000	–	200	=	800		950
Difference					500	=	500

In month 3, when there is a run-down in stock, the opposite happens. Under absorption costing the amount of fixed overhead brought forward from last month is greater than the amount of overhead carried forward to next month. The month then becomes over-burdened with more than one month's share of overhead. Profit is therefore lower than under marginal costing, where the charge is just one month's overhead, and no more.
A reconciliation again:

	Closing stock		*Opening stock*		*Decrease in stock*		*Profit*
	£		£		£		£
Absorption costing	325	–	1 625	=	(1 300)		1 550
Marginal costing	200	–	1 000	=	(800)		2 050
Difference					500	=	500

When sales match production and there is no change in stock levels, as in month 1, the two methods produce the same amount of profit. This is because under absorption costing, the amount of overhead deferred to next year in closing stock is *exactly equal* to the amount of last year's overhead charged to this year in opening stock. In effect the charge is the amount of overhead incurred during the month. As marginal costing also charges this amount we can expect profits under the two systems to be equal.

	Closing stock		*Opening stock*		*Change in stock*		*Profit*
	£		£		£		£
Absorption costing	325	–	325	=	0		1 500
Marginal costing	200	–	200	=	0		1 500
Difference					0	=	0

The larger the fluctuation in stock levels the greater will be the discrepancy in profits between the two systems. Although fluctuations are common in the short-term, in the *long-term* sales and production are usually equal to each other i.e. there is no *continuous* build-up or depletion of stock. Taking one period with the next then, total profits under the two systems should be equal. In our example, production is 3 000 units over the three months, and sales are also 3 000 units. The quarterly total profits should then be the same. We can see below that this is so.

Month	*Absorption costing profit*		*Marginal costing profit*
	£		£
1	1 500		1 500
2	1 450		950
3	1 550		2 050
Total profit	4 500	=	4 500

Advantages of Marginal Costing

1. Decision-making

One distinction between the fixed and variable components of costs is that *fixed costs are unavoidable* in the short-term whereas *variable costs are avoidable.* Managers are able to influence the levels of variable cost but not fixed cost since they are *sunk* costs, already incurred. In short-term decision-making it is best to ignore these irrelevant costs and look only at the variable costs associated with different alternatives. A marginal costing system highlighting contribution is therefore likely to be of more use for decision-making than one including irrelevant fixed costs. Decision-making and relevant costs is considered in the next chapter.

2. More Meaningful Results

Under absorption costing it is possible for a business suffering from a slow-down in sales and build-up of stock to show a healthy profit for the year. This is because a large amount of the year's fixed overhead is not charged, being carried forward in the large stock figure. If sales pick up in the following year, profits may actually *fall* — because the year is over-burdened with a large amount of overhead from the previous year in addition to that year's overhead. Under marginal costing such anomalies can never occur. *Profits and sales always move in the same direction.* If the selling price and cost structure remain unchanged, an increase in sales always leads to an increase in profit, and vice-versa. This is because marginal costing profit is influenced by sales volume only whereas under absorption costing profit is a function of both sales *and* production volume.

Absorption costing flatters the results of an accounting period in which there is a build-up of stocks. Marginal costing does not do this. As a result its profit figure in a period of poor sales is more realistic and alerts management to the problem. Under absorption costing the problem may be hidden in an inflated profit figure, giving management a false sense of achievement.

3. Inter-year Comparison

For the above reason, comparison of profit from one year to another is more meaningful under marginal costing.

4. Performance Evaluation

Large businesses are often *de-centralized* into autonomous divisions, for example by function, product or sales area. The manager of each individual division is responsible for its performance. This is frequently monitored by top management, for control purposes. The two most widely used measures of performance are divisional sales and divisional profit. Under absorption costing, as mentioned in 2 above, it is possible for an increase in sales to *decrease* profit. A manager is not likely to have much faith in a costing system which rewards his good performance by showing a fall in profit! Worse still, he may be tempted to manipulate profit, by varying the level of stocks. For example, he may inflate it by deliberately building up stocks just before the year-end. No such temptation exists under marginal costing. The results, taking one year with the next, are also fairer and more meaningful.

5. No need to forecast

Under absorption costing, overhead recovery rates are based on forecasts. If actual activity does not turn out to be exactly as forecast, an incorrect amount of overhead is changed to the income statement. Although an adjustment is made for under(over) absorption later in the statement, closing stock is valued *before this* i.e. with the incorrect amount of overhead charged to it. The balance sheet figure for stock is therefore also 'wrong'. No such problems arise with marginal costing.

Which Method to Use?

It seems clear from the above that marginal costing is the more suitable for day-to-day running of a business. Which is the better system for *external reporting*? In external reporting an important requirement is *consistency* — from year to year for the same business and also between businesses. A choice has to be made and stuck to. In the UK the official recommendation is to use absorption costing (UK SSAP 9 Stocks and work-in-progress). This does not mean to say that marginal costing is made redundant. It is widely used by internal management for decision-making, performance evaluation, and control. It would be fair to say that financial accountants are more concerned with absorption costing, management accountants with marginal costing.

Asset or Expense?

In recent years the debate has centred on whether production overhead embodied in stock is an *asset or expense*. If it is considered an asset the amount should be included in stock and shown in the balance sheet, as in absorption costing. If it is considered an expense it should be written off to the income statement and excluded from the balance sheet, as in marginal costing. The definition of asset then becomes central to the debate. The problem is that accountants are not in agreement over the definition. The disagreement centres around whether assets are best described as *cost-obviators* or *revenue-producers*. An item of expenditure is *cost-obviating* if by its spending *the need to incur some future cost is averted.* Spending money on fixed production overheads in one year does not reduce the amount that needs to be spent on those overheads in future years — they are therefore *not* cost-obviating. As such they should be wholly written off to the income statement. This definition of asset supports marginal costing. An item of expenditure is *revenue-producing* if by its spending *the firm's future revenues are boosted.* Firms do not spend money on fixed factory overheads just for the sake of it. They do so because it is necessary for the production of goods — goods which will ultimately bring in revenue. Any goods which remain unsold at the end of a year should therefore be charged their share of overhead as this expense will contribute to future revenue. This definition supports absorption costing.

Examination Questions

Questions usually ask for comparative income statements under the two systems. A reconciliation of the different profit figures, with an explanation, is sometimes also asked for. Essay questions on the theoretical disagreements between the two systems are more a feature of professional examinations than those at this level. You should however be prepared to write about the disagreement over the interpretation of the matching concept, as outlined at the start of the chapter. The dispute about the best definition of asset is not so important at this stage, although knowledge of it will help you to appreciate the difference between the two systems more fully.

Questions

19.1 Monteplana Ltd produced the following financial statement for the year ended 31 December 19_3:

	£	£
Sales (100,000 units)		300 000
Less		
Direct materials	100 000	
Direct labour	40 000	
Variable factory overhead	10 000	
Fixed factory overhead	100 000	250 000
Manufacturing profit		50 000
Less		
Selling and distribution expenses	30 000	
Administrative expenses	30 000	60 000
Net Loss		10 000

There were no opening or closing stocks of either finished goods or work-in-progress. The factory plant had a production capacity of 200 000 units per annum.

As a result of the net loss arising in 19_3, the sales director maintained that the loss had arisen through not operating the plant at full capacity and that an extensive advertising campaign would increase sales significantly. Thus the board of directors agreed that £40 000 would be spent on an advertising campaign in 19_4, and that the plant would be worked to full capacity producing 200 000 units.

The following results were achieved in the financial year ended 31 December 19_4.
(1) 130 000 units were sold at the 19_3 price.
(2) All factory variable expenses increased directly in proportion to output.
(3) There was no increase in selling and administrative expenses except that due to increased advertising.
All the directors agreed that in order to pursue a policy of consistency, stocks of finished goods should continue to be valued at the full manufacturing unit cost.

The accountant stated that he would prefer to see stock valuation including manufacturing variable costs only.

Required:
(a) An income statement for the year ended 31 December 19_4 on the agreed basis of valuing stocks. (5 marks)
(b) An alternative income statement for the year ended 31 December 19_4 using the accountant's suggestion as the basis of valuing stock. (5 marks)
(c) (i) Use accepted accountancy principles to explain the 'correctness' of the argument regarding the stock valuation of the directors.
(ii) Write a memorandum which the accountant could submit to the directors in an effort to persuade them to change to his policy for stock valuation. The memorandum should explain the shortcomings of the present policy and the advantages which would accrue from the change. (10 marks)
(20 marks)

Advanced level Accounting, AEB

19.2* The data below relate to a company which makes and sells one product.

	March	*April*
	units	units
Sales	4 000	6 000
Production	8 000	2 000
	£	£
Selling price per unit	80	80
Variable production costs, per unit	40	40
Fixed production overhead incurred	96 000	96 000
Fixed production overhead cost, per unit, being the predetermined overhead absorption rate	12	12
Selling, distribution and administration costs (all fixed)	40 000	40 000

Required:

(a) present comparative profit statements for each month using:
  (i) absorption costing,
  (ii) marginal costing; (14 marks)

(b) comment on the following statement using, for purposes of illustration, if you wish, figures contained in your answer to (a):
  'Marginal costing rewards sales whereas absorption costing rewards production.' (6 marks)

(20 marks)

Chartered Institute of Management Accountants

19.3 C. Jones & Co. have traditionally used an absorption costing approach to valuing stocks in their final accounts. The firm's accountant wishes to assess the differences, if any, that the use of a marginal approach might have produced.

Opening stock on 1 January 19_3 was 700 units valued at £12 000; this figure is to be used for both methods.

	19_3	19_4
Fixed factory overhead (£)	14 000	16 000
Direct labour cost/unit (£)	6	7
Direct material cost/unit (£)	8	8
Variable overhead/unit (£)	4	5
Sales (units)	2 200	2 300
Selling price/unit (£)	25	32
Production (units)	2 400	2 400

You are asked to:

(a) Draw up the manufacturing and trading accounts for 19_3 and 19_4 adopting each method, and (21 marks)

(b) Use your answer to explain why the profits are different under each method. (9 marks)

(30 marks)

Advanced Level Accounting, London

19.4 (a) Explain the meaning of (i) absorption costing, (ii) marginal costing, (iii) contribution. (6 marks)

(b) A firm which uses cost plus (full cost) pricing makes 100 each of a range of products each month. The unit costs of the whole range are shown at the top of the next page.

	J	*K*	*L*	*M*	*N*
	£	£	£	£	£
Direct materials	10	12	13	16	19
Direct labour	8	9	10	13	13
Variable overhead	4	5	7	9	10
	22	26	30	38	42
Fixed overhead	3	4	5	7	8
	25	30	35	45	50
Profit (20%)	5	6	7	9	10
	30	36	42	54	60

Market conditions have moved against the firm and competitors are charging the following prices for the whole range, beginning with J: £21; £34; £38; £51; £40.

Show how the firm can still compete at the new prices, and earn itself an overall profit of £200 per month by producing K, L and M. Explain fully how this can be so. (6 marks)

(c) Why is the marginal costing approach not suitable for analysing long-term decisions? (3 marks)

(15 marks)

Advanced Level Accounting, London

19.5 The Jolly Jodphurs Company is situated in Hampshire and manufactures riding trousers of a distinctive design. The company has been operating for some years, utilizing an overhead absorption technique to reflect the charging of manufacturing overheads into production costs. The management have recently received a report, however, from a member of staff who attended a short course on accounting techniques. This report highlighted another technique for dealing with the treatment of the fixed portion of manufacturing overheads — the variable approach. The management are impressed by the report and have decided that, as a special exercise, the accounts for the financial year just ended should be shown under both techniques, and have accordingly asked you, the company's accountant, to undertake this task.

The following information is relevant to the year ended 31st May, 19_5:

Detail	*Budgeted*	*Actual*
Production in pairs	24 000	15 000
Sales in pairs	21 000	18 000
Direct material cost	£120 000	£165 000
Direct labour cost per hour	£5	as per budget
Direct labour hours	2.5 per pair	30 000 in total
Fixed manufacturing overhead	£54 000	£4 000 per month
Fixed administration overhead	£96 000	£120 000
Variable selling expenses	£19 950	as per budget basis

Additional information:

(1) Selling price is £35 per pair.

(2) At present, fixed manufacturing overheads are absorbed via a direct labour hour rate basis, based upon the budgeted level of activity. Variances are transferred to the Profit and Loss Account of the year.

(3) On 1st June, 19_4, opening stocks of finished goods consisted of 4 000 pairs valued at a production cost of £106 000. This production cost value reflected costs as follows:

direct materials	£10 per pair
direct labour	£12 per pair
fixed manufacturing overhead	£4.50 per pair

Finished goods are charged out on a F.I.F.O. basis.

Required:

(a) (i) Prepare a Profit and Loss Account for the year ending 31st May, 19_5, using the fixed overhead absorption approach as employed by the Company; (8 marks)

(ii) Prepare a Profit and Loss Account for the year ending 31st May 19_5 using the variable approach; (7 marks)

(iii) Explain the reason why the profits you have calculated in (i) and (ii) above differ and apply your explanation to account for this difference. (3 marks)

(b) Compare the under/over absorption arising when fixed manufacturing overheads are absorbed via a direct labour hour rate basis, as in (a) (i) above, with the under/over absorption arising if those overheads were absorbed,

(i) via a unit of output absorption rate.

(ii) via a prime cost percentage absorption rate.

Where appropriate calculations are to be made to 3 decimal places. (5 marks)

(23 marks)

Institute of Chartered Accountants, Foundation

19.6* The Bright and Clear Cream Company produces four types of face cream viz.: Spot Cleanse, Dew Drops, Wrinkle Whacker and Line Out.

The creams are produced in a complex which consists of two production departments, through which each cream passes, and a general service department.

Unfortunately, due to inherent production problems, not all of the creams produced always satisfy quality control criteria for classification as superior quality; these sub-standard quality creams are sold at reduced prices.

Below are budgeted details relating to the year ending 30th June 19_5:

	Cream:			
Detail	*SC*	*DD*	*WW*	*LO*
Selling price per jar:				
Superior quality	£2.96	£4.36	£2.34	£2.96
Sub-standard quality	£0.60	£0.72	£0.70	£0.60
Production — number of jars	3 000	2 000	6 000	4 000
Prime cost of production per jar	£0.80	£1.40	£1.00	£1.20

It is anticipated that all jars produced will be sold with 10% being of substandard quality.

The fixed overhead per annum will total £18 920 comprising £5 280 for Production Department 1, £10 560 for Production Department 2 and £3 080 for the General Service Department. The General Service Department fixed overhead is apportioned to the Production Departments on the basis of direct labour hours worked; total fixed production overhead is absorbed into product costs via a direct labour hour rate.

An analysis of the budgeted production schedule reveals the following spread of hours

Production Department	*Total*	*SC*	*DD*	*WW*	*LO*
Number 1	4 000	1 200	1 400	600	800
Number 2	5 600	1 600	2 400	800	800

Despite the fact that the details above have been extracted from the budgets for the forthcoming year, the management still feel uncertain about some of the assumptions upon which the forecasts have been made. The management is also unsure of the policy to adopt regarding the sale of the sub-standard products.

Given these doubts and uncertainties, the management has requested that you:

(a) calculate the budgeted cost per jar of each product and the total budgeted profit for the year based on the assumption that the production/sales of sub-standard products are as budgeted. (8 marks)

(b) assuming that the details are as expected, comment on the proposals that Dew Drops should be discontinued as it may be unprofitable. (Any surplus operating capacity arising will not be utilised.) (8 marks)

(c) discuss the relative merits of absorption and variable costing with particular reference to the case of Dew Drops. (5 marks)

(21 marks)

Institute of Chartered Accountants, Foundation

19.7 'Decisions made about the future of products on the basis of production costs when production overhead has been allocated and apportioned can be misleading' said the accountant to the managing director.

You are required, as the assistant accountant, to write a short report to the managing director in which you should comment on the reasons for the validity of the above statement and also include in your report an explanation of the following terms:

(a) production cost
(b) production overhead
(c) cost allocation
(d) cost apportionment

(15 marks)

Chartered Institute of Management Accountants

19.8 'While the financial accountant is interested in absorption costing, the management accountant is interested in marginal costing'. Discuss. **(20 marks)**

Author's Question

Solutions

19.1 (a)

MONTEPLANA LTD.

Income Statement for the year ended 31 December 19_4 under Absorption Costing

	£	£
Sales (130 000 × £3)		390 000
Less		
Direct materials	130 000	
Direct labour	52 000	
Variable factory overhead	13 000	
Fixed factory overhead	100 000	
	295 000	
Less closing stock (W_1)	103 250	
Cost of goods sold		191 750
Gross profit		198 250
Selling and distribution expenses	70 000	
Administration expenses	30 000	100 000
Net profit		£98 250

W_1 Unit production cost $= \frac{295}{200} = £1.475$

Value of closing stock = 70 000 units @ £1.475
= £103 250

(b)

MONTEPLANA LTD.

Income Statement for the year ended 31 December 19_4 under Variable Costing

	£	£
Sales		390 000
Less		
Direct materials	130 000	
Direct labour	52 000	
Variable factory overhead	13 000	
	195 000	
Less closing work (W_2)	68 250	
Total variable cost		126 750
Contribution		263 250
Fixed factory overhead	100 000	
Selling and distribution expenses	70 000	
Administration expenses	30 000	200 000
Net profit		£63 250

W_2 Unit production cost $= \frac{195}{200} = £0.975$

Value of closing stock = 70 000 units @ £0.975
= £68 250

(c) See text.

19.3 (a)

C. JONES & CO.

Manufacturing and Trading Account — Absorption costing — for the years ended

	31 December 19_3		*31 December 19_4*	
	£	£	£	£
Direct material		19 200		19 200
Direct labour		14 400		16 800
Prime cost		33 600		36 000
Variable overhead	9 600		12 000	
Fixed factory overhead	14 000	23 600	16 000	28 000
Factory cost of production c/d		57 200		64 000
Sales		55 000		73 600
Opening stock	12 000		21 450	
Factory cost of production b/d	57 200		64 000	
	69 200		85 450	
Less closing stock (W_1)	21 450		26 666	
Cost of goods sold		47 750		58 784
Gross profit		£7 250		£14 816

Working

W_1 *Valuation of closing stock*

First we need to determine *unit production cost*. There are two methods of doing this, as illustrated in the text. Both are shown below.

Method 1

Unit production cost $\frac{£57\ 200}{2\ 400 \text{ units}}$ = £23.833 $\qquad \frac{£64\ 000}{2\ 400 \text{ units}}$ = £26.66

Method 2

			£			£
Per unit:						
Direct material			6			7
Direct labour			8			8
Variable overhead			4			5
Fixed overhead	$\frac{14\ 000}{2\ 400}$	=	5.833	$\frac{16\ 000}{2\ 400}$	=	6.66
Unit full cost			23.833			26.66

The two methods produce the same answer of course.

Next it is necessary to calculate the number of units of closing stock.

	31 December 19_3	*31 December 19_4*
	Units	*Units*
Opening stock	700	900
Produced	2 400	2 400
Available for sale	3 100	3 300
Sold	2 200	2 300
∴ Closing stock	900	1 000

We can now value it as: 900 × £23.833 = £21 450 1 000 × £26.66 = £26 666

Manufacturing and Trading Account — Marginal costing — for the years ended

	31 December 19_3		*31 December 19_4*	
	£	£	£	£
Direct material		19 200		19 200
Direct labour		14 400		16 800
Prime cost		33 600		36 000
Variable overhead		9 600		12 000
Variable cost of production c/d		43 200		48 000
Sales		55 000		73 600
Opening stock	12 000		16 200	
Variable cost of production b/d	43 200		48 000	
	55 200		64 200	
Less closing stock (W_2)	16 200		20 000	
Variable cost of goods sold		39 000		44 200
Contribution		16 000		29 400
Fixed factory overhead		14 000		16 000
Gross profit		£2 000		£13 400

W_2 *Working*

Valuation of closing stock

First we need to determine unit variable cost.

Method 1 $\frac{£43\ 200}{2\ 400 \text{ units}}$ = £18 $\frac{£48\ 000}{2\ 400 \text{ units}}$ = £20

Method 2

Per unit:		
Direct material	8	8
Direct labour	6	7
Variable overhead	4	5
Unit variable cost	18	20

Value of closing stock 900 × £18 = £16 200 1 000 × £20 = £20 000

(b) Since production exceeds sales in both years profit under absorption costing is higher than under marginal costing. For an explanation of this, see text.

Since the only difference between the two systems is in the valuation of stock the different profit figures can be reconciled through stocks.

	+(−) in stock	*Profit*	*+(−) in stock*	*Profit*
Absorption costing	9 450	7 250	5 216	14 816
Marginal costing	4 200	2 000	3 800	13 400
Difference	5 250	5 250	1 416	1 416

19.4 (a) See text.

(b) *Contribution Statement*

	Product				
	J	*K*	*L*	*M*	*N*
	£	£	£	£	£
Market price	21	34	38	51	40
Less variable cost	22	26	30	38	42
Contribution	(1)	8	8	13	(2)

The above statement shows that it is worth producing K, L, and M in the short run since revenue covers variable cost and provides a contribution to the firm's fixed costs. It is not worth producing J and N since revenue does not cover even their variable cost.

Profit Statement

	K	L	M	Total
	£	£	£	£
Sales	3 400	3 800	5 100	12 300
Less variable cost	2 600	3 000	3 800	9 400
Contribution	800	800	1 300	2 900
Less fixed overhead				
(3 + 4 + 5 + 7 + 8) × 100				2 700
Profit				£200

(c) Marginal (variable) costing advocates production of a good so long as variable costs are covered and a contribution is made towards fixed overhead. While this is acceptable in the short term it is not so in the long term. In the long term *all* costs have to be covered, both fixed and variable, if a firm is to survive. Long-term decision making must therefore be based on *full cost*, not variable cost only.

19.5 (a) (i) THE JOLLY JODPHURS COMPANY

Profit and Loss Account for the year ending 31st May 19_5 — Absorption costing basis

	£	£
Sales		630 000
Opening stock	106 000	
Direct materials	165 000	
Direct labour (30 000 × £5)	150 000	
Fixed manufacturing overhead (W_1)	27 000	
	448 000	
Less closing stock (W_2)	22 800	
	425 200	
Under-absorbed overhead (48 000 − 27 000)	21 000	
Cost of goods sold		446 200
Gross profit		183 800

	£	£
Variable selling expenses (19 950 × $\frac{18}{21}$)	17 100	
Fixed administration overhead	120 000	137 100
Net profit		£46 700

Workings

W_1 Overhead absorption rate $= \dfrac{£54\ 000}{24\ 000 \times 2.5}$

$= £0.90$ per direct labour hour

Overhead absorbed = 30 000 hours × £0.90 = £27 000

W_2 *Determination of unit production cost*

Method 1 (in 000s)

$$\frac{165 + 150 + 27}{15} = \frac{342}{15} = £22.80$$

Method 2

	£
Direct material $\frac{165\ 000}{15\ 000}$	11.00
Direct labour hours $\frac{30\ 000}{15\ 000} = 2$	
Direct labour cost 2 hours × £5	10.00
Fixed manufacturing overhead $\frac{27\ 000}{15\ 000}$	1.80
	22.80

	Units
Opening stock	4 000
Produced	15 000
Available for sale	19 000
Sold	18 000
Closing stock	∴1 000

Valuation of closing stock 1 000 × £22.80 = £22 800

(ii) THE JOLLY JODPHURS COMPANY

Profit and Loss Account for the year ending 31st May 19_5 — Variable Costing basis

	£	£
Sales		630 000
Opening stock (4 000 @ £22)	88 000	
Direct materials	165 000	
Direct labour	150 000	
	403 000	
Less closing stock (1 000 @ £21)	21 000	
	382 000	
Variable selling expenses	17 100	
Variable cost of goods sold		399 100
Contribution		230 900
Fixed manufacturing overhead	48 000	
Fixed administration overhead	120 000	168 000
Net profit		£62 900

(iii) Since the only difference between the approaches is in valuation of stock the different profit figures can be accounted for through the movement in stocks.

	+(−) in stock	*Profit*
	£	£
Absorption costing	(83 200)	46 700
Variable costing	(67 000)	62 900
Difference	16 200	16 200

(b) (i) *Rate per unit of output*

$$\text{Budgeted absorption rate} = \frac{£54\ 000}{24\ 000} = £2.25 \text{ per trouser}$$

	£
Overhead incurred	48 000
Absorbed (15 000 × £2.25)	33 750
Under-absorption	14 250

(ii) *Percentage of prime cost*

$$\text{Budgeted absorption rate} = \frac{£54\ 000}{£120\ 000 \text{ material} + £300\ 000^{*} \text{ labour}} \times 100$$

= 12.857% of prime cost

* Budgeted labour cost = 2.5 hours × £5 × 24 000 trousers
= £300 000

	£
Overhead incurred	48 000
Absorbed (£315 000 × 12.857%)	40 500
Under-absorption	7 500

PART III
Management Accounting

CHAPTER 20

Decision-making and Relevant Costs

Financial accounting and the system of absorption costing include historic costs. When it comes to making decisions about the future, historic costs which have already been incurred are irrelevant. The accountant is more interested in *avoidable future costs*. Such information is not available from the financial accounts. However, not all future costs are relevant to a particular decision. Decision-making is a process of choosing among competing alternatives each with their own set of costs and revenues. Those costs which are the same under each alternative are irrelevant — because they are not affected by the decision taken. A relevant cost is therefore a *future differential* cost.

An example will help to illustrate. Let us take a company reviewing its policy of purchasing its fleet of vehicles and considering leasing as an alternative. The annual costs per vehicle associated with each alternative are:

	Purchase	*Lease*
	£	*£*
Initial outlay	10 000	—
Monthly rental	—	250 a month
Petrol and running costs	500	500
Tax and insurance	600	600

All four costs are future avoidable costs. However out of these only the first two are relevant costs. Since the petrol, running costs, tax, and insurance are the *same whichever alternative is chosen* they are irrelevant to the decision.

To summarize, for a cost to be relevant to a decision it must be:
(1) a future cost, *and*
(2) a differential cost i.e. its level must be different for each of the alternatives under consideration.

The above applies equally to benefits.

It is the responsibility of the management accountant to identify and separate the differential from the common costs and revenues under each alternative, and present them to management in the form of a differential cost statement. Such statements are widely used in practice and often asked for in examination questions. They can be used for both short-run (tactical) decisions and long-run (investment) decisions. The main distinction is that in the short-run the firm is limited to a fixed amount of capacity and has certain fixed costs — those associated with land, capital, and certain types of labour. These fixed costs are not relevant costs because they are unavoidable in the time period under consideration. The relevant costs are the differential variable costs. In the long run all costs are variable, so that the fixed costs irrelevant in the short run become relevant in the long run. This chapter is concerned mainly with short-run decisions. Long-run capital investment decisions are considered in Chapter 24.

Short-run decisions are many and varied but some of the more important ones, which we shall look at in this chapter include:

(1) dropping a segment
(2) accepting or rejecting an order
(3) decision-making in the face of a limiting factor

Dropping a Segment

A segment is an identifiable unit of a business such as a particular product, branch, or sales area. Let us take a firm producing three products — two profitable and one unprofitable — and examine the relevant considerations in the decision on whether to drop the unprofitable product.

Example

General Components Ltd. manufacture three components A, B, and C, used in the helicopter industry. The estimate of costs and revenues for each for the coming financial year are as follows:

	A	*B*	*C*	*TOTAL*
	£000	*£000*	*£000*	*£000*
Sales	200	150	100	450
Cost of goods sold	100	75	60	235
Gross profit	100	75	40	215
Less expenses				
Factory overhead	40	30	20	90
Selling and distribution costs	15	12	15	50
Head office administration expenses	20	15	10	37
Total expenses	75	57	45	177
Net profit (loss)	25	18	(5)	38

The factory overhead and 50 per cent of the head office administration expenses are fixed and have been apportioned to the products on the basis of sales value.

Should the company cease producing Component C? At first sight it appears so. Let us now consider the proposal more carefully.

The first point to note is that the factory overhead and fixed element of the administration expense will continue to be incurred and their levels unchanged whether or not C is dropped. They are therefore *irrelevant* in the context of the decision. In contrast, the selling and distribution costs and costs of goods sold are *avoidable* and therefore *relevant*. Whether or not the company gets any sales revenue from C will also be affected by the decision — it is therefore relevant. From this we can prepare a

Differential cost statement if C is dropped

	£000	*£000*
Sales		100
Less differential costs		
Cost of goods sold	60	
Selling and distribution costs	15	
Variable administration expenses	5	80
Differential profit		£20

The above statement tells us that C should not be dropped since it is *contributing* £20 000 to the factory overhead and head office administration expenses. If C were dropped (on the basis of the income statement incorporating irrelevant costs) the £20 000 would no longer be covered by C and would have to be absorbed by components A and B thus decreasing their profitability. Total profits of the company would thus fall from £38 000 to £18 000.

Accepting an Order

Another common type of decision in business is whether or not to accept a special order at a price below the normal selling price.

Example

Fred manufactures wooden clogs. Each unit costs:

	£
Direct material	3
Direct labour	1
Fixed overhead	2
	6

He receives a large order from abroad to supply 1000 clogs at £5. Should he accept?

On the basis of the above statement he should not. However the fixed costs are irrelevant. Fred is committed to incurring them whether or not the order is accepted. As such, they should be ignored.

Differential cost statement if order is Accepted

	£	£
Sales		5 000
Less relevant costs		
Direct material	3 000	
Direct labour	1 000	4 000
Differential profit		£1 000

Fred should accept the order — he is £1 000 better off.

Although fixed costs are usually irrelevant in short-term decision-making, they need not *always* be so. If in the above example Fred has to purchase machinery for £800 and incur £600 for insurance and supervision costs to satisfy the export order, these fixed costs now become relevant since they are both future costs *and* differential costs. The differential cost statement would look as follows:

	£	£
Sales		5 000
Less relevant costs		
Direct material	3 000	
Direct labour	1 000	
Additional machinery	800	
Insurance, supervision	600	5 400
Differential loss		£(400)

The order is no longer worthwhile.

Decision-making in the Face of a Limiting Factor

Sometimes a firm cannot satisfy its full market demand because of bottlenecks in production. Output may be limited by some scarce factor — this could be a shortage of a particular type of material or component, skilled labour, machinery, or a shortage of cash. In such a situation management should choose that output which makes the most profitable use of the scarce factor.

Example

Expansion Ltd, which makes three products A, B, and C has recently been enjoying a period of increasing demand and profitability such that all its machines are now working at full capacity. A further increase in demand is expected in the next year but management will now have to make a decision on which of the three products to cut back on. The information given at the top of page 310, is available:

	Product		
	A	*B*	*C*
Market demand (units)	1 000	600	600
Contribution per unit	£16	£9	£10
Machine hours per unit	4	3	2
Total machine hours required	4 000	1 800	1 200

If there were no limiting factors the company should produce up to market demand for each product since they all provide positive contributions. Suppose however that plant capacity is limited to 6 100 machine hours. 7 000 hours (being 4 000 for A, 1 800 for B plus 1 200 for C) are required to produce up to demand for each product. In this situation, management has to set priorities for the three products. Under normal circumstances the criteria to use would be contribution per unit. By this the priority would be A £16, C £10, B £9. However, when one factor is scarce this solution is wrong. In order to make the best possible use of the scarce factor the products should be ranked not in terms of *total* contribution but *contribution per unit of the scarce factor.*

Per unit:	*A*	*B*	*C*
Contribution	£16	£9	£10
Machine hours required	4	3	2
Contribution per machine hour	£4	£3	£5
Ranking	2	3	1

At £5 contribution per machine hour product C uses the scarce factor most efficiently. C should therefore be given top priority and produced up to market demand. Product A is next best and should also be produced to its demand limit. The balance of machine hours available should be alloted to B. The optimum product-mix may be presented as follows:

Product	*Units produced*	*Machine hours used*	*Cumulative machine hours used*
C	600	1 200	1 200
A	1 000	4 000	5 200
B	∴ 300	900	6 100

The quantity of B produced is found by working back from machine hours usable. Since 900 hours are left after allocation to C and A, the quantity is found by $\frac{900}{3} = 300$ units

By optimum mix is meant that it is not possible to increase total contribution by re-arranging the output mix in any way.

Exercise

To check your understanding of the above, work out the optimum product-mix if, as a result of a breakdown in some of Expansion Ltd's machines, capacity is further reduced to only 4 000 machine hours.

Answer

Product	*Units produced*	*Machine hours used*	*Cumulative machine hours used*
C	600	1 200	1 200
A	700	2 800	4 000
B	0	0	4 000

In situations where there are *two* limiting factors the optimum solution cannot be found by this method. Instead the accountant has to use linear programming techniques which involves constructing a set of simultaneous linear equations reflecting the scarce factors, then solving them. Where *three or more constraints* exist at the same time advanced mathematical techniques involving matrix algebra have to be used, along with computers to solve them. You are not expected to know these, but will meet them in Management Accounting papers at professional level.

Other Examples

It is not possible to look at *all* the instances of decision-making where the concept of relevant costing can be applied — nor indeed is that necessary. Among its more common other uses are decisions on:

- making a product internally or buying from outside
- selling a by-product or further processing it
- buying fixed assets or leasing

The Long Term

You should be clear that while it is sufficient for an alternative to be accepted in the short run if it covers all variable costs and provides a contribution, firms can not accept such a situation for *all* products *all* of the time. *In the long run all costs have to be covered,* both fixed and variable, if a firm is to survive.

Non-financial Factors

Decisions are not made on financial grounds alone. Some factors cannot be expressed in financial terms but may be important to the decision. Consider a factory which has always manufactured its own components. A quotation comes in from a specialist manufacturer offering to supply a particular component below its own production cost. On financial grounds it should stop making and buy from outside. However, there are certain *qualitative* factors which cannot be converted into money terms and the accountants' report to management should mention these. Buying from outside might well involve closure of part of the factory — with consequent redundancies. Management should therefore consider whether the potential conflict with the unions is worth the financial cost savings. Industrial action may, after all, be costly too. Buying from outside will also increase dependance on other firms and decrease the amount of *control* the firm has over delivery times, quantity and quality of supplies. If the product in question is a key component it might be worthwhile to produce internally even though it is at a higher cost.

To take another example, when faced with a large order below normal selling price management should take into account the possibility of further orders or breaking into new markets. Examination questions often ask for identification of relevant non-financial factors to a given decision (usually after the numerical part).

Social Responsibility Accounting

An important development in recent decades has been a re-consideration of the motives of the firm. The traditional view is that the only motive is profit maximization. It is now realized that there may be more than one motive. The effect of a business decision affects not only profits accruing to owners but also its employees, consumers, and in some cases the environment. In practice, firms try to balance conflicting interests with one another. Decisions taken in this way may not lead to maximum profits. For example, a firm may keep open an unprofitable segment out of a sense of responsibility to the local community and/or a desire to avoid the adverse publicity and resentment that goes with a closure. Again, a business may install pollution-reducing devices, thereby reducing profits, out of a sense of responsibility to the environment and/or reaction to local environment protection pressure groups. This is a complex and growing field of study called Social Responsibility Accounting. See question 20.3.

Questions

20.1* A company currently makes and sells 1 000 units per month of its product. The selling price is £55 per unit, and unit costs are: direct labour £3; direct materials £7; variable overheads £4. Fixed costs per month are £16 200.

The firm receives two special export orders for completion in the same month. Order A requests 500 units at a special price of £6 500; order B requires 600 units at £12 000. Order A will require no special treatment, but order B will demand extra processing at a cost of £5 per unit. The firm has sufficient productive capacity to undertake either A or B in addition to its current production.

(a) Show the firm's profits for the month if
   (i) normal production only takes place
   (ii) order A is accepted
   (iii) order B is accepted. (12 marks)

(b) Explain why a company will generally accept an order which makes a positive contribution towards overheads. (8 marks)

(c) Before accepting an order based upon marginal cost prices, what safeguards must a firm adopt? (5 marks)

(25 marks)

Advanced Level Accounting, London

20.2 From one basic raw material a company produces two different grades of a product known as 'Crude' and 'Refined'. The company's direct labour wage rate is £3 per hour and it absorbs overhead into the cost of its two grades of product by means of variable and fixed overhead rates per 100 kilogrammes produced. The budgeted costs and selling prices for each grade are as follows:

	Crude *100 kgs* £	*Refined* *100 kgs* £
Direct material	20.0	20.0
Direct wages	18.0	30.0
Variable production ovehead	3.6	7.5
Fixed production overhead	24.0	40.0
	65.6	97.5
Selling prices	80.0	105.0

For the year ending 30th June, 19_5, the company's effective annual production capacity is 120 000 labour hours and its estimated fixed production overhead costs total £480 000. Its sales policy is to sell 75% of its capacity in the more profitable grade and 25% in the less profitable grade.

Required:

(a) state on which grade of product the company should concentrate to obtain the highest profit—show your calculations;

(b) present a statement for management which shows the expected sales, variable costs (by element of cost) and contribution for each grade of product together with the overall net profit which can be expected for the year ending 30th June, 19_5, if the company's present sales policy is followed. Budgeted fixed selling and administration costs are £90 000; **(16 marks)**

Chartered Institute of Management Accountants

20.3 Eurasifrac, a multi-national company of diverse interests, was reviewing a number of its activities in order to determine possible courses of action.

(1) The company owned a coal mine where increased geological difficulties had resulted in the full cost per ton of coal mined rising from £70 to £90 in the last year. The current market price of coal was £80 per ton, and was likely to remain at that level in the forseeable future. The normal level of output was 10 000 tons per annum. A director has argued that the mine should be closed, so that the company's profits would increase. All of the employees should be made redundant.

(2) A factory owned by the company was located in a rural environment close to a small town. The local community had complained that poisonous effluent was being discharged in a river passing through the town. Scientific tests had shown that fish were being killed, and that seepage of poison had occurred into agricultural and residential land adjacent to the river.

Summarised Revenue Statement of the Factory
for the last three years

	Year I	*Year II*	*Year III*
	£M	*£M*	*£M*
Sales	10.0	12.0	15.0
less			
Variable costs	5.0	6.7	9.1
Fixed costs	4.0	4.1	4.1
Profit	1.0	1.2	1.8

The fixed costs include £3M of the parent company costs allocated to the factory annually.

The local community had requested that the pollution be stopped, but the company replied that the factory was not very profitable. In order to eliminate the poisonous effects a capital outlay on new plant of £4M over three years would be required.

(3) Over the past two years the company had stockpiled a very scarce material known as Igoxi, which it used in a high-technology process. The material had cost £6.50 per lb and all of the stock-pile of 10 tons had been purchased at this price. The material was not used in normal production, but only on special contract orders.

In the last three months world demand had increased the market price of Igoxi to £10 per lb.

Required:
Prepare a report advising the company as follows:

(a) Whether the company should proceed to close the coal mine. (8 marks)

(b) Whether the company can justify continuing to operate the factory and allow the river to remain polluted. (10 marks)

(c) What should be the basis of valuing the stock of Igoxi:
   (i) for balance sheet purposes.
   (ii) for production purposes. (7 marks)

(25 marks)

Advanced Level Accounting, AEB

20.4* Morro and Son, a small but specialized engineering business, manufacture and sell three products; M, R, and S. For the year ending 30 June 19_2 the activity programme is expected to be:

Product	*Direct Materials*	*Direct Wages*	*Overhead (25% Fixed)*	*Sales*	*Total Quantities*
	£	£	£	£	Units
M	4 000	8 000	16 000	40 000	400
R	19 200	12 000	24 000	72 000	600
S	12 000	12 000	24 000	60 000	600

Required:

(a) Calculate the profit for the year ending 30 June 19_2 if actual activity were as expected. (3 marks)

(b) Calculate the *change* in the profits for the year if the business were to accept a sub-contract from a larger firm to produce an additional 50 units of product S at a selling price of £90 each. Assume that the resources would be available subject to the need to buy additional machinery at a cost of £2 300 which, it is estimated, would have a scrap value of £300 after its useful life of 4 years; use of this machinery would incur annual running costs of £300 per annum. (6 marks)

(c) Calculate which of the products would provide the largest profit if existing direct labour (as inferred by direct wages in the table above) could be applied to the exclusive production of M, R, or S without any change in the total fixed overheads. It may be assumed that the same type of machining and labour is required in the production of all three products; direct labour receives the same rate of remuneration whichever product is manufactured. (8 marks)

(d) A brief report comparing the *total* profits for the business for the year under the existing programme as modified by proposal (b) and under proposal (c); state the practical considerations to be borne in mind before deciding whether or not to adopt either change from the original plan. (8 marks)

(25 marks)

Advanced level Accounting, AEB

20.5 Aut plc produces Umn, a product made popular by a recent television series, the selling price of which is £50. The unit cost structure based on the present level of production/sales of 100 000 units is:

	£
Direct materials	20
Direct labour	5
Variable overhead	2
Fixed overhead	8

The present level of production represents 100% of capacity working a single shift. The Marketing Manager estimates that at the present price the quantity sold during the next year could be increased by 50%.

A second shift has been proposed. This would increase production capacity to 180 000 Umns per annum, fixed costs increasing by £550 000 per annum. A shift work premium of 20% would be payable to the direct workers engaged on the additional shift; however, if production was at least 150 000 Umns per annum, the whole of the direct materials used would qualify for a discount of 10%.

Required:

(a) Calculate whether it would be profitable for Aut plc to add the second shift. (9 marks)

(b) Calculate the minimum annual increase in production/sales of Umn necessary to justify the additional shift. (6 marks)
(c) Outline any additional factors that would need to be considered before a final decision is made. (6 marks)
(21 marks)

Institute of Chartered Accountants, Foundation

(Attempt this question only when you know the break-even formula.)

20.6* The annual flexible budget for Rodo Limited, is as follows:

Level of activity	40%	60%	75%	100%
Costs	*£000*	*£000*	*£000*	*£000*
direct labour	104	156	195	260
direct material	64	96	120	160
production overhead	46	54	60	70
administration, selling, and distribution overhead	28	32	35	40
	242	338	410	530

Depressed trading conditions have caused management to consider whether the factory should be closed down temporarily and re-opened to coincide with the anticipated upsurge in demand expected sometime in the following year. Current production output is only 50% of capacity with a forecast annual sales revenue of £250 000 at that level of production. Informed sources forecast that in the twelve months following the re-opening date, sales could run at 80% of capacity and at an increased selling price per unit which would generate a total sales revenue of £480 000.

Closure of the factory for twelve months would, it is estimated:
(1) reduce the fixed element of overhead expenses to £25 000 per annum;
(2) incur plant maintenance costs of £4 000 per annum;
(3) entail closing down costs (e.g. redundancy payments) of £8 000.
Re-opening the factory after such a long period of closure would involve costs (e.g. training new personnel) which are estimated at £6 000.

Required:
(a) A financial statement showing the variable costs, contribution, fixed costs, and profit or loss at 50% and 80% levels of activity. (16 marks)
(b) A statement of the costs which would be incurred if the factory were closed and subsequently re-opened. (3 marks)
(c) Advise the company, with reasons, as to the course of action they should take, on the basis of the information given. (6 marks)
(25 marks)

Advanced Level Accounting, AEB

(Attempt only when you know Budgeting.)

20.7* A local authority owns and controls a multipurpose leisure/conference hall with adjacent bars and restaurants, in a seaside holiday resort. The authority has received requests for the letting of the hall from
(1) the organizers of an international Modern and Latin American dance championship, and
(2) a firm of exhibition organizers which wants to mount an exhibition of hotel and catering equipment.
The estimates of income and costs are shown below.

Dance championship

Dates hall required: Monday 16th May to Saturday 21st May, 19_8, inclusive.

Income: £200 per day rent plus 25% of box office takings from visitors who pay £5 entry fee per day to watch the championships. From past experience of running this event, the organizers estimate the number of dance competitors, who do not pay at the box office, will be 1 200 (200 per day) and that there will be 14 000 paying visitors over the six days.

30 stalls can be let to traders who use the concourse adjoining the hall. The traders sell dance shoes, clothes, records, and videos. Stall rents vary with size but if all are occupied, the rental income received by the authority for the whole period of six days will be £5 000.

Some events are to be filmed for showing on television at a later date for which the authority will receive a fee of £3 000.

Bars and restaurants can expect to take £3 per person per day for *each person using the hall.*

Hotel and catering equipment exhibition

400 stand units can be erected and dates required are Sunday 15th May to Wednesday 18th May, 19_8, inclusive. Sunday is the preparation day for the businesses renting stands for the exhibition from the organizers. The exhibition is to be open to the trade and public on the Monday, Tuesday and Wednesday. Stands are dismantled during Wednesday evening.

The exhibition organizers believe that all the stands will be let although some exhibitors will take two or more units to constitute larger stands. Exhibitors' employees average two per stand unit per day with exception of the preparation day (Sunday) when the average is six per stand unit.

Although open to the public, the exhibition is primarily for the trade, i.e. for buyers of hotel and catering equipment, which is what prompted the organizers to select a holiday resort. The exhibition organizers are offering £8 000 rent for the four-day period plus 20% of receipts from visitors. It is expected that 4 600 visitors will each pay £2.50 to enter the exhibition over the three-day period.

It is estimated that all the exhibitors' employees will spend £6 each per day in the bars and restaurants and that each visitor to the exhibition will spend an average of £2.

Authority employees, some of whom are temporary part-time, staffing the hall, bars and restaurants are listed below. Box office staff are engaged on other duties within the hall when it is not open to the public. Assume that the weekly payments are variable with the days the hall is in use and are based on a 6-day working week.

	Weekly wage £	*Number required for duty*	
		Dance championship	*Exhibition*
Managers	300	4	2
Box office staff	200	9	6
Attendants/security staff	150	20	20
Restaurant and bar staff	200	10	6
Restaurant and bar staff	120	100	60

Variable costs:

Energy costs £200 } per day the hall is in use
Cleaning contractors £300 }

Employee-related costs are 10% of *total* variable staff costs.

Fixed costs are expected to be incurred as follows:

	Per annum £
Manager and support staff permanently on site	60 000
Electrical, lighting and maintenance staff	100 000
Depreciation on fittings and equipment	80 000
Insurance	20 000

A gross profit of 45% is expected from all bar and restaurant receipts; the gross profit represents sales less cost of food, beverages and drinks.
Ignore inflation and value added tax.

Required:

(a) prepare a comparative statement showing the income and expenditure relating to letting the hall for
  (1) the dance championship, and
  (2) the exhibition; (12 marks)

(b) calculate the average surplus contribution per day of use for each proposal; (2 marks)

(c) recommend to the authority which proposal should be accepted, together with **two** reasons supporting your choice; (5 marks)

(d) list **three** factors which the authority should consider—these may not necessarily be of a financial nature. (6 marks)

(25 marks)

Chartered Institute of Management Accountants

20.8 The manager of a small business has received enquiries about printing three different types of advertising leaflet. Information concerning these three leaflets is shown below:

Leaflet type	*A*	*B*	*C*
	£	£	£
Selling price, per 1 000 leaflets	100	220	450
Estimated printing costs:			
Variable, per 1 000 leaflets	40	70	130
Specific fixed costs, per month	2 400	4 000	9 500

In addition to the specific fixed costs a further £4 000 per month would be incurred in renting special premises if any or all of the above three leaflets were printed.

The minimum printing order would be for 30 000 of each type of leaflet per month and the maximum possible order is estimated to be 60 000 of each leaflet per month.

Required:

(a) (i) Examine and comment upon the potential profitability of leaflet printing. Make whatever calculations you consider appropriate. (8 marks)

  (ii) Assuming that orders have been received to print each month 50 000 of both Leaflet A and Leaflet B calculate the quantity of Leaflet C which would need to be ordered to produce an overall profit, for all three leaflets, of £1 800 per month. (4 marks)

(b) It is possible that a special type of paper used in printing the leaflets will be difficult to obtain during the first few months. The estimated consumption of this special paper for each type of leaflet is:

  Leaflet A 2 packs per 1 000 leaflets
  Leaflet B 6 packs per 1 000 leaflets
  Leaflet C 16 packs per 1 000 leaflets

  Advise the manager on the quantity of each leaflet which should be printed in order to maximise profit in the first month, if 50 000 of each type of leaflet have been printed, there remains unfulfilled orders of 10 000 for each type of leaflet and there are 170 packs of special paper available for the rest of the month. (5 marks)

(c) 'If the manager of the above business wastes ten packs of special paper then the cost to the business of that waste is simply the original cost of that paper.'
  Critically examine the validity of the above statement. (5 marks)

(22 marks)

Chartered Association of Certified Accountants

20.9 What do you understand by the term 'Relevant Costing'. Illustrate its application to the following decisions:
(a) make or buy
(b) dropping a segment
(c) decision-making in the face of a scarce factor. **(20 marks)**

Author's Question

Solutions

20.2 A typical question on decision-making in the face of a limiting factor. Be careful with the table provided. The *'unit'* figures represent production *per 100 kgs* of each grade, not per unit. This distinction is important when making the necessary arithmetic calculations in part (b).

(a) *Budgeted Contribution Statement per 100 kg*

	Crude		*Refined*	
	£	£	£	£
Selling price		80.0		105.0
Less variable costs:				
Direct material	20.0		20.0	
Direct wages	18.0		30.0	
Variable production overhead	3.6	41.6	7.5	57.5
Contribution		38.4		47.5

	Crude	Refined
Labour hours required	$\frac{£18}{3} = 6$	$\frac{£30}{3} = 10$
Contribution per labour hour	$\frac{38.4}{6} = £6.40$	$\frac{47.5}{10} = 4.75$

The company should concentrate on *'Crude'* since this yields the highest contribution per limiting factor — labour hours.

(b) *Workings*

W_1 It is first necessary to calculate the number of units produced of each grade, and *revenue* obtained from them.

Grade	*Proportion of labour hours devoted*	*Production per 100 kgs.*	×	*Selling price*	=	*Revenue*
Crude	$\frac{3}{4}$	$\frac{90\,000}{6} = 15\,000$		80		1 200 000
Refined	$\frac{1}{4}$	$\frac{30\,000}{10} = 3\,000$		105		315 000

W_2 It is also necessary to work out the budgeted *fixed production overhead* using the overhead absorption rates given.

Overheads absorbed:		£
Crude	15 000 × £24	360 000
Refined	3 000 × £40	120 000
Total fixed production overhead		480 000

Budgeted Income Statement for the year ending 30th June 19_5

	Crude		*Refined*		*Total*	
	£000	*£000*	*£000*	*£000*	*£000*	*£000*
Sales (W_1)		1 200		315		1 515
Less variable costs:						
Direct material	300		60		360	
Direct wages	270		90		360	
Variable production overhead	54	624	22.5	172.5	76.5	796.5
Contribution		576		142.5		718.5

	£000	£000
Less fixed costs		
Fixed production overhead (W_2)	480	
Selling and administration costs	90	570
Net profit		£148.5

20.3 REPORT

To: Directors of Eurasifrac

(a) *Coal Mine*

It is necessary to know the *variable* cost of coal mined. If this is less than the market price of £80 it may be worth keeping the mine open in the hope that the geological difficulties are overcome or that the price of coal increases.

The social effects of closure must be considered. If the mine is in a town where other industries are expanding it will be easier to stop operations and make redundancies than if the town is heavily dependant on coal for jobs. The effect of any redundancy payments on the firm's finances must also be considered before a decision is reached.

(b) *Pollution of river*

Your claim that the factory is not profitable is not borne out by the figures. Excluding the £3 million allocated overheads from the parent Company, the true profit of the factory was £4 m in year 1, £4.2 m in year 2, rising to £4.8 in year 3. Sales have also increased. There seems to be a strong case for the instalment of a pollution-reducing device. Not only can the company afford it but it is also worthwhile in terms of the benefit to the local environment. The company has no right to pollute the river, kill fish, and damage nearby land, and if you shirk your responsibility on this you risk the escalation of local protest, with the adverse publicity which goes with this.

(c) *Igoxi*

(i) Stock should be valued at the lower of cost and net realizable value, in line with SSAP 9, i.e. at £6.50 per lb.

(ii) The stock should be charged to the income statement at historic cost, £6.50. The current market price of £10 represents the opportunity cost of use, but the historic cost concept prevents it from being entered anywhere in the books.

20.5 (a)

	One Shift		*Two Shifts*	
	100 000 Umns		*150 000 Umns*	
	£000	£000	£000	£000
Sales		5 000		7 500
Less variable costs:				
Direct materials	2 000		2 700 (W_2)	
Direct labour	500		800 (W_3)	
Variable overhead	200	2 700	300	3 800
Contribution		2 300		3 700
Fixed overhead		800 (W_1)		1 350
Profit		£1 500		£2 350

Workings

W_1 Fixed overhead = Overhead absorption rate × Units produced
= £8 × 100 000
= £800 000

W_2	£000
Direct materials cost	3 000
Less volume discount, 10%	300
Relevant cost	2 700

W_3 Direct labour cost:

Normal shift	100 000 × £5	500
Additional shift	50 000 × £6	300
Total cost		800

The above statement suggests that it would be profitable for Aut plc to add the second shift. Profit rises by £850 000.

(b) This can be found by applying the break-even formula. First calculate contribution per unit.

	£	£
Sales		50
Less variable cost		
Direct materials	20*	
Direct labour £5 × 1.2	6	
Variable overhead	2	28
Contribution		22

* Since production is going to be below 150 000 Umns the materials do not qualify for the volume discount.

Now apply the break-even formula:

$$\text{Break-even sales volume of additional shift} = \frac{\text{Additional fixed costs}}{\text{Incremental unit contribution}}$$

$$\frac{£550\ 000}{£22} = 25\ 000 \text{ units}$$

Answer: The minimum increase in production/sales necessary to justify the additional shift is 25 000 Umns.

OPTIONAL: It is possible to *check* the answer by calculating profit at the sales level of 125 000 Umns. Profit at this level should be equal to the current profit of £1 500 000.

	Calculation	*£000*	*£000*
Sales	125 000 × £50		6 250
Less variable costs			
Direct materials	125 000 × £20	2 500	
Direct labour:			
normal shift	100 000 × £5	500	
additional shift	25 000 × £6	150	
Variable overhead	125 000 × £2	250	3 400
Contribution			2 850
Fixed overhead			1 350
Profit			£1 500

(c) Additional factors that should be considered before a decision is made:
(1) Is the increase in demand likely to be *permanent*? If it is not it may not be worth increasing production capacity.
(2) Are the men willing to work the necessary overtime?
(3) The fixed costs increase of £550 000 presumably represents production overhead. Management would need to consider any resultant increase in the non-manufacturing overhead such as increases in distribution costs and administrative expenses.

20.8 (a) (i) First find the contribution provided by each type of leaflet.

	A	*B*	*C*	*Total*
Per Thousand Leaflets:	£	£	£	£
Selling price	100	220	450	
Variable costs	40	70	130	
Contribution	60	150	320	

It is a good idea to now find the profit/(loss) position for the maximum and minimum monthly order sizes expected.

Minimum Orders — 30 000 leaflets

Contribution (× 30)	1 800	4 500	9 600	15 900
Specific fixed costs	2 400	4 000	9 500	15 900
Profit/(loss)	(600)	500	100	—
Rent				4 000
Total loss				£(4 000)

Maximum Orders — 60 000 leaflets

Contribution (× 60)	3 600	9 000	19 200	31 800
Specific fixed costs	2 400	4 000	9 500	15 900
Profit	1 200	5 000	9 700	15 900
Rent				4 000
Total profit				£11 900

Comments The leaflets are not equally attractive. In the absence of any limiting factor, C is the most attractive at a contribution of 32 pence per leaflet, followed by B at 15 pence, and finally A at only 6 pence. The potential does not exist for the business to make a profit out of leaflet printing, but only if order sizes are greater than minimum. The managers should try and press the Enquirers for a commitment to future orders and then repeat the above calculation. If we assume that the same quantity of each leaflet is to be produced it is possible to calculate the precise break-even order size.

$$\text{Break-even point} = \frac{\text{Total fixed costs}}{\text{Average contribution per leaflet}}$$

$$\frac{2\,400 + 4\,000 + 9\,500 + 4\,000}{\dfrac{0.06 + 0.15 + 0.32}{3}} = \frac{£19\,900}{£0.1766} = 112\,684 \text{ leaflets (approx)}$$

$$\text{Required order size of each leaflet} = \frac{112\,640}{3} = 37\,561 \text{ (approx)}$$

The maximum profit potential is £11 900.

(ii)

	£
Required profit	1 800
Rent	4 000
Required contribution	5 800

First calculate the existing contribution from leaflets A and B from order sizes of 50 000.

	A	*B*	*Total*
	£	£	£
Contribution per 1 000 (× 50)	3 000	7 500	
Less specific fixed costs	2 400	4 000	
Contribution towards rent	600	3 500	4 100
Required Contribution			5 800
Shortfall, to be provided by C			1 700

C's contribution must be large enough to cover:

	£
Specific fixed costs	9 500
Contribution towards rent and required profit	1 700
	11 200

Each leaflet provides a contribution of 32 pence.

$$\text{Required quantity of C} = \frac{11\,200}{0.32} = 35\,000$$

(b)

	A	B	C
Contribution per pack of paper	$\frac{60}{2} = £30$	$\frac{150}{6} = £25$	$\frac{320}{16} = £20$
Ranking	1	2	3

Quantity of paper required to produce unfulfilled order

	Packs
A 10 × 2	20
B 10 × 6	60
C 10 × 16	160
Total packs required	240
Packs available	170
Shortage	70

The manager should rank the leaflets by looking at contribution per pack of paper. This leads to the solution above of concentrating on A, then B, and finally C.

Type	*Production*	*Packs used*	*Cummulative packs used*
A	10 000	20	20
B	10 000	60	80
C	5 625*	90	170

* Production of C $= \frac{90}{0.016} =$ 5 625 leaflets

(c) The statement is not correct. Since the special paper is scarce its value extends beyond mere historic cost. Wastage of the 10 packs reduces the number of C type leaflets that can now be produced.

Production of C possible $= \frac{90 - 10}{0.016} =$ 5 000 leaflets

The business has lost the opportunity to earn contribution on 5 625 − 5 000 = 625 leaflets.
Contribution foregone = 625 × 0.32 = £200

∴ Relevant cost = Historic cost + £200 opportunity cost.

Note that if the paper was *not* scarce the statement would be true.

CHAPTER 21

Budgeting and Budgetary Control

We do not live our life from day to day without any consideration about the future. We *plan* — from major things such as our career to small things such as what we are going to do tomorrow and over the week-end. The first is a long-term plan, the second a short-term plan. The same is true of business. However, here the plan is expressed in financial terms and is more formal and deliberate — in a process known as Budgeting. *A budget is a detailed plan of action for a future period.* It may cover both the near and distant future.

Long-term and Short-term Budgets

The long-term budget is a financial translation of proposed future capital investments, development of new products and abandonment of existing ones, breaking into new markets, and so on. It looks several years ahead e.g. 5-year

Plan. Each year it is broken down into more detail for the next year in an *operating plan.* This is the short-term budget. These may in turn be divided into quarterly or monthly budgets. The long- and short-term budgets should not be thought of as being separate from each other. They are inter-related. When the annual budget is prepared, a lot of the decisions affecting activity such as the fixed asset base and the products and markets the business is selling in will already have been made in the long-term plan. In turn, the events of a particular budget year may cause the long-term plan to be amended.

Apart from investment in fixed assets (which we look at in Chapter 24) long-range planning, somestimes called *Strategic* or *Corporate planning,* is not in the syllabus of most bodies at this level. Examination questions tend to concentrate on short-term budgeting and it is this we shall be looking at in this chapter.

Functions of Budgets

1. *Planning* — Forward planning forces managers to formally consider alternative future courses of action, evaluate them properly and decide on the best alternative. It also encourages managers to anticipate problems *before* they arise giving them time to consider alternative ways of ovecoming them when they do arrive. Such an exercise tends to produce better results than decisions made in haste.

2. *Co-ordination* — Left to their own devices, department managers may make decisions about the future which are *incompatible* or even in conflict with other departments. For example, Sales may be planning to extend the credit period in order to stimulate sales to a point beyond the bank overdraft arrangements. Budgeting helps to avoid such conflicts by encouraging managers to consider how their plans affect other departments and how the plans of other departments affect them.

3. *Control and performance evaluation* — While budget preparation aids planning, *the way budgets are used* helps in control and performance evaluation. The system of calculating deviations from budget i.e. variances, after the event *fosters cost-consciousness* amongst workers and managers and highlights areas of over- and, more importantly, under-achievement. The use of budgets for control and performance is considered in detail in the next chapter, Standard Costing and Variance Analysis. The behavioural aspects of budgetary control are considered at the end of this chapter.

4. *Participation* — By actively involving managers at all stages of the hierarchy, the process of budgeting brings the *different levels closer together.* The junior members feel that they have a say in the running of the organization — this leads to increased job satisfaction and consequently productivity. It has been said that the actual *process* of budgeting is as beneficial as the budget itself.

Who is Involved?

The *budgetees,* who prepare and are responsible for their budget, are the departmental line managers. They may or may not involve their sub-ordinates depending on their style of management and relationship with their juniors. In converting the budget into money terms they may enlist the help of an accountant. The person whose function it is to co-ordinate the many individual budgets of the line men is the appointed *Budget Officer,* normally an accountant. In large public companies budgeting for the whole organization can be a very complex process indeed, co-ordination of which is far beyond the limits of any one person. Here, a *Budget Committee* may be set up, comprising several high level executives in charge of the major functional divisions of the business.

Preparation of the Budget

A number of stages can be identified in the preparation of a budget.

Stage 1 — Identification of:
(1) the *key aims* for the coming year, and
(2) any major *external changes* likely to affect the business and communicating these to the budgetees so that they know what overriding factors to keep in mind when preparing their budgets. These will be largely gauged from the long-term corporate plan.

Stage 2 — Determination of the *key factor* or *limiting factor*. Every business has some factor which eventually limits its growth. In most cases it is sales demand. The key factor has two significances in budgeting. Firstly, it is the point at which the process *starts*. The rest of the budget is built around it. The reason for this is obvious — it would be pointless to budget for an activity level of 100 000 units if sales demand is expected to be 20 000 units. Secondly, it is the most important single sub-budget. An error in the key factor budget would throw out all the subsidiary budgets. We met the concept of the key factor in the previous chapter, Decision-making and Relevant Costing. When used in the context of budgeting it is sometimes called the *principal budget factor*. If the principal budget factor happens to be production level attainable, the Production Budget is constructed first and the rest of the budget built around it.

Stage 3 — Assuming sales is the limiting factor, preparation of the Sales Budget. Unfortunately this is usually the most difficult budget to prepare, because of the many external influences which govern its level over which the firm has no control. Before the budget is attempted a sales *forecast* is usually made, by product type and geographical area. There are two broad methods of doing this:

(i) By *asking the sales managers* of each product and area to estimate next year's likely sales. The responses are simply added together to give the total for the firm
(ii) By using *mathematical and statistical techniques* of interpolating the future from the past taking into account expected changes in market conditions.

Large companies may use both methods. One advantage of the first method is that it actively involves lower-level managers in the budgeting process.

Stage 4 — Initial preparation of the subsidiary budgets. These include the production budget, direct materials budget, direct labour budget, production overhead budget, selling and distribution budget, administration budget, capital expenditure budget, and cash budget.

Stage 5 — *Review and co-ordination* of the subsidiary budgets by the Budget Officer or Budget Committee. Their function is to check that there are no inconsistencies or conflicts between the many subsidiary budgets. For example, if the capital expenditure budget includes large amounts for the replacement of assets in a month when the liquidity position is poor, the budget has to be sent back to the budgetee with a note of the problem and amendment required. In this way the budgets get sent back and forth until the co-ordinator is satisfied that all the individual budgets are in harmony with each other.

Stage 6 — The individual subsidiary budgets are consolidated into a single *Master Budget*, presented in the form of a budgeted income statement and balance sheet.

Stage 7 — The work is now presented to the Board of Directors for approval. If they are not satisfied with any aspect of it, perhaps because some budgetees have been over-optimistic or pessimistic or they suspect slack or padding (explained later) they will return it to the Budget Committee for amendment. The Committee will have to return the subsidiary budgets to the budgetees and stages 3, 4, 5, and 6 repeated. On completion these revised budgets are again presented to the Board. If approved, the budgets are finalized.

Although the budgeting is 'finalized' on director approval, in one sense the process of budgeting never ends. A budget is prepared under certain basic assumptions about the future. Any change in these should lead to the budget being revised. Some organizations operate a *continuous* or *rolling budget* where as one quarter unfolds any change in market conditions cause the budgets of subsequent quarters to be updated.

Examination Questions

Examination questions ask mostly for the preparation of a Cash Budget and/or Master Budget from information supplied. Questions on other types of budgets are relatively uncommon. Let us now look at the cash budget.

Cash Budget

As we saw in Chapter 12, Ratio analysis and the Interpretation of Accounts, a large profit does not in itself make for a healthy business. Liquidity is just as important. The cash budget is an attempt by management to ensure that the company does not run into liquidity problems in the future. It involves estimating receipts and payments implied by the other budgets to find the balance in hand or overdrawn at the end of each month or quarter. Apart from the master budget the cash budget is the last to be prepared since it depends critically on the plans in the other budgets. Its format is as follows:

Pro-forma

Cash Budget

	January	*February*	*March*	*April*	. . .
Receipts					
Cash sales					
Credit sales					
Capital					
Other receipts					
Total receipts					
Payments					
Material					
Wages					
Overheads					
Fixed assets					
Total payments					
Net cash flow					
Balance b/f					
Balance c/f					

Note that:

(i) Net cash flow is given by total receipts less total payments. When receipts > payments there is a net inflow, when payments > receipts there is a net outflow.

(ii) The balance c/f in one month is the balance b/f in the next month

(iii) Expenses of a non-cash nature such as *bad debts* and *provisions* for depreciation and doubtful debts are not included.

Having estimated the likely cash balances at the end of each month arrangements can be made for the required level of bank overdraft during months in which the company is expected to be in the red. Bank managers are far more willing to entertain requests for a loan or overdraft from a business which has taken the trouble to plan future cash flows in advance than requests from a business which has suddenly found itself short of liquid resources. Another benefit of the cash budget is that months of large surpluses are revealed. Plans can then be made in advance for their investment in the short-term money market — idle cash balances represent an *opportunity cost* in terms of lost interest.

The cash budget has become increasingly important since the large number of bankruptcies due to insolvency during the stagflation (economic recession coupled with high inflation) of the 1970s. This has reflected itself in the increasing frequency with which they now appear in examination questions.

Examination Technique

Preparation of budgets asked for in examination questions is really quite a simple affair. There is nothing intrinsically difficult or complicated in the exercise. You might find it helpful to adopt the following 3-step procedure:

(1) Having read the question a first time get down your *outline* to the budget on paper i.e. fill in the format without any figures.
(2) Read the question again, this time more slowly and deliberately, taking each budget item in turn and filling in the *figures* implied by them in your format. Separate workings often need to be made — remember to reference these to your main budget.
(3) Perform the necessary additions and subtractions to arrive at your completed budget.

Fixed and Flexible Budgeting

One of the functions of budgeting stated at the start of the chapter was performance evaluation and control. Actual performance of each responsibility centre is compared to its budget to evaluate performance. Let us take a firm which budgeted for a monthly production level of 1 000 units, for which the materials purchasing manager was allocated a spending of £10 000. Actual activity during the month was better than expected because of an unexpected increase in sales. 1 100 units were produced at a material cost of £10 800. Under a *fixed budget* the comparison would be:

Budgeted spending	Actual spending	Variance
£10 000	£10 800	£(800) *Adverse*

Such a system would hardly gain the support and co-operation of the materials purchasing manager. Surely he should be evaluated not on the activity level budgeted but the actual level achieved. Under this flexible budgeting system all costs are translated from budgeted activity level to actual activity level. These figures are then used to evaluate performance. Under this system the comparison for our materials purchasing manager is:

Flexed budget spending	Actual spending	Variance
£11 000	£10 800	£(200) *Favourable*

Credit will now be given to him for spending less than budget for the higher level of activity.

Under a flexible budget, costs react differently to changes in activity depending on whether they are of a fixed, variable, or semi-variable nature. Fixed costs stay the same at all activity levels while variable costs increase directly with output. With semi-variable costs only the variable element changes. Have a go at the following exercise.

Exercise

Given:	Maximum production level	10 000 units
	Direct materials cost	£5 per unit
	Direct labour cost	£4 per unit
	Fixed overhead	£20 000
	Power — standing charge	£1 000
	variable element	£0.25 per unit

Prepare a flexible budget for production levels 7 000, 9 000 and 10 000 units.

Answer

Production level (units)	7 000	9 000	10 000
% of maximum capacity	70%	90%	100%
	£	£	£
Direct materials	35 000	45 000	50 000
Direct labour	28 000	36 000	40 000
Fixed overhead	20 000	20 000	20 000
Power *	2 750	3 250	3 500
	85 750	104 250	113 500
* Standing charge	1 000	1 000	1 000
Variable element	1 750	2 250	2 500
Power total	2 750	3 250	3 500

It is fairly easy to flex a budget for fixed costs and variable costs. The difficulty arises with semi-variable costs. In examination questions you are not likely to be given the amount of the fixed element of a semi-variable cost. It has to be deduced by calculating the change in total cost from one activity level to another and from this working out the variable element *per unit*. The balance must represent the fixed element and this will be the same at all activity levels. See question 21.4.

Behavioural Aspects of Budgeting

A common charge levied against accountants is that in preparing their budgets and designing control and evaluation systems they do not give sufficient attention to *human behaviour*. Accountants have long suffered an image of being boring, heartless, and devoid of human feelings. This is certainly not the case, but the image is unfortunately sometimes justified. Especially in the past, accountants have tended to concentrate on achieving professional and technical excellence in their work at the expense of proper consideration of how their proposals are likely to affect the *people* they are intended to help/control. At the start of the chapter we looked at four claimed advantages of budgeting. In 1953 *Argyris* challenged this traditional view in a now famous study in which he found that, far from being a help, budgets had a *disfunctional* effect on performance and were widely regarded with suspicion and hostility by employees. (By dsyfunctional is meant that results are actually worse than if no budget had been set.) Since Argyris' path-breaking article, the behavioural aspects of budgeting and accounting control systems has been a fertile area for research. The studies have centred on three controversial points:

(1) *Tightness of budget* — How easy or difficult to achieve should a budget be set?
(2) *Way in which the budget is used* — To what extent should the budget be used as a performance evaluator?
(3) *Participation* —To what extent should budgetees (people responsible for achieving a budget) participate in its setting?

Let us look at each of these points in turn.

1 Tightness of Budget

The question here is whether it matters if the budget is set tight or loose. *Hofstede* (1968) has found that a budget will lead to improved performance *only if it is set at a particular degree of tightness.* A loose budget will encourage inefficiency; a very tight budget will cause the budgetee to perceive it as impossible and unattainable and may have a negative dysfunctional effect. The only budget that will be a motivator to efficiency is one that is set a *little* tighter than the budgetee's expectations. These findings are largely similar to an earlier study on the subject by *Stedry* (1960). He pointed out that one implication of these findings is that a 'good' budget should produce plenty of adverse variances. If management sets a budget which is not expected to be achieved should it then be used for *planning* purposes? Stedry thinks not, suggesting that firms should produce *two* budgets each year — a tight one for motivation and control and a more realistic one for planning. Good advice perhaps, but there are practical problems in adopting this, not least of which is the resulting increase in cost and complexity of the budgeting process, which in most companies is already a complex and expensive exercise.

2 How the Budget is Used

Hopwood (1976) found that different companies attach different weight to the budget. He identified two broad styles of performance evaluation — *budget-constrained* and *profit-conscious.* In the first, budget achievement is the only consideration in evaluating a manager; in the second a broader more long-term view is taken — adverse variances are tolerated so long as they are felt to be temporary or for the long-term good of the company. In his research Hopwood found that budgetees regarded management adopting the budget-constrained style with suspicion. They resented the whole process of budgeting — it was there to 'shoot them down if they failed to perform'. He also found that a narrow budget-constrained style gave rise to decisions which, while worth making to a budgetee about to be evaluated, were not in the long-term interests of the organization a a whole. For example, fear of an adverse variance sometimes led to urgent maintenance work being postponed to a future budget year. However, this critical delay increased the amount of spending needed in the future period. The art of good management is to encourage a state of *goal congruence,* in which the aims of each individual correspond to the aims of the organization as a whole. If management focuses exclusively on the budget, it may lead to budgetees becoming obsessed with meeting the budget as an end in itself at the expense of goal congruence. *Churchill, Cooper, and Sainsbury* (1964) found that undue emphasis on budget achievement led managers to regard it as a strait-jacket. As a result they conformed to plans laid down for them even when subsequent changes in the environment made those plans sub-optimal. Such behaviour is clearly not desirable and is the cost of an evaluation system that is narrow and inflexible.

Likert and Seashore (1968) have pointed out the cost in *human terms* to budgetees evaluated in a narrow manner. They found that they suffered from increased tension and anxiety about achieving targets, and that this led to higher levels of absenteeism and staff turnover. Hopwood found that the more flexible profit-conscious style avoided such problems. The general consensus now is that evaluation of managerial performance is a complex task for which using one single measure is inadequate. For example, the manager of a Production Department is expected not only to meet his budget with regard to costs, but also to maintain a good working relationship between himself and employees, between the employees themselves, to meet production deadlines on time, and to maintain the quality of the product. It is impossible, even dangerous, to attempt to evaluate all of these criteria by using a single index of performance. A comprehensive performance evaluation should encompass achievement with regard to *non-financial* objectives as well as the budget.

3 Participation

The question here is to what degree budgetees should participate in the setting of the budget. It is felt that an authoritarian style of management, where the budget has been imposed from the top without any participation or consultation at all is a bad thing. Budgetees and workers, being unable to relate to the budget might reject it without even attempting to conform. The benefit of some participation is that it makes budgetees feel involved in the whole process and removes some of the distrust which exists between management and workers. In 1960 however *Vroom* claimed that the relationship between participation and performance was not so simple. Participation was not beneficial in all cases — it depended on several factors including personalities of the budgetee and assessor, type of organization, and organization structure. For example, a de-centralized organization was more conducive to participation than a highly centralized one, Following Vroom's findings several pieces of research have been done specifically on this point but the results do not point to a common conclusion.

While participation seems in most cases to lead to an improvement in worker-attitudes and a better climate of industrial relations there is a danger in allowing budgetees too much freedom in setting their own budget. This is the problem of *slack* or *padding*. It is natural for a manager allowed to set his own budget to overstate costs and understate revenues so that the budget is not difficult to achieve; he builds into the budget a certain amount of slack which is in effect an *insurance* that the budget will be reached. *Lowe and Shaw* on a study of sales budgets in 1968 found clear evidence of such padding and also found that the problem was likely to be greatest where the remuneration system was directly tied to sales performance and achievement of the budget. Other studies have confirmed this finding. Management can reduce the amount of slack by remunerating and evaluating employees by criteria other than just budget achievement i.e. by adopting a profit-conscious style.

Another possible solution is to adopt a technique known as *Zero-Base Budgeting,* recommended by *Phyrr* in 1970. Under normal budgeting the starting point for next year's budget is *this years'* adjusted for expected changes in the level of activity and inflation. The procedure accepts previous years' expenditures as being necessary without question. Any padding built into the budget in previous years is therefore likely to be repeated in future years. It also encourages managers of efficient cost centres to waste surplus funds towards the end of the budget year in the fear that if they do not spend the whole of there allowance, it will be reduced in future years. In order to overcome these problems, Phyrr advocated an alternative system of budget-setting in which previous years' figures were to be ignored and each year's budgets were to start from a *base of zero.* Managers in presenting their budgets for approval would have to justify the *whole* of their expenditure, not just the increment. The mere fact that an item of expenditure was incurred last year would not *in itself* be accepted as a reason for approving its spending next year. Such an approach, Phyrr believed, would reduce the amount of slack in two ways:

(i) managers would not propose as large an expenditure bill in the knowledge that it would be subject to tight scrutiny
(ii) any padding that *is* proposed is likely to be detected and rejected. In the traditional system, padding is approved without scrutiny.

Unfortunately, most companies have not adopted zero-base budgeting, because:

(i) its proper implementation would burden it with additional expenditures. Re-evaluating each item of expenditure from scratch every year is no mean task
(ii) its implementation has in some instances been resisted by managers for fear that they will lose the luxury of their safety padding.

No doubt the work on the three areas discussed above will continue and new evidence will throw further light on them. It seems that, after a slow start, accountants are finally waking up to their responsibility to take people into account when designing their control systems.

References

Argyris, C., 'Human problems with budgets', *Harvard Business Review,* January - February 1953.
Churchill, N. C., Cooper, W. E., and Sainsbury, T., 'Laboratory and field studies of the behavioural effects of audits', In *Management Controls,* Bonini, E. C., Jaedicke, R. K., and Wagner (Eds.) McGraw-Hill, 1964.
Hofstede, G. H., *The Game of Budget Control*, Tavistock, 1968.
Hopwood, A. G., *Accountancy and Human Behaviour*, Prentice-Hall, 1976.
Lowe, E. A., and Shaw, R. W., 'An analysis of managerial biasing: Evidence from a company's budgeting process', *Journal of Management Studies,* October 1968.
Likert, R., and Seashore, S.E., 'Making cost control work', In Solomons, D. (Ed.) *Studies in Cost Analysis,* Sweet & Maxwell, 1968.
Phyrr, P. A., 'Zero-base budgeting', *Harvard Business Review*, November - December 1970.
Stedry, A. C., *Budget Control and Cost Behaviour*, Prentice-Hall, 1960.
Vroom, V. H., *Some Personality Determinants of the Effects of Participation*, Prentice–Hall, 1960.

Questions

21.1 B. Howe plans to set up a new business commencing 1 September 19_5. The timetable of activities planned for the first four months is:

(1) 1 September 19_5: transfer £40 000 into a business bank account.
(2) 1 September 19_5: purchase of machinery £4 500, vehicles £3 600, and premises £16 000. Immediate payment by cheque from the business bank account.
(3) 20 September 19_5: purchase of goods £4 000 followed by a further £6 400 before the end of the month and thereafter £8 000 each month. Payment for the first purchase will be on 2 October 19_5. Subsequent purchases will be paid for two months after each transaction.
(4) In September 19_5 sales are expected to be £8 000 and £10 000 for each month thereafter. Debtors will pay for goods three months after each transaction.
(5) On 31 December 19_5 stocks on hand will be valued at £4 000.
(6) Wages of £300 per month will be payable on the last day of the month.
(7) General expenses of £100 per month will be payable during the month following.
(8) £11 000 will be raised by a sale of private investments and paid into the business bank account during mid December 19_5.
(9) £460 insurance and rates for the four months will be payable in November 19_5.
(10) Drawings by cheque will be £160 per month.
(11) Depreciation of vehicles will be at the rate of 20 per cent per annum, and on machinery at 10 per cent per annum.

Required:

(a) A cash budget (including bank) to show the monthly balance available from September to December 19_5. (14 marks)
(b) The budgeted trading and profit and loss accounts for the first four months of trading, and a budgeted balance sheet as at 31 December 19_5. (16 marks)

(30 marks)

Advanced Level Accounting, London

21.2* Ian Spiro, formerly a tax-driver, decided to establish a car-hire business after inheriting £50 000. His business year would be divided into budget periods each being four weeks.

He commenced business on a Monday the first day of period 1, by paying into a business bank account £34 000 as his initial capital. All receipts and payments would be passed through his bank account.

The following additional forecast information is available on the first four budget periods of his proposed business venture.

(1) At the beginning of period 1 he would purchase 6 saloon cars of a standard type; list price £6 000 each, on which he had negotiated a trade discount of 11%.

(2) He estimates that four of the cars will be on the road each day Monday to Friday inclusive, and at week-ends all six cars will be on the road. Hire charges as follows:

Weekday rate	£10 per day per car
Weekend rate	£18 per day per car

He estimates that this business trading pattern will commence on the Monday of the second week of period 1, and then continue thereafter. All hire transactions are to be settled for cash.
Note: a week-end consists of Saturday and Sunday. All remaining days are week-days.

(3) An account was established with a local garage for fuel, and it was agreed to settle the account two periods in arrear.
The forecast gallon usage is as follows:

Period 1	*Period 2*	*Period 3*	*Period 4*
200	200	400	500

The fuel costs £1.80 per gallon.

(4) Servicing costs for the vehicles would amount to £300 per period, paid during the period following the service. Servicing would commence in period 1.

(5) Each of his vehicles would be depreciated at 25% per annum on a reducing balance basis.

(6) Fixed costs of £200 per period would be paid each period.

(7) He had agreed with a local firm to provide 2 cars on a regular basis, Monday to Friday inclusive, as chauffeur driven cars. The agreed rate was £60 a day (per car) payment being made in the following period. This contract would not commence until the first day of period 2, a Monday.

(8) Drawings: Periods 1 & 2 £400 a period
Periods 3 & 4 £800 a period

(9) Wages and Salaries:
 (i) Initially he would employ 3 staff, each on £320 a budget period. Employment would commence at the beginning of period 1.
 (ii) On commencement of the contract the two additional staff employed as chauffeurs would each receive £360 a budget period. Payments are to be made at the end of the relevant period.

(10) In anticipation of more business being developed he planned to buy a further three cars for cash in period 4. The cars would cost £6 500 each and it was agreed he would be allowed a trade discount of 10%.

Required:

(a) A detailed cash budget for the first four budget periods. (11 marks)

(b) An explanation as to why it is important that a business should prepare a cash budget. (8 marks)

(c) Identify how a sole proprietor may finance a forecast cash deficit distinguishing between internal and external financial sources. (6 marks)

(25 marks)

Advanced Level Accounting, AEB

21.3 A company's estimated pattern of costs and revenues for the first four months of 19_7 is as follows:

Costs and Revenues: January - April 19_7
(£000)

Month	*Sales*	*Materials*	*Wages*	*Overheads*
January	410.4	81.6	16.2	273.6
February	423.6	84.8	16.8	282.4
March	460.8	93.6	18.3	306.7
April	456.3	91.2	18.6	304.5

(1) One quarter of the materials are paid for in the month of production and the remainder two months later: deliveries received in November 19_6 were £78 600, and in December 19_6, £74 800.
(2) Customers are expected to pay one-third of their debts a month after the sale and the remainder after two months: sales expected for November 19_6 are £398 400, and for December 19_6, £402 600.
(3) Old factory equipment is to be sold in February 19_7 for £9 600. Receipt of the money is expected in April 19_7. New equipment will be installed at a cost of £38 000. One half of the amount is payable in March 19_7 and the remainder in August 19_7.
(4) Two-thirds of the wages are payable in the months they fall due, and one-third a month later: wages for December 19_6 are estimated at £15 900.
(5) £50 000 of total monthly overheads are payable in the month they occur, and the remainder one month later: total overheads for December 19_6 are expected to be £265 200.
(6) The opening bank balance at 1 January 19_7 is expected to be an overdraft of £10 600.

Required
(a) Using the information above, prepare the firm's cash budget for the period January - April, 19_7. (16 marks)
(b) Provide a statement to show those items in part (a) which would appear in a budgeted balance sheet as at 30 April 19_7. (9 marks)
(25 marks)

Advanced Level Accounting, London

21.4 The Marketing Director of W Limited is dissatisfied with the variances reported to him on the basis of actual costs being compared with a fixed budget for the costs attributed to the marketing function. He seeks your help and asks you to prepare for him a flexible budget for the calendar year 19_7, based on the following information which is stated for an estimated sales level of £10 million unless stated otherwise.

Fixed costs:	*£000*
Salaries—Sales representatives	200
Sales office	60
Salary-related costs	32
Rent	100
Depreciation of furniture	5
Depreciation of cars	67
Insurance	20
Advertising	250
Variable costs:	
Sales representatives' commission	64
Salary-related costs—$12\frac{1}{2}$% of commission	8
Sales representatives' ordinary expenses	25
Bad debts	100
Stationery and postage	50
Agency fees	80

Semi-variable costs:
Telephone rentals £2 000, metered calls £14 000; Sales representatives' car expenses excluding depreciation: fixed £7 000, variable £48 000

Sales promotions: the budget figures are to be based on the costs given below which relate to the years 19_2 to 19_5 and the estimates for 1986.

Year		*Costs*		*Sales*
		£000		*£million*
19_2		384		4.2
19_3		402		5.1
19_4		368		3.4
19_5		450		7.5
19_6	Estimate	478	Estimate	8.9

Ignore Inflation

Required:
(a) prepare a flexible budget for sales levels of £9m., £10m., and £11.5 m.; (12 marks)
(b) calculate the total marketing cost allowance, assuming sales of £10.75 m. (3 marks)
(15 marks)

Chartered Institute of Management Accountants

21.5* Home Counties Appliance PLC manufactures three types of lawnmower: manual, diesel, and electric. The production costs are as follows:

Models	*Manual*	*Diesel*	*Electric*
	£	£	£
Materials	15	22	30
Labour (£4 per hour)	16	20	20
Variable overhead	4	5	6
Fixed Overheads	8	10	10
Total costs	43	57	66
Selling Price	50	65	75
Profit	7	8	9
Expected maximum demand	10 000	5 000	2 000

Maximum labour hours available 60 000 hours for the year. Fixed overheads are allocated at £2 per labour hour.

Required:
(a) Prepare a budget to maximize profit for the coming year. (14 marks)
(b) Discuss why and on what basis you have prepared this budget. (6 marks)
(20 marks)

Institute of Chartered Accountants, Foundation

21.6 A company producing and selling a single product expects the following trading results for the year just ending:

		£000	*£000*
Sales			900
Costs: Materials: direct		200	
Labour: direct		120	
indirect fixed		38	
Other production overhead:	variable	50	
	fixed	80	
Administration overhead:	fixed	78	
Selling overhead:	variable	63	
	fixed	44	
Distribution overhead:	variable	36	
	fixed	20	
			729
Net profit			171

Budgets are now being prepared for the year ahead. The following information is provided:

(1) A selling price reduction from £9 to £8 per unit is expected to increase sales volume by 50%.
(2) Because of increased quantities purchased a 5% quantity discount will be obtained on the purchase of raw materials. Material usage per unit of output is expected to be 98% of the current year.
(3) Hourly direct wage rates will increase by 10%. Labour efficiency should remain the same. 20 000 units will be produced in overtime hours at a premium of 25%. Overtime premium is treated as a direct cost.
(4) Variable selling overhead is expected to increase in total proportionately with total sales revenue.
(5) Variable production and distribution overhead should increase in total in proportion to the increase in sales volume.
(6) Fixed overhead is forecast at 20% above the level for the current year.
(7) Monthly production will be scheduled so that finished goods stocks at the end of a month are sufficient to meet sales quantities forecast for the following one and a half months.
(8) Materials will be purchased so that closing stocks of materials at the end of a month are sufficient to meet production requirements in the following month.
(9) Monthly sales for the first six months are forecast as:

Month	*1*	*2*	*3*	*4*	*5*	*6*
000 units	10	12	15	11	12	12

You are to assume that:

(i) Prices and efficiency have been at a constant level throughout the year just ending.
(ii) Stocks of materials and finished goods at the end of the current year are consistent with the above assumptions for the year ahead e.g. closing stocks of raw materials will be sufficient for production requirements in month 1 of the new year.

Required:

(a) Prepare a budgeted profit statement for the year ahead in marginal costing format. (10 marks)
(b) A monthly production budget for the first quarter of the new year. (4 marks)

Chartered Association of Certified Accountants **(14 marks)**

21.7* The balance sheet of KQV plc at 31st May, 19_5, is expected to be:

	£000	*£000*	*£000*
Fixed assets, at cost		6 000	
Less depreciation provision		900	5 100
Current assets:			
Materials stock (27 000 lbs)		270	
Work-in-progress		30	
Finished goods stock (9 000 units)		450	
Debtors		660	
Cash at bank		10	
		1 420	
Less creditors payable within one year:			
Creditors for materials	300		
Corporation tax	165		
Proposed dividend	105	570	850
			5 950
Ordinary shares of £1 each, full paid			700
Reserves: Retained profit			5 250
			5 950

Additional information:

(1) The company manufactures and sells a single product, the selling price of which during the year to 31st May, 19_6 is expected to be £100. During this year, it is forecast that 120 000 units will be sold and 121 000 units manufactured. Sales should be spread evenly throughout the year.

(2) Work-in-progress should remain unchanged in value during the year.

(3) In manufacturing one unit of product, 2 lbs of material and 3 hours of labour are required. It is expected that the material price per lb. will be £10, and the wage rate per hour, £4. Purchases of materials should be made evenly throughout the year.

(4) During the year to 31st May 19_6, the following overhead expenses should be paid in cash:

	£000
Manufacturing	1 698
Administration	3 540
Distribution	2 100

(5) Depreciation of fixed assets is at the rate of 10% per annum of cost, and the depreciation charge for the year is to be divided between manufacturing, administration and distribution in the ratio of 8:1:1. No fixed assets are likely to be purchased during the coming year.

(6) The stock of materials at 31st May, 19_6 is planned to be 25 000 lbs.

(7) The stock of finished goods is to be valued at forecast manufacturing cost, which includes the cost of materials, wages and manufacturing overhead (including the proportion of depreciation), but does not include administration or distribution expenses.

(8) All sales and purchases of materials are on credit. Debtors are required to pay their accounts in the month following the month of sale, and the company is required to pay creditors' accounts within a similar period of time.

(9) During the year to 31st May, 19_6 the existing liabilities for corporation tax and proposed dividend will be paid, and at the year end provision should be made for corporation tax at the rate of 50% of the net profit for the year, and for a dividend of 10% on the ordinary share capital. It is not proposed to issue any share or loan capital, or to repay any, during the year.

Required:

(a) a forecast profit and loss account of KQV plc for the year to 31st May, 19_6; and (25 marks)

(b) a forecast balance sheet at that date. (15 marks)

(40 marks)

Chartered Insitute of Management Accountants

21.8 Outline

(a) the objectives of budgetary planning and control systems. (7 marks)

(b) the organization required for the preparation of a master budget. (10 marks)

(17 marks)

Chartered Association of Certified Accountants

21.9 'Budgeting aids management in planning, controlling, co-ordinating, and motivating.'

Discuss this statement and explain any conflicts that may exist between the four objectives mentioned. **(20 marks)**

Institute of Chartered Accountants, Foundation

21.10 In response to a request from the managing director of a company, you are required to explain how a system of budgetary control could be introduced. **(20 marks)**

Advanced Level Accounting, London

21.11 How can budgets motivate workers? **(20 marks)**

Institute of Chartered Accountants, Foundation

Solutions

21.1 (a)

B. HOWE

Cash Budget September – December 19_5

	September	*October*	*November*	*December*
	£	£	£	£
Receipts				
Capital	40 000			11 000
Trade debtors		—	—	8 000
	40 000	—	—	19 000
Less Payments				
Machinery, vehicles, premises	24 100			
Trade creditors		4 000	6 400	8 000
Wages	300	300	300	300
General expenses		100	100	100
Insurance and rates			460	
Drawings	160	160	160	160
	24 560	4 560	7 420	8 560
Net cash flow	15 440	(4 560)	(7 420)	10 440
Balance b/f	—	15 440	10 880	3 460
Balance c/f	15 440	10 880	3 460	13 900

(b)

B. HOWE

Budgeted Trading and Profit and Loss Account
for the four months ending 31 December 19_5

	£	£
Sales		38 000
Less cost of goods sold		
Purchases	34 400	
Less closing stock	4 000	30 400
Gross profit		7 600
Less Expenses		
Wages	1 200	
General expenses	400	
Insurance and rates	460	
Depreciation on vehicles (3 600 × 20% × $\frac{4}{12}$)	240	
Depreciation on machinery (4 500 × 10% × $\frac{4}{12}$)	150	2 450
Net profit		£5 150

B. HOWE

Budgeted Balance Sheet as at 31 December 19_5

	£ Cost	£ Dep'n	£ Net
Fixed assets			
Premises	16 000	—	16 000
Machinery	4 500	150	4 350
Vehicles	3 600	240	3 360
	24 100	390	23 710
Current assets			
Stock		4 000	
Debtors		30 000	
Bank		13 900	
		47 900	
Less Current liabilities			
Creditors	16 000		
General expenses owing	100	16 100	
Working capital			31 800
Net assets			£55 510
Financed by:			
Capital			51 000
Add Profit			5 150
			56 150
Less Drawings			640
Capital employed			£55 510

21.3 (a) *Cash Budget for the period January - April 19_7*

	Jan £	Feb £	Mar £	Apr £
Receipts				
From Debtors (W_1)	399 800	405 200	414 800	436 000
Sale of equipment				9 600
	399 800	405 200	414 800	445 600
Less payments				
Materials (W_2)	79 350	77 300	84 600	86 400
Wages (W_3)	16 100	16 600	17 800	18 500
Overheads (W_4)	265 200	273 600	282 400	306 700
New equipment			19 000	
	360 650	367 500	403 800	411 600
Net cash flow	39 150	37 700	11 000	34 000
Balance b/f	(10 660	28 550	66 250	77 250
Balance c/f	28 550	66 250	77 250	111 250

Workings

W_1 *Receipts from Debtors*

Month	*Sales*	*Cash received*				*(b) Owing at 30 April*
Nov.	398 400	265 600				
Dec.	402 600	134 200	268 400			
Jan.	410 400		136 800	273 600		
Feb.	423 600			141 200	282 400	
Mar.	460 800				153 600	307 200
Apr.	456 300					456 300
		399 800	405 200	414 800	436 000	763 500

W_2 *Payments to material suppliers*

Month	*Purchases*	Jan	Feb	Mar	Apr	Owing at 30 April
		Cash paid				
Nov.	78 600	58 950				
Dec.	74 800		56 100			
Jan.	81 600	20 400		61 200		
Feb.	84 800		21 200		63 600	
Mar.	93 600			23 400		70 200
Apr.	91 200				22 800	68 400
		79 350	77 300	84 600	86 400	138 600

W_3 *Wages*

Month	*Incurred*	Jan	Feb	Mar	Apr	Owing at 30 April
		Wages paid				
Dec.	15 900	5 300				
Jan.	16 200	10 800	5 400			
Feb.	16 800		11 200	5 600		
Mar.	18 300			12 200	6 100	
Apr.	18 600				12 400	6 200
		16 100	16 600	17 800	18 500	6 200

W_4 *Overheads*

Month	*Incurred*	Jan	Feb	Mar	Apr	Owing at 30 April
		Overheads paid				
Dec.	265 200	215 200				
Jan.	273 600	50 000	223 600			
Feb.	282 400		50 000	232 400		
Mar.	306 700			50 000	256 700	
Apr.	304 500				50 000	254 500
		265 200	273 600	282 400	306 700	254 500

(b) *Budgeted Balance Sheet Extract as at 30 April 19_7*

	£	£	£
Fixed asset			
Equipment			38 000
Current assets			
Trade debtors		763 500	
Bank		111 250	
		874 750	
Current liabilities			
Trade creditors	138 600		
Wages owing	6 200		
Overheads owing	254 500		
Owing for equipment	19 000	418 300	456 450

21.4 (a)

W LIMITED

Flexible Marketing Budget for 19_7

	Sales levels (£m) 9	10	11.5
	£	£	£
Fixed costs			
Salaries — sales representatives	200 000	200 000	200 000
— sales office	60 000	60 000	60 000
Salary-related costs	32 000	32 000	32 000
Rent	100 000	100 000	100 000
Depreciation of furniture	5 000	5 000	5 000
Depreciation of cars	67 000	67 000	67 000
Insurance	20 000	20 000	20 000
Advertising	250 000	250 000	250 000
Telephone rentals	2 000	2 000	2 000

Sales representatives' car expenses	7 000	7 000	7 000
Sales promotions (W_2)	300 000	300 000	300 000
	1 043 000	1 043 000	1 043 000
Variable costs			
Sales representatives' commission	57 600	64 000	73 600
Salary-related costs	7 200	8 000	9 200
Sales representatives' ordinary expenses	22 500	25 000	28 750
Bad debts	90 000	100 000	115 000
Stationery and postage	45 000	50 000	57 500
Agency fees	72 000	80 000	92 000
Telephone, metered calls	12 600	14 000	16 100
Sales representatives' car expenses	43 200	48 000	55 200
Sales promotions (W_1)	180 000	200 000	230 000
	530 100	589 000	677 350
Total marketing budget (fixed + variable)	1 573 100	1 632 000	1 720 350

Workings

W_1 *Sales promotion*

We can find the variable element of this semi-variable cost by noting the *change* in the cost as activity level changes. As sales falls from the maximum of £8.9m to the minimum of £3.4m cost falls from £478 000 to £368 000.

$$\therefore \text{Variable element} = \frac{478\,000 - 368\,000}{8.9 - 3.4}$$

$$= \frac{110\,000}{5.5} = \text{£20 000 per £m of sales}$$

From this we can work out the variable element of this cost at the different activity levels.

Sales	*Variable element*
£m	*£000*
9	180
10	200
11.5	230

W_2 To find the *fixed* element in the sales promotions costs:

At a sales level of £8.9m

	£000
Total cost	478
of which variable element is 8.9 × 20	178
Fixed element is	∴ 300

This is the *same* at all activity levels.

Check:

Sales level		£3.4m		£7.5m
		£000		*£000*
Total cost		368		450
Variable element	3.4 × 20 =	68	7.5 × 20 =	150
Fixed		∴ 300		∴ 300

(b) *At a sales level of £10.75 million*

	£
Fixed cost	1 043 000
Variable cost * $\frac{589\,000}{10} \times 10.75$	633 175
Total marketing cost allowance	£1 676 175

* or $\frac{677\,350}{11.5} \times 10.75$

21.6 (a) *Budgeted Profit Statement in marginal costing format*

	£000	£000
Sales (900 × $\frac{8}{9}$ × 1.5)		1 200
Less variable costs		
Direct materials (200 × 1.5 × 0.95 × 0.98)	279.3	
Direct labour*	204.6	
Variable overheads:		
Production (50 × 1.5)	75	
Selling (63 × $\frac{1\,200}{900}$)	84	
Distribution (36 × 1.5)	54	696.9
Contribution		503.1
Less fixed (period) costs		
Indirect labour (38 × 1.2)	45.6	
Production overhead (80 × 1.2)	96	
Administration overhead (78 × 1.2)	93.6	
Selling overhead (44 × 1.2)	52.8	
Distribution overhead (20 × 1.2)	24	312.0
Profit		£191.1

* *Direct labour*

	Units 000s
To be produced	150
During overtime	20
During normal hours	∴ 130

	£000
Normal working (120 × 1.1 × 1.3)	171.6
Overtime (120 × 1.1 × 0.2 × 1.25)	33.0
Total cost	204.6

(b) *Production Budget (units)*

	Month 1	2	3
Units to be sold	10 000	12 000	15 000
Planned closing stock	19 500 (W_1)	20 500 (W_3)	17 000 (W_4)
Total units required	29 500	32 500	32 000
Less planned opening stock	16 000 (W_2)	19 500	20 500
Units to be produced	13 500	13 000	11 500

Workings

W_1 12 000 + $\frac{1}{2}$ of 15 000 = 19 500
W_2 10 000 + $\frac{1}{2}$ of 12 000 = 16 000
W_3 15 000 + $\frac{1}{2}$ of 11 000 = 20 500
W_4 11 000 + $\frac{1}{2}$ of 12 000 = 17 000

CHAPTER 22

Standard Costing and Variance Analysis

Standard costing is the setting of pre-determined levels of costs and revenues, which then represent a target for achievement. *Variances* are the difference between actual results and standards. Conceptually, standard costing is similar to budgeting. The only difference is one of degree. While budgets relate to the activities of the firm as a whole, standard costs relate to individual cost units. For example, if the budgeted manufacturing cost is £6 000 for an output of 1 000 units, the standard cost is £6 per unit. This can be analysed into standard material cost, standard labour cost, and so on.

Usefulness

Like budgeting, standard costing is a *managerial aid to planning and control.* By setting cost standards and comparing actual costs to standards, managers and workers are made cost-conscious since they know that they will be evaluated on their performance. In this way standard costing promotes efficiency.

Types of Standard

In the previous chapter we saw that management has to make a decision on whether to set a tight, loose, or medium budget. So it is with standards. Again there are three types.

Basic Standards

These are standards which are left unchanged for many years. Since they are not updated they are not suitable as the basis for budgeting from year to year. Their main function is to highlight *trends* over time. For example, the effect of the introduction of new technology on productivity can be gauged by observing the change in labour efficiency variances over time.

Ideal Standards

Ideal standards represent maximum performance and are consistent with a very tight budget. As we saw in the last chapter, such standards are likely to be regarded as unattainable by employees and the resulting mass of adverse variances might discourage them and serve as a disincentive to effort. As a result they are not often used.

Currently Attainable Standards

These represents costs that should be incurred under *normal efficient operating conditions*. They are consistent with a medium to tight budget. Thus while not easy to achieve, they are by no means impossible. This is because, unlike ideal standards, allowances are made for normal wastage of materials, machine breakdowns, and some labour inefficiency. They are tight enough to motivate and be taken seriously by employees, yet not too tight that they cannot be used for the setting of budgets. Unlike the other two types, currently attainable standards can therefore be used for *both planning and control.* Because of this most budgets are prepared under this type of standard.

Setting Standard Costs

Setting standard cost is a complicated task involving a large number of people including engineers, technicians, management, and workers. Four separate standards have to be established to arrive at standard unit cost.
These are:

	£
Standard material cost	x
Standard labour cost	x
Standard variable overhead cost	x
Standard fixed overhead cost	x
Standard unit cost	£x

In multi-product firms, the above has to be done for each type of product. Although setting standard cost is a complicated exercise, it is imperative to get it right because incorrect standards will throw up variances that have little meaning and cannot be used as the basis for performance evaluation and control.

Standard Material Cost

This is determined by the type and quantities of materials used and the price of each. The first should be set by engineers, technicians, and other members of the Production Department. It should take into account normal wastage. The standard price should be obtained from the Purchasing Department, who should quote not current but *expected* prices during the period in which the standards are to apply. Thus there is some element of guesswork in their estimate.

Standard Labour Cost

This is determined from the grades of direct labour required to manufacture a product from start to finish, time for each operation and the wage rate of each grade. To establish the first two *time and motion studies* could be conducted for each product. These should allow for an element of labour inefficiency through idle time, poor concentration, and fatigue. The wage rate of each grade should be forecast by supervisors and management.

Standard Overhead Cost

Overhead standards are established by using the information generated in pre-determining overhead absorption rates, describes in Chapter 16.

$$\text{Standard variable overhead cost} = \frac{\text{Budgeted variable overhead}}{\text{Budgeted output}}$$

If the absorption method is the rate per unit of output the standard variable overhead cost is in fact equal to the overhead absorption rate. If the method is the rate per labour hour or machine hour the absorption rate has to be multiplied by the standard labour or machine hours to arrive at total standard variable overhead cost. The above applies similarly to standard fixed overhead cost.

Since separate overhead absorption rates are calculated for each cost centre, the total standard overhead cost has to be found by multiplying the appropriate absorption rate by time spent in each cost centre, then adding these together.

Variance Analysis

Let us now look at variance analysis, which is about:
(1) *measuring deviations of actual performance from standards*, and
(2) *analysing their possible causes* so that corrective action may be taken.
There is almost no end of possible variances that may be computed. They all have one thing in common however — they represent the *difference between what was and what should have been*. We shall be looking at some of the more important variances in this chapter, demonstrating their calculation with an example and mentioning possible causes. Adverse or unfavourable variances are bracketed, with the letter A next to them. Favourable variances have the letter F next to them.

Material Variances

Consider the following information:

Standards

Material price	£4 per kg.
Usage	5 kg. per unit

During a given period, 100 units of the finished article were produced. The material purchase price was £3.80, total used 525 kg.

Since the cost of material used is determined by both price and usage it is possible to also calculate two material variances.

The *Price Variance* is the *difference between the standard price and actual price paid multiplied by the quantity of materials purchased.*

£(4.00 − 3.80) × 525 kg = £105 F

Since the purchase price was £0.20 per kg less than expected we have a favourable variance.

Possible Causes
(a) Unexpected fall in market price (b) Efficiency by purchasing department taking advantage of special offers and large volume discounts (c) Purchase of inferior quality material.

The *Usage Variance* is the *difference between standard quantity and actual quantity used multiplied by the standard price.*

Standard usage = 100 units × 5 kg = 500 kg.
Variance = (500 − 525) kg × £4 = £(100) A

Since 25 kg more material was used than expected the variance is adverse.

Be careful
1. The under (over) usage is multiplied by the *standard*, not actual price. If we used actual price, the computation of the usage variance would be affected by the efficiency or inefficiency of the purchasing department. Since we are trying to *separate* the price variance from the usage variance, we must not do this. We have already performed a calculation for the price variance and bringing it into our calculation again would be double-counting it.

2. If budgeted output was not 100 units we should not compare budgeted total usage to actual usage. The budget should first be *flexed* to the actual level of activity. This flexed amount (representing standard usage) should then be compared to the actual to determine variance.

Illustration

Budgeted output	110 units
Budgeted usage, 110 × 5 kg	550 kg
Actual output	100 units
Actual usage	525 kg

Under a fixed budget the variance is:

(550 − 525) kg × £4 = £100 F.

This is wrong. The standard amount of material that *should* have been used is

$$550 \text{ kg} \times \frac{100}{110} = 500 \text{ kg}.$$

This flexed amount should be the basis for the comparison. Now the variance is

(500 − 525) kg × £4 = £(100) A.

Possible Causes

(a) Inferior materials leading to excessive waste
(b) Abnormal losses in production
(c) Poor stock control and pilferage

A favourable price variance often leads to an unfavourable usage variance. The cheaper supplies obtained may have been from a disreputable supplier selling poor quality material or 'seconds'. This lead to excessive wastage.

Standard material price and usage variances should be calculated for *each type* of material used.

Labour Variances

Consider the following information:

Standards

Wage rate	£6 per hour
Time per unit	2 hours

The 100 units produced used 190 direct labour hours at a wage rate of £6.25.

Since the total wage bill is determined by two factors — quantity of labour used and wage rate — the variance can also be split in two (as with materials).

The *Rate Variance* is the *difference between the standard wage rate and actual wage rate multiplied by the actual number of hours worked.* (Note the similarity with the material price variance.)

£(6.00 − 6.25) × 190 hours = £(47.50) A

Since the rate turned out to be higher than expected the variance is adverse.

Possible Causes

(a) Trade unions successfully negotiating a larger wage increase than management had anticipated
(b) A scarcity of a particular type of skilled labour which necessitated an increase in rates to attract personnel
(c) Use of a higher grade of labour than normal for some operations.

The *Efficiency Variance* is the *difference between the standard time for actual production and actual time taken multiplied by the standard wage rate.* (Note the similarity with the material usage variance.)

Standard time = 100 units × 2 labour hours
= 200 labour hours
Variance = (200 − 190) hours × £6 = £60 F

Since 10 less hours than expected were worked the variance is favourable.

As with the material usage variance, note again that:

1. The under (over) use is multiplied by the *standard*, not actual wage rate.
2. The budget should be *flexed* to the actual activity level before comparison between standard and actual is made.

Possible causes

(a) The large increase in pay may have boosted worker morale and employer-employee relationships

(b) Use of better grades of labour than standard may have speeded up operations of those processes
(c) Less time than usual was lost by workers being idle because of machine breakdowns and bottlenecks in production (caused by poor scheduling or late delivery of components)
(d) Workers working with better quality material to that budgeted

Overhead variances are more difficult to understand, mainly because they are of an abstract nature. Let us look at them.

Variable Overhead Variances

The *variable overhead variance* is the *difference between the standard variable overhead absorbed for the activity level achieved and the actual variable overhead incurred.*

Illustration

Budgeted variable overhead	£330
Budgeted output	110 units
Standard variable overhead per unit	£3
Actual production	100 units
Variable overhead incurred	£380

First, we need to flex the budget to the level of activity achieved. Variable overheads should have been

$£330 \times \frac{100}{110} = £300$. This represents the standard variable overhead

This represents the standard variable overhead — 100 units × £3 = £300.

Variable overhead variance = £300 − £380
= £(80) A

The allowed expenditure for an output of 100 units was £300. Since actual expenditure was £380 we have an adverse variance of £80.

When variable overheads accrue on the basis of direct labour hours or machine hours it is possible to analyse them into the expenditure and efficiency variances. Suppose that the standard variable overhead was not £3 per unit but 2 hours at £1.50 per direct labour hour. Remember from our labour variance example that direct labour hours budgeted was 200 hours, actually worked 190 hours.

The *Expenditure* (or spending) *Variance* is the *difference between the standard and actual variable overhead per direct labour hour multiplied by the number of direct labour hours worked.*
Since variable overheads now vary with labour hours it is necessary to flex the budget *on this basis.*

Actual variable overhead per direct labour hour $= \frac{£380}{190 \text{ hours}} = £2$ per hour

The standard is £1.50 of variable overhead per direct labour hour. There is therefore an adverse expenditure variance of

£(0.50) × 190 hours = £(95) A

Another approach to calculating the expenditure variance is to see it as the difference between the budgeted overhead adjusted to the level of operations and the actual overhead incurred. By this approach:

	£
Variable overhead absorbed, 190 hours × £1.50 =	285
Incurred	380
Variance	£(95) A

Possible Causes

(a) Indirect materials costing more than expected, or usage being greater than expected
(b) Indirect labour being paid more than expected or efficiency being lower than expected
(c) Charges for utilities such as electricity and power increasing.

The total of the variable overhead expenditure variance in itself has little meaning. For example, a nil variance does not necessarily mean that everything went according to plan. A large adverse variance on indirect materials could have been offset by a large favourable variance on indirect labour. For the variance to be useful to management, the cost accountant needs to prepare a report setting out the variance of *each cost item.*

Illustration

Item of cost	*Flexed budget (Allowed cost)*	*Incurred (Actual cost)*	*Variance*
	£	£	£
Indirect materials	x	x	x
Indirect labour	x	x	x
Repairs	x	x	x
:	:	:	:
:	:	:	:
Total	x	x	£(95) A

The *Efficiency Variance* is the *difference between the standard and actual input hours multiplied by the standard variable overhead rate.*
Because fewer labour hours than expected were worked we could expect there to be a favourable efficiency variance.

Labour hours variance is 200 − 190 = 10 hours F
Efficiency variance = 10 hours × £1.50 = £15 F

Possible Causes
Since this variance arises from the efficiency of labour its causes are the same as those mentioned under labour efficiency variance.

Note that:

	£
Variable overhead expenditure variance	(95) A
Variable overhead efficiency variance	15 F
Variable overhead total variance	£(80) A

Fixed Overhead Variances

Illustration

Budgeted fixed overhead	£1 100
Budgeted output	110 units
Standard fixed overhead per unit	£10
Actual production	100 units
Fixed overhead incurred	£1 250

The total *fixed overhead variance* is the *standard fixed overhead absorbed by actual production less the actual fixed overhead incurred.*

(100 units @ £10) − £1 250
1 000 − 1 250 = £(250) A

This is the same as saying that there has been a £250 under-recovery of fixed overhead. Under-recovery is caused either by excessive expenditure or by budgeted production not being achieved. The total fixed overhead variance can therefore be split into two parts to reflect this — through the expenditure and volume variances.

The *Expenditure* (or spending) *Variance* is simply *the difference between the budgeted and actual fixed overhead.* It is not necessary to flex the budget this time since fixed overheads do not vary with output.

Variance is £1 100 − £1 250 = £(150) A

Possible Causes

(a) A greater than expected increase in factory occupancy costs
(b) An increase in insurance or any other fixed factory cost

The total of the fixed overhead variance in itself has little meaning — for the same reason as for the total variable overhead variance. Again, the cost accountant should prepare a statement showing the variance on each cost item.

Illustration

Item of cost	*Flexed budget (Allowed cost)*	*Incurred (Actual cost)*	*Variance*
	£	*£*	*£*
Rent	x	x	x
Rates	x	x	x
Insurance	x	x	x
Depreciation	x	x	x
:	:	:	:
:	:	:	:
Total	x	x	£(150) A

If the budgeted volume of production, 110 units, had been achieved, then the only variance would have been excessive expenditure. However, there is a shortfall in production, implying under-absorption. The extent of this under-absorption reflects the volume variance.

The *Volume Variance* is given by *budgeted cost less the standard cost absorbed by production achieved.*

£1 100 − (100 units × £10)
1 100 − 1 000 = £(100) A

Where actual output exceeds plan the volume variance is favourable.

Possible Causes

(a) Over-estimation of sales demand leading to a slow-down in production
(b) Industrial action slowing down production
(c) Production being held up by machine breakdowns, poor scheduling of work, or delays in receiving materials and components

Note that:

	£
Fixed overhead expenditure variance	(150) A
Fixed overhead volume variance	(100) A
Fixed overhead total variance	£(250) A

The cause of the volume variance is that production did not match up to expectations. This can be caused by:
(1) inefficiency of work, and/or
(2) capacity available and paid for but not utilized.
It is possible to further split the volume variance into two parts to reflect this, through the efficiency and capacity variances.

(1) The *Efficiency* (or productivity) *Variance* is the *difference between standard hours and actual hours multiplied by the standard fixed overhead rate per direct labour hour.*
Since only 190 hours were worked when the standard was 200 hours, we have a favourable efficiency variance.

Standard fixed overhead rate per direct labour hour =

$$\frac{\text{Standard fixed overhead per unit}}{\text{Standard labour hours per unit}}$$

$$\frac{£10}{2} = £5$$

Variance = (200 − 190) hours × £5
= £50 F

Possible Causes
Same as for labour efficiency variance.

(2) The *Capacity Variance* is the *difference between the capacity available and capacity used, multiplied by the standard fixed overhead rate per direct labour hour.*
On the budget of 110 units at 2 direct labour hours per unit, capacity available for production was 220 direct labour hours. Since actual hours worked was only 190 hours, the firm has failed to make use of 30 hours of available capacity.
Variance = (220 − 190) hours × £5
= £(150) A
If the 30 hours had been worked an additional 30 × £5 = £150, fixed overhead would have been absorbed by production, resulting in a nil capacity variance.

Possible Causes
Same as for fixed overhead volume variance.

Note that:

	£
Fixed overhead efficiency variance	50 F
Fixed overhead capacity variance	(150) A
Fixed overhead volume variance	£(100) A

Sales Variances

Standard costing and variance analysis is not concerned solely with costs but revenues as well. Consider the following information:

	Budget	*Actual*
Selling price	£60	£59
Quantity	120 units	125 units
Total revenue	£7 200	£7 375

Since revenue is a function of both price and quantity it is possible to calculate two separate variances for sales.

The *Price Variance* is the *difference between the standard price and actual price multiplied by the actual sales volume.*
£(59 − 60) × 125 units = £(125) A
The adverse variance indicates that selling price was lower than planned.

The *Volume Variance* is the *difference between the actual and planned sales volume multiplied by the standard price.*
(125 − 120) units × £60 = £300 F
Since 5 more units than budgeted were sold the variance is favourable.

Interpretation — As there is an inverse relationship between selling price and quantity sold, the adverse price variance has led to a favourable volume variance.

With income variances, when the actual is greater than the planned, the variance is favourable. For this reason I have written the actual before the planned in the formula. With cost variances the reverse is true. The planned is therefore written before the actual in the formula.

With the growing popularity of marginal costing for internal management purposes, a new set of sales variances have recently come into use which calculate the impact of the variances not on total revenue but on *contribution* or profit margin. *Sales margin variances* do not feature in examinations at this level but you will meet them at a later stage in your studies.

Alternative Approach to Calculation

In some questions the nature of the information given makes it awkward to adopt the approach we have used so far in variance calculations. Consider the following information:

Standard direct labour cost per unit, 3 hours at £4.50 per hour
Actual total direct labour use, 2 000 hours at a cost of £9 315
What is the wage rate variance?

By the approach we have used so far

Rate variance = (Standard wage rate − Actual wage rate) × Actual hours worked

$$\text{Actual wage rate} = \frac{£9\ 315}{2\ 000}$$
$$= £4.6575$$

This is when things become awkward. The actual wage rate does not come to a simple figure. In some cases it can run to many more decimal places. An alternative method in these situations is as follows:

	£
Standard cost for actual hours, 2 000 × £4.50 =	9 000
Actual cost	9 315
Rate variance	£(315) A

We have got to our answer by avoiding any awkward figures. The reasoning behind each route is essentially the same; the only difference is in the nature of the calculation. Performed accurately, our original method will produce the same answer.

Check:

Rate variance = £(4.6575 − 4.50) × 2 000
= £0.1575 × 2 000
= £(315) A

Which is the better method to use? They are equally good. You can either:

(1) use our original method for all calculations
(2) use the second method for all calculations
(3) use the first method as a general rule, resorting to the second when the figures become awkward.

I have adopted approach (3) in my worked solutions to the questions.

One Other Possible Cause

Note that one other possible cause of any variance is that the original standard set is unrealistic. It might be too tight, too loose, or it might not have been updated to take recent changes into account.

Standard Costs and Selling Prices

Standard, rather than actual, costs are often used as the basis for setting selling prices. In this way it is ensured that efficiencies in production are rewarded in the form of a larger profit margin and that inefficiencies are not passed on to the consumer in the form of higher prices. Raising prices because of inefficiencies is, in any case, not a good idea since it may erode the competitive position of a business.

Examination Questions

Examination questions require you not only to compute variances but also *interpret* them and comment on possible causes. In this, look out for *inter-relationships.* For example, a favourable material price variance caused by the purchase of inferior quality material is likely to lead to excessive wastage and an adverse usage variance. Students tend to become so absorbed in their variance calculations that they give little time to analysis and possible causes. Do not make this error — it will cost you marks in an examination.

With regard to the calculations it is desirable but not necessary for you to memorize the formulae. If you understand a variance you will be able to work out the formula for yourself. If you are really stuck go back to basics, adopt a common sense approach, and ask yourself the question 'what is the difference between what was and what should have been?' This will often lead you to the right answer. A check on whether sub-divisions of a variance add up to the total variance is recommended e.g. whether the variable overhead expenditure variance plus the efficiency variance equals the total variance.

Departmental Performance Reports

It is common for cost accountants to prepare performance reports from variances for each responsibility centre at regular intervals. Such reports separate those variances that are significant from those that are not. Management attention can then be focused on areas where variances are exceptionally large — this system is known as *Management by Exception.*

Performance reports should distinguish *controllable costs* from *non-controllable costs.* The departmental manager should be held responsible only for those costs which he can influence. This is an obvious point but also a very important one. A manager will not co-operate with an evaluation system which assigns responsibility to him over costs his department incurs but which he cannot control. Thus the manager of a production department can in most situations be justifiably assigned responsibility over material usage and labour efficiency variances but not over material price or wage rate variances. A material price variance is the responsibility of the purchasing department, and wage rates are set by negotiations between unions and management. An example of a possible format for a departmental performance report is shown below.

Performance Report for Month

Cost centre: Production C

Manager: ______

	Budget	*Actual*	*Variance*	*Percentage Variance*
Production — hours	x	x	x	x
units	x	x	x	x

	Flexed budget £	*Actual cost* £	*Variance in month* £	*Variance in year* £
Controllable costs				
Direct material	x	x	x	x
Direct labour	x	x	x	x
Indirect labour	x	x	x	x
Other variable overheads	x	x	x	x
Non-controllable costs				
Rent and rates	x	x	x	x
Light and heat	x	x	x	x
Depreciation	x	x	x	x
Other fixed overheads	x	x	x	x

Analysis of Variances (C = controllable)

		In month		*In year*	
		C	Non-c	C	Non-c
Direct material:	Price		x		x
	Usage	x		x	
Direct labour:	Rate		x		x
	Efficiency	x		x	
Variable overhead:	Expenditure	x		x	
	Efficiency	x		x	
Fixed overhead:	Expenditure		x		x
	Volume	x		x	

As mentioned in the last chapter, it is important that the manager has faith in the evaluation system and sees it as a device to help him rather than judge or blame him. It would help if the manager has participated in the setting of the budget. Also, he is more likely not to fear the report if he knows that he will be evaluated on a *profit-conscious* rather than *budget-constrained* style. In addition to the traditional financial measures, the evaluation should encompass *non-financial qualitative measures* such as relationship with employees, the meeting of production schedules on time, and maintaining product quality.

Having digested the report the manager should investigate significant variances to identify their causes. Corrective action should then be taken. This final act is one of the rewards of an effective system of standard costing. Businesses do not take the trouble and expense of maintaining a standard costing system just for the sake of it; it is not an end in itself. It is a means to an end. The end is cost-minimization and control.

Questions

22.1 South Wales Refractories Ltd., manufacturers of special bricks for the steel industry, use a standard cost system. The following information was extracted from the firm's books for the month of March 19_4:

	Budget for March	*Actual Usage for March*
Labour		
Direct Skilled Labour	400 hrs at £3.50 per hour	420 hrs at £3.80 per hour
Direct Unskilled Labour	800 hrs at £2.50 per hour	750 hrs at £2.60 per hour
Materials		
Steel	50 tons at £90 per ton	55 tons at £85 per ton
Chrome Ore	120 tons at £150 per ton	130 tons at £160 per ton

Required

(a) An explanation of the purpose of standard costing, including the factors which must be taken into account in setting standards. (8 marks)

(b) The standard and actual cost of production for the month of March. (3 marks)
(c) Calculate the following variances from standard:
  (i) direct wage rate variances;
  (ii) labour efficiency variances;
  (iii) material price variances;
  (iv) material usage variances. (8 marks)
(d) Comment on the material usage and material price variances calculated in (c), giving one possible reason for the variance in each case. (6 marks)

(25 marks)

Advanced level Accounting, AEB

22.2 A manufacturing company operates a system of standard costing. Information concerning its Department A is as follows:

	Budgeted	*Actual*
Total variable overheads (£)	400 000	500 000
Total fixed overheads (£)	600 000	560 000
Volume of production (standard machine hours)	10 000	12 000
Units produced	200	280

(a) Calculate (i) the standard variable overhead rate;
  (ii) the standard fixed overhead rate;
  (iii) the standard hours to produce one unit. (3 marks)
(b) Using your answers to (a) calculate:
  (i) total variable overhead variance;
  (ii) variable overhead spending variance;
  (iii) variable overhead efficiency variance; (10 marks)
(c) Using your answers to (a) calculate:
  (i) total fixed overhead variance;
  (ii) fixed overhead spending variance;
  (iii) fixed overhead volume variance. (10 marks)

(23 marks)

Advanced level Accounting, London

22.3* Sun plc has budgeted to produce 5 000 units of Beam per month. On this basis the standard cost per Beam is set as follows:

Direct materials	50 kilos at £0.18 per kilo
Direct labour	45 minutes at £1.60 per hour
Fixed overhead	£0.80 per unit

For the month of May the actual production was 4 800 Beams and the actual costs incurred for the month were:

Direct materials 241 000 kilos at a total cost of £43 300
Direct labour 3 400 hours at a cost of £5 500
Fixed overhead incurred £4 140

Mr Ray, the Management Accountant, has asked you to calculate the variances for the month and prepare a report briefly giving reasons for each variance.

Required:
Calculate the variances and prepare the report asked for by Mr Ray.

(15 marks)

Institute of Chartered Accountants, Foundation

22.4 A single product company operates a standard costing system. Its production budget for May 19_4 was as follows:

		£
Materials:	(A) 5 000 lbs	2 500
	(B) 7 500 lbs	2 250
Labour:	1 000 hours	4 000
		8 750
Fixed overheads		1 500
Production (5 000 units) cost		10 250

Actual results for May 19_4 were as follows:

Materials:	(A) 6 000 lbs	2 400
	(B) 6 000 lbs	2 400
Labour:	900 hours	4 500
		9 300
Fixed overheads		1 500
Production (4 700 units) cost		10 800

Required:

(a) Analyse the variances. (12 marks)

(b) Discuss how standard costing can help in planning and control. (13 marks)

(25 marks)

Institute of Chartered Accountants, Foundation

22.5* D Limited currently makes and sells only one product, but a new additional product is contemplated for July. An extract from the standard cost of the existing product is given below, together with other relevant details for Period 3.

Direct material:	$3\frac{1}{3}$ metres at £12 per metre
Direct labour:	4 hours at £4.40 per hour
Variable production overhead:	£2.75 per direct labour hour

The company absorbs variable production costs on the basis of standard hours of production and operates its variance analysis on marginal costing principles.

Production:	2 400 units equivalent to 9 600 standard hours of production
Direct material:	Opening stock 5 000 metres
	Closing stock 8 000 metres
	Purchases — 5 000 metres at £11.50 per metre
	6 500 metres at £12.20 per metre

Direct wages incurred were £47 500 for 10 000 hours worked.
Variable production overhead incurred: £28 500.

Required:

(a) calculate variances for material, labour and variable overhead which would be useful to management; (10 marks)

(b) identify to which of the variances calculated in (a) above, the following statements refer and comment briefly whether the explanation could be acceptable:

  (i) 'Normally the buyer purchases at list price less 20% but because the quantity ordered was greater than usual, the price was list price less 25%.'

  (ii) 'The flow of work was much better following the appointment of an additional production supervisor.'

  (iii) 'Higher wage costs resulted in higher employer's National Insurance contributions.'

(iv) 'The wastage rate allowed for in the standard was exceeded.'
(v) 'An expected increase of 10% over the previous year's rate of pay had actually been 15%.' (10 marks)

(20 marks)

Chartered Institute of Management Accountants

22.6 What are standard costs? Explain their use regarding the following:
(a) overhead absorption
(b) planning
(c) control
(d) performance evaluation **(20 marks)**

Author's Question

Solutions

22.1 (a) See text.

(b)

	Standard	*Actual*
Labour	£	£
Direct skilled	1 400	1 596
Direct unskilled	2 000	1 950
Materials		
Steel	4 500	4 675
Chrome ore	18 000	20 800
Cost of production	£25 900	£29 021

(c) (i) *Direct wage rate variances*

			£
Skilled	£(3.50 − 3.80) × 420 hours	=	(126) A
Unskilled	£(2.50 − 2.60) × 750 hours	=	(75) A
			(201) A

(ii) *Labour efficiency variances*

Skilled	(400 − 420) hours × £3.50	=	(70) A
Unskilled	(800 − 750) hours × £2.50	=	125 F
			55 F

(iii) *Material price variances*

Steel	£(90 − 85) × 55 tons	=	275 F
Chrome ore	£(150 − 160) × 130 tons	=	(1 300) A
			(1 025) A

(iv) *Material usage variances*

Steel	(50 − 55) tons × £90	=	(450) A
Chrome ore	(120 − 130) tons × £150	=	(1 500) A
			(1 950) A

(d) See text.

22.2 (a) (i) Standard variable overhead rate $= \frac{\text{Budgeted variable overhead}}{\text{Budgeted machine hours}}$

$$\frac{£400\ 000}{10\ 000} = £40 \text{ per machine hour}$$

(ii) Standard fixed overhead rate $= \frac{\text{Budgeted fixed overhead}}{\text{Budgeted machine hours}}$

$$\frac{£600\ 000}{10\ 000} = £60 \text{ per machine hour}$$

(iii) Standard hours $= \dfrac{\text{Budgeted machine hours}}{\text{Budgeted output}}$

$\dfrac{10\ 000}{200} = 50$ hours

	£
(b) (i) Standard variable overhead, £40 000 × $\frac{280}{200}$	560 000
Variable overhead incurred	500 000
Total variable overhead variance	60 000 F
(ii) Variable overhead absorbed, 12 000 machine hours × £40	480 000
Incurred	500 000
Variable overhead spending variance	(20 000) A
(iii) Standard machine hours, 10 000 × $\frac{280}{200}$	14 000
Actual	12 000
Machine hours variance	2 000 F
Variable overhead efficiency variance 2 000 hours × £40	80 000 F
Check:	
Variable overhead spending variance	(20 000) A
Variable overhead efficiency variance	80 000 F
Total variable overhead variance	60 000 F
(c) (i) Standard fixed overhead, 12 000 × £60	720 000
Actual	560 000
Total fixed overhead variance	160 000 F
(ii) Budgeted fixed overhead	600 000
Actual	560 000
Fixed overhead spending variance	40 000 F
(iii) Budgeted fixed overhead	600 000
Standard fixed overhead absorbed	720 000
Fixed overhead volume variance	120 000 F
Check:	
Fixed overhead spending variance	40 000 F
Fixed overhead volume variance	120 000 F
Total fixed overhead variance	160 000 F

22.4 (a) *Material price variances*

	Standard	*Actual*
A: Price per lb.	$\dfrac{£2\ 500}{5\ 000\text{ lbs.}} = £0.50$	$\dfrac{£2\ 400}{6\ 000\text{ lbs.}} = £0.40$

Price variance = (Standard price − Actual price) × Actual quantity
= (£0.50 − £0.40) × 6 000 lbs.
= £600 F

	Standard	*Actual*
B: Price per lb.	$\dfrac{£2\ 250}{7\ 500\text{ lbs.}} = £0.30$	$\dfrac{£2\ 400}{6\ 000\text{ lbs.}} = £0.40$

Price variance = (£0.30 − £0.40) × 6 000 lbs.
= £(600) A

Material usage variances

A: Standard quantity per unit $= \dfrac{5\ 000\text{ lbs.}}{5\ 000\text{ units}} = 1$ lb.

Standard usage = 4 700 units × 1 lb. = 4 700 lbs.
Usage variance = (Standard usage − Actual usage) × Standard price
= (4 700 − 6 000) × £0.50
= £(650) A

B: Standard quantity per unit $= \dfrac{7\ 500 \text{ lbs.}}{5\ 000 \text{ units}} = 1\tfrac{1}{2}$ lbs.

Standard usage = 4 700 units × $1\tfrac{1}{2}$ lbs. = 7 050 lbs.
Usage variance = (7 050 − 6 000) × £0.30
= £315 F

Labour rate variance

Standard rate $= \dfrac{£4\ 000}{1\ 000 \text{ hours}} =$ £4 per hour

Actual rate $= \dfrac{£4\ 500}{900 \text{ hours}} =$ £5 per hour

Rate variance = (Standard rate − Actual rate) × Actual hours
= (£4 − £5) × 900
= £(900) A

Labour efficiency variance

Standard time per unit $= \dfrac{1\ 000 \text{ hours}}{5\ 000 \text{ units}} =$ 0.2 hours

Standard time for actual production = 4 700 units × 0.2
= 940 hours

Efficiency variance = (Standard time − Actual time) × Standard wage rate
= (940 − 900) × £4
= £160 F

Fixed overhead expenditure variance

Budgeted cost	1 500
Actual cost	1 500
Variance	—

Fixed overhead volume variance

Budgeted cost	1 500
Standard cost absorbed 1 500 × $\dfrac{4\ 700}{5\ 000}$	1 410
Variance	£(90) A

(b) See text.

CHAPTER 23

Break-even Analysis

Contribution Revisited

We have already met the concept of contribution in the context of marginal costing. It is time to look at it again, from a slightly different angle this time. Consider the following story. Joe Bloggs sets up a factory manufacturing leather jackets. Each jacket incurs variable costs of £40 and and Joe sells at £60. The fixed costs of the factory are £20 000 a year.

Consider Joe's financial position when, on setting up the factory, the first jacket is sold. At first thought he has made a profit of £20 on it. But is this really profit? Revenue from the jacket has covered variable costs, but what about the £20 000 fixed costs? It has not covered them. Joe is in a large loss position.

	£
Total revenue	60
Less variable costs	40
Contribution	20
Less fixed costs	20 000
Loss	£(19 980)

The surplus of revenue over variable cost is known as *Contribution*. This goes towards covering the fixed costs, in this case by £20. The question to ask is 'How many jackets does Joe need to sell before he can start to earn a profit?' To do this, Joe has to earn enough contribution on sales to recover all the fixed costs first. This is known as the *break-even point* and can be found by the formula.

$$\frac{\text{Fixed costs}}{\text{Contribution per unit}} \text{ or}$$

$$\frac{\text{Fixed costs}}{\text{Total revenue per unit} - \text{Variable cost per unit}}$$

$$\text{In this case, } \frac{£20\,000}{£60 - £40} = \frac{£20\,000}{£20} = 1\,000 \text{ units}$$

Joe has to sell 1 000 jackets a year to break even. At this point he will be neither suffering a loss nor enjoying a profit. Sales past 1 000 start earning profit. The £20 received in excess of variable cost is now true profit since it does not have to go towards covering fixed costs — all fixed costs have by now already been covered. At a sales level of 1 100 units for example:

	£
Total revenue	66 000
Less variable costs	44 000
Contribution	22 000
Less fixed costs	20 000
Profit	£2 000

It is now possible to see that contribution on sales past the break-even point has earned clear profit.

Sales past break-even	×	Contribution per unit	=	Profit
100 units	×	£20	=	£2 000

From this we can conclude that:

(1) when total contribution is *less than* fixed costs, losses are suffered
(2) when contribution is *greater* than fixed costs, profits are enjoyed
(3) when contribution is exactly *equal* to fixed costs there is neither profit nor loss — we are in a break-even position.

The Break-even Chart

It is possible to represent the break-even point on a chart which shows the levels of fixed cost, variable cost, and total revenue at all output levels from zero to capacity. This provides a visual impression of the critical relationship between costs, volume, and profit. For this reason break-even analysis is sometimes referred to as cost-volume-profit analysis or CVP analysis for short.

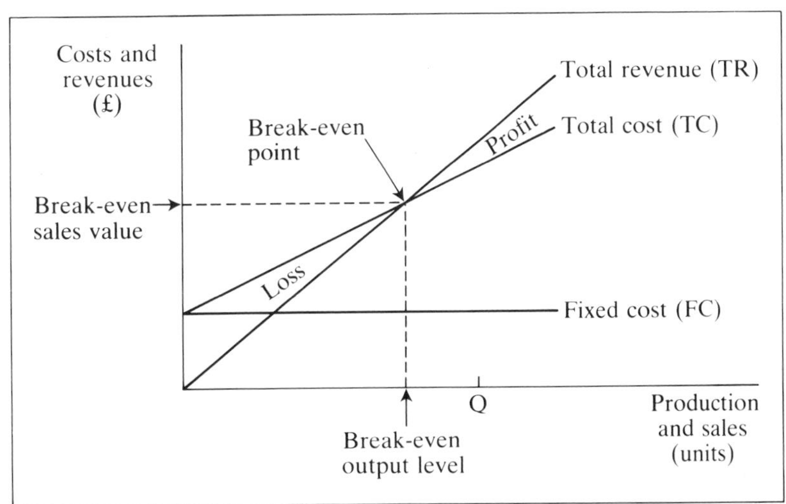

Note from the chart on page 357 that:

(1) fixed costs are a constant in relation to production level
(2) variable costs are indicated by the area above fixed costs and below total costs. They increase directly with output
(3) total revenue increases directly with sales volume
(4) the slope of the total revenue line is greater than that of variable cost because for each unit produced and sold selling price is greater than variable cost.
(5) At an output level of zero, loss is equal to the whole of fixed costs. As the firm starts to produce and sell, fixed costs are gradually recovered and consequently losses get smaller, until the break-even point. Thereafter additional sales earn increasing amounts of profit
(6) At all points *before* break-even total cost is greater than total revenue
(7) At all points *after* break-even total revenue is greater than total cost
(8) At the break-even point, where the two lines intersect, total revenue is exactly *equal* to total cost and profit is zero.

Entrepreneurs do not set up in business to break even. They set up to make a profit. Output levels in excess of break-even point earn this profit. The amount by which such an output exceeds break-even point is known as the *margin of safety*. On the chart; at an output level of Q units, the margin of safety is indicated by the distance between the break-even output level and Q. The greater the margin of safety the greater are profits and the safer is the firm's position.

Construction

Questions on this topic usually ask for construction of a break-even chart from information supplied. In this, the following steps should be followed.

Step 1
Calculate total cost at various levels of output. There is no need to do this at *all* levels since the relationship between output and cost is assumed to be linear. Choose these output levels — zero, capacity and one in between. For example for Joe's factory we would write:

Output (units)	*FC* £	*VC* £	*TC* £	*TR* £
0	20 000	0	20 000	0
750	20 000	30 000	50 000	45 000
1 500	20 000	60 000	80 000	90 000

Step 2
Select suitable *scales* for axes

Step 3
Draw axes.
Plot lines in the following order:
FC — horizontal at given level.
TC — from workings. Having marked your three points join them with a ruler. If it does not come to a straight line check your calculations.
TR — Same as for TC.

Step 4
Label the break-even point.

If you are asked to state the amount of profit or loss at a particular output level, do not be tempted to answer this from the chart. Since profit is the difference between two lines you will not be able to state it precisely. It is better to do a little calculation of total revenue minus total cost for an accurate answer.

Limitations

Users of break-even charts should be aware of their limitations to prevent the possibility of false conclusions being drawn from them. These limitations lie in the assumptions which underlie them, most of which are suspect. The assumptions are as follows:

1. The cost functions are linear

In practice this is not so for either fixed cost or variable cost, in either the short run or long run — as the economist will tell us. From a given asset base, as output expands in the short run the rate of increase in variable cost initially *falls* as the firm benefits from *increasing returns* to the variable factors. Eventually a point is reached when *diminishing returns* set in — this *increases* the rate of increase in variable cost. The short run cost function is therefore *non-linear*. In the long run, when time is allowed for changes in the scale of operations, again businesses do not experience constant costs. In the early stages of growth *economies of scale* are reaped as the firm benefits from increased specialization of men and machines (technical economies) and enjoys certain other benefits like discounts on bulk-buying (trading economies), and cheaper loans (financial economies). At very large levels of output however *diseconomies* set in of an administrative and managerial nature as the organization becomes too large and unwieldy for efficient management. The long run cost function is therefore also non-linear.

With *fixed costs* the assumption that they are constant over the whole range of output from zero to maximum capacity is unrealistic. In reality fixed costs are stepped, as shown below.

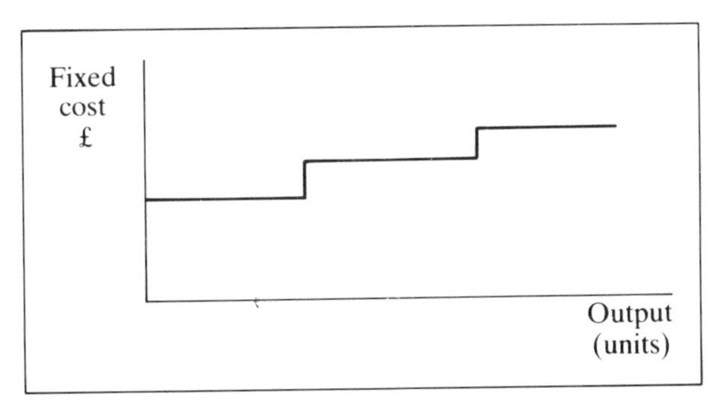

2. The revenue function is linear

While this may be so for a firm operating in a perfectly competitive market, where *market imperfections* exist (as they do in the majority of markets) economists will at once tell us that firms have to *reduce price* in order to sell more. This gives us a curvi-linear revenue function, as shown below.

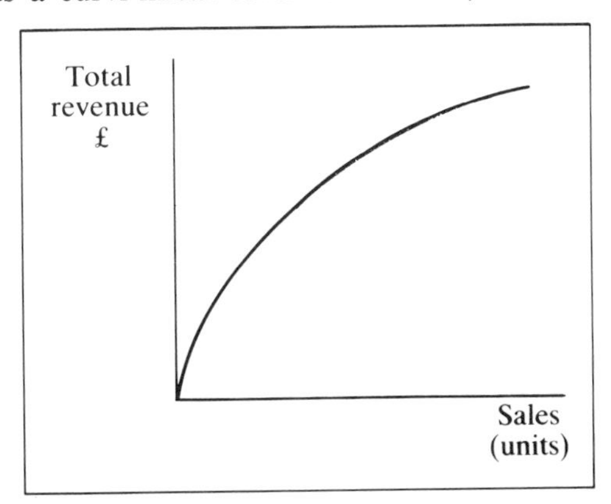

3. Volume is the only factor affecting costs and revenues

In practice costs may also be affected by a number of other factors such as inflation, technological change, and an increase in workers' productivity. Revenue may be affected by the need to change prices in response to a change in market conditions. The break-even chart ignores these and makes the *ceteris paribus* assumption that all other factors affecting costs and revenues remain constant.

4. A single product is sold

Break-even charts cannot handle multi-product situations. A multi-product firm earning different amounts of contribution on each product will find that there is *more than one* break-even point, this depending on the *sales mix*.

5. All output is sold

The break-even chart does not incorporate the possibility of changing stock levels.

Usefulness

Given that in the short term the firm's capacity is fixed, and range of output limited, break-even charts do have value because in this limited range the extent of the curves in the cost and revenue functions are so slight that they can be approximated as being linear. Management is often concerned with decision-making at the margin. Over this limited range the functions are pretty much linear. For this reason, despite the unrealistic assumption of linearity, break-even analysis does have relevance in the real world. The range over which the assumptions hold true is known as the *relevant range*. Strictly speaking when drawing the chart the accountant should only include the functions within this range, and not extend them to very low and very high levels of output.

Although the break-even chart as presented in this chapter cannot handle multi-product situations and changing stock levels, more complicated versions can be adapted for use even in these situations.

Break-even charts are an excellent way for the accountant of a firm to present financial information to management, who may be non-accountants. Most non-accountants prefer to look at information in the form of charts and diagrams rather than a table of figures or financial statements.

Perhaps the greatest value of the chart is its *highlighting of the underlying relationship between costs, volume, and profit*. In so doing it provides an excellent framework for exploring the effect on the firm's finances of management following different courses of action. In this way the chart is a useful tool for decision-making. For example the effect of an increase in wages would be to increase the slope of the variable cost curve. This would increase the break-even point and reduce profit, as shown in the chart below.

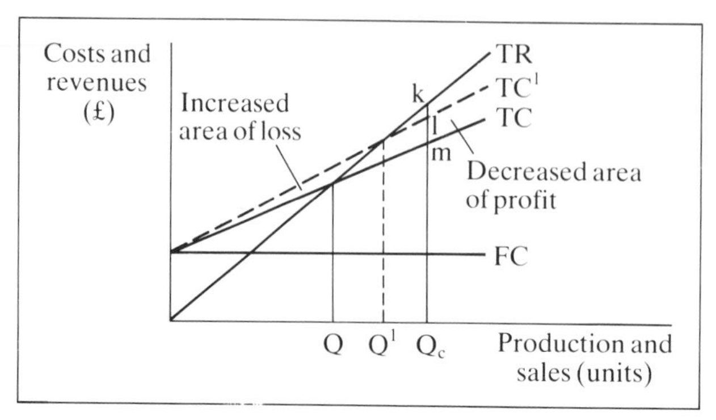

The dotted total cost function TC' represents the new level of costs after the change. The break-even output level is increased from Q to Q'. If the firm is currently producing Q_c the amount of profit is reduced from km to kl, the margin of safety from $Q_c - Q$ to $Q_c - Q'$.

As an useful exercise you might like to construct break-even charts to represent the following:

(i) an increase in fixed costs
(ii) a decrease in selling price
(iii) a decrease in variable costs

Examination Questions

Questions usually ask for the construction of a break-even chart from information supplied. You may also be asked to represent the effect of a given change on the chart and the break-even point. You will probably need to use the formula to calculate the precise break-even point. If asked for the sales level necessary to achieve a given profit target you can find this by adapting the formula thus:

$$\frac{\text{Fixed costs} + \text{target profit}}{\text{Contribution per unit}}$$

After the graphical and numerical parts, an evaluation of break-even analysis is often asked for, allowing you to demonstrate your knowledge of its limitations and uses.

Questions

23.1 XYZ Industries has introduced a new product. It is estimated that the fixed costs will be £16 740 per year, and that the variable costs will be £18 per tonne. The selling price will be £45 per tonne. Output is expected to be 900 tonnes per year.

(a) Calculate:
  (i) The amount of 'contribution' per tonne;
  (ii) The break-even output and income. (6 marks)

(b) Prepare a break-even chart showing clearly the angle of incidence, the break-even point, and the margin of safety at the expected level of output. (6 marks)

(c) Describe briefly the main limitations of break-even charts. (8 marks)

(20 marks)

Advanced level Accounting, London

23.2* A firm producing a single product sells everything which it produces. Fixed costs are £4 000, variable costs per unit are £0.40 and selling price per unit is £0.80.

Required:

(a) Draw a break-even chart to show costs and revenues at output levels of 5 000, 10 000, 15 000, 20 000 and 25 000 units. (5 marks)

(b) Show clearly the break-even point, the angle of incidence and the margin of safety at an output of 25 000 units. (3 marks)

(c) *Calculate* the break-even output if:
  (i) prices increase by 10 per cent (2 marks)
  (ii) prices remain at £0.80 per unit, but fixed costs increase by 5 per cent. (2 marks)

(d) Briefly outline the limitations of break-even charts as management tools. (8 marks)

(20 marks)

Advanced level Accounting, London

23.3 Mr Brown runs a shoe shop in a residential area of North London. His income statement for the year ending 31 March 19_3 is as follows:

		£
Sales [5 000 units at £20 each]		100 000
Cost of sales [5 000 units at £12 each]		60 000
		40 000
Rent, rates, lighting, and heating	20 000	
Shop assistant's salary	5 000	25 000
		£15 000

Mr Brown has been offered a larger shop in a new shopping centre. Rent, rates, lighting, and heating of the new shop will be £30 000 p.a. He would need an extra shop assistant. He reckons his sales would increase by 25%, but he would have to spend £2 000 p.a. on advertising.

Required:
(a) Calculate Mr Brown's
  (i) existing break-even point
  (ii) break-even point of proposed new shop, and
  (iii) income statement of the new shop if all the assumptions hold.
(13 marks)
(b) Discuss how cost-volume-profit analysis can help in decision-making.
(9 marks)
(22 marks)

Institute of Chartered Accountants, Foundation

23.4* Winners Ltd. sell matching hat, scarf and gloves sets to 'cash and carry' wholesalers at £6.00 per set using sales personnel who are rewarded on a fixed salary plus commission basis. The following forecasts are made for the year ending 31 December 19_2:

	£
Invoice cost to Winners Ltd. per set	4.70
Sales commission per set sold	0.30
Fixed expenses	
Salaries	21 220
Rent	6 600
Other	8 280
	36 100

Consideration is being given to adjusting the rates of commission payable and to the possibility of abolishing commission and increasing basic salaries.

Required:
On the assumption that all expense and revenue relationships would remain unchanged except where specified, answer each of the following questions independently:
(a) If commission were increased to 35p per set, what increase in sales value and sales units would be necessary to break even? (6 marks)
(b) What would be the net profit or loss if
  (i) 35 000 sets were sold with commission unchanged at 30p per set;
  (ii) 55 000 sets were sold but each salesman were to receive 30p plus an additional commission of 10p per set sold in excess of the break-even point? (8 marks)
(c) If commission were discontinued and salaries increased by a total of £9 595 per year
  (i) what would be the value of sales necessary to achieve break-even point?

(ii) how many units would need to be sold to achieve a target net profit of £17 000 for the year? (7 marks)

(d) State **one** reason for, and **one** against, the company adopting the plan (given in (c)) in times of fluctuating demand rather than the original salary plus commission plan. (4 marks)

(25 marks)

Advanced level Accounting, AEB

23.5 Perriwinkle Ltd manufacture and sell a single product and the following summarised information represents the original forecast profit budget and the subsequent actual results for the year ended 30 April 19_6.

	Budget £		*Actual* £
Sales (Selling price £15 per unit)	105 000	(Selling price £13.50 per unit)	101 250
Direct materials	21 000		23 000
Direct labour	14 000		16 000
Variable manufacturing overhead	10 500		11 000
Fixed manufacturing overhead	16 000		18 000
Gross profit	43 500		33 250
Variable sales overhead	7 000		8 000
Other fixed costs	12 000		12 000
Net profit	24 500		13 250

Additional information:

(1) The company had prepared the profit budget on the basis that 7 000 units would be produced and sold. The number of units actually sold during the year was 7 500.

(2) No stocks of finished goods were held and there was no work in progress.

Note: It should be assumed that all expense and revenue relationships remain unchanged except where specifically identified.

Required:

(a) Calculate the budget volume of sales units necessary to achieve the budget break-even point in 19_5/6. (4 marks)

(b) Calculate the volume of sales units to achieve the actual break-even point. (4 marks)

(c) Prepare a break-even chart to illustrate the budgeted and actual sales/costs relationships for 19_5/6. Identify the break-even points. (8 marks)

(d) Calculate the sales variance for 19_5/6 distinguishing between the sales price variance and the sales volume variance. (5 marks)

(e) Briefly outline the limitations of break-even analysis. (4 marks)

(25 marks)

Advanced level Accounting, AEB

23.6 (a) Explain to a non-accounting colleague how you would calculate the break-even point of a company manufacturing and selling one type of product. (6 marks)

(b) 'If a company reduces its selling price by 10% and sales volume increases by 11% then the profit earned by the company would not change.'
Examine the validity of the above statement. (3 marks)

(c) The management of a company is considering automating most of its manufacturing operations. This change would result in a significant

reduction in variable costs, but the increase in fixed overheads would be such that, at current levels of activity, profits would not change.
Discuss the possible effects of this proposed change on the future profits of the company. (4 marks)

(d) Consider the effect on a company's reported profit of an increase in production volume with no corresponding increase in sales volume. (4 marks)

Chartered Association of Certified Accountants **(17 marks)**

Solutions

23.1 (a) (i) Contribution = Price − variable cost
= £45 − £18
= £27

(ii) Break-even output = $\frac{\text{Fixed costs}}{\text{Contribution per tonne}}$

$\frac{16\ 740}{27} = 620$ tonnes

Break-even income = 620 × £45
= £27 900

(b) *Workings for chart below*

Output (tonnes)	*FC* £	*VC* £	*TC* £	*TR* £
0	16 740	0	16 740	0
450	16 740	8 100	24 840	20 250
900	16 740	16 200	32 940	40 500

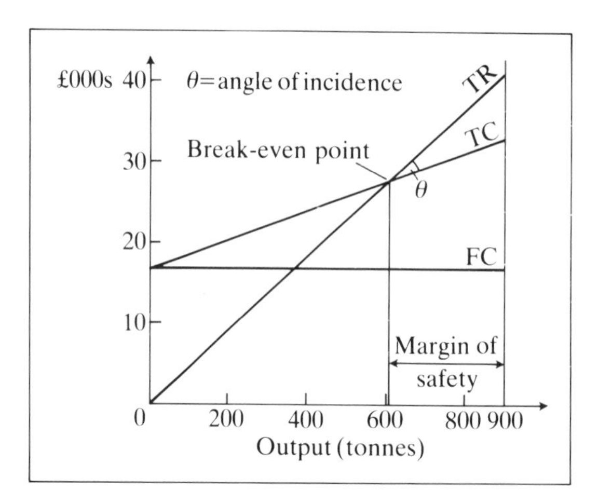

(c) See text.

23.3 (a) (i) Existing break-even point = $\frac{25\ 000}{20 - 12}$ = 3 125 units

(ii) Fixed costs of proposed new shop:

	£
Rent, rates, lighting, and heating	30 000
Two shop assistants*	10 000
Advertising	2 000
	42 000

* It is assumed that the second assistant will be paid the same salary as the first.

Break-even point = $\frac{42\ 000}{20 - 12}$ = 5 250 units

Mr. Brown would have to sell an additional 2 125 units to cover the increase in fixed costs.

(iii) *Forecast income statement of the new shop*

	£	£
Sales (6 250 units @ £20)		125 000
Cost of sales (6 250 @ £12)		75 000
Gross profit		50 000
Less Expenses		
Rent, rates, lighting and heating	30 000	
Salaries	10 000	
Advertising	2 000	42 000
Net profit		£8 000

It seems that the move to the larger shop in the shopping centre would *not* be a good idea — net profit is expected to decrease, by £7 000. The 25% increase in sales is not enough to compensate for the large increase in fixed costs.

(b) See text.

23.5 (a & b) *Working*

	Budget £	*Actual* £
To find variable cost per unit:		
Direct materials	21 000	23 000
Direct labour	14 000	16 000
Variable manufacturing overhead	10 500	11 000
Variable sales overhead	7 000	8 000
Total variable cost	52 500	58 000
÷ by number of units	7 000	7 500
Variable cost per unit	£7.50	£7.733̇
Break-even sales volumes	$\frac{16\,000 + 12\,000}{15 - 7.50}$ = 3 733 units	$\frac{18\,000 + 12\,000}{13.50 - 7.733̇}$ = 5 203 units

(c) *Workings for chart below*

Budgeted

Output	*FC*	*VC*	*TC*	*TR*
0	28 000	0	28 000	0
3 500	28 000	26 250	54 250	52 500
7 000	28 000	52 500	80 500	105 000

Actual

Output	*FC*	*VC*	*TC*	*TR*
0	30 000	0	30 000	0
3 500	30 000	27 067	57 067	47 250
7 500	30 000	58 000	88 000	101 250

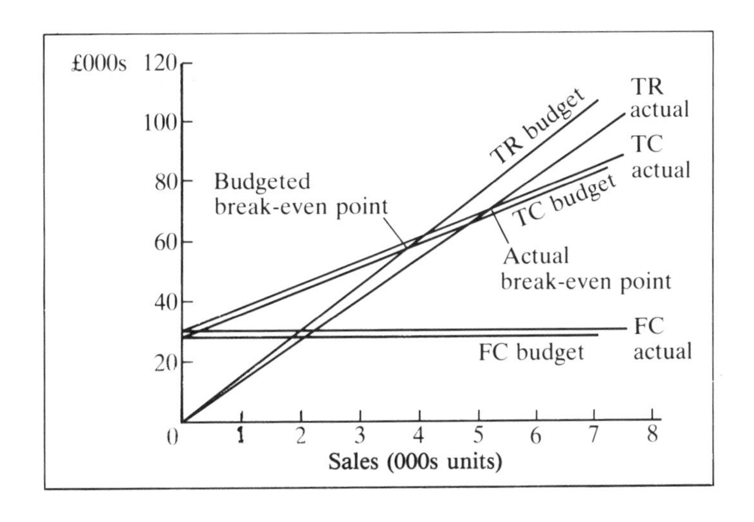

(d)

			£
Budgeted sales revenue	7 000 @ £15	=	105 000
Actual sales revenue	7 500 @ £13.50	=	101 250
Total sales variance			(3 750) A

This can be split into:

Sales price variance = £(13.50 − 15.00) × 7 500 units
= £(11 250) A

Sales volume variance = (7 500 − 7 000) × £15
= £7 500 F

Check: Price variance	(11 250) A
Volume variance	7 500
Equal to total sales variance	(3 750) A

(e) See text.

CHAPTER 24

Capital Investment Appraisal

In contrast to business decisions considered so far, such as dropping a segment, accepting a special order, and decision-making based on break-even analysis, which are short-term, investment decisions are long-term i.e. the effects are felt over several years. Capital investment is concerned with the *type and mix of fixed assets* employed by a firm. When a fixed asset is due for replacement a decision has to be taken on which of several competing assets to purchase. When a business is planning for expansion, investment decisions have to be taken regarding plant and machinery and land and buildings. Such decisions are usually taken by top management for three reasons:

(1) they usually involve very large sums of money
(2) the quality of the decisions taken affect the profitability of the firm for many years
(3) having purchased an item of fixed asset or embarked on a long-term project the decision is usually irreversible. To find subsequently that the wrong decision has been taken and attempt to change it could prove to be very costly.

Given the crucial importance of 'getting it right' management, in selecting between alternatives, do not choose on the basis of feelings or hunches but use tried and tested techniques and concrete financial data.

Methods

Several techniques are available to help in the decision-making process. They vary in complexity from simple crude methods such as *payback* and *accounting rate of return* to more sophisticated techniques using discounted cash flow principles such as *net present value* and *internal rate of return.* These are described and evaluated in this chapter.

Payback

The simplest method is payback. This ranks projects by the time it takes for the expected net cash inflows to pay back the initial outlay. By net cash inflows is meant cash inflows less cash outflows.

Example

Stone PLC is considering investing £1 million on one of two competing projects. Details are as follows:

	A	*B*
	£000	*£000*
Initial outlay	1 000	1 000
Expected net cash inflows:		
Year 1	450	200
2	550	500
3	250	600
4	150	300

The estimated residual value of both projects after four years is zero. The cost of capital is 10%.

Payback periods

Project A = 2 years

Project B = 2 years + $\frac{300}{600}$ of year 3 = $2\frac{1}{2}$ years

By this criteria, the company would select Project A. The payback method prefers projects whose returns are concentrated in earlier years. The main limitation of such a narrow criteria is that it does not take account of monies received *after* the payback period i.e. it ignores the longer-term profitability of projects. In our example the rejected project B in fact returns more than A over the full four year period — £1.6 million compared to £1.4 million. These drawbacks are overcome by our second method.

Accounting Rate of Return (ARR)

The criteria here is profitability rather than speed of return. The ARR is given by

$$\frac{\text{Average annual profit}}{\text{Average investment}} \times 100$$

Only revenues and costs flowing from the investment should be included in the calculation. The average annual net cash inflow from project A, in £000, is

$$\frac{450 + 550 + 250 + 150}{4 \text{ years}} = £350,$$

for project B $\frac{200 + 500 + 600 + 300}{4 \text{ years}} = £400.$

To calculate the average annual *profit* we need to account for depreciation in addition to the cash flows given. By the straight-line method the annual charge is £250 (000). The average annual profit is therefore £100 for project A, £150 for B. The average investment, in £000s, is its book value at the mid-point of the project's life i.e. $\frac{1000}{2} = £500$. This gives us:

For project A, ARR $= \frac{£100}{£500} \times 100 = 20\%$

For project B, ARR $= \frac{£150}{£500} \times 100 = 30\%$

While ARR is a more comprehensive method than payback it still suffers from one major problem — *it ignores the time value of money.*

What we have done in our calculations so far is to add together monies expected in year 1 to that expected in year 2, and so on. But monies in different time periods are worth different amounts, for two reasons:

(1) money received earlier is worth more than money received later since once received, it can be invested to earn return
(2) inflation reduces the purchasing power (real value) of money over time.

The two methods so far have failed to account for this. In both, cash flows from *different years* are added together. Since £1 received in year 1 is worth *more* than £1 received in year 2, mathematicians will at once tell us that we cannot add them together, in the same way that we cannot add apples to bananas or £ to $. In the latter case the two are added by first converting one in terms of the other by means of an exchange rate between the two. What is needed is a similar exchange rate such that £s received in the future can be converted back to what they are worth today, the time of the initial outlay, so that we can compare like with like.

Discounted Cash Flow (DCF)

It is possible to do just this by *discounting,* the purpose of which is to reduce the value of future cash flows to their present day value by using an appropriate discount factor.

Taking an interest rate of 10% per annum, how much will £1 invested today be worth in one year's time? £1 + £0.10 = £1.10. And in two years' time? £1.10 + £0.11 = £1.21. This process, which you have probably met before, is known as Compounding.

Discounting is the opposite of compounding. It asks the question 'Given that the rate of interest is 10 per cent how much is £1 received in one year's time worth today?'

$\frac{£1}{£1.10}$ = £0.9091. And £1 received in two years' time?

$\frac{£1}{£1.21}$ = £0.8264. The compounded values are calculated by the formula $A = P(1 + i)n$, the discounted values by

$$P = \frac{A}{(1 + i)^n},$$

where P is the principal (original sum invested), A the sum to which it will amount, i the rate of interest, and n the number of years.

Despite the fact that DCF techniques are more complicated than the first two methods, firms still use them because, in practice, the time value of money is an important consideration, especially in times of high interest rates and inflation. We did not meet this problem in short-run decisions because the elements of interest and inflation over short periods of time are usually insignificant. Over a long period of time they are not and should therefore be brought into the calculations. There are two specific DCF methods — NPV and IRR.

Net Present Valve (NPV)

The estimated future cash flows are discounted at the minimum rate of return acceptable to the firm. This total sum expressed in today's £s, is compared to the initial outlay. If it is greater the project is worthwhile. The criteria for setting the minimum acceptable rate of return is discussed later in the chapter.

Illustration

Let us evaluate project A on the assumption that the minimum acceptable rate of return is the cost of capital, 10%.

Year	*Cash flow*	*Discount factor*	*Present value*
	£000	*at 10%*	*£*
0	(1 000)	1.0000	(1 000 000)
1	450	0.9091	409 095
2	550	0.8264	454 520
3	250	0.7513	187 825
4	150	0.6830	102 450
		NPV	+ 153 890

The calculation tells Stone PLC that the project will add to the value of the company by £153 890 at today's money value.

Present value of expected net cash inflows – Initial outlay = NPV of project

£1 153 890 – £1 000 000 = £153 890

This would be compared with the NPVs of competing projects, the one with the largest NPV being selected. Where NPV is negative the project should be rejected.

Internal Rate of Return (IRR)

The IRR, or *yield,* is the true interest rate earned on a project. It is given by that interest which, when applied to the future cash flows, reduces the NPV of the project to zero. It has to be found by trial and error.

Illustration

For Project A

Year	*Cash flow*	*Discount factor*	*Present value*	*Discount factor*	*Present value*
	£000	*at 18%*	*£*	*at 19%*	*£*
0	(1 000)	1.0000	(1 000 000)	1.0000	(1 000 000)
1	450	0.8475	381 375	0.8403	378 135
2	550	0.7182	395 010	0.7062	388 410
3	250	0.6086	152 150	0.5934	148 350
4	150	0.5158	77 370	0.4987	74 805
		NPV	+ 5 905	NPV	(10 300)

The IRR is between 18% and 19%. This return is compared to the minimum acceptable rate. If it is *greater* the project is worthwhile. Note how the return using discounted cash flow is lower than that obtained by the simple ARR method (20%) which does not take the time value of money into account.

The IRR represents the maximum a firm is willing to pay for finance. (Economists amongst you will recognize the similarity of this to Keynes' concept of the *marginal efficiency of capital*, which also represents the maximum rate of interest a firm is prepared to pay for investment funds.)

Where projects are mutually exclusive and all have an IRR greater than the minimum acceptable rate of return, the project with the largest IRR is to be selected.

The Minimum Acceptable Rate of Return

A common criteria is *cost of capital* to the firm. In practice, businesses raise finance through several sources each with a different cost attached to it. The cost of capital then has to be calculated as the weighted average cost.

Example

A company has the following capital structure:

Source	*Cost*	*£*
Ordinary shares	12%	60 000
Debentures	8%	30 000
Bank loan	10%	10 000

What is its cost of capital?

Answer

Source	*£000*	*Weight* ×	*Cost* =	*Weighted cost*
Ordinary shares	60	6	12	72
Debentures	30	3	8	24
Bank loans	10	1	10	10
	100	10		106

Divide by sum of weights ÷ 10
Weighted average cost 10.6%

The company's cost of capital is 10.6%.

Economists advocate the use of the *opportunity cost* concept in setting the minimum acceptable rate. By this criterion, the rate should be at least equal to the return the firm could obtain if it invested the funds outside the business.

Example

The company above could earn a return of 14% if it invested externally. A project offering a return of 12% would be accepted by the cost of capital criteria, but rejected by the opportunity cost criteria. Accepting the project would be a bad decision in the sense that the opportunity would be lost of earning a better return on the capital in an alternative use.

In addition, the minimum acceptable rate of return should be adjusted in line with the degree of *risk* attached to various projects. Risky projects should be evaluated with a higher rate than safe projects, to compensate for the additional risk.

Comparison of Methods

Only the DCF methods are theoretically sound. ARR suffers from the failure to take the time value of money into account. Payback also suffers from this, and in addition fails to take relative profitability of projects into account. It may seem surprising then that payback is the most widely used method in industry. This is partly because of its simplicity and also because in times of rapid change when forecasting becomes particularly hazardous projects offering a quick return are favoured. Another possible reason for the popularity of payback is that man is motivated by the short-term. Ambitious young managers who want to work their way up the corporate ladder in as short a time as possible display a preference for projects offering quick spectacular returns, rather than those equally profitable in the long run but whose returns are more spread out. In most situations management uses more than one method before reaching a decision. In major investments involving very large sums of money all four methods may be used.

Limitations

All methods of investment appraisal suffer from the fact that the figures used in the calculations are only estimates. One of the main problems in practice is quantifying future cash flows likely to emanate from different projects. In a dynamic world it is not possible to do this with certainty. Since the timescale in investment decisions is long rather than short, forecasting is made even more difficult. The correctness of decisions taken often relies on the quality of the original forecast. In this respect DCF methods are at a disadvantage to the simple crude methods since in addition to cash flows, estimates have to be made about the future course of interest rates and inflation.

The other main limitation of the techniques presented in this chapter is that they do not incorporate *non-financial factors* such as the *social worthwhileness* of projects and degree of risk. It should be said however that more advanced methods *can* take these into account. Investment decisions in the public sector for example often try to attach money values to social costs and benefits emanating from a project, such as construction of a ring-road, in an exercise known as *Cost-Benefit Analysis*. Risk can also be allowed for in more complicated methods.

Examination Questions

Examination questions require you to advise on which of two or more mutually exclusive investments should be selected. The method(s) of appraisal to be used is specified.

Questions

24.1 A company has the following capital structure with each type of finance having the cost as shown:

		£000
Ordinary shares	(20%)	1 000
Preference shares	(16%)	600
Debentures	(10%)	400

Debenture interest is allowable against corporation tax, which is 40%.
The company currently has three investment projects under review, details of which are given below. However, only two can be undertaken.

Project	*Arrow*	*Dart*	*Spear*
Initial Cost (£)	18 000	22 000	24 000
Cash Flows (£)			
Year 1	7 000	6 500	8 200
Year 2	11 000	7 000	10 400
Year 3	11 300	8 500	10 800
Year 4	11 500	12 800	11 600
Year 5	11 900	14 300	12 000

(a) Calculate the company's cost of capital. (5 marks)

(b) Rank the investment projects in order of preference using: (i) Payback. (ii) NPV; use your answer to (a) as the discount rate. (17 marks)

(c) Refer to the table below:

Present Value Factors:

	15%	16%	17%	18%	19%	20%
Year 1	0.870	0.862	0.855	0.847	0.840	0.833
Year 2	0.756	0.743	0.731	0.718	0.706	0.694
Year 3	0.658	0.641	0.624	0.609	0.593	0.579
Year 4	0.572	0.552	0.534	0.516	0.499	0.482
Year 5	0.497	0.476	0.456	0.437	0.419	0.402

State, with reasons, the two projects you advise the company to select. (8 marks)

(30 marks)

Advanced level Accounting, London

24.2 (a) Explain the relationship between Net Present Value (NPV) and Yield (Internal Rate of Return). (4 marks)

(b) A firm is considering an investment project costing £12 500. The estimated annual cash flows accruing at the end of each year are:

Year 1	£2 500	Year 3	£5 700
Year 2	£4 600	Year 4	£7 000

If the company has to borrow money to finance the project, is the maximum rate of interest it should pay for finance: 16%, 18%, 20%? Give reasons for your answer.

Table of Factors

Period	16%	18%	20%
1	0.862	0.847	0.833
2	0.743	0.718	0.694
3	0.641	0.609	0.579
4	0.552	0.516	0.482

(11 marks)
(15 marks)

Advanced level Accounting, London

24.3* Roadwheelers Ltd were considering buying an additional lorry but the company had not yet decided which particular lorry to purchase. The lorries had broadly similar technical specifications and each was expected to have a working life of 5 years.

The following information was available on the lorries being considered:

(1)

	Lorries		
	BN	*FX*	*VR*
	'Roadhog'	*'Sprinter'*	*'Rocket'*
Purchase price	£40 000	£45 000	£50 000
Estimated scrap value after 5 years	£8 000	£9 000	£14 000
Fixed costs other than depreciation	£	£	£
Year 1	2 000	1 800	1 500
Year 2	2 000	1 800	1 500
Year 3	2 200	1 800	1 400
Year 4	2 400	2 000	1 400
Year 5	2 400	2 200	1 400
Variable costs per road mile	6p	8p	7p

(2) The company charges 25p a mile for all journeys irrespective of the length of journey, and the expected annual mileages over the 5 year period are:

	Miles
Year 1	50 000
Year 2	60 000
Year 3	80 000
Year 4	80 000
Year 5	80 000

(3) The company's cost of capital is 10% per annum.

(4) It should be assumed that all operating costs are paid and revenues received at the end of the year.

(5) Present value of £1 at interest rate of 10% per annum:

Year 1	£0.909
Year 2	£0.826
Year 3	£0.751
Year 4	£0.683
Year 5	£0.621

Required

(a) (i) Appropriate computations using the net present value method for each of the lorries under consideration. (14 marks)

(ii) A report to the directors of Roadwheelers Ltd advising them as to which specific lorry should be purchased. (6 marks)

(b) A brief outline of the problems encountered in evaluating capital projects. (5 marks)

(25 marks)

Advanced level Accounting, AEB

24.4 Rainy plc is considering investing in a machine to manufacture a new line of umbrellas. The following data has been assembled in respect of the investment:

(1) Market research has just been carried out at a cost of £20 000. The study estimated the revenue from the new umbrella and the effect on existing products to be:

Year	*Revenue from new umbrella*	*Lost revenue from existing products*
	£000s	*£000s*
1	100	30
2	120	25
3	140	10
4	120	—

(2) The annual variable costs associated with expected sales and savings from reduced production of existing products are expected to be:

Year	*Variable costs of making the new umbrella*	*Costs saved on existing products*
	£000s	*£000s*
1	60	20
2	65	15
3	70	5
4	60	—

(3) Fixed costs such as rent, rates, etc. which are unaffected by the investment will be £50 000 per year.

(4) The machine to be used will cost £120 000 payable immediately. It will be depreciated using the straight line method. The residual value will be nil.

(5) The cost of capital is 12%.

Required:

(a) Calculate the NPV of the project. Should Rainy plc invest? (10 marks)

(b) *Briefly*, explain why the NPV method is superior to the ROCE and Payback approaches. (5 marks)

(15 marks)

Institute of Chartered Accountants, Foundation

24.5* The Rovers Football Club are languishing in the middle of the First Division of the Football League. The Club has suffered a loss of £200 000 in their last financial year and whilst receipts from spectators have declined over the last five years, recently receipts have stabilised at approximately £1 000 000 per season. The Club is considering the purchase of the services of one of two new football players, Jimmy Jam or Johnny Star.

Jimmy Jam is 21 years old and considered to be a future international footballer. He is prepared to sign a five year contract with Rovers for a salary of £50 000 per annum. His present club would require a transfer fee of £200 000 for the transfer of his existing contract. With J. Jam in the team the Rovers Club would expect receipts to increase by 20%.

Johnny Star is 32 years old and a leading international footballer who is prepared to sign for Rovers on a two year contract before retiring completely from football. He would expect a salary of £200 000 per annum and his present club would require a transfer fee of £100 000 for the transfer of his existing contract. Rovers believe that as a result of signing Star receipts would increase by 40%.

The rate of interest applicable to the transaction is 12% and the following is an extract from the present value table for £1:

	12%
Year 1	0.893
Year 2	0.797
Year 3	0.712
Year 4	0.636
Year 5	0.507

It should be assumed that all costs are paid and revenues received at the end of each year.

Required:

A report, incorporating an evaluation of the financial result of engaging each player by the net present value method, providing the Rovers Football Club with information to assist it in deciding which alternative to adopt. Indicate any other factors that may be taken into consideration. **(18 marks)**

Advanced level Accounting, AEB

24.6 Compare and contrast discounting with non-discounting methods of investment appraisal. Illustrate your answer with examples. **(20 marks)**

Advanced level Accounting, London

Solutions

24.1 (a)

Source	£	*Cost* %	× *Weight*	*Weighted cost* %
Ordinary shares	1 000	20	10	200
Preference shares	600	16	6	96
Debentures	400	6*	4	24
	2 000		20	320
				÷ 20
		Weighted average cost 16%		

* The effective cost of the debentures is reduced by 40% since the interest payments are tax-deductible.

(b) (i) *Payback*

Project	*Payback period*
Arrow	2 years
Dart	3 years
Spear 2 + $(\frac{5\ 400}{10\ 800})$ of year 3	$2\frac{1}{2}$ years

The project with the shortest pay-back period is to be preferred.

Ranking
1 Arrow
2 Spear
3 Dart

(ii) *Net Present Value*

Year	*Discount factor at 16%*	*Arrow* Cash flow £	*Arrow* PV £	*Dart* Cash flow £	*Dart* PV £	*Spear* Cash flow £	*Spear* PV £
0	1.000	(18 000)	(18 000.0)	(22 000)	(22 000.0)	(24 000)	(24 000.0)
1	0.862	7 000	6 034.0	6 500	5 603.0	8 200	7 068.4
2	0.743	11 000	8 173.0	7 000	5 201.0	10 400	7 727.2
3	0.641	11 300	7 243.3	8 500	5 448.5	10 800	6 922.8
4	0.552	11 500	6 348.0	12 800	7 065.6	11 600	6 403.2
5	0.476	11 900	5 664.4	14 300	6 806.8	12 000	5 712.0
		NPV	+ 15 462.7	NPV	+ 8 124.9	NPV	+ 9 833.6

The project with the higher NPV is to be preferred.
Ranking: 1. Arrow
2. Spear
3. Dart

(c) By both methods the company should select Arrow and Spear, and reject Dart. The problem with Dart is that its returns are concentrated in the later years of its life when the present value of cash flows are most reduced and there is the greatest danger of the project suffering from obsolescence. In this respect, Dart is also the most *risky* of the three projects.

24.2 (a) See text.

(b)

Year	Cash flow	Discount factor at 16%	PV £	Discount factor at 18%	PV £	Discount factor at 20%	PV £
0	(12 500)	1.000	(12 500.0)	1.000	(12 500.0)	1.000	(12 500.0)
1	2 500	0.862	2 155.0	0.847	2 117.5	0.833	2 082.5
2	4 600	0.743	3 417.8	0.718	3 302.8	0.694	3 192.4
3	5 700	0.641	3 653.7	0.609	3 471.3	0.579	3 300.3
4	7 000	0.552	3 864.0	0.516	3 612.0	0.482	3 374.0
		NPV	+ 590.5	NPV	+ 3.6	NPV	+ (550.8)

The maximum interest the company should pay for finance is 18% since the real return on the project is fractionally over 18% but below 19%. Paying 20% would not be worthwhile since the net present value of future cash flows discounted at this rate gives a negative value i.e. the return is less than the cost of finance.

24.4

RAINY PLC

(a)

Year	*Additional Revenue £000*	*Additional Variable cost £000*	*Net cash flow £000*	*Discount factor at 12%*	*PV £*
0			(120)	1.0000	(120 000)
1	70	40	30	0.8929	26 787
2	95	50	45	0.7972	35 874
3	130	65	65	0.7118	46 267
4	120	60	60	0.6355	38 130
				NPV	+ 27 058

Notes

(i) The £20 000 market research has already been spent and is therefore *irrelevant* to this future decision. It is a *'sunk'* cost.

(ii) Fixed costs do not feature in the calculation since their level is not affected by the decision to invest or not.

(iii) Rainy plc will make an overall surplus on the proposed investment in the new line of umbellas — net present value is a positive £27 058.

(iv) If there are no competing projects yielding a higher return the company *should* invest in the machine.

(b) See text.

Miscellaneous Essay Questions

Part I: *Financial Accounting*

1. Jack Thompson has completed his first year in business as a sole trader. The profit for the year is rather more than Jack had anticipated because certain fixed assets appear to have been valued at more than their resale value. In discussion his accountant mentions that profit is calculated on the basis that the firm is a 'going concern'.

During the year Jack has established several useful business contacts and has obtained the custom of several large firms which he firmly believes will become loyal customers. As a result Jack has asked his accountant to include goodwill as one of the assets of the business.

Required:

(a) An explanation of the term 'going concern' and how it affects the calculation of profit. Illustrate your answer by reference to the matter discussed in the first paragraph above. (12 marks)

(b) A reasoned reply to Jack Thompson concerning his proposal to include goodwill as an asset of his business. (12 marks)

(24 marks)

Advanced level Accounting, AEB

2. *Required:*

(a) define

(i) a Provision;

(ii) a Revenue Reserve; (5 marks)

(b) give one example of each; (2 marks)

(c) state briefly what you consider to be the main difference between a Provision and a Revenue Reserve; (4 marks)

(d) state where you would expect to find them in the financial statements of a company. (4 marks)

(15 marks)

Chartered Institute of Management Accountants

3. 'Net profit can be as high or low as the financial accountant wishes to make it.' Comment on this statement. **(20 marks)**

Advanced level Accounting, London

4. The managing director of a limited company has been told by the company's auditors that published financial statements should comply not only with relevant Acts of Parliament, but also with *statements of standard accounting practice* (SSAPs).

(a) Examples of areas covered by SSAPs include: (1) depreciation, (2) research and development expenditure, and (3) stocks and work in progress. Explain the reasons for standardizing the accounting procedures in relation to *one* of these areas. (8 marks)

(b) Explain the significance of SSAPs to the accounting profession and the users of accounting information. (12 marks)

(20 marks)

Advanced level Accounting, London

Part II: *Cost Accounting*

5. 'The cost accountant is an important person in the management sphere, but the financial accountant is a mere keeper of records.'
Is it possible to justify this statement? Give reasons for your answer.

(20 marks)

Advanced level Accounting, London

6. (a) Describe the role of the cost accountant in a manufacturing organization. (8 marks)
(b) Explain whether you agree with each of the following statements:
(i) 'All direct costs are variable.'
(ii) 'Variable costs are controllable and fixed costs are not.'
(iii) 'Sunk costs are irrelevant when providing decision-making information.' (9 marks)

(17 marks)

Chartered Association of Certified Accountants

7. 'There is no such thing as a *true* cost, since the cost of a product depends upon the accounting conventions used.' Comment on this statement.

(20 marks)

Advanced level Accounting, London

Part III: *Management Accounting*

8. What is management accounting? How does it differ from (a) financial accounting, and (b) cost accounting? **(20 marks)**

Advanced level Accounting, London

9. The management process centres upon the key activities of planning, organization, co-ordination, command and control. How does the work of the cost and management accountant contribute to the management process?

(20 marks)

Advanced level Accounting, London

The Professional Bodies

Given the many different branches of accounting it is easy to understand why accountants tend to specialize in a particular branch. Because of this there is no single professional body for accountants — in the United Kingdom there are *six*, reflecting the fact that the accountant is a very diverse animal. He is to be found in industry, commerce, public practice, local government, clubs, charities, schools, hospitals, anywhere in fact where people and money are involved. It is difficult to describe a picture of the typical accountant — there is no such thing.

The different professional bodies emphasize different aspects of the accountant's work. Financial accountants, the largest body of accountants, belong mostly to the *Institute of Chartered Accountants,* of which there are three — in England & Wales, Scotland, and Ireland. They are separate from one another with their own rules and regulations and conditions of entry. Generally, to qualify, the trainee has to undergo a period of rigorous training (minimum of three years) in a firm of accountants and pass the professional examinations of the Institute. Once qualified members, designated by the letters ACA, are allowed to work in private practice and are empowered to audit (check and certify) the accounts of limited companies before they are published. Some eventually leave to work in industry.

The specialist body for cost and management accountants is the *Chartered Institute of Management Accountants.* Their student members are also required to serve an apprenticeship and pass the Institute's examinations, but here the training must be acquired in industry or commerce (not in an accountant's practising office) and the examinations are orientated towards cost and management accounting. Members, designated by the letters ACMA, work mostly in industry. Given the nature of their work, their role in the organization is often more than just an accountant — they are actively involved in management process. A lot of industrial accountants are elected on to the Board of Directors of companies.

A further important body, and one which allows its trainees to work in either industry or the profession is the *Chartered Association of Certified Accountants.* Again members, ACCAs, are admitted only after they have gained the necessary experience and passed the Associations's examinations. The appeal of this qualification is its versatility — members can work in industry and the profession and are also empowered to audit the accounts of limited companies. (In contrast, management accountants cannot carry out this audit function.)

The professional body for public accountants is the *Chartered Institute of Public Finance and Accountancy.* Public accountants, IPFAs, work in the public sector — central or local government, and nationalized industries. A common position reached by members is Treasurer — of a local authority, area health authority, or government department.

In recognition of the need for some expertise in the lower levels of the accounting function, in 1980 the four chartered bodies set up the *Association of Accounting Technicians.* This was to provide a professional body for accountancy support staff such as clerks and assistants to accountants. Membership, designated by the letters MAAT, is gained by passing a set of examinations and completing three years approved experience. As might be expected, the examinations are not as demanding as those for accountants aiming for chartered status. Members work in all sectors of the economy, in the offices of practising accountants, industry, commerce and government. In the final stage of the examination students are required to select one of three routes to qualification — the Accounting Practice stream, Industry and Commerce, and the Public Sector stream.

INDEX